DREAM WORK

in Psychotherapy *and* Self-Change

BOOKS BY ALVIN R. MAHRER, PH.D.

How To Do Experiential Psychotherapy: A Manual For Practitioners
(1989)

The Integration Of Psychotherapies: A Guide For Practicing Psychotherapists (1989)

Therapeutic Experiencing: The Process of Change (1986)

Psychotherapeutic Change: An Alternative Approach To Meaning And
Measurement (1985)

Experiential Psychotherapy: Basic Practices (1983/1989)

Experiencing: A Humanistic Theory Of Psychology And Psychiatry
(1978/1989)

Creative Developments In Psychotherapy (1971, Editor with L. Pearson)

New Approaches To Personality Classification (1970, Editor)

The Goals Of Psychotherapy (1967, Editor)

A NORTON PROFESSIONAL BOOK

DREAM WORK

in Psychotherapy *and* Self-Change

ALVIN R. MAHRER, Ph.D.
Professor of Psychology
University of Ottawa

W·W·NORTON & COMPANY · *NEW YORK* · *LONDON*

Published simultaneously in Canada by Penguin Books Canada Ltd,
2801 John Street, Markham, Ontario L3R 1B4

Printed in the United States of America.

First Edition

Library of Congress Cataloging in Publication Data

Mahrer, Alvin R.
    Dream work in psychotherapy and self-change / Alvin R. Mahrer. —
1st ed.

    "A Norton professional book."
    Bibliography: p.
    Includes indexes.
    1. Dreams—Therapeutic use.   2. Behavior therapy.
3. Psychotherapy.   I. Title.
    [DNLM: 1. Behavior Therapy.   2. Dreams.   3. Psychotherapy.   WM
460.5.DB M216d]
RC489.D74M34   1990   616.89′14—dc20   89-16033

ISBN 0-393-70089-5

W. W. Norton & Company, Inc., 500 Fifth Avenue, New York, N.Y. 10110

W. W. Norton & Company Ltd., 37 Great Russell Street, London WC1B 3NU

1 2 3 4 5 6 7 8 9 0

CONTENTS

GUIDELINES FOR READERS

THIS BOOK IS FOR PEOPLE who want to work on their own dreams and for psychotherapists who want to use dreams in their work with patients.

If you want to work with your own dreams, my purpose is to show you how to do it so that you can bring about changes in the very core of the person that you are, and so that you can be and behave in ways that fit the kind of person that you can become. All you need is readiness and willingness to work on your own dreams. You do not need any special knowledge of dreams or personality theory. This book will give you the background you need, and it will provide you with the skills. It has enough examples for you to become reasonably proficient.

Whether you work on your own dreams or are a psychotherapist who uses dreams in your work with patients, the theory and just about all the methods are the same. When I give training workshops for people who want to work on their own dreams, many of these people are interested in the rationale and the theory. Besides, using the methods usually depends on having a reasonable understanding of the relevant rationale and theory. Therefore, if you want to work on your own dreams, you will probably want to read those parts of the chapters that deal with the rationale and theory. However, some of the methods of working with dreams are appropriate only for psychotherapists and patients. Since these are identified, you can skip them if you wish.

I hope that some psychotherapists reading this book can be persuaded to adopt my approach to dream work. In order to persuade you, I have presented the actual stepwise practices you can use with your patients, as well as the theory of dreams and dreaming that is the foundation for these practices, and I have compared this approach with other theories and practices of dreams, dreaming, and dream work.

It would be appealing to say that this way of using dreams can be blended into most psychotherapeutic approaches. But that is not true. Whether or not you use dreams in your work, this way of using dreams can be cordial if the following three propositions make sense to you or if you can "bracket" your way of understanding dreams and entertain these three propositions in reading this book:

(1) The dreaming person may be described as having entered into a new and qualitatively different personality state. In contrast, virtually all other approaches see the dreaming person as essentially the same personality as the awake person but with reduced "defenses."

(2) Deeper personality processes may be grasped by entering into the dream state. This means that you will probably be unable to grasp or be privy to these particular deeper personality processes by standing outside the dream and talking about it or trying to figure out what the dream "means."

(3) Deep-seated and profound personality change occurs to the extent that you can "be" or "experience" the deeper personality processes contained in the dream. This means that you will probably be unable to undergo this kind of deep-seated and profound personality change by standing outside the dream and trying to do something therapeutic.

If you can welcome these three propositions, then I believe you will find this way of using dreams helpful in your psychotherapeutic work. Psychotherapists with a Gestalt approach are already cordial to these three propositions. So too are therapists using my experiential approach (Mahrer, 1972, 1978a, 1978c, 1980a, 1980b, 1983a, 1983b, 1984, 1985a, 1985b, 1986a, 1986c, 1989a, 1989b, 1989c, 1989d; Mahrer & Boulet, 1986). For these experiential psychotherapists, the book extends experiential psychotherapy into the realm of dreams.

The book has three purposes. One is to provide a useful way for people to work on their own dreams. Personal dream work is precious to me, and I hope that you will use this approach in undergoing your own personal change over the course of your life. My hope is that if you and I both spend time using our dreams as vehicles for opening up personal change processes, we can participate in a gentle avenue of collective social change. Here is a quiet avenue that is a distinctive alternative to organizations, movements, governments and our usual means of trying to effect social change (Mahrer, 1970, 1971b, 1972b, 1973, 1975, 1986b, 1989a).

The second is to introduce a way of working with dreams that is profoundly powerful and extremely useful in psychotherapy. I have given pieces and bits of this experiential approach in other writings (Mahrer, 1966, 1971a, 1975, 1986d, 1987a, 1987b), but it is presented here in its entirety and is compared and contrasted with most of the other ways of working with dreams in psychotherapy.

Finally, the third purpose is to offer an experiential theory of dreams and dreaming. There are a few major theories of dreams and dreaming, such as the psychoanalytic, Jungian, Gestalt, and Daseins-analytic, and there are lots of other variations and side theories. My purpose is to propose an alternative comprehensive approach based upon my own humanistic-existential theory of human beings and experiential theory of psychotherapy.

Is this book complete in and of itself? Do you need any special background in order to use the methods? If your aim is to do your own personal dream work, this book is complete. If you are interested in the understanding of what dreams are, how they come about, and the other theoretical issues surrounding dreams, this book should be enough to provide the experiential approach to these issues.

I know that many people work on dreams with a single other person or with a group. Nevertheless, the picture I had in mind as I wrote this book is a single person working on her own dreams by herself. If you wish, you can translate this into your own picture of working with a partner or even with a group. When the picture is that of a psychotherapist and patient, those are the words I used. I prefer those words to others such as "client" or "counselor" or words designating a particular approach such as "psychoanalyst."

With regard to the verbatim excerpts and recorded dreams in the appendix, these were taken from my own patients, from the patients of my interns and postdoctoral trainees, and from my own dreams. In addition to the standard contractual agreements to permit use of this material, I used several means of insuring confidentiality. Since my aim was to use this material to show the reader how to do dream work, I retained the spirit of the verbatim material while taking plenty of liberty in deleting and modifying names, dates, situations, personal expressions, and anything else that might identify the dreamer.

I teach this way of working with dreams to doctoral students, interns, postdoctoral trainees, and participants in workshops. It helps to talk with them about what is clear and what is unclear, about where the problems are and what needs more work, about extensions and modifications, about the theory and the methods. My real talk about all this is with Dr. Patricia Gervaize, my wife, but I am grateful to these persons for their interested help, and to Susan E. Barrows for her constructively merciless editing of the manuscript. However, the development of experiential dream work will continue beyond this book. Accordingly, I invite you to let me know your thoughts and ideas by writing to me at the School of Psychology, University of Ottawa, Ottawa, Canada K1N 6N5.

DREAM WORK

in Psychotherapy *and* Self-Change

CHAPTER 1

The Usefulness
of Dreams

THIS CHAPTER ANSWERS four questions:

(a) What are the valued relationships between dream theory, dream research, and dream practice?
(b) Is working on one's own dreams doable and useful?
(c) Is dream work a big part of most psychotherapies?
(d) What are the actual steps in the experiential approach to dream work?

THE CONTRIBUTION OF DREAM THEORY
AND RESEARCH TO THE PRACTICE OF
DREAM WORK

You can emphasize dream theory or research or practice. When I emphasize practice, dream theory and research become useful to the extent that they offer sound contributions to practice. This gives us an interesting perspective on dream theory and research.

Dreams Accommodate Very Easily to Just About
Any Theory

From this perspective, a theory is a way of making sense of, understanding, and explaining dreams and dreaming. If we look at theory in this way, then dreams and dreaming accommodate very easily to just about any theory. If you are inclined to think in terms of neurology, dreams can easily be understood as the product of neural activity generated by cholinergic nerve cells in the pontine gigantocellular field activating the forebrain to make sense of essentially random activation originating in the hindbrain (Hobson & McCarley, 1977). But dreams and dreaming also easily accommodate to other neurological theories, to chemical, physiological, information-processing theories, and to theories emphasizing repressed sexual fantasies, per-

1

sonal Godliness, feelings and reactions to the therapist, archetypes, symbolic birth processes, changes in cognitive structures, resolution of personal problems, messages from the spirit world, prophesies of the future, and just about any theory that you like. Once you are fond of some theory, dreams accommodate in a friendly way (Ehrenwald, 1966).

In the same way, the proponents of one theory can attack the very heart of a rival theory and it will make very little difference. For example, the dean of the Daseinsanalytic theory of dreams can attack the basic tenets of the Freudian dream theory:

> . . . in the observable phenomena of dreaming, there is not the slightest factual evidence for the existence of either the "dream work" postulated by Freud, or any infantile instinctual desires of the sort supposed to produce dreams from within an individual unconscious. Even the central notion of "dream symbolism" collapses as soon as inadmissible suppositions are no longer confused with empirical facts. (Boss, 1977, p. 7)

But dreams accommodate so easily to virtually any theory that they are essentially impervious to attacks:

> That the language of dreams is symbolic was for Freud such a self-evident assumption, supported by a widely held, age-old tradition, that it hardly occurred to him to question its validity. (Stern, 1977, p. ix)

Once you think of a theory of dreams and dreaming as another way of making sense of, understanding, and explaining dreams, then nearly any theory will do. I prefer to think of theory in terms of its contribution to practice rather than in terms of its comparative ability to explain dreams.

"Practice-Justification Theory"

Theory can be used to contribute to the practice of dream work. This is the use of theory that I value because it advances practice by opening new avenues of what can be done with dreams. But most theories of dreams and dreaming are merely ways of justifying and rationalizing what the practitioner is inclined to do with dreams anyhow. It is "practice-justification theory." While this is not the kind of relationship with practice that I value, it is exceedingly common.

If you like using dreams to prophesize the future, then accept a theory that dreams foresee future events. If you are drawn toward providing patients with interpretive insights into their innermost fears and deepest wishes, then justify this with a theory that dreams tap unconscious impulses and psychodynamics. If you want to disclaim responsibility for your actions, then hold to a theory that dreams are divine inspirations and psychic solutions to personal problems. If you find it important to connect yourself to forces that are bigger than you, that are grand and mysterious, then have a theory that dreams come from universal forces that connect you with other people from other times. If you are drawn toward enacting the role of other people and things, then have a theory that each element in a dream is a projection of yourself, and assert that the goal is to re-own the projection; then you can be a delivery boy or a bathtub or a license plate. If you like looking up the meaning of esoteria in scholarly books, then choose a theory that includes archetypal material requiring library research to uncover the hidden meaning of the symbols. If you are a therapist who likes to be the center of attention, then use a theory in which just about everything in dreams is really a symbol of the therapist (cf. Gillman, 1980). If you like talking with patients about childhood sexuality, use a Freudian theory where even a dream feeling that you have been here before can express childhood sexuality:

> In some dreams of landscapes or other localities emphasis is laid in the dream itself on a convinced feeling of having been there once before. (Occurrences of '*déjà vu*' in dreams have a special meaning.) These places are invariably the genitals of the dreamer's mother; there is indeed no other place about which one can assert with such conviction that one has been there once before. (Freud, 1900, p. 399)

A great deal of what passes as dream theory is, from this perspective, merely a way of justifying whatever actions or practices the therapist finds important to carry out.

Neither Dream Practice Nor Theory Have Progressed Much Over The Last 100 or 2000 Years

When I began serious concentrated reading about dreams, I was surprised by how few books were available, by the absence of dream journals, and by the long history of dream writings. The earliest writings seem to have been on Egyptian papyrus dating from the 12th dynasty around 2000–1790 B.C. (Wolff, 1952, cf. O'Neill, 1976; Van de Castle, 1971; Webb, 1979), followed by a little trickle of literature throughout the centuries. We know precious little about dreams, but we have known it for perhaps 2000–4000 years.

With regard to both theory and practice, we owe our greatest debt to one man whose contributions were monumental. He was perhaps the first person who dedicated his life's work to the study of dreams. His major book, entitled *The Interpretation of Dreams*, provided the first comprehensive review of the distinguished history of dreams over the past 1000 years or more, drawing material both from his scholarly knowledge of historical writings on dreams and also from his own personal work with dreams. He is to be credited with our understanding of dreams as wish fulfillment, with wishes as the expression of deeper processes that were present in waking behavior but more evident in dreams. His clinical contributions included the understanding of dreams as symbols and the interpretation of these dream symbols by studying the dreamer's associations. Through his study of the dreamer's associations, he framed the relationships between dream symbols, dream thoughts, and mechanisms by which the dream thoughts were converted into the manifest dream images. Perhaps the essence of his contribution is given in the following quotation from his writings: "Those who are skilled in dream interpretation discern the dream wishes through the veil of symbols" (Wolff, 1952, pp. 21–22).

It is a little disconcerting to realize that all of this refers to the work of Artemidorus of Daldi, and also to Sigmund Freud. Artemidorus lived around 140 A.D. Freud was great, but he was not the first (Artemidorus, 1975; Mahrer, 1986d; Parker & Parker, 1985; Rycroft, 1979; Wolman, 1979; Woods & Greenhouse, 1974). About the only difficulty a 2000-year-old dream practitioner would have in the contemporary dream scene would be using our technical jargon. Indeed, Artemidorus might have made the same comment when he reviewed the history of dream theory and practice 2000 years ago.

Most of today's dream theory and practice of dreams was familiar several thousand years ago. Wolff (1952) describes a series of interpreted dreams, based on the idea that a series of dreams offers interpretive advantage over a single dream and yielding an overall interpretation quite in keeping with a psychoanalytic approach—except that the work dates back nearly 4000 years! Approximately 2000 years ago, the leading dream theorists and practitioners had a system of symbolic interpretive meanings that is essentially still used today. For example, a woman's garment, a ship, a sea, or a female animal were understood as symbolic of a loved woman. The student of symbolic dream interpretation could examine manuals in India from approximately 1500 to 1000 B.C. (O'Neill, 1976), clay tablets from roughly the same era (Van de Castle, 1971), or Egyptian papyrus (Webb, 1979; Wolff, 1952). A somewhat embarrassing case may be made that there has been very little change in dream theory and practice over the last one or two or even three thousand years.

What about the short run? Freud's monumental work on dreams was published in 1900, and he concluded in 1931 that nothing new had been produced in the intervening years:

> Freud himself stated sadly in 1931 that after the first publication of his book in 1900, "nothing new or valuable as regards the conception of dreams, either in material or in novel point of view," has been produced. (Wolff, 1952, p. 1)

Wolff concurred that very little had been accomplished beyond Freud's work. Fleiss (1953) reinforced this conclusion by noting only some revival in clinical use of dreams, and the general consensus today is that genuine progress in clinical dream theory and practice has been slight (Khan, 1976).

The Usefulness of Research Depends on Its Contribution to the Practice of Dream Work

There are various ways of looking at the usefulness of dream research. When I look at its usefulness in terms of its contribution to practice, a little bit of research has high usefulness while most has to find justification on other grounds.

Biological (neurological, physiological) dream research contributes essentially nothing to the clinical practice of dream work. When we look at the clinical practice of dream work, almost nothing has been or can be gained from biological research on dreams. In the existential-humanistic theory on which the experiential approach is based, it is assumed that phenomena such as the "human body" or "dreams" are open to description and understanding from multiple perspectives which are not necessarily causally related to one another; no system of constructs is reducible to some other system of constructs that is assumed to be basic or fundamental (Mahrer, 1962,

1989a). This means that no construct system can own the human body or dreams. Neither the human body nor a dream is basically biological any more than it is chemical or existential or religious. Neurological or physiological research on dreams is no more causally related, basic, or fundamental to psychological modes of description and understanding than existential research is causally related, basic, or fundamental to neurological or physiological modes of description and understanding. Accordingly, from this perspective, biological research contributes essentially nothing to psychological practices of dream work.

In contrast, virtually all biological dream researchers hold to quite different assumptions. They believe in a hierarchy of sciences wherein psychological constructs are reducible to biological (neurophysiological) constructs that are held as basic and fundamental. Eventually, they believe, the cumulative findings of biological dream research will provide the scientific foundation for a firmly based, biologically grounded practice of dream work:

> . . . I can conceive that in some sense the primitive biological process of the REM state periodically provides the "energy" to illuminate the screen as well as the projector mechanism to crank the film, and possibly the film itself. . . . For physiological answers to such questions as how the scripts of dreams are written, or the film produced, or why the entire process takes place, we can only wait hopefully and expectantly, but still very much in the dark. (Snyder, 1969, p. 24)

In the meantime, biological dream researchers act as if the domain of dreaming is to be owned and studied by biological dream researchers while the clinical study of dreams themselves may, for now at least, be the domain of the clinicians (cf. Jones, 1968; Murray, 1965). Yet their faith is that neurological and physiological constructs are of course basic and fundamental, and all psychological constructs can and will be reducible to those of neurology and physiology. It is this faith that underlies their innocent-appearing concern that the findings of psychological dream research and biological dream research should at least be "consistent" with one another:

> We hope to demonstrate that data about dream physiology can help us to understand more clearly the process of dreaming. A basic premise of our work is that hypotheses about various aspects of nervous system function should be consistent. Findings in the area of neurophysiology

should not contradict or be contradicted by psychological hypotheses.
(Greenberg & Pearlman, 1980, pp. 85–86)

But what is to be done if psychological and biological findings are
not consistent, if indeed one is taken to contradict the other? Here is
where the innocent-appearing consistency guideline gets tough. If
you accept a hierarchy of the sciences, then biology is typically basic
and fundamental to psychology, and "consistency" means that the
softer psychological findings must accommodate to the more fundamental biological findings. This is rather acceptable to psychoana-
lytic-psychodynamic theories and practices of dreaming and dreams,
for they accept the neurophysiological grounding (Greenberg &
Pearlman, 1975a, 1975b, 1978; Reiser, 1984; Winson, 1985).

My position is that there is no causal relationship between psychological and biological theories of dreaming and dreams, neither one
being necessarily basic or fundamental to the other. Accordingly,
biological dream research can offer little or nothing to the psychological practice of dream work. Even with regard to the Freudian theory
of dream practice, a few theories lean in support of this position:

> . . . the use of physiological variables to test a psychological theory
> provides only an indirect test of the theory. A direct test would involve
> only the psychological variables. In the case of Freud's dream theory, a
> direct psychological test has yet to be made. (Vogel, 1978, p. 1534)

Stern (1977) holds that Boss takes the same position wherein neurological and physiological research have little or no relevance to the
Daseinsanalytic practice of dream work:

> Dr. Boss has little if any use for the voluminous body of sleeping and
> dreaming that has accumulated in recent years. [These studies] strike
> Boss, though he does not deny their incidental interest, as entirely
> beside the point where an understanding of the nature of dreaming is
> concerned. (Stern, 1977, pp. vii–viii)

So we are left with a dilemma when psychological and biological
dream research findings are not "consistent" with one another. How
do we resolve the "inconsistency"? A case in point is the thoroughly
neurophysiological description of dreams offered by Hobson and Mc-
Carley (1977; see also McCarley & Hobson, 1977). Central to this
description is their activation-synthesis hypothesis in which the
dream is mere neural activity generated by cholinergic nerve cells. As

discussed by Fiss, Hobson and McCarley have presented, " . . . a theory which reduces the dream almost literally to 'ash' by virtually physiologizing it out of existence" (1983, p. 148; cf. Fiss, 1979; Labruzza, 1978). There is a sharp "inconsistency" between the evidence accepted by the neurologists and physiologists and the evidence accepted by the clinicians. Fiss puts the sharp inconsistency as follows: " . . . the proposition that the formal characteristics of dreaming are neurophysiologically determined runs contrary to evidence that dreams, even over the course of an entire night, are remarkably coherent, not at all disconnected, and thematically interrelated" (1983, p. 148). Is there an inconsistency, and if so, what is to be done to resolve the inconsistency?

From the perspective of our existential-humanistic theory of human beings, there is no inconsistency. If a neurophysiological theory of dreaming and dreams does not accept dreams as expressing material from a collective unconscious, there is no "inconsistency," for "cholinergic nerve cells" and "collective unconscious" are constructs from different conceptual systems. On the other hand, if you are a neurophysiologist, you might hold to the belief that the "inconsistency" must be resolved. Either there are no scientifically grounded thematic interrelationships across dreams or the psychological thematic interrelationships are to recast in the more basic and fundamental constructs of neurology and physiology. This is their position.

The position I accept is that biological (neurological, physiological) dream research can and does contribute essentially nothing to the clinical practice of dream work. The experiential theory of dream practice will be advanced by good changes in the experiential theory of dreaming and dreams and in the underlying existential-humanistic theory of human beings. Neither the existential-humanistic theory of human beings nor its experiential theory of practice are causally related to, reducible to, or grounded in the constructs of biology, neurology, or physiology. Accordingly, biological dream research can and does contribute essentially nothing to the clinical practice of dream work.

Research that aims at testing theories of dreaming contributes essentially nothing to the clinical practice of dream work. There are lots of different theories of dreaming. Consider just a few, for example, dreaming frees the brain of excess cell connections that accumulate during the waking day (Crick & Mitchison, 1983), dreaming provides energy and stimulation for the psychic processes of everyday life (Koestler, 1964), dreaming protects sleep, dreaming reflects changes in a large community of persons, or dreaming serves an adaptive, adjustive, organizing function. Research can set out to confirm or disconfirm any of these theories or to see which of a number of theories best fits some "scientific" findings. The trouble is that virtually none of this research has much chance of contributing anything of real measure to the clinical practice of dream work.

This kind of research has its eyes fixed on the parent theory of dreaming and not on clinical practice. The derivation of hypotheses is done so as to establish a series of logical steps down from the theory to the hypothesis, or down from several competing theories to alternative testable hypotheses. Once the findings are in, they are used to run back up the logical ladder and to confirm or disconfirm some theory or theories. This research is not aimed at nor can it contribute to clinical practice. It has enough trouble justifying itself as a way of testing hypotheses so as to confirm or disconfirm theories (Mahrer, 1985a, 1988a).

Research cast within one theory of practice contributes very little to other theories of practice. Some research grows out of and bears implications for theories of clinical practice. The trouble is that in general the implications are limited to that particular theory of practice, so the research is indeed useful for that theory of practice but has little or no usefulness for other theories of practice.

Research may suggest that the dreams of persons who typically have trouble remembering dreams are characterized by more "unconscious anxiety" than the dreams of those who easily recall their dreams, and this line of research may have implications for what to expect in actual dreams and how to use the presence of "unconscious anxiety" in dreams (e.g., Eisenstein, 1980). However, this research is cast within a psychoanalytic framework, and would be of little or no use in the experiential theory of practice, which has no place for the psychoanalytic construct of "unconscious anxiety." Similarly, research cast within a Jungian theory of practice may indicate that the same archetypal image appears in a series of dreams, and therefore the use of this series of dreams is warranted. Such research may be useful for a Jungian practice of dream work but it would be of questionable value in a Gestalt or experiential or Freudian theory of dream practice.

Research comparing groups of people contributes essentially nothing to the clinical practice of dream work. It is appealing for some researchers to see how the dreams of one group differ from the dreams of some other group. There is almost no end to the kinds of groups that can be compared. Typically the research moves on to whatever group is "in season." Accordingly, researchers are drawn toward comparing the dreams of black-skinned people and white-skinned people, prostitutes and nuns, Russians and Americans, smart people and dumb people, people diagnosed as psychotic and those diagnosed as normal, gay and straight people. Recently the interest has moved to comparing the dreams of women with all sorts of other groups and subgroups (Hall, 1966; Hall & Domhoff, 1963; Koch-Sheras, 1985; Kramer, Whitman, Baldridge, & Ornstein, 1970; Krippner, Posner, Pomerance, & Fischer, 1974; Stukane, 1985; Van de Castle, 1971; Winget, Kramer, & Whitman, 1972). Such research has little yield in contributing to the advancement of the clinical practice of dream work.

Research on the clinical practice of dream work will likely contribute to the clinical practice of dream work. Yet this kind of research has been egregiously overlooked. There is precious little study of what occurs in dream work (Mahrer, 1979, 1985a; Werman, 1978).

One way of doing such research is to investigate the actual procedures in clinical practice. Dream work can be organized into given conditions, operations, and consequences so that the interrelations among the three can be examined (Mahrer, 1985a, 1988a, 1988c). For example, a considerable portion of dream work in many approaches relies on some idea of what the actual dream consists of, yet we are limited to the person's verbal report of the dream and consequently lose what may be regarded as valuable data (cf. Webb & Cartwright, 1978). What a boon it would be to clinical practice if we had a "dream recorder," some instrument that recorded the actual dream as it was occurring (Mahrer, 1979).

I have placed the actual practice of dream work as uppermost, and proposed that the usefulness of dream theory and research is to be gauged in terms of their contribution to this practice. Let us now turn to a major kind of dream practice: the use of dreams in self-change.

THE USE OF DREAMS IN SELF-CHANGE

If you want to undergo profound personal change, probably the best way is to work with your own dreams. Learn this experiential method and then work with your own dreams.

Psychotherapy and Personal Dream Work

Is psychotherapy something the person should go through in order to get ready for doing personal dream work? Are there any significant ways that psychotherapy helps prepare the person for personal dream work? My answer is that psychotherapy is not at all necessary, by and large is not helpful at all, and in a few instances may offer little more than some mild encouragement for the person to work on her own dreams after psychotherapy is over.

Perhaps the only time that I encourage a patient to work on her own dreams is when this issue comes up in the last part of a session where we consider possible new ways of being and behaving. It happens rarely. In psychoanalytic therapy there are hints that an occasional patient might take an interpretive look at some dreams when therapy is over (Bonime, 1962). Jungian therapists are an exception, for it is somewhat common that Jungian therapists would " . . . follow this practice of encouraging their analysands to continue to interpret their own dreams after termination of the analysis" (Mattoon, 1984, p. 159). In general, psychotherapists seldom offer substantive encouragement for patients to do personal dream work on any serious basis after therapy is over.

Nor do patients in therapy acquire the necessary skills to do their own personal dream work. In experiential psychotherapy the therapist shows the patient how to carry out each step in dream work, but the therapy is not intended to teach dream work skills. Training workshops in learning the explicit skills of experiential dream work are much better than loads of experiential sessions when it comes to acquiring actual skills. I believe that the patient in psychoanalytic therapy likewise learns insufficient skills to work on his own dreams, although some disagree: "Dream interpretation in analysis is, or should be, a skill passed on to the patient" (Ullman, 1962b, p. xvii; cf. Bonime, 1962). Once again, Jungian therapy may be the exception. Jung saw his therapy as schooling the patient in the necessary dream work skills to that he might, in the later stages, ask " . . . them to work out the interpretation as well. In this way . . . the patient learns how to deal correctly with his unconscious without the doctor's help" (Mattoon, 1984, p. 159).

In general, with perhaps the exception of some Jungian therapists, most therapists neither provide solid encouragement nor learned skills for personal dream work. It appears that psychotherapy is minimal and unnecessary preparation for personal dream work.

The Value and Importance
of Personal Dream Work

Some therapists work regularly on their own dreams. Jourard (1976) writes that he wants to have competence in the skills he expects his patients to acquire, but the more common reason is to undergo their own personal change. Leaders such as Freud, Jung, and Perls worked on their own dreams to uncover their innermost nature:

> Perhaps the greatest legacy of Sigmund Freud was not his theory of dreaming and his conceptualizations about psychotherapy, but his personal search. Freud was trying to understand his own dreams and the secrets that he kept from himself. (Corriere, Karle, Woldenberg, & Hart, 1980, p. 50)

This is why I do dream work. I use my dreams to obtain what psychotherapy is supposed to offer. I do regular dream work because of its effects on the very person that I am and can be, not because I am a psychotherapist. In the same way, I offer every person the opportunity to use dream work for their own personal betterment. It enables you to undergo change both at the deepest levels of personality and also at the level of actual ways you behave in your world. I am echoing the words of Jung here:

> Although Jung deemed dream interpretation to be essential to psychotherapy, he considered it also to be a valuable education for persons who do not undergo psychotherapy. For such persons, the widening of consciousness resulting from the incorporation of unconscious contents through dream analysis enhances development of their personalities. (Mattoon, 1984, p. 4)

Use dream work because of the good it provides for you personally. But there is much more. An existential-humanistic theory of social change holds that social worlds and social phenomena are a function of collective human beings, and the nature and extent of changes in these social worlds and phenomena depend on the nature and extent of the personal change in collective individual human beings (Mahrer, 1970, 1971b, 1972b, 1973, 1975, 1989a, 1986b). As you are undergoing your own personal actualization and integration through regular dream work, you are also engaging in a massively powerful process of quiet social change. Since the existential-humanistic theory places great value on both personal and social change, dream work is an alternative to psychotherapy, religion, politics, and war.

Advantages of personal dream work over psychotherapy. Perhaps the main advantage is that you are free of the therapist. Your work is not impeded, inhibited, twisted, deflected or suffocated by the problems, well-meanings, intrusions, limitations, or personal involvements of a therapist (Mahrer, 1971c, 1978b, 1980a, 1982, 1985c, 1986a, 1986b, 1986e, 1989a, 1980c; Mahrer, Dessaulles, Gervaize, & Nadler, 1987; Mahrer & Gervaize, 1983). You use effective methods rather than a therapist who is supposedly more authoritative and knowledgeable than you are. "These ways require some effort and some courage, and, sometimes, some friends, but they do not require any expert knowledge . . . nor do they require the help of anyone who possesses expertise . . . " (Jones, 1979, p. 2).

On the other hand, many dream approaches require a therapist. Most notably the psychodynamic/psychoanalytic approach holds that dream work rests on effective interpretation. Patients cannot provide their own interpretations: " . . . interpretation of one's own dreams carries difficulty because of the dreamer's psychological blind spots, which dream interpretation is designed to illumine" (Mattoon, 1984, p. 159). According to these approaches, the therapist is essential, and herein lies the problem. The therapist will encase you in a relationship, envelop you with interactions. You and the therapist will conjointly entwine one another in a relationship in which you fulfill one role, the therapist another, and you both get caught in the web spun by the two of you. Once you and a therapist build a relationship with one another you are caught in the jaws of that relationship, and you sacrifice what could be gained from dream work.

In other words, if you want to gain something useful from working with your dreams, do your own personal dream work. If you want to become involved in some sort of role relationship, become involved with a psychotherapist. The advantage of personal dream work is that you have a good chance of gaining what dream work has to offer while being free of the role relationships that are essentially insured in nearly every psychotherapy in which patient and therapist talk with one another about dreams.

There is a pocket of exception however. For some people, the role relationship is compelling. It is very important to get into a relationship where they are understood and accepted by an understanding and accepting parental figure, or where they are able to talk about themselves for years with a person who gives 50 minutes of absolute attention, or where they are told the real meaning of their dreams by a doctor who knows the secrets of the mind.

If you are drawn toward using dreams as the ticket into interesting relationships, I suggest that you sample a dream group. There are many who describe the interpersonal advantages of dream groups (Bonime, 1984; Bynum, 1980; Corriere, Karle, Woldenberg, & Hart, 1980; Eckhardt, Zane, & Ullman, 1971; Greenleaf, 1973; Hall, 1966; Perlmutter & Babineau, 1983; Regush & Regush, 1977; Rossi, 1972; Stewart, 1969; Ullman, 1987; Ullman & Zimmerman, 1979). In terms of potential for offering a richer class of satisfying role relationships, dream groups are superior to the standard array of patient-therapist role relationships. In terms of bypassing the problems of patient-therapist role relationships, personal dream work is the safest bet of all.

Another advantage of personal dream work over therapeutic dream work is the greater opportunity to acquire the skills of working on dreams. You can read books and articles about whatever way you are using. You can join with others in the learning of these skills. You can take classes or attend workshops that train you in these skills.

In addition, personal dream work is considerably less expensive than therapeutic dream work, and is something you can continue the rest of your life. Finally, personal dream work is far more efficient. If you spend five or six hours a month on personal dream work, most of that time can be concentrated on actual dream work. In contrast, five or six therapy hours will likely offer little or no time on dreams.

All in all, I am convinced of the advantages of personal dream work over the typical interactive role relationships of being a patient talking with a therapist.

How and Where to Gain the Skills
of Personal Dream Work

Doing personal dream work takes skills. It seems clear that most people cannot just "do" dream work and that, with the probable exception of the Jungian approach (Hillman, 1967), most patients in most therapies will not acquire the requisite skills. How and where can people gain the skills to do personal dream work?

Most of the books on personal dream work hold that you can gain the necessary skills by following the guidelines described in the book, typically involving the use of a set of questions coupled with a set of procedures (e.g., Delaney, 1981; Faraday, 1972, 1974; Garfield, 1977; Gendlin, 1986; Krippner & Dillard, 1988; Miller, Stinson, & Soper, 1982; Morris, 1985; Reed, 1985; Regush & Regush, 1977; Taylor, 1983). Even using an interpretative approach, you might provide your own interpretations: "The basic tenet of this book is that you can become your own dream authority and in so doing improve the quality of your life" (Regush & Regush, 1977, p. 79).

I agree that several ways of working with one's own dreams can be learned by following the guidelines laid down in the books. In fact, the present book aims at doing the same thing. If you want to learn sufficient skills to do experiential dream work, this book should be enough.

I foresee the time when there will be workshops, seminars, classes dedicated to training people to develop the skills of personal dream work. They will be offered by psychotherapy clinics and centers and, as the importance of personal dream work catches hold, they will be taught in high schools, colleges, and universities. Some of these skill-training workshops, seminars, and classes are available now. Many more will, I believe, be available soon.

In the meantime, I encourage readers to gain the skills of experiential dream work by studying the guidelines of this book and by getting together regularly with one or more other personal dream workers to improve your skills. I suggest taping personal dream work sessions and discussing selected excerpts with an eye toward improving your skills.

Some Practical Guidelines For
Personal Dream Work

One of the advantages in most approaches to meditation and contemplation is that you can do it just about anywhere. In experiential dream work, however, you need a room where you can make noise — lots of noise — and no one outside the room can hear you, nor should you hear noise from outside the room. I use an office that is sound-proofed and wrapped in corridors sealed off by doors at the ends.

Schedule a regular time for your dream work. Set aside two or three hours every week or so. One of the advantages of regular dream work is that you will be less inclined to retreat into dream work when your life is falling apart or you are in an especially rotten state. Feel free to vary the time and day and number of sessions per month, but designate some sort of moderately regular schedule, rather than trying to do dream work when the inclination strikes or limiting the time available by starting at 7:30 PM knowing that you intend to watch that special television program at 8:30 PM.

If you do dream work with a partner, choose someone with whom there is a high degree of mutual respect and trust (Mattoon, 1984, p. 160), and where you are both at about the same level of skill. Select someone with whom your private lives will not intrude into the dream work sessions, and where the dream work sessions will not intrude into your private lives. In short, stay away from spouses, people with whom you live, and friends. Choose someone with whom you can terminate the sessions, or who can terminate the session with you, and still you feel all right. Clearly it is quite special to find and work with such a partner.

Alternate whose dream to work on. Use your dream for one or two sessions and then proceed to the other person's dream for one or two sessions. Stay with the dream work. That is, do not veer off into psychotherapeutic games where one fulfills the role of therapist and the other of patient.

When you have developed a sufficient skill level, perhaps after a year or so, I suggest that you say goodbye to the partnership. The main reason for having a partner is to gain adequate skills to carry on dream work by yourself. On the other hand, there is no denying the appeal of working on dreams with another person or group. You can experience a sense of deep sharing, of safe equality with another person, of community, of all the experiencings that accrue to dream work with others. The choice is yours.

THE SPECIALNESS OF DREAMS IN PSYCHOTHERAPY

Are dreams regarded as special in the various psychotherapies? What determines whether dreams are or are not regarded as special?

The Specialness of Dreams in Experiential Psychotherapy

Dreams hold a very special place in experiential psychotherapy. There are at least three ways in which dreams earn this special status.

Dreams are the purest and most trustworthy expression of your deeper potentials. As a therapist, I know of nothing that can compare with dreams in touching the patient's innermost personality processes (cf. Altman, 1969; Garma, 1966; Hall, 1947; Rosenthal, 1980; Scott, 1982; Weiss, 1986). Jung puts this in simple eloquence:

> The dream gives a true picture of the subjective state, while the conscious mind denies that this state exists, or recognizes it only grudgingly. . . . (The dream) simply tells now the matter stands. (1933, p. 5)

It is an expression relatively uncontaminated by patient or by therapist:

> The dream as the experience of an involuntary psychic process not controlled by the conscious outlook presents the inner truth and reality as it is; not because I presume it to be thus, nor as I wish it to be, but simply as it is. (Jung, 1961, p. 49)

It is almost solely the uncontaminated production of the dreaming existence, the innermost personality processes, the deeper potentials:

> They are especially useful in the analysis of existence because it is in the dreaming existence that the individual is totally in charge. The dreamer alone writes the script and produces the dream itself. Dreams are the best example of the world construction of the individual existence while it is relatively uninfluenced by the world of reality or by input from others. (Mendel, 1980, p. 394)

If you are inclined to work deeply and rapidly, to open up deeper personality processes right away, rely upon dreams as the very best way, as Freud's "royal road to the unconscious," as the purest and most trustworthy expression of your deeper potentials.

Dreams are an especially efficient and effective way of starting experiential sessions. The first step in every session of experiential psychotherapy is for the patient to attain a state of strong feeling. The feeling may be pleasant or unpleasant, but it is to be strong. How do we arrive at that state? How does the session start in order for the patient to reach a state of strong feeling? We start by inviting the patient to see what feeling is here right now, and then allowing that feeling to occur, to happen. That is one beginning place. The other is whatever is front and center on the patient's mind, as long as it is connected with some feeling. Then, beginning in one of these two starting places, we move toward the state of strong feeling. The dream is an especially efficient and effective starting point, for the person is already having strong feelings. Somewhere in the dream, the dreamer is having a strong feeling. That is special.

There is a disclaimer clause, however. A dream is a very special starting place except when the patient is already caught in some feeling state or is already compellingly focused on something that is front and center in his mind. The patient is already exhilarated or disconsolate, sexually aroused or annoyed. The therapist may not have to see if the patient has something front and center on his mind because he is already attending to the recent letter from the attorney or the look on his mother's face or the cracking open of the marriage. Under these conditions, the usual starting places are best. But when there is no immediate feeling state or feelinged attentional center, the dream is an especially efficient and effective starting point.

In experiential psychotherapy, dreams are effective and useful for every patient and in every session. It does not matter how you describe the patient. It may be an initial session or a subsequent one. The patient may be young or old, therapeutically sophisticated or naive. It is irrelevant whether the patient is tranquil or upset, seems happy or sad, or acts in a way that seems weird and bizarre. Dream work can be useful with anyone:

> Hallucinating, wildly agitated, she was denudative, smeared herself and the walls of seclusion rooms with menstrual blood, and was destructive of property and sometimes assaultive. During more than 15 years of psychotherapeutic work with her, I found the role of dreams in treatment an important one. . . . Thus . . . it is apparent that dreams can be used in the treatment of schizophrenia. (Kafka, 1980, p. 102)

In the dream, the patient has already made the radical shift into being the deeper potential. In experiential sessions, one of the important tasks is for the patient to disengage from and let go of the ordinary operating personality in which she lives and behaves and functions. The patient is to make the radical shift into being the deeper potential—a whole new, deeper personality—and to give up being the person that she is from moment to moment in her daily life. This is a momentous shift, a profound step in each session of experiential psychotherapy.

What is so very special about dreams is that you as the dreamer have already undergone this radical shift. You have disengaged from your ordinary waking personality and are now being and behaving from within a deeper potential. This momentous shift has occurred quietly in your dream world.

It is momentous and radical because it is the direction of valued change from the perspective of experiential theory. That is, a major direction of change is being able to let go of the ordinary personality that you are, to let go of these operating potentials, and to be the deeper potentials. Merely being these deeper potentials, as you are in the dream world, is a radical change that is more precious in our valued direction of change.

In our theory of human beings (Mahrer, 1989a), the deeper potentials represent what you can be, your direction of change. The world of the deeper potentials far outstrips the world of the ordinary, waking, operating personality in what we refer to as integration and actualization. Undertaking the radical shift into the deeper potentials of the dream world is a giant step toward what you are capable of becoming. This view of the dream world is not, however, shared by all existentialists:

> . . . the world of dreaming is, despite its apparent fluidity, narrower, more closed in and hermetic, than the waking world . . . the mode of awakeness surpasses the dreaming mode in existential richness and freedom. . . . (Stern, 1977, pp. xvi–xvii)

The Specialness of Dreams in the Field of Psychotherapy

Dreams have a special place in experiential psychotherapy. What about the field of psychotherapy in general? Do dreams enjoy a special place in most psychotherapies? Does dream work take up a large measure of therapeutic time in most approaches?

Dreams become unspecial as the conscious (ego, operating) personality is increasingly regarded as preeminent. In the existential-humanistic theory on which experiential dream work is built, the deeper personality is preeminent over the operating personality, and because dreams are the expression of the deeper personality, dreams are very important indeed.

A similar case can be built for Freudian psychoanalysis. In its classical form, the deeper personality processes were preeminent over the conscious ego processes. The ego was puny, and virtually everything the person did was determined predominantly by unconscious processes. Because dreams were the royal road to the unconscious, dreams were very special indeed.

In today's version of most therapies, however, the conscious, thinking, behaving personality is the star, and important changes are to occur in this conscious, functioning personality. It is to be strengthened, made more insightfully aware. Its cognitive processes are to be improved, its behavior modified, its problems reduced. If there are stored memories or residual behaviors or processes less available to the conscious personality, they can be obtained and used to improve the functioning of the conscious personality. In almost all contemporary therapies, the conscious operating personality is preeminent. As the axis of change shifts to the conscious functioning personality, dreams are divested of their specialness, so that dreams are decidedly not special in most contemporary psychotherapies.

The same shift is occurring in most psychoanalytic/psychodynamic schools. Beginning perhaps with Alexander (1930), dreams were widened into serving as the expression of normal, ordinary wishes of the more or less conscious functioning ego (Adler, 1938, 1958, 1974; Gold, 1979), as well as from the deep and powerful unconscious. As this trend has developed into the current emphasis on ego psychology, there has been decreasing specialness given to dreams in psychoanalytic therapies (Altman, 1969; Eisler, 1953; Greenson, 1970; Rapaport, 1959):

> (Many psychoanalysts) . . . consider the dream no more important than any other manifestation of the patient's unconscious. This latter view of the dream may be due to: (1) the development of ego psychology, (2) emergence of new views on narcissism, and (3) other formulations which have drained interest away from the id and toward the ego and self. (Eisenstein, 1980, p. 319)

If the dream is less used as a royal road to the unconscious, perhaps it can be used for other purposes such as an interesting way of introducing the patient to free association:

> The interchange between patient and analyst is the heart of the therapeutic endeavor. In this interchange, dreams are not only a rich source of data; they can also, because of their bizarre nature, become the best means of introducing the patient to the activity of free association, a seemingly abstruse aspect of a strange new experience. (Bonime, 1962, p. 1)

But why use free association to dreams? If the important activity is free association, perhaps there are more useful things to associate to than the outmoded and somewhat useless dream:

> While free association to dreams is likely to lead to one or more complexes, it has no advantage over free association to any other mental content or external stimulus in identifying complexes. (Mattoon, 1984, p. 55)

The trend has been away from latent psychoanalytic dream content and toward straightforward manifest meaning (Hall, 1966; Hall & Van de Castle, 1966; Pulver & Renik, 1984; Ullman, 1962a; Warner, 1987). In psychoanalysis, dreams have largely lost their specialness, receding into merely one of a number of sources of interesting clinical information (Arlow & Brenner, 1964; Bonime, 1969; Cirincione, Hart, Karle, & Switzer, 1980; Kardiner, 1977; Levay & Weissberg, 1979). If the patient happens to mention a dream, it is used in pretty much the same way as any other useful material by, for example, a client-centered or rational-emotive therapist (cf. Doweiko, 1982).

An insignificant proportion of psychotherapeutic time is taken up with dream work. If we look at psychotherapy in general, at all the therapists doing all sorts of therapies, my impression is that a tiny proportion of time is given to dream work. It is safe to say that dreams are not special in the field of psychotherapy.

The big exception is Jungian therapy. In this approach, a good measure of therapeutic time is awarded to dream work, and dreams are thereby special. Similarly, in experiential therapy, somewhere between 10 and 20 percent of the sessions are given to dream work, and in these sessions most of the time is directed toward working with and from the dream. My impression from the literature is that the use of dreams has receded to an almost insignificant proportion of therapeutic time in psychoanalytic therapies. Even in those sessions where the patient brings up a dream, a large proportion of the psychoanalytic session deals with material that is only distantly related to the dream. Yet many psychoanalytic therapists still claim that the dream is regarded as more significant in psychoanalytic therapies than in other therapies (Langs, 1980). The reassuring claim is that dreams are still very special, even though just about everything else is also special: "The dream has maintained its cardinal place in analysis, but it shares importance with the transference, free association, and the real world in which the patient lives" (Eisenstein, 1980, p. 327). All in all, an insignificant proportion of therapeutic time is given to dream work, with the exception of Jungian therapy, experiential therapy, and occasional psychoanalytic therapists.

In many approaches, dreams are used in the same way as most other therapeutic material. In this sense, dreams are not so special (Snyder, 1970). The patient may report a dream or a recent incident or just about anything else, and the therapist will listen to the material in essentially the same way the therapist listens to any other client-centered material or Gestalt material or rational-emotive material (Doweiko, 1982). Within Langs' psychoanalytic approach, " . . . a dream report requires no modification in the therapist's approach to the patient's communications" (1980, p. 359).

If you listen to therapeutic material by paying attention to the degree of completeness, clarity, or symbolization in what the patient says, you will do the same whether the patient is talking about her history, herself, a recent incident, a dream, or just about anything else (cf. Corriere, Karle, Woldenberg, & Hart, 1980). If you are a psychoanalyst of the object relations school, you might give the same interpretive response to a dream as to nearly any other kind of reported recent incident:

> He had dreamed: I was driving an old car I had years ago and came to a place where I wanted to get up to some bridge over to where I was going. I could go up on a lift, but there was a side road up a steep hill that I could get up by and I decided to go up that way. I commented, "It looks as if you decided not to accept help but to get up by your own way, to do it yourself." (Guntrip, 1969, p. 345)

If the dream can tell you nothing new about a patient, the dream is not very special. Object relations analysts already understand that dreams basically portray either the traditional psychoanalytic oedipal conflict or the basic object relations conflict (Kohut, 1977). According to Freud, dreams merely express the patient's erotic wishes, thereby not telling us much that is new about the patient:

> The more one is concerned with the solution of dreams, the more one is driven to recognize that the majority of the dreams of adults deal with sexual material and give expression to erotic wishes. (Freud, 1900, p. 396)

In many ways, it appears that dreams and dream work do not hold a special place in the field of psychotherapy. The exceptions seem to be Jungian and experiential psychotherapies and perhaps some psychoanalytic therapists, but in general it seems that dreams have receded to the status of an interesting historical remnant.

HOW TO USE DREAMS:
THE STEPS IN EXPERIENTIAL
DREAM WORK

Using dreams means going through a series of steps. Follow the same series of steps in each session, whether you are a therapist working with a patient's dream or a person working on your own dream by yourself or with a partner.

The steps in a session of experiential dream work are the same as the steps in a session of experiential psychotherapy because they are the steps of experiential change. We go through the same four steps whether it is an ordinary session, a session that starts with a dream, or a personal dream work session.

The first step in a session of experiential psychotherapy is the attainment of a level of strong feeling. This means that whatever the patient is experiencing, it is occurring to a strong degree, fully, intensely, genuinely. Bodily sensations are likewise strong and full and intense. This occurs at step 3.3 in the process of dream work (Figure 1). Both experiential dream work and ordinary sessions of experiential psychotherapy aim at achieving this as the first step.

Once the patient attains the level of strong feelings, the next step in an ordinary experiential session is for the therapist to discern (listen for) the inner, deeper experiencing which is then opened up, brought forward, and expressed in its welcomed good form. In short, the step is that of "appreciating" the newly present deeper experiencing. In experiential dream work, this corresponds to step 4.1 (Figure 1).

Now that the patient and therapist have sensed, felt, "appreciated" the deeper experiencing, the next step is for the patient voluntarily and actively to disengage from the ordinary, continuing personality in which she typically lives in daily waking life, and to enter into being the deeper experiencing. This is accomplished within the context of earlier life situations. In both experiential therapy and dream work, this consists first of identifying the earlier life situation (step 4.2, Figure 1) and then being the experiencing in the context of the earlier life situation (step 4.3, Figure 1).

SELECTING AND RECOUNTING THE DREAM

1.1 Select dream as the target of therapeutic work
1.2 Patient recounts dream

IDENTIFYING RECENT SITUATIONS

2.1 Identify connected recent situations
2.2 Identify feelinged moments in recent situations

ATTAINING THE DREAM EXPERIENCING

3.1 Identify and clarify peak moment
3.2 Enter into peak moment
3.3 Open up dream experiencing in both peaks
3.4 Identify single common dream experiencing

BEING THE DREAM EXPERIENCING

4.1 Be dream experiencing in dream peak moments
4.2 Identify earlier life situation
4.3 Be dream experiencing in earlier life situation
4.4 Be dream experiencing in recent life situation

BEING-BEHAVIOR CHANGE

5   Being-behavior changes in imminent extratherapy world
5.1 Rehearsal for reality
5.2 Behavioral commitment

Figure 1. Steps in a Session of Experiential Dream Work

The patient has now become a different personality, has now had a taste of what it is like to be the deeper experiencing in the context of an early life situation. The final step, in both experiential psychotherapy and dream work, is for the patient to be and to behave as this new experiencing within the context of the imminent extratherapy world. The patient is to get a taste and a sample of what it can be like to be this new experiencing and to behave as this new experiencing, all within the context of tomorrow and next week in the world outside the therapy room (step 5, Figure 1), culminating in a "rehearsal for reality" (step 5.1) and a final "behavioral commitment" (step 5.2, Figure 1).

A Summary Overview of the Steps in Experiential Dream Work

We follow these steps whether dream work occurs in an experiential therapy session or in personal dream work. Accordingly, I will be referring to therapist and patient. If you do personal dream work, substitute yourself for both therapist and patient.

Dream work begins with proper recording of the dream (see Chapter 2). In the session, the first step is to select the dream as the target of therapeutic work (1.1, Figure 1).

The next step (1.2) is for the patient to recount the dream. The proper ways for the patient to recount the dream and for the therapist to receive the dream are discussed in Chapter 2. Once the dream is recounted, therapist and patient then proceed from the dream to recent life situations. Beginning with the dream, therapist and patient identify a few recent life situations (step 2.1), and then identify the feelinged moment in the recent life situations (step 2.2). Steps 2.1 and 2.2 are discussed in Chapter 3.

We now turn to the dream itself. In step 3.1 (Chapter 6), you are to identify where the moment of peak feeling is in one of the dreams or episodes and to clarify what is occurring in this moment of peak feeling. The patient is then to enter into the peak moment, to live and exist as if she were actually the dreamer in the peak moment. This is step 3.2; it is discussed in Chapter 6 also. In step 3.3, discussed in Chapter 9, the patient and therapist are to open up the dream experiencing, to allow it to come forth, to sense and feel its presence. It is here that the patient is in the throes of feeling and experiencing. Once you do this in one peak moment, repeat the process in the other moment of peak feeling. Step 3.4 (also in Chapter 9) consists of identifying the single common experiencing present in both peaks. We know the dream experiencing and can put it into words.

Step 4 (Chapter 10) consists of actually being the dream experiencing in its welcomed and accepted, appreciated good form. It begins by being the wholesome dream experiencing back within the context of the dream itself (step 4.1). Step 4.2 occurs when therapist and patient identify an earlier life situation appropriate for the undergoing of the dream experiencing. Here is a remote situation in which the dream experiencing might have occurred, could or should have occurred, began to occur, or occurred in part. Finally, the patient is to be given an opportunity to be the dream experiencing within the context of the recent life situations identified in step 2 (step 4.4).

The last step in the session is for the patient to gain an experiential taste and sample of what it can be like to be the wholesale new dream experiencing, to behave as and from the dream experiencing, and to do so within the context of the live and real imminent extratherapy world. This is "being and behavioral change," step 5, and it is discussed in Chapters 11 and 12. A few of these new behaviors may be actually carried out. They are real possibilities, or at least they may be refined into real possibilities. This is step 5.1, rehearsal for reality. In any case, the session ends with some commitment to carry out some behavior. The behavioral commitment, step 5.2, is the culmination of the session of experiential dream work.

CHAPTER 2

Recording, Recounting, and Receiving the Dream

THIS CHAPTER DEALS WITH our answers to these practical questions:

(a) If I have trouble remembering dreams, what can I do to help me remember?
(b) How do I select a dream to record and work with? What are the characteristics of useful dreams for recording?
(c) When I am recording a dream, what should I try and include?
(d) How is it most useful for the patient to recount the dream and for the therapist to receive the dream?
(e) What does the therapist do when the patient engages in "talking about" the dream? Is "talking about" the dream useful or essentially useless for dream work?

RECORDING THE DREAM

Dream work begins with recollecting and recording the dream. There are some skills in doing both well.

Priming The Dream Pump:
How To Remember Dreams

If you haven't remembered a full-fledged dream in many years or you are a little worried because it has been almost a month without a real dream, there are some ways of priming the dream pump. However, explaining why you forget is not one of them.

Explanations of why some people do not remember their dreams typically tell you almost nothing about what to do. One of the longest running explanations is that people who do not remember their dreams tend to be people who do not remember lots of things anyhow. In the last 50 or 100 years we have called these people "repressors," which means that they generally do not remember what they do not remember. Psychologists like to see how these people fare on the myriads of tests, scales, inventories, assessment and evaluation devices. The result is an almost endless supply of personality traits, characteristics, and dimensions from an almost endless number of vocabularies and personality language systems. We have loads of explanations, most of them variations on the general theme that people who do not remember dreams are characterized by unspecified personalities of people who do not remember dreams.

In addition, there are some more intricate explanations, but they likewise do not tell you much about what to do. For example, suppose that the dream is supposed to provide you with a resolution of some personal problem. Remembering the dream would then be a step toward resolving the problem. But if the problem is resolved, then you do not have to remember the dream because you do not have a problem that needs resolution (cf. Cartwright, 1974, 1979; Greenberg & Pearlman, 1980). That is an interesting explanation for not remembering a dream, but it tells you very little about what to do to remember one.

Another explanation is that you do not remember dreams because they are threatening, and therefore deserve to be forgotten (cf. Schonbar, 1961), and also because they are fantastic and strange, and therefore are difficult for your memory apparatus to work on:

> In the forgetting and distortion of dreams during waking life it is important to distinguish between that which is due to the resistance to and repression of a specific dream thought or dream content and that which is due to the incapacity of the conventional memory schemata to retain the fantastic general quality and the strange language of dreams. (Schachtel, 1947, p. 17)

Still another explanation is that the remembering of a dream will be blocked if the dreams from prior sessions were not adequately interpreted:

> Sometimes, it appears to me that, if the dreams brought to one session have not been interpreted adequately, the patient's remembering of subsequent dreams is inhibited. (Mattoon, 1984, p. 149)

Not remembering dreams is interesting to try and explain, and we have lots of explanations. Yet these explanations are not expressly geared to helping the person do something to remember dreams.

Practical guidelines for remembering dreams tend to be provided by those who promote work on one's own dreams (e.g., Delaney, 1981; Garfield, 1977; Weiss, 1986). Those suggested below are practiced in the experiential approach.

Schedule a regular time for dream work. If you work on your own dreams, schedule a regular session every week or every two weeks or so. You know that on Thursday, nine days from now, you have your session of dream work at 7:00. If you work with a partner, you know that every Thursday at 7:00 you will be working on dreams, and that next Thursday will be your evening. You will find that dreams tend to be remembered when there is a regularly scheduled dream work session (cf. Mattoon, 1984).

Before going to sleep, get yourself ready to remember a dream. There are at least two ways of doing this. In experiential dream work, this consists of preparing equipment. Someday we may have a workable "dream recorder" that you put on or plug in so that your dreams are recorded effortlessly as you are dreaming (Mahrer, 1979, 1988a). In the meantime, if you use an alarm, have one that is gentle rather than one that blasts you out of bed. Place the alarm within easy reach so that you can turn it off almost without waking up, and certainly without having to get out of bed.

Use a tape recorder. Place it within easy reach so that all you have to do is push one button and you are recording. If you use pen and paper, make sure that you can turn on a light and write down your dream with a minimum of effort, and certainly by remaining in bed (cf. Black, 1971; Garfield, 1976).

There is a second way of getting ready to remember a dream. While it is not expressly used in the experiential approach, it cannot hurt, and it has the virtue of a distinguished history. For over a few thousand years, many cultures have used everything from direct suggestion to authority figures who command the person to remember dreams, often coupled with the promise of gifts or the penalty of torture, as well as all sorts of helpful rituals for placing the person in the proper frame of mind (de Becker, 1968; Eliade, 1960; Lorand, 1974; Meier, 1967; Von Gruenbaum & Caillois, 1955). Here is one such ritual used before the time of Christ:

> The Egyptian magician tried to procure dreams by magic prayers, magic drawings, and magic rites. The latter was accomplished by writ-

ing magic names on a linen bag, folding it up, and making it into a lamp wick, which was then saturated with oil and set alight. Before this magic light a magic formula was spoken. (Wolff, 1952, p. 10)

More contemporary versions of these ancient practices are often credited to Cayce (Bro, 1968), whose method of "incubating" a dream included the person's focusing attention on having a dream when he sleeps, framing a question that the dream is to answer, and trying to concentrate one's sheer will on getting a dream to occur. These methods have been refined and developed by Delaney (1981), Faraday (1974), Lifton (1976), and others, but the general idea remains that of taking a few minutes before sleeping and framing a question or topic for the dream, together with concentrating your attention on the sheer having of a dream.

Each time you awaken, record anything you can of the dream. There is a window of about two to four seconds. It occurs just as you are emerging from the dream state into the waking state. During these first few seconds of awakening, record something about the dream. Let your attention focus on the dream state in which you just lived (cf. Gendlin, 1986; Mendel, 1980). Then record something, anything at all of what occurred in the dream. Train yourself to do this; " . . . immediately upon awakening (either during the night or in the morning) train yourself to turn inward to allow any residual dream feelings or images to rise to the surface. To do this, lie quietly, minimize movement, and avoid distraction" (Ullman & Zimmerman, 1979, p. 93). Dedicate about 30 seconds to daily recording so that the dream occupies the first 30 seconds of each awakening.

Here are the recordings of an older man who said that he had perhaps three dreams in his whole life:

(Day 1) I don't remember anything. I have no memory of the dream. Nothing. (Day 2) There was a dream. A dream. There was a dream. But I don't remember anything. (Day 3) I think I had a long dream. Lots happened. I think it was pleasant. Can't remember a damned thing . . . (Day 4) There were people. Something was far away. I think somebody did something . . . That's all . . . (Day 5) I felt special. Felt special. Can't remember . . . (Day 6) There was a clock. White. A big clock. Really huge white clock . . . that's all. . . .

On the seventh day he remembered a full dream in detail. But you will notice that he assiduously focused on the dream in his attempts to record something. The trick is concentrating your attention on the dream, and recording. You may remember nothing but a residual feeling of being special, or a glow of sexual feeling, or even just feeling kind of good. It is all right to begin with only the tail of the feeling (e.g., Corriere, Karle, Woldenberg, & Hart, 1980, pp. 13–14).

Just make sure you record whatever is here as you are starting to enter into wakefulness. It may be the tail end of the dream. It may seem much more tied to movement from a dream state to a state of wakefulness. Make sure that you record it even though such images are compelling in their own right and may constitute indications of the receding away of the dream world as you move into the waking world. Here are two such recordings:

> Like seeing a painting, a large canvas, oil. But the thing was, it was bubbling, heating up, and so everything was oozing into everything else, and you can't see what the picture was.

> I see an opening, a slit, like the vagina of a little baby, only the opening is long, maybe 10 or 12 inches, and something is going down the opening. It's like a fissure or a well opening and something went back down and now it's all closed up.

You must not let your attention wander to other topics such as the ordinary preoccupations of your waking personality: "I have to pick up Sam and Joe this morning. . . . I wonder if my mother-in-law slept OK. . . . Is it raining?" Do not let your attention go to the way you are feeling right now as you are becoming awake: "My cramps are still bothering me . . . I have to pee . . . I'm still sleepy, really tired. . . . My mouth feels awful!" Do not have thoughts "about" the dream: "Were there two peaks? I just remember one. . . . That's the first one I remember in color. . . . There was a bush in the dream, a little bush, very pretty. I think I should record that. . . . Hey! I had a dream. I haven't had one in months. I remember the dream."

Just record anything you can of the dream, and start putting your attention on the dream the very first few seconds you are awakening. That primes the dream pump and allows you to receive a full dream.

What to Record in Order to Have a Good Dream
To Work With

Each dream approach has its own answer to the question of what to record. Do you record just what you remember of the dream itself? Do you record more than what happened in the dream? What else is useful to record? Here is the succinct Jungian guideline: "In addition to the dreams themselves, the dreamer records the personal associations to each dream, whatever archetypal amplifications become available . . . " (Mattoon, 1984, p. 46). Below are some guidelines for what to record in order to have a good dream to work with in the experiential approach.

Some dreams are quite useful to work with, and some dreams are quite useless. In the experiential approach you can rather easily divide most dreams into useful and not useful. Jung leaned in the opposite direction: "In analyzing tens of thousands of dreams, Jung found that some message can be gleaned from nearly every dream . . . " (Mattoon, 1984, p. 4). So did Freud: " . . . I am asserting that there are no indifferent dream instigators—and consequently no 'innocent' dreams. . . . Dreams are never concerned with trivialities. . . . The apparently innocent dreams turn out to be quite the reverse when we take the trouble to analyse them. . . . (Freud, 1900, pp. 182–183). On the other hand, I would say that only certain dreams and dream recordings are useful (cf. Cohen, 1974a, 1974b).

Record and work with a dream from the last few days or so. There are several reasons for this. One is that the dream experiencing is still rather fresh, still active and rather close. Second, I have greater trust in the accuracy, detail, and completeness of a recently recorded dream. Dreams from weeks or years ago tend to be more in the nature of interesting memories than good descriptions.

I suggest that you not work with dreams that happened weeks or months ago, or treasured dreams from when you were a child, or that dream you remembered from when you were in the hospital after the accident years ago or after your uncle killed himself. Nor would I advise working on a dream a little and then returning to do more work on that dream some years later:

Three years later, the slow and painful accumulation of evidence . . . had brought her to a new approach to this introductory dream. She recalled the dream . . . vividly, with details she had not at first reported, and accompanied by associations and interpretive readiness that made the dream a rich source of spontaneous insight. (Bonime, 1962, p. 119)

The patient's bringing up of old dreams can be quite useful in the same way that whatever the patient talks about may be quite useful, but experiential dream work calls for a recent dream rather than an old one.

The dream should have several peaks of feeling, episodes, scenes. The rule is that a useful dream has at least two moments when there was a rising-up of feeling. Over here the feeling was like this, and in this other part of the dream I felt like that.

Usually this means two feelings, one in each of two tandem vignettes or scenes. In one scene I felt excited and happy and in the other scene I was curious and filled with awe. Sometimes the two risings-up of feeling occur in the same general situation. We were on the battlefield and I was really scared when I heard the enemy nearby, and then they appeared and we fought and I was excited and felt really alive.

The two feelings may have the same content. When the enemy is heard nearby the feeling is that of being scared, and then the enemy soldiers take out their guns and aim at you and again you are scared. That is all right because you have located two different moments. Also, the feeling need not be absolutely intense. All you need is to locate where the feeling rises up or peaks, even if the intensity is only moderate.

Be rigid in applying this guideline. If the dream has only one rising-up or peak of feeling, do not use it for dream work. The dream may seem unusual or compelling or intriguing. Nevertheless, if there is only one peak moment of feeling, do not work with it. The dream may have the special characteristic of being a recurrent one, and clinicians stamp recurrent dreams as warranting therapeutic work:

Such a dream is of special importance for the integration of the psyche. (It refers) to something that has been in existence for a long time and is particularly characteristic of the mental attitude of the individual. (Mattoon, 1984, p. 84)

Even so, do not use a recurrent dream when it has only a single peak of feeling.

When you refuse to use such single-peak recurrent dreams, the person may be on the lookout for another part to the recurrent dream, and every so often another part can be found:

Pt: I had that same dream again. I've had it all my life. It's always the same. I am tiny, I mean, really little, maybe a few inches big, and I'm in a huge thimble, an old one, big, huge, and there is this massive thumb above me and it's just the size of the opening, and I can't get away. Too big, can't escape. The thumb comes down and I know it's going to crush me. I always wake up scared as hell. I had it this morning, and I woke up terrified. But then I remembered something else. Never had anything like that. I was working for a farmer, and he gave me this salt shaker, only it was filled with some sort of mysterious concoction that was hot and sizzled. The salt shaker was wood, and carved. I had to go out in a field and spread this stuff on mushrooms cause they were poisonous. It was amazing. I poured the stuff on, and the mushrooms went away. There were hundreds.

Now you have a recurrent dream with two peaks of feeling, and it can be used. The reason why two peaks are necessary is that you can get at the dream experiencing in one peak, get at the dream experiencing in the other peak, and use whatever seems to be common across both peaks. How to do this is described in Chapter 6. What is important here is that dreams with several peaks are to be used because it makes it considerably easier to arrive at a dream experiencing in which you can have confidence.

Use dreams regardless of content, apparent cause, or apparent meaning. Do not dismiss recording and using a dream because you think the content is everyday, mundane and banal. Do not dismiss a dream because the content is fantastic and unrealistic. Do not dismiss a dream because of its content, for the usefulness of dreams has nothing to do with the nature of the content.

Do not dismiss a dream because you are convinced that the nature of the experiencing is obvious or that the "meaning" is transparent. The usefulness of a dream has virtually nothing to do with your thought about its obvious meaning, and the dream should be recorded and used in spite of your certainty of its meaning.

Do not dismiss a dream because you believe it came out of "deep" sleep or because your sleep was "light." Dreams that come while you are taking a nap are just fine. Sometimes you will record a one-peak dream, fall right back asleep and have another dream. If this second dream also has one peak of feeling, you can use the two dreams. However, I prefer to use dreams coming from a single sleep state.

Do not dismiss a dream because you think you know what "caused" it. Last night you had that great moment of making up with your cousin after all those years. Your dream was all about making up with a close friend. Record the dream. No matter how certain you are of what accounted for the dream, record it. Do not dismiss a dream because you think it was caused by eating pickles and ice cream, or because you have the flu, or because you are menstruating, or any other supposed cause. Do not dismiss a dream because you know the dream was prompted by something as you were sleeping: the cat walked over your back, the room became cold as snow blew in through the open window, your husband dropped the glass in the bathroom, and all of this occurred as you were dreaming. These dreams have traditionally been understood as responses to stimuli occurring during your sleep:

> What is the *stimulus* to which the dream responds? Sometimes there is an actual sensory stimulus, like the alarm clock . . . in this case the dream comes under the definition of an illusion; it is a false perception, more grotesquely false than most illusions of the day. A boy wakes up one June morning from a dream of the Day of Judgment, with the last trump pealing forth and blinding radiance all about— only to find, when fully awake, that the sun is shining in his face and the brickyard whistle blowing the hour of four-thirty A.M. (Woodworth, 1929, p. 480)

Aside from what the cause is, record these dreams and use them.

Describe the dream in detail, especially what is occurring in the peaks. The more detail the better. The appendix includes some dreams as they were actually recorded. Make sure that your recording is as detailed, for sparse and terse summaries are essentially unusable in our approach, although they can be used in psychoanalytic and psychodynamic approaches. For example, the following summary of three or four dream episodes was adequate for Binswanger (1958): "While on a trip overseas, she jumped into the water through a porthole. The first lover (the student) and her present husband attempted resuscitation. She ate many cream-filled chocolates and packed her trunks" (p. 321). This is Binswanger's own synthesis of a dream reported to him by his patient, and is so far from a detailed dream report that it is of no use for experiential work.

We cannot use a tight condensation such as, "I was in Paris and German spies watched me" (Garma, 1987, p. 15), yet that was sufficient for psychoanalytic interpretation. The therapist used his background information that the dream " . . . occurred during World War II at the time of the German occupation in Paris. A man who was married to a woman with a German name had in a previous social gathering courted a French woman" (p. 15). On the basis of this background information, Garma arrives at an interpretation: "Paris represents the French woman and the German spies represent the man's wife, who had a German surname and was very watchful and disagreeable with him during that gathering" (p. 16).

For experiential work, make sure that you detail what is occurring in the peaks of feeling. It is all right to mention what you can of the rest of the dream, but try hard to describe as much as you can about the peaks. Tell about the scene and situation, the sights and sounds, the colors and the odors, everyone's behaviors and movements. Describe what everyone is doing and how they are doing it. Make sure that you describe everything that is occurring inside: the thoughts and ideas in you, the images in your head during the peak, and especially as much as you can describe about your feeling. Tell what the feeling is in connection with and something about when the feeling was strongest. The peak is the richest part of the dream, and must be given plenty of description.

If you record as you are awakening, you can do a good job. Otherwise, the details will slip away and you will be left with a bare skeleton of what happened. This was illustrated when a woman brought a recording of what she introduced as a fine two-peak dream. We listened to the recording of one episode and the peak. Then we heard the following:

> . . . Then, in the next part, I'm in a castle, and this man is with me.
> . . . There is a dwarf and he looks at my bracelet and I feel good.
> . . . What happened? Trying to think. . . .

She was dismayed. That was all there was to the second part of the dream. She had been sure that much more happened in this second part. Although she was convinced that much more had happened in the second part, she could recollect nothing, and she was embarrassed that she had not recorded more about the dream. While she was talking, the cassette recorder was silently moving on until we heard the following, none of which the patient had remembered until the recorder announced:

> . . . I remember. This guy comes up to me. He's a dwarf . . . he looks at my opal bracelet. It's gold, with opals all over, maybe eight of them. I am standing and there is a bright table lamp, and this dwarf is sitting in a chair and my hand is on the table, and he is holding my hand. The dwarf had been placed in a spell. I mean he was really the owner of the castle, but he was placed in a spell and made into the dwarf, and the dwarf is looking for someone to be his bride and to make him into the rightful owner of the castle. He inspects the bracelet and he looks at me. He has been searching for years for someone with the right gold bracelet to release him from the spell, and I'm the person because the look in his eyes tells me that. My feeling is that I am excited; in fact, I am so excited that I can hardly stop shaking. I will be the wife of this man. It's excitement that I will release him and make everything the way it should be. I'm shaking I'm so excited.

The moral is to make sure that you provide plenty of description of what is occurring in the peak moments of feeling, and to describe the dream as fully as you can.

Record the bits and pieces as they come to you rather than trying to organize the dream in a logical sequence. Start recording with whatever is front and center right now, whether it is from the beginning or middle or end of the dream. As more bits and pieces come to mind, describe them. Recording which part comes first in the actual dream is much less important than catching and describing whatever else comes to you in any order.

In some approaches, you are asked to review the dream in your mind before actually recording it in some sort of logical sequence (cf. Regush & Regush, 1977). Do not follow that guideline in experiential work. What is important is that you end up with as much as you can, not that you present the dream in some kind of logical sequence.

Do not record or use your waking feelings, thoughts, explanations, or bodily sensations. The only useful information from the waking person will consist of "connecting" recent events, but what these are and how to get them will be mentioned shortly. With this exception, we do not use the waking person's thoughts and feelings about the dream. You may be drawn to providing descriptions of how you feel on awakening, thoughts about the dream, explanations, and immediate bodily sensations. These are not useful for dream work: "I have a feeling of being scared, ominous, like something is going to happen, like the dream makes me this way." "I feel like I got heartburn, from the dream I bet." "That was another erotic dream like the one I recorded last time." "More of that theme of being taken care of and nurtured." "Funny that I have a thought about wanting to call my cousin even though I haven't even thought of him in years."

Unusual bodily sensations on awakening are very interesting, but they add little to dream work and need not be recorded. You may wake up with a cold wet sensation on your face, or a burning sensation on your leg, or a painful sensation in the crook of your elbow. We do not use these because they are a part of the awake person and tell us very little about the dream itself. On the other hand, some approaches will go from the pain in the elbow to the patient's thoughts about the pain and then to an interpretation about what the patient is like:

> Another patient wakes up feeling that he has been dreaming, but recalls only the experience of pain in the crook of his elbow, which continues to ache after he awakens. He associates this pain with punishment from a teacher who made him stand in front of a class for an inordinate period holding heavy books without dropping them. . . . This man faces therapy as if it were a painful, extended punishment. (Bonime, 1962, p. 3)

Everything you record is to provide a description of the dream itself. There is one exception, and that is our next topic.

Linkages: What They Are and How to Get Them

In the experiential approach, just about everything in the dream is a context wherein you have some kind of experiencing. If you are going to experience being closed in, you need some situational context appropriate for that experiencing. What occurs in the dream is largely the right kind of scenery, the proper situation, the cordial context for whatever is the experiencing. This is close to Hall's idea that the dream setting portrays the way the person looks at the world:

> The dream setting may portray the ways in which the dreamer looks at the world. If he feels that the world is closing in on him, he dreams of

cramped places; if the world appears bleak, the dream setting is bleak. (Hall, 1965, p. 227)

When you record the dream, the experiential approach accepts that there are simple connections between what is in your dream and what was in your life in the last few days or so. If your dream included your being cramped into a small seat in a car, then some part of this probably links up with a situation in your recent life. You were in such a position or perhaps someone mentioned being cramped. The question to ask yourself is where and when, in the last few days or so, you had any contact whatsoever with pieces or bits of the dream.

If some connection or linkage comes to you as you are recording the dream, record it. If, on the other hand, you finish recording the actual dream, then keep going so that you end the recording with two or three linkages. Make sure that you have two or three "linkages." Here are some verbatim examples from actual recordings:

Lake. Lake. The sign said "Lake." Oh, I remember, Jan and I watched that old movie and we tried to remember the actress's name. Veronica Lake. That's it.

She wore a dress with those swirls on it. That fabric. I remember. The fabric of the woman's dress in the dream, that's the same fabric on the antique chair I looked at in the shop yesterday. Yeah.

Policeman. Where? Did I see a policeman? Think about one? Sure. I was walking Sam's dog, and the policeman in the car last night. He wanted to know what kind of dog it was. I didn't know.

The old lady that was holding the fish. She is real old. That's the old lady the guy helped across the street on Saturday. Lots of traffic. Same kind of frail old lady. Real old.

The fellow walked into the cell with a fruit salad. Fruit salad. At the buffet yesterday there was this huge fruit salad. I told Bill that I was going to eat the whole thing.

Balls, little balls. Where did I see little balls like that. They were light, not metal. Right. In the mall on Friday. We walked by the pantomimists and one was juggling ping-pong balls. He had some on his mouth and shot them in the air and caught them in his mouth. He was good.

My name was listed but it was scratched out. A name scratched out. Scratched out. Not a name, but I remember at breakfast the old price was scratched out and I tried to see what it was. Same scratched out.

Notice that some of the dream bits or elements are the things you actually saw in the dream, e.g., the fabric of the dress of the woman in the dream is the same fabric on the antique chair in real life. Other linkages will be to the descriptive term or phrase you used in describing the dream element. For example, in the dream is an old lady holding a fish. In recent life you may have seen that exact old lady perhaps. But maybe you also had some contact with some "old lady" although perhaps not this exact one. In the last day or so you may have seen or thought about or had contact with the lake in your dream. But you described it as a "lake," and the word "lake" occurred in the last day or so when you recollected the actress's name as "Veronica Lake."

Here is an excerpt from the recorded dream of a person searching for a linkage:

> That baby. Advanced or something. She's singing and dancing, and she's just a baby. Hard to believe . . . baby, little one, just a tiny little thing. Did I see a baby like that? See a baby like that. That baby, just a little baby. I can't get anything. Did someone talk about a baby? Did I think about a baby? Baby. Sure. Yeah. Kelly called last night from Montreal, and she is pregnant. She's going to keep the baby. Her age. We talked about her baby. Sure.

The linkage might have been to the baby that she saw in the dream, or it might have been to the word "baby" which, although it was not spoken in the dream, was used in describing what occurred in the dream.

Sometimes you have a choice in selecting what part of the dream object to use. Try out one part after another to find some linkage:

> There was this little white dog that came bouncing along with the thick white fur and the s-shaped black mark on the side. Did I have contact with a little white dog like that? . . . Little white dog . . . little dog, some little dog . . . can't remember, can't. . . . Fur, white fur. Did I see some fur like that? Someone wearing white fur? . . . S-shape. A mark. Oh! That kid, student, that's the same mark. On his t-shirt. The same s shape. Black. That's it.

Use the parts of bizarre and unusual things that occur in the dream. Freud was ingenious in showing how all sorts of clever mechanisms work to combine interesting aspects into a single bizarre or unusual figure or object in the dream. We need not be concerned about these mechanisms, for we are merely looking for the linkages from the dream to recent life events. But we can use Freud's underlying belief that some parts of the dream are comprised of a blending or combination of several different incidents or situations from recent life events:

> If in the course of a single day we have two or more experiences suitable for provoking a dream, the dream will make a combined reference to them as a single whole; it is under a necessity to combine them into a unity. . . . Many experiences such as this lead me to assert that the dream-work is under some kind of necessity to combine all the sources which have acted as stimuli for the dream into a single unity in the dream itself. (Freud, 1900, pp. 178–179)

We are concerned with working in the other direction, on the understanding that a single dream element can be comprised of several pieces from recent life events. Even if something seems bizarre and unusual, the experiential version of Freud's thesis is that different parts of the image may be used to link to recent life events (Mahrer, 1971a, 1975). For example, here is a patient recording two linkages from a dinosaur in the dream:

> I never saw a dinosaur. Not even a little one. Nothing like that. In a magazine? No . . . "Dinosaur." The word. Someone say it? In class yesterday. That new guy. Mrs. Anderson read out the names of the class, and she mentioned this guy Oser, and she asked his first name and he said "Dean," and she laughed and said Dean Oser like it was Dinosaur, and everyone laughed. . . . Yeah, and the dinosaur had black leathery skin and it was old and cracked. That's the same thing, exactly the cracked leather on Dad's favorite chair down in the basement, and I asked him if it's OK for me to sit in it while he was fixing the furnace, and he got all funny, the same exact cracked old leather on the dinosaur.

Suppose that in the dream you are outside a saloon with some buddies, and the bunch of you are going to go inside the saloon. The swinging doors are heavy and slab-like, of cement or concrete, and you are a little surprised by the ease with which they open when one of the group pushes them aside and walks through. In your waking world you probably had no contact with swinging doors like that. No matter how unusual or bizarre the element, you can use aspects or parts to arrive at linkages. For example, when recently have you had any contact with swinging doors? "The new house, model house. Bob mentioned the swinging doors were kind of silly, between the kitchen and the laundry room." Or, you can ask yourself where you had contact with concrete like that. "When we were driving home from the model homes, I saw a cemetery, ugly, row on row of tombstones, same look of ugly concrete slabs, and I hated them. Just about the same shape like in the dream." The idea is to start with what occurs in the dream, no matter how bizarre, and go from there to where you had contact with that very thing.

Exclude linkages from peak moments and from the therapy situation. The purpose of getting linkages is to locate recent life situations where the dream experiencing may have been activated to some degree (Chapter 3). Any part of the dream may be used to go from the dream to these recent life situations. There is, however, one exception. Do not use connections from what is occurring in this moment of strong feeling. Exclude the nature of the peak feeling. Exclude the actions that are occurring in this peak moment. Exclude the objects and persons here in the peak moment. The reason is that what is occurring in this moment of peak feeling is much better used as an expression of the deeper experiencing than as a way of identifying recent life situations where that experiencing may have stirred.

In the dream of the saloon, if the moment of peak feeling is when all of you are inside the saloon and you are filled with fear when the bartender aims a gun directly at you and pulls the trigger, then exclude getting linkages from what occurs in that peak moment. Do not use the feeling of fear or bartender or gun.

There is a different explanation for excluding linkages from dream elements that more or less directly express the therapy situation. I am referring to the appearance of the therapist in the dream, or perhaps objects from the therapy office itself. In our approach, the preference is for real life situations in the person's own extratherapy world rather than in the part of that world involving therapy and therapist. Our way of using these recent life situations places much greater usefulness on extratherapy than in-therapy situations. If the patient's dream experiencing consists of ripping apart and assaulting, and if the dream connects to recent incidents involving his hated enemy at work, the big fellow driving the truck, and the statue of Hercules in the therapist's hallway, I find that the therapist can do a much better job of enabling the patient to undergo the dream experiencing within situations other than ripping apart and assaulting in the therapist's hallway. Accordingly, I prefer excluding linkages to therapy and therapist when there are plenty of other connections available in the dream.

Use simple, direct linkages rather than a loose flow of thoughts and ideas starting from the dream. The question you are asking yourself is, "In the last day or so, where did I have contact with or see or think about or have something to do with that very thing in the dream?" The linkages are simple and direct. The fruit salad in the dream was the fruit salad from the buffet yesterday. There was an old lady in the dream, and you had contact with an old lady like that yesterday. The word "Lake" on the sign in the dream is the same word you remembered last night when you recalled the actress's name, Veronica Lake.

In the psychoanalytic/psychodynamic approach, the patient engages in a flow of thoughts and ideas starting from something in the dream. I find that such a flow of thoughts and ideas seldom culminates in some recent experience and rarely in the same recent experience obtained by our method of simple direct linkages. Here are some associative flows starting with fruit salad, old lady, and lake:

Fruit salad reminds me of fruits, homosexuals, and I think of the two men in the next apartment. They moved in about a month ago, and I expect we will be getting at my own homosexuality soon because I was raised by my mother and had so little contact with my father. I haven't heard from him lately even though I wrote him and asked if he wanted to come to my wedding next June.

The old lady is holding a fish. Don't know the symbols. Wise old lady and the fish, penis, no, symbol of Christianity. But I'm thinking about my aunt, the older sister. She was the wise one and she introduced me to thinking and I read the bible with her. Values. I'm indebted to her. Wonder if I've been drifting away from what she represented in my life.

The lake was serene and lovely, calm. Peaceful. That's sure not been the way my life has been going lately. It's just the opposite. Like all my old craziness is coming back, and I'm at loose ends again. I don't have any time to myself. Always running, and like my motor is just racing wild.

When your attention is concentrated on the fruit salad or old lady or lake in the dream, you can connect that to where it occurred in the last day or so. However, once you proceed from the fruit salad to

some other interesting thought, and from that to some other interesting thought, you will have very little chance of locating some connection between the fruit salad and when you had contact with fruit
salad in the last day or so.

RECOUNTING AND RECEIVING
THE DREAM

The aim of recounting the dream is for the person to make the
dream alive and real again, ready to enter into, and for the therapist
to do the same thing, i.e., to be ready to enter into an alive and real
dream life.

A patient may bring a cassette and use the cassette recorder that I
have in my office. Sometimes the patient brings a cassette and the
recorder. Often the patient will bring the typed or written recounting
of the dream. In any case, the recounting is in the present tense, and
the aim is to make the dream present, alive, detailed, and real:

> To achieve the proper state of attentiveness, the analyst must repeated-
> ly encourage the reawakened dreamer to visualize the entities that have
> appeared in the light of his dreaming existence, then describe what he
> has visualized in the most minute detail . . . it is, pure and simple, a
> way of apprehending more and more succinctly what someone has
> actually dreamed. . . . (Boss, 1977, pp. 163–164)

The Therapist Receives the Dream by Taking the
Perspective of the Dreamer

The therapist listens with eyes closed and mouth shut. Mainly, the
therapist tries to see and feel and do what the dreamer is seeing and
feeling and doing, and this is what the patient is to do also. The
therapist keeps mouth closed because the main job is to be reasonably
close to what happened in the dream by trying to take the vantage
point of the dreamer (cf. Ullman & Zimmerman, 1979). This means
the therapist must tolerate a lot of ambiguity because the conditions
of recording were not those that necessarily emphasize clarity and
logical organization. The guideline for the therapist is to try and be
quiet while being as much as possible in the dream and inside the
dreamer.

Occasionally you will be very confused, and the sheer confusion
pulls you out of the dream. Then, occasionally, interrupt the recounting and get clarification:

Pt: . . . and then she turned into a bush and started blooming, and I grabbed her by the hand and said that I'm scared. . .

T: (Pulled out of the dream) I'm mixed up. You're with the little girl and the woman from the organization, and then one turned into the bush?

Pt: The woman just turned into a bush, but I knew it was still her, and I reached out and held her hand. When she turned into a bush I don't know what happened to the little girl.

T: Oh. OK. I see . . . OK.

The Recorded Dream Is More Useful Than Telling the Dream to the Therapist

In the experiential approach, we work with the actual dream as much as possible. Since we cannot literally be with the dreamer as he is undergoing the dream, we compromise by working with the recorded dream, and we hope that the recording is a good one. When the cassette is playing the recorded dream, the therapist concentrates on the dream that is being described. When the patient is recounting the dream, the therapist's attention is on the dream that is being portrayed. In general, most of the therapist's attention is on the dream itself rather than on the person who is doing the recounting. This is one reason why we would welcome some kind of dream recorder that could provide a living record of the dream as it is occurring.

In some other approaches, however, the important data consist in how the patient is being right here and now as she talks about the dream to the therapist. The therapist's attention is largely on the patient who is telling about the dream rather than on the described dream. Even bringing a written recording of the dream is thereby open to interpretation as, for example, resistance:

> The written dream is a modification of the fundamental rule of free association. . . . It is primarily a resistance . . . an effort to gain distance from the dream. . . . (Langs, 1980, p. 346)

In such an approach, the importance of the dream lies in how the patient uses the dream and how the patient is being in talking with the therapist (Breger, 1980; Langs, 1971, 1978a, 1978b). The reporting itself is the main feature: "The dream as reported is part of the dreamer's process" (Corriere, Karle, Woldenberg, & Hart, 1980, p. 12), and allows the therapist to make inferences based on the way the patient talks about the dream: " . . . the therapist may observe the links between the patient's prior and subsequent associations, and the manifest dream, and the extent to which there are or are not evident connections" (Langs, 1980, p. 359).

In our approach, the important material consists of the recorded dream, and the therapist's attention is mainly on the dream. In some other approaches, the important material consists of the patient who is talking to the therapist about the dream, and the therapist's attention is mainly on the patient. There are sharp differences.

How the Therapist Works With the Patient's "Talking About" the Dream

Occasionally patients will merely talk about a dream. It may happen in the beginning of the session, before they recount the dream itself, or later, when they mention something about a dream in a typical experiential session. How does the therapist work with such "talkings about" a dream?

Prefatory talking about the dream followed by the actual recounting: no problem. In the beginning of a session, it is common for patients to engage in some prefatory talk about the dream. When that is over, they then get to the recounting of the dream. As long as the prefatory talk is followed by the actual recounting of the dream, there is no problem. Indeed, one kind of prefatory talk is quite helpful as perhaps citing a recent event to which the dream may be connected. This is where the patient mentions the recent event and often connects it with the dream. When you are ready to use the dream experiencing in a recent scene (step 4.4, Figure 1), this information may well be useful:

Pt: I'd never been with a baby, not for more than a few minutes. Well, yesterday was the first time. My friend Edna had to go be with her father suddenly, and she begged me to take care of her baby, not even a year old. Tommy. I spent the whole day with him. I'd never done anything like that. I never spent a day like that in my life. It was all new, everything. So naturally I had a dream. "I was a mother and there was this baby . . . "

Pt: Yesterday I had a huge fight with my mother-in-law. I hate that woman. I hate being in the same room with her. I've never been able to tolerate her since Ned and I got married. She's always looked down on me. So we had this big fight. (Pause) And this morning I had a dream about it. It was awful. I was still fighting with her only in the dream we were killing each other. "Mabel and I had this fight, a real fight, with swords and we were . . . "

In addition, patients may talk about all sorts of other topics before the actual recounting of the dream. They may mention how the dream included a childhood friend whom they haven't thought about for years, how this dream was unusual because it was in vivid color, how the theme of this dream is so much like the theme of the last batch of dreams, how he happened to remember the dream while shaving, how she had two dreams to choose from and they both are good. As long as all this is in the beginning of the session and is followed by the recounting of the dream, the therapist can treat it as mere prefatory material followed by the actual recounting.

In the beginning of the session, the dream can be just another topic the patient talks about. Every session of experiential psychotherapy begins with the therapist showing the patient how to start with whatever feeling seems to be present here and now, or with whatever is front and center on the patient's mind, as long as it is connected with some feeling. Starting from here, the first stage of the session is completed when the patient attains a level of genuinely strong feeling. Suppose that the patient starts with attention on a dream, and "talks about" the dream. When this happens, the therapist uses this in the same way the therapist uses any other thing that may be front and center on the patient's mind in the beginning of the session. The therapist listens for the feeling that is here, as she allows the patient's words to be as if they were coming in and through the therapist. Once the therapist listens in this experiential way, the therapist then does what she would do with anything the patient talks about in the beginning of the session. That is, if the patient starts the session by "talking about" the dream, the therapist listens for the feeling and then opens the way for the patient to move in the direction of strong feelings.

Pt: (In a heavy, slow manner) I had another dream about being the outsider, and I felt rotten when I woke up. I'm always the odd one out, even in my dreams. I don't think it's ever going to stop. What the hell's the use.

T: (As above words are as if they are coming in and through the therapist, there is a feeling of almost crying.) There's a feeling here of almost crying. All right, what the hell, let the tears come if that is all right.

Pt: It's always the same . . . (light crying) . . . I feel so helpless . . .

The opening instructions invite the patient to attend to any feelinged center that is on his mind; if the patient "talks about" a dream, the therapist listens for the feeling:

Pt: Well we might as well get to the dream. I had this one about a well, and pushing a baby down into the well. It is my damned sibling rivalry with my younger brother, and there's no disguise. I've always hated him from the beginning and I wanted him to get back inside the womb and never born. It's that damned sibling rivalry.
T: (As these words come in and through the therapist, there is a pronounced feeling of anger at the brother.) Oooh, I feel this anger toward him. OK, then let it happen. You can be angry at him.
Pt: No I can't! It's like a cancer in me and I feel this way toward every man that I should be close to. Like my own son. I resent him! I wish he'd just go away! Yesterday he just glared at me and I wanted to kill him! I could have throttled that bastard!!

When the patient "talks about" a dream, you as experiential therapist listen for the feeling in the same way you would if the patient talked about his cancer or the nagging worry about losing money or the way he caved in when his sister yelled at him. If the patient talks on and on about one dream after another, you have loads of opportunity to listen for the feelings that go with each of the statements. We do not let this go on for most of the session and then "interpret" this as a "compulsion" or explain it as a way of preventing the therapist from saying what the therapist wants to say:

> That this was quite a serious compulsion was evident from the fact that for a long time my assertion that these dreams were a waste of time since he never made any use of them, made no impression on him. By cramming sessions with dreams he was seeking to prevent my saying anything that might stir up anxiety. (Guntrip, 1969, p. 298)

Instead of recounting the dream as it was recorded, patients may select all sorts of interesting things about the dream to talk about. They may talk about its recurrent theme, how unusual it was that the childhood chum appeared in a cameo role, how realistic or utterly absurd it was, how interesting that one object turned into another. In all of this, the therapist allows the words to be as if they are coming in and through her, and listens for the feelings that are present.

Patients may talk about the sheer remembering or forgetting of the dream. They say, "I wanted to bring a dream, and I had one this morning, first time in weeks, but I forgot it as soon as I woke up." "I had a dream and it was so vivid that I thought I'd remember it, but it went away. I can't remember at all." If there are feelings accompanying these statements, the therapist uses the feelings. If there are no feelings, the therapist allows the patients to turn to other ways of beginning the session. We do not draw interpretive inferences from their talking about remembering or forgetting the dream:

> If a patient is aware of dreaming at the time and then forgets it, he is at least in contact with his fantasy life, which is better than having it totally cut off. One patient, an entirely intellectual financial expert, had only about half a dozen dreams in some three years of analysis, and made only superficial if useful adjustments of personality. (Guntrip, 1969, p. 299)

Talking about a dream much later in the session. Almost always, if we are going to work with a dream, it is introduced in the beginning of the session when we start with whatever feeling is here or with whatever feelinged attentional center may be present. Even though the sessions are open-ended and may go on for several hours or so, it is seldom that the dream is recounted long after the beginning of the session.

In other approaches, especially where sessions are time-limited to around 50 minutes, mentioning a dream toward the end of a session may very well be interpreted in terms of relationship maneuvers or resistance (Bonime, 1962). In experiential psychotherapy, sessions go on till we have finished our work. Accordingly, if a dream is introduced and fully recounted after 30 or 40 minutes, we work on the dream. If the patient merely mentions a dream later in the session, we listen in the same we listen to anything else the patient says. In a similar way, Langs (1980) treats the patient's recalling a dream later in a session as just another instance of patient behavior.

We have reached the point where the person has recounted the dream. You may be alone in a room, working on your dream. You may be working with a partner. You may be a therapist working with a patient. Dream work has begun.

CHAPTER 3

Connections Between Dreams and Waking Life

IN THE SESSION, YOU HAVE selected the dream as the target of work (step 1.1, Figure 1), and the dream has been recounted (step 1.2). The next steps are to identify the recent life events that are connected with the dream (step 2.1) and to identify the moment of heightened feeling in these recent life events (step 2.2). This chapter answers two questions: (a) How may recent life events help us to understand and explain much of what occurs in dreams? (b) What methods are useful to go from the dream to the particularly useful parts of recent life events?

HOW RECENT LIFE HELPS US TO EXPLAIN AND UNDERSTAND DREAMS

Many theories share the general belief that there is some kind of connection between recent life and dreams. Experiential theory shares in this belief.

Pieces of Significant Recent Situations Will Occur in the Dream

Lots of dream theorists, researchers, and practitioners agree that bits and pieces of recent life events will show up in your dream (e.g., Foulkes, 1985; Hartmann, 1967; Hunter & Breger, 1970; Lane & Breger, 1970; Witkin & Lewis, 1965). Some of these things may show up intact so that the cigarette lighter that you lost yesterday may show up as the very same lighter in the dream. Often the thing from recent life shows up in a somewhat modified form, but perhaps close enough to impress you that what occurred in recent life can show up in your dream. It may occur as a different cigarette lighter, but still a cigarette lighter. Things that occur in your recent life will tend to show up in your dream, more or less directly.

But not everything in your daily life will show up in the dream, and that poses the question: Why would this particular thing show up in the dream? Suppose that you actually had a meal at a restaurant where you had smoked salmon, and the conversation among the four people at the table drifted to a mutual acquaintance who recently published a botanical monograph. How could you predict that your dream might include smoked salmon or a botanical monograph?

Experiential theory has no way of making such a prediction. If some kind of inner experiencing were activated in that recent situation, our prediction is that some specific part or parts of the situation would likely occur in the dream. But our theory is unable to say which part or parts would occur in the dream. It might be the smoked salmon. It might be a botanical monograph. But it also might be the glasses of the woman sitting across from you, the design on the dinner plate, the waiter, four or so people sitting at a table, the clock on the wall of the restaurant, or indeed any part of the whole situation. We are unable to predict that the dream will include a botanical monograph.

On this question, Freud's theory has a much more powerful answer. To begin with, he says that the dream will take up those parts of the recent situation that drew your attention:

> . . . our dream-thoughts are dominated by the same material that has occupied us during the day and we only bother to dream of things which have given us cause for reflection in the datetime. (Freud, 1900, p. 174)

Some element of a recent situation will be "food for thought" because it is connected to a large number of dream thoughts. Of all the elements in the scene in the restaurant, it is the botanical monograph which earns the honor and therefore is taken up into the dream:

> . . . the elements "botanical" and "monograph" found their way into the content of the dream because they possessed copious contacts with the majority of the dream-thoughts, because, that is to say, they constituted "nodal points" upon which a great number of the dream-thoughts converged, and because they had several meanings in connection with the interpretation of the dream. (Freud, 1900, p. 282)

Experiential theory allows us to say that the dream will likely include some part of a recent situation in which a deeper experiencing was active. But we have no idea which part of that recent situation will be included in the dream. In contrast, Freud's theory is powerful enough to identify which particular part of the recent situation will likely be taken up into the dream.

Recent Life Activates Deeper Processes That are Expressed in the Dream

According to experiential theory, deeper potentials for experiencing are activated in very particular moments a day or so before the dream. Deeper potentials work to organize the situation, to give it meaning, and once the situation is present the deeper potential is in turn given experiential life.

It is an ancient and widespread idea that recent life activates deeper processes that are then expressed in the dream, although approaches vary a great deal in what they regard as the nature of the deeper processes. Some of our contemporary approaches include the ancient idea that deep-seated bestial tendencies and impulses can be stirred up during the day, and these are then expressed in dreams. One of the earliest to enunciate this idea was Lucretius (97–55 B.C.) (Wolff, 1952). But the deeper processes may also consist of the activated physiological stirrings of internal bodily organs:

> Thomas Hobbes (1588–1650) . . . believed with Aristotle that dreams are caused by inner physiologic changes which are imperceptible in the waking state, where they are overwhelmed by our daily life impressions. During sleep the messages of the internal organs are translated into dream images. (Wolff, 1952, p. 27)

The internal organs know when a tumor is starting, an infection is present, a woman is pregnant or is at a particular point in the menstrual cycle (e.g., Hertz & Jensen, 1975; Schultz & Koulack, 1980; Sirois-Berliss & De Koninck, 1982; Swanson & Foulkes, 1967).

But the activated deeper processes can include more than bestial tendencies or the changes in internal bodily organs. One of the most common notions of the nature of these activated deeper processes is that they consist of thoughts, feelings, and sense perceptions that are more or less unconscious during the day and which are then expressed in the dream:

> [Dreams] include, according to Jung, subliminal thoughts and feelings, as well as sense-perceptions that are too weak to reach cognitive awareness. (Mattoon, 1984, p. 35)

Freud also holds that recent life events activate deeper thoughts, ideas, feelings, and wishes that are then expressed in the dream. His genius allowed him to penetrate into the various ways that these activated deeper processes were modified and expressed indirectly rather than directly. Yet it all starts with something real in the recent life event. Words that occur in the dream come from words in recent life events, and these are then altered in clever ways:

> . . . the dream-work cannot actually *create* speeches. However much speeches and conversations, whether reasonable or unreasonable in themselves, may figure in dreams, analysis invariably proves that all that the dream has done is to extract from the dream-thoughts fragments of speeches which have really been made or heard. It deals with these fragments in the most arbitrary fashion. (Freud, 1900, p. 418)

Freud discerned the many transmutations, symbolizations, displacements, condensations, combinations, transformations, conversions, and so on that take place so that, for example, words from everyday life may be expressed in the dream in comical and bizarre ways.

> The work of condensation in dreams is seen at its clearest when it handles words and names. It is true in general that words are frequently treated in dreams as though they were things, and for that reason they are apt to be combined in just the same way as are presentations of things. Dreams of this sort offer the most amusing and curious neologisms. (Freud, 1900, pp. 295-296)

Accordingly, the word "autoeroticism" may occur in the dream, according to Freud, as a person kissing a car. In the same way, all manner of mechanisms modify the recent life event into something else so that, for example, a tall person may occur in the dream as a short person or a white urn may occur as a black urn:

> Dreams feel themselves at liberty, moreover, to represent any element by its wishful contrary; so that there is no way of deciding at a first glance whether any element that admits of a contrary is present in the dream-thoughts as a positive or as a negative. (Freud, 1900, p. 318)

Regardless of the mechanism for converting the recent life thoughts into dreams, Freud relied mainly on the thought. Other psychoanalysts complicate this process enormously by holding that the important recent event is not only the deeper process itself, the thought, but also the manner in which the person was thinking it (e.g., sluggishly, conflictually, enthusiastically), and the somatic state of the person at the time (e.g., with heavy head, agitated body, or upset and nauseous) (Silberer, 1951, 1955).

Yet the commonality is that recent life activates deeper processes that are then expressed in the dream. This is both an ancient and a popular current way of explaining and understanding what occurs in the dream, and experiential theory is also included here. But there are further ways of explaining and understanding dreams in terms of recent life events.

Recent Life Includes Conscious Behaviors, Wishes, Thoughts and Feelings Which Are Then Expressed in Dreams

It is not necessarily "deeper" processes, activated in the last day or so, that lead to the dream. Cicero believed that conscious behaviors, thoughts, and feelings in waking life are the cause of dreams; " . . . according to him, dreams originate only in the thoughts and activities of the waking state" (Wolff, 1952, p. 19). Many dream approaches embrace this way of understanding and explaining dreams.

But which behaviors, thoughts, and feelings will be expressed in the dream, and what does the dream do with the conscious behaviors, thoughts, and feelings from recent life? Are they merely reflected in the dream, or are they worked over or modified in some way? The answers depend in part on one's notions of the use of dreams and dreaming.

One answer to these questions is that whatever conscious waking behaviors, thoughts, and feelings tend to preoccupy the person will be taken up in the dream. Greenberg and Pearlman (1980) explicitly studied this matter by looking at a series of their own dreams; they concluded that many of these recent life preoccupations were indeed taken up in the dreams, often just lifted out and expressed directly:

Sometimes the dreams portrayed the actual situations in which we were emotionally involved and sometimes they seemed to present a picture of certain thoughts with which we had been preoccupied. This was most dramatic in the dreams of one of us after his father died after the beginning of the vacation. The preoccupation with grief and attempts to cope with it pervaded both waking and dreaming. (p. 88)

Another answer is that recent life contains moments when the person disguised or hid some feeling, and the dreamer can observe all of this, i.e., can go over these moments once again. "While sleeping, the dreamer watches the way he or she disguised feelings and lived through images during the day" (Corriere, Karle, Woldenberg, & Hart, 1980, p. 27).

Perhaps the most widely used answer is that feelings and wishes which are not adequately or fully expressed in recent life tend to be taken up and expressed more adequately and fully in the dream. Freud accepted the idea of the dream expressing wishes, but he considered these as more or less unconscious. In classical academic psychology, wishes and desires were regarded as relatively conscious, and the accepted explanation was that those recent life wishes and desires that were not "satisfied" were then expressed in the dream:

> . . . the wish gratified in the dream is one that has been left unsatisfied in the daytime. . . . The desires that are satisfied during the day do not demand satisfaction in dreams; but any desire that is aroused during the day without being able to reach its conclusion is likely to come to the surface in a dream. (Woodworth, 1929, p. 482)

This notion is accepted in many contemporary dream approaches. Accordingly, the dream " . . . is a neutral releasing activity in which feelings that were not expressed, or not fully expressed during the day, try to come to completion through expression" (Corriere, Karle, Woldenberg, & Hart, 1980, p. 60). The dream is thereby understood as an adaptive enterprise, using material from recent life that is worked over, both in terms of its conscious and unconscious implications:

> A dream is prompted by some reality stimulent or day residue. . . . The dream is an adaptive effort and constitutes a working over, directly and indirectly, of the conscious and unconscious implications of the day residue. (Langs, 1980, p. 338)

The experiential theory declines this explanation of the relationship between recent life and dreams. We lean toward the importance of deeper potentials that are active in recent life, and prefer to emphasize these deeper (and thereby more or less "unconscious") potentials rather than conscious behaviors, wishes, feelings, and thoughts. Yet there is another accepted explanation to our question.

Recent Life Is Balanced and Compensated by
Dream Life

If the conscious waking life is one way, the dream life balances and compensates. "Dreams, I maintain, are compensatory to the conscious situation of the moment . . . " (Jung, 1974, p. 40). "I have made it a practical rule always to ask, before trying to interpret a dream: What conscious attitude does it compensate? As may be seen, I thus bring the dream into the closest possible connection with the conscious state" (Jung, 1933, p. 18); "what they really do is to present images or actions which effectively compensate 'the conscious attitude' of the dreamer" (Henderson, 1980, p. 376). It is a kind of homeostasis:

> . . . just as the "physical metabolism" carries out the task of guaranteeing the constancy of physiological events, so have the multiform events, occurring within the sub-conscious and unconscious spheres, the dreaming process included, effectuate the psycho-affective homeostasis. (Lowy, 1942, p. 65)

We need the dream life to provide a homeostasic balance to waking life. Otherwise we might become "desiccated automata":

> Dreaming, in the literal and metaphorical sense, seems to be an essential part of psychic metabolism—as essential as its counterpart, the formation and automatization of habits. Without this daily dip into the ancient sources of mental life we would probably all become desiccated automata. (Koestler, 1964, p. 181)

The problem is how to describe the waking life so as to see what it is the dreaming life will balance and compensate. Perhaps we can say that a person's conscious waking life is practical and coldly realistic so that his dream life would be lofty and romantically fantasy-laden. If the waking life is cerebral, perhaps the dream life would be sensuously feelinged. If one's waking world is frenetically impulsive, the dream world may be saturninely heavy and slow. Even if we accept the idea of homeostatic balance and compensation, we must still be able to describe the waking life in some way so that the dream life can be seen as a balancing compensation.

It is here that Jungian dream theory provides helpful dimensions for describing a person's waking life. But systems of grand polarities are by no means restricted to Jungian dream theory. In the approach of Corriere, Karle, Woldenberg, and Hart (1980), one such polarity is that from cognition to feeling/expression so that if waking life is dominated by thinking/cognition, the dream life balances this with feeling/expression:

> Feelings are left incomplete when cognitive functioning substitutes for matched expression. During dreaming the opposite process slowly begins to occur. Expression tries to substitute for cognition. It is the body's natural healing system against an unbalanced state. (p. 29)

The object-relations psychoanalytic school offers yet another grand polarity wherein the waking world subjects the ego to a sea of threats and dangers, and the dream world provides a safe haven, a place where the ego may be maintained safely against the waking world:

> Dreaming is the maintenance of an internal world, withdrawn from the outer world, in which the outer world including the analyst may not be allowed to share. . . . The dream world is to a considerable extent a defensive artifact, a struggle to maintain an ego in face of dangers from outer reality. . . . As a wish-fulfillment it is primarily an expression of the wish to remain in being, by having a world to live in when the real outer world is largely lost to the inner core of the self. (Guntrip, 1969, pp. 299–300)

The several dream approaches differ in just how recent life events are related to and help explain and understand dreams, but there is a long-established commonality among many dream approaches that there is a solid and useful connection between recent waking life and what happens in the dream. Experiential theory shares in this commonality and has its own way of making sense of this connection.

GOING FROM THE DREAM TO RECENT LIFE SITUATIONS

We now reverse the matter, and look into the ways that we can go from the dream to recent life situations.

Some Commonly Used Methods

In the experiential approach, the recent life situation is to be identified in the actual recording of the dream. As described in Chapter 2, recording the dream includes picking out a few specific elements or bits of the dream and asking yourself where and when in the last day or so you had some contact or connection with those. The camera in the dream is the camera you were looking for yesterday when your visitors were getting ready to leave and you wanted to take a picture. The yellow fire hydrant came up in the conversation in the committee meeting yesterday at work. The beard occurred when the fellow from the other department kidded you about not recognizing that he shaved off his beard. This is our way of finding the recent life situations.

A second method takes place in the conversation between patient and therapist. As represented in the Jungian approach, the therapist asks the patient to identify where in recent life the patient had similar thoughts, preoccupations, or experiences to those coming from the meaning or interpretation of the dream rather than from bits and pieces contained in the dream itself:

> In many of his examples . . . (Jung) . . . appeared to follow the practice of asking the dreamer, after the amplifications had been gathered, to describe the experiences and mental preoccupations of the day before the dream. Sometimes the dreamer's or the interpreter's intuition selects the relevant experience or preoccupation. . . . (Mattoon, 1984, p. 78)

A third method uses the patient's thoughts and ideas starting from the dream. The patient "free associates" from selected aspects of the dream. Listening to this series of thoughts and ideas, the therapist tries to make a connection to the patient's recent life. Again, this psychoanalytic method almost always yields different recent life situations than would be obtained by the experiential method. However, the psychoanalytic and the experiential methods would likely flag similar recent life situations when the associations start with a specific item from the dream and link directly to where that occurred in recent life, rather than proceeding through the usual flow of thoughts and ideas. For example, in working on one of his own dreams, Freud began with a dirty syringe from the dream and linked this directly to a recent situation involving a dirty syringe:

> This was yet another accusation against Otto, but derived from a different source. I had happened the day before to meet the son of an old lady of eight-two, to whom I had to give an injection of morphia twice a day. At the moment she was in the country and he told me that

she was suffering from Phlebitis. I had at once thought it must be an infiltration caused by a dirty syringe. I was proud of the fact that in two years I had not caused a single infiltration. . . . (Freud, 1900, p. 118)

A fourth method is for the therapist to predecide what recent life situation is important and to presuppose that the dream must therefore link to that situation. There is little to figure out in this method, for the therapist already decides that the important recent life event is that the patient is starting psychoanalytic therapy, has just had a miscarriage, has just accepted a position of high responsibility, or is losing the psychoanalytic therapist who is going on a month's vacation. The dream is then connected to the preselected important recent life event.

These are four methods commonly used to connect the dream to recent life situations. Almost always, different recent life situations will be flagged depending on which method you use.

Life Situations From the Last Few Days, Weeks or Months, or Long Ago

Is it useful to connect the dream to life situations that occurred in the last few days, or perhaps in the last few weeks or months, or even many years ago? How may we explain the occurrence in the dream of specific objects and events from long ago?

The preference is for life situations from the last few days. In the experiential approach, dreams reflect deeper potentials that are alive and active. This leads me to stay with the last day or so because my impression is that this particular deeper potential was probably not the alive and active one a week or month or year ago.

Freud also links the dream to recent life events, those in the last day or so:

. . . in every dream it is possible to find a point of contact with the experiences of the previous day. . . . The question may be raised whether the point of contact with the dream is invariable the events of the *immediately* preceding day or whether it may go back to impressions derived from a rather more extensive period of the most recent past. . . . I am inclined to decide in favour of the exclusiveness of the claims of the day immediately preceding the dream. . . . (Freud, 1900, 165–166)

In general, Jung also uses the same guideline. If, however, the dream is an especially big one, a significant one, then Jung allows the connected life situations to be from weeks or even months ago:

> The conscious situation, in Jung's view, includes the happenings in the dreamer's life the previous day or two, especially those that have had or might be expected to have a marked emotional impact. A dream of more far-reaching significance may reflect a conscious situation that embraces the days, weeks, or even months preceding the dream. (Mattoon, 1984, p. 75)

However, how may we explain the occurrence of remote old elements in the dream? How do we go from these bits and pieces to recent life situations? Suppose that your father died when you were 11 years old, and your dream included your father exactly as he was when you were a child. Or suppose your dream included the toy truck you had as a child, or the elementary school teacher, or the little girl from a few doors down where you lived in the small town as a child.

We use these dream elements in the same way we use any other elements from the dream, i.e., by asking when and where in the last few days you had any contact with that. The little girl from your childhood was named Selma, and yesterday your friend from work called to say that she had named her baby Selma. That is when you had the fleeting thought about the little girl from your childhood. Or, the dream included your elementary school teacher and you connect her with the lady waiting behind you in the grocery checkout counter, the one whom you momentarily thought looked just like your second grade teacher. The dream included your deceased father, and you connect him with the incident yesterday when your husband said that he hated mowing the lawn, and you laughed and said that your father always said the same thing. Freud used the same procedure in identifying recent life situations when the dream includes objects and figures from long ago:

> The frequency with which dead people appear in dreams and act and associate with us as though they were alive has caused unnecessary surprise and has produced some remarkable explanations which throw our lack of understanding of dreams into strong relief. Yet the explanation of these dreams is a very obvious one. It often happens that we find ourselves thinking: "If my father were alive, what would he say to

this?" Dreams are unable to express as "if" of this kind except by representing the person concerned as present in some particular situation.
(Freud, 1900, p. 429)

Jung used a different explanation for the occurrence in the dream
of early objects and figures. In his approach, these may occur because
some childhood experiences were forgotten, either because they were
connected to unacceptable childhood impulses or because they were
relatively insignificant:

> . . . memories of past waking experiences often appear as dream im-
> ages. They may be memories that were once conscious, perhaps in
> childhood, but subsequently were forgotten. Some memories may be
> represented because they are related to unacceptable impulses and,
> hence, are painful, or because they are not sufficiently important to be
> remembered consciously. (Mattoon, 1984, p. 36)

Neither the experiential nor the psychoanalytic approaches would
argue much with this line of thought. However, as indicated by
Greenberg and Pearlman (1980), we would add the working guideline that these early fragments were activated and occurred again in
the last day or so.

METHODS FOR IDENTIFYING THE
FEELINGED MOMENTS IN THE RECENT
LIFE SITUATIONS

The patient has started the session by recounting the dream. Your eyes
are closed and the patient's eyes are closed. The recording included two
or three linkages. Now what? According to Figure 1, the next step (2.2)
is to identify the feelinged moments in the recent life situations.

Why We Identify the Feelinged Moments in the
Recent Life Situations

You know that the dark wood from the dream connected to the
time yesterday when the beautiful bar came up in the conversation
with your sisters, and you recollected the lovely dark wood in the bar.
The work of this step is to identify when and where the feeling rose
up in that recent moment. Somewhere in that situation with your
sisters some kind of feeling rose up in you. It may have felt good or it

may have felt bad. We want to know what was happening when the feeling was strongest.

At this point, we have no idea about the nature of the dream experiencing. All we know is the dream and two or three connected recent life situations. But when we do uncover the nature of the dream experiencing (step 3, Figure 1), then the next step (step 4) is for the person to disengage from the ordinary continuing personality, the operating domain, and to enter into being the deeper dream experiencing. For this to happen, we have to know exactly when and where the person is to be the dream experiencing in the recent life situation. It is in this feelinged moment that the dream experiencing, according to our theory, might have occurred. This is the moment when the dream experiencing was activated, when it was stirred up but did not occur openly, when it may have started to come forth but not all the way or not in a good way, in a way that we regard as integrated and actualized. Our job is to try and identify that feelinged moment in the recent life situation.

The Instructions

The instructions are essentially the same whether the person is working by herself or with a partner or a therapist. The aim of the instructions is to start with the recent life situation and to locate the moment of peak feeling in the situation.

T: You said that the dark wood in the dream was the same dark wood in the bar from the old house where you grew up, and you briefly thought about that dark wood and the bar when you and your sisters were talking yesterday. The next thing is for us to find when the feeling was strongest then. It might have been any feeling at all, good or bad, and the feeling may have been very strong or even kind of mild. But there was some moment there in talking with them or when they were talking when there was some kind of feeling in you. Is this OK? Is it all right for you to look for this moment? Are you ready?

The instructions so far tell the person what we are going to do and invite the person's cooperation. After all, it is the person who will be doing the work. Almost always, the person will agree. The task then is to look for the feeling and what was happening in that moment, which may have little or nothing to do with the dark wood.

T: The feeling probably has no connection with the dark wood. But in that scene there was some feeling, something in the whole scene with your sisters, talking together. What kind of feeling was in you in that whole scene there? There was some feeling that came in you.

If it seems warranted, the therapist may explain that the dream connects with some particular moment in that general scene, a moment that is signalled by the rising up of feeling:

T: The dream connects to some moment in that scene with your sisters. The important moment is when there was some feeling in you. That is the moment we are looking for.

The patient has a right to know the whole story about what to do and how to do it. On the other hand, back-and-forth discussions about the reasons for the reasons are hardly tied to what to do and how to do it. Give the patient all that can help her locate the moment in the scene when the feeling rose up.

Pt: Well, Edna's stretched out on the sofa and giving her usual performance. We are her audience. I know I do it to myself. She's not a bad person, and I just naturally become like a little mouse.

We are getting closer. Now we should uncover the nature of the feeling and what was occurring in that moment.

T: Sounds like you weren't feeling so great. Is that when the feeling is strongest? When she's holding forth? What is she saying? Or what are you doing?
Pt: It's when she asks if the coffee is ready. She doesn't ask. She orders. I feel like a servant. Actually I could feel my stomach tighten when she just about, she asked me. Actually commanded me. She looks at me with that sort of intent tough look like no one better disobey her. That's when.

That is enough. The instructions merely tell the patient to look for the feelinged moment in the scene, invite the patient's readiness and willingness, and then work with the patient in identifying the moment. Once you locate one moment, start with the next linkage and do the same for that one. Whether you are a therapist or working with your own dreams, the aim is to look for what was happening in that scene when a feeling was occurring.

Some Helpful Guidelines

There are some helpful guidelines that make it easier to find the feelinged moment in the recent scene. The person who works on her own dreams should know about these guidelines; the therapist can do things to put these helpful guidelines into action. One guideline is that the feelinged moment in the recent scene usually has little or nothing to do with the linkage that connected to the recent scene. The person who works on her own dream should understand this; the therapist should make this clear to the patient:

T: The antenna in the dream. That was the antenna on your car yesterday, when you tried to pull it up and it was stuck. In that whole scene with the car, that scene, when was the moment when there was some feeling? It may have nothing at all to do with the antenna. Or maybe it did. What was happening there?

Pt: I was feeling hurt. I had a fight with my brother-in-law, and I was just hurt, feeling alone. I wanted to go for a long ride and the damned radio never worked. I was unhappy about the whole car anyhow, and I bought it from him, used. It never worked. It was in the shop more than I had it. The clutch was just fixed. I wanted my money back or something. I hated that car.

In fact, the actual moment of heightened feeling usually has nothing to do with the dream object or figure:

T: OK, so the ballet slippers are like the slippers of the woman at the Women's Center. Something happened at the place, probably had nothing to do with the woman and the slippers. But there was a feeling there, somewhere.

Pt: I felt threatened. Have no idea why. It's a lesbian drop-in center, and most of them looked like they don't go for a lot of shit. I have no idea. I was threatened.

T: Some time especially?

Pt: There was a woman I think I met once. She didn't recognize me, but maybe she knew Jan. I don't know. When I saw her, she looked like an animal on the scent. More ferocious than anything. We didn't talk. She didn't even see me, but I could feel my heart pumping when I saw her over there, and I was threatened. I barely got out of there. I felt suffocated.

On the other hand, sometimes the feelinged moment just comes tumbling out. In the actual recording, he says the following: "That old man who walks around dizzy and then passes out. That dizziness is what happened to me in the afternoon when I came home from work. I almost passed out. Got real dizzy all of a sudden and I was scared." In looking for the feelinged moment, the therapist inquires as follows:

T: What happened when you were dizzy? You were scared? Where was this? What is going on?

Pt: I came home and looked at the mail and I was in the kitchen, and suddenly I got dizzy. I couldn't stand up and the walls were going every which way. I almost passed out and I had to just sit on the floor and I put my head on the floor. I was scared as hell that something was really wrong with me. I was really scared, I mean I was scared as hell that something snapped in my head, like blood vessels or something. I couldn't even open my eyes, everything was going round. It was awful!

We now have a clear picture of the moment of strong feeling.

Often, however, it is difficult to go from the general scene to the moment of strong feeling. Take your time, and slowly look for the moment:

T: The "Florida" in the dream connects to Mary. She just came back from Florida, and you chatted with her yesterday.

Pt: Nothing happened. She just mentioned Florida. There was no feeling.

T: Maybe not around "Florida." But in talking with her. There was some feeling.

Pt: No, we just talked about her brother and the business. Nothing.

T: (We could easily leave this linkage go. The therapist tried once more.) It may not have been some particular thing. Just how were you feeling?

Pt: I had cramps. Bad. I was up most of the night. It was OK then, but I felt like I wanted to go to bed. I could barely follow her. Wait! I remember when she was telling about the business. That's what she was talking about. I felt so nauseous. I could barely hear her. I could almost throw up!

Most people are skilled at keeping the moment fuzzy and vague, especially when the feeling is unpleasant. You can make a stab at locating the moment, but sometimes it cannot be found so easily. Occasionally the patient will start to have the feeling right here in the session, and then the moment will come back:

T: The lawn mower is Jack's, and you and Sally were there, and a couple of the other neighbors. When did you have some kind of feeling in that whole scene there?

Pt: We were just talking. Nothing special. I felt all right.

T: There was probably some feeling. How did you feel?

Pt: I felt all right.

T: Maybe it would help to describe what was happening there, what you were doing and talking about. Sometimes it's hard to find exactly when the feeling was high. It's hard.

Pt: Well, I was not saying much. Greta was there. She's the new one, just moved in. They were talking about things, the new zoning or something. (And then with some tenseness) The city's starting in again.

T: That sounds a little tense.

Pt: That means more damned meetings! I hate those damned meetings! I just hate them. Doug said that we're going to have to do something. I just froze up inside and I wanted to get the hell away from there! Sally loves all those damned neighborhood meetings and they drive me crazy. I saw that Sally got all excited. I could have killed her!

Sometimes the feeling is a delightful one. Good feelinged moments are useful too. Make sure that you allow the moments to be good ones:

T: So the scene is being in the car with Marilyn. What was the moment when there was a feeling? Any kind, good or bad.

Pt: I don't have a car, and Marilyn loves to drive. We were going to get a hamburger. She (laughs hard), she can yell! This guy in the truck cut her off and she yelled! Yipes! She screamed bloody murder. She gave him hell! He yelled at her and she called him a damned fucker! I got embarrassed! I huddled down in the seat so no one can see me. She's great! We laughed like hell!

The feeling may be a quiet inside feeling, not tied to any action or interaction. It can occur when you are alone:

T: So the walrus is something you read about in the paper. You are alone in the living room . . .

Pt: Yeah, I don't usually read there. I was reading, and I was slumped back in the chair and just reading, and I remember my Dad would take a nap in the living room. He'd put the paper over his face and he'd sleep, and Mom used to kid him about being near-sighted when he read. (Quiet light crying) I miss him. I miss my Daddy. . . . I felt sad just thinking about him and his naps, and it only lasted a few seconds.

Now you have identified moments that can be used later, in step 4.4. When you grasp the nature of the dream experiencing, you can then "be" this dream experiencing in the context of these recent moments. But this step comes later.

A Few Common Problems and
What to Do About Them

It usually takes some time before patients include linkages in their recordings. I find that people who work on their own dreams do better than patients. Until patients include linkages in their recordings, the question is whether or not the therapist can get these linkages in the session. My impression is he cannot. The time to get linkages is when you are recording the dream, not in the dream work session. I still occasionally try to find some useful linkages in the session, but in general that does not work.

If the patient's recounting contains no linkages, I go over the way of recording linkages, and sometimes the linkages do indeed come tumbling out:

T: Remember the lady with the limp? You can ask yourself where and when yesterday you had some contact with a lady with a limp, or with someone with a limp. Just see some connection like that and record it, that's all. And get two or three of them. It can be the limp or the lady herself. In the dream she was a cleaning lady, so ask yourself when and where you had some connection with a cleaning lady yesterday. Or she was a short woman, with white hair . . .

Pt: She was the bag lady from yesterday. I live downtown, and there are women all over who live there and this one and I, we are not really friends, but we say hello to each other, and every other day or so we meet as I go to work by the church where they go in the morning. And the limp is when I left work yesterday and I fell on the ice and hurt the knee that was operated on when I was a kid, and I limped all the way home. Limped! I was scared that I had done something to it.

A second problem is when the patient goes from the recent life situation to other topics and never gets at the feelinged moment in the scene. In the recording, the white pants connected to the white pants worn by his friend yesterday. In the session, you and the patient are starting to look for the recent life situation on your way to looking for the feelinged moment:

T: Yesterday. He's wearing the white pants. What was going on? Where was this? What is happening?

Pt: He just came over. He didn't say anything, just showed up. I think it was in the afternoon because I left work early to do some shopping. Everyone takes off, and I had so many hours. So I decided to go shopping and just be by myself. I haven't taken off in months. And all I bought was some light bulbs (laughs).

This is not a difficult problem. Just show the person how to look for the feelinged moment back in the scene with the white pants:

T: All right. But stay in the scene with old white pants, and let yourself look for what was happening, what you were feeling. It may not even have anything to do with him or the pants.

Pt: I wanted to be alone. I wanted to do the tiles in the bathroom, at least figure out, lay it out, the design. He comes in and, I felt intruded. But I didn't say anything. I made some coffee and listened to his stuff about the car he's having trouble with. I never said anything. I felt . . . I should have said something when he just came in. But I didn't.

In general, I stay with the search for the feelinged moment, and I decline to drift along with the patient onto one topic after another. On the other hand, many other therapies invite the patient to start from the dream and to proceed to whatever other topics seem to come along:

> The analyst, whose first responsibility is therapy, and only secondarily dreams, must attend to the "irrelevant" material, even though it seems unrelated to the dream, because, as a result, the patient may be enabled to arrive more quickly at recognition of a problem area. (Mattoon, 1984, p. 57)

In the psychoanalytic procedure, the patient is to go from the dream to some associated connection, often from the last day or so ("day residue"). The fellow, Joe, in the dream, is connected to talking with Joe yesterday, and the argument in the dream is connected to seeing the television program in which everyone was arguing. In our approach, we would make the same connections from the dream to recent life. Here is where the sharp differences occur. The psychoanalytic therapist would then want more associations in order to get some ideas about the patient's feelings, hidden wishes, and symbolic meanings connected with Joe and arguments:

> The patient may connect the people, scenes, and actions in the dream to various day residues: "Joe was in the dream because I talked to him yesterday and I guess there was an argument because I saw that tv program last night where everyone was arguing." While associations to day residues may often prove useful, when the patient stops with them he is communicating, "This is all the dream means, it has nothing to do with my feelings about Joe or what he represents, nothing to do with my wish to argue." (Breger, 1980, pp. 8–9)

From the perspective of the experiential therapist, the patient could talk all day long about his feelings and hidden wishes about Joe and about arguing. Yet none of this would bring us closer to the feelinged moment in talking with Joe yesterday or to the feelinged moment watching the television program in which everyone was arguing. The solution to this problem is to look for the feelinged moments in the recent life incidents, and to decline all sorts of interesting connected topics or associations.

Another problem occurs when the patient becomes so embroiled in the recent incident that the choice is whether to stay with this material or to turn to the search for the feelinged moment. For example, the dream included a bridge, and the linkage was to the recent incident when his brother is telling how worried he was riding his motorcycle over a bridge. As we went further into this incident, looking for the feelinged moment, the patient became increasingly filled with a sense of fondness toward his brother. Soon he was talking to his brother, expressing his warmth and closeness. This immediate experiencing took center stage, and the dream work receded in importance. The rest of the session was an ordinary experiential session rather than a dream work session. This does not happen often, but occasionally the therapist will have the option of working with the experiential material in the recent incident or identifying the feelinged moment and proceeding with dream work.

We have now identified the feelinged moments that occurred in recent life situations, probably a day or so before the dream. The next step involves getting at the dream experiencing. But before we get to that, it is important to discuss the useful data for dream work from the perspective of the various dream approaches.

CHAPTER 4

Useful Data for Dream Work

WHAT ARE THE USEFUL DATA for dream work? Are some parts or aspects of the dream more useful than others? This chapter is introductory, for it deals with the kinds of data that many approaches consider useful, as well as comparing the experiential answer with those of other dream approaches.

THREE WAYS OF LOOKING AT A DREAM, AND THE DISTINCTIVE DATA PROVIDED BY EACH

The thesis of this section is that there are at least three ways of looking at a dream, each of which yields its own unique data (Figure 2). You can look at the dream from the perspective of the dreamer. That is, the person (and the therapist too) can get inside the perspective of the dreamer in the dream. Secondly, you can look at the dream from the perspective of the awake person in the session. Now you are not the dreamer; you are an awake person who is talking about the dream. Or, thirdly, you can look at the dream from the perspective of the therapist. Whichever perspective you use, you are thereby privy to distinctive data and lose data available from the other perspectives. This is a serious thesis indeed, for it has direct implications for the data you will use and lose, as well as for the methods of obtaining whatever data you select.

The Distinctive Perspective of the Dreamer

In the experiential approach, the absolutely precious data consist of the experiencings that are here in the dream. If we want to grasp the dream experiencing, we must get inside the perspective of the dreamer, for the dream experiencing is accessible only from the dreamer's perspective (Figure 2). The waking person cannot get at the dream experiencing, nor can the therapist.

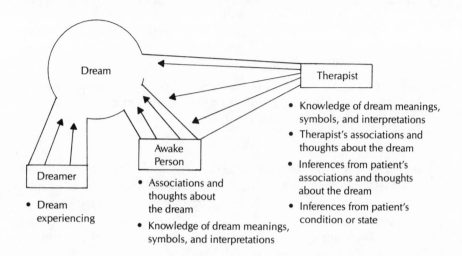

Figure 2. Three Ways of Looking at a Dream, and the Data Provided by Each

The dreamer is in a qualitatively different, deeper personality. In the existential-humanistic theory of personality that underlies experiential psychotherapy (Mahrer, 1989a), there is a sense of I-ness, the heart of the innermost identity or self. When you are awake, this sense of I-ness is in the personality that is the more or less conscious, thinking, behaving, functioning you. This is the operating personality. But there is also a deeper personality (see Figure 3). The potentials for experiencing that comprise this deeper personality are not directly tied to what you think and feel and experience in your waking life. Deeper potentials have an influence, but not the same direct influence that is your operating personality. The I-ness remains in your waking operating personality when you are awake and being the operating personality. But when you dream, that center of I-ness moves out of the operating personality and enters into the deeper personality. You are literally a qualitatively new and different personality in the dream world.

This means that in the dream world you will tend to be and behave as a qualitatively different person. The experiencings in your dream world are different from the experiencings that are you in your waking world. If your waking personality is predominated by experiencings of defiance and rebellion, control and conquest, these will tend to be absent from your dream world. If your waking world is charac-

terized by strangeness and lunacy, by ways that impress others as mad
and crazy, the person you are in the dream world will be free of all
that. In commenting on this point, Kafka (1980) cites the work of
Eisler (1953):

> In Eisler's paper . . . there is a reference to a psychotic patient who in
> her dreams repairs the psychosis so to speak. It is as if the dreaming
> ego were nonpsychotic while her waking ego was psychotic. . . .
> (Kafka, 1980, p. 103)

In the vocabulary of psychoanalytic/psychodynamic theory, we
can say that the very core of the ego has moved out of the conscious
and preconscious realm and has entered into the unconscious realm.
In the vocabulary of object relations, we can say that in the dream
state the observing ego has detached from other ego aspects and has
entered even further into the libidinal unconscious (cf. Fairbairn,
1951, 1958; Padel, 1987). Although neither of these approaches
accepts that the dreamer is in a qualitatively different and deeper
personality than the waking person, the idea is not new. It has long
been noted that there are parallels between the dreaming state and
what is termed a state of insanity — in both the person is literally "out
of his mind." That is, in both state the person has left the ordinary
everyday personality and has entered into a qualitatively different,
deeper personality. In 1867, Griesinger spelled out some of the similarities:

> Wilhelm Griesinger was one of the first to compare the state of dream-
> ing to that of insanity. Dream and insanity alike show an incoherence
> of intelligence and project subjective internal reactions and images of
> the senses upon images of the external world. For the dreamer as well
> as for the insane the absurd becomes truth, frustrations experienced in
> reality are removed, and wishes are gratified. In dream as in insanity
> the idea of time vanishes. (Wolff, 1952, p. 31)

Among contemporary approaches, there are also those who regard
the dream state as qualitatively different from the waking state, as a
separate kind of existence, truly a wholesale other way of being:

> At one time he exists as a dreaming being; at another, as a waking
> being. Waking and dreaming are two equally autochthonous, though
> different possibilities or modes of existing of an ever-integral and
> whole human being. (Boss & Kenny, 1987, p. 150)

Clinical theorists such as Fromm-Reichmann (1958) and Blum (1976) also see the dream state as qualitatively different from waking, as a state of regression, similar to the supposed state of primitives or psychotics. Reviewers of dream research likewise see a basis for regarding the two states as qualitatively different (Fisher, 1965; Hartmann, 1965; Jones, 1964; Snyder, 1963).

The dreamer's perspective offers a unique access to the experiential reality of the dream world. The question is not so much whether dream events are real, but rather where one stands when asking the question. Almost always, the question of the "reality" of the dream events is asked from the standpoint of the waking person. Accordingly, Descartes can pronounce dreams as just as real as waking events:

> . . . René Descartes (1596–1650), in his *Meditations*, says that 'there exist no certain marks by which the state of waking can ever be distinguished from sleep', because dreams may be so vivid that they may be confounded with reality. (Wolff, 1952, p. 27)

Contemporary dream theorists can likewise pronounce dreams as real, but again, it is a question that is asked only from the world of the waking person:

> Any fundamental consideration of "reality" . . . will end in assigning a reality to what we dream that is autonomous yet equal in importance to waking reality. For what impinges on us as dreams is no different from what we see while waking, in that it too comes to being in the light of human perception and persists "there." (Boss, 1977, p. 183)

Once we ask this question from the perspective of the dreamer, then I agree heartily with Condrau and Boss that dream events are indeed real:

> If we judge our dreams not from the external, alien standpoint, but we allow the dream phenomena to be simply in their immediate givenness, it is obvious that what we dream is perceived neither as images nor as symbols. We experience what confronts us in dreaming as real entities. . . . (Condrau & Boss, 1971, p. 513)

Waking persons are inclined to probe into whether or not dreams are real. But I know of no symposia or journals in which dreamers presented their views on the reality of the waking world. In the experiential view, the dreaming person is living in a world that is qualitatively different from and essentially unavailable to the waking person, and the dreaming person is in the vicinity of experiencings that are essentially unavailable to the waking person.

These exceedingly precious deeper experiences are the treasure of the dream world, the data that are crucial for us, and they are accessible only from within the dream world (Figure 2).

Access to the distinctive data of the dream world is through the perspective of the dreamer. If the dreamer is understood as inside the deeper personality rather than the operating personality (Figure 3), and if you value the experiencings of the deeper personality, and if the experiencings of the deeper personality are accessible only from within the dreamer's perspective, then it seems to follow that the waking person (and the therapist) must get inside the perspective of the dreamer.

The extreme emphasis on getting inside the dreamer's experiential world separates this approach from many others. To grasp the experiencings of the dreaming person, you must get inside the existence of that dreaming person: "All mental experiences—perception, rememberance [sic], thinking, dreaming, and also feeling—are relations of an existing human being and his world" (Buytendijk, 1967, p. 255; cf. Lifton, 1976).

Jung likewise saw the futility of reading the dream from the perspective of the conscious waking person; " . . . we are dealing with something like a text that is unintelligible not because it has a facade, but simply because we cannot read it" (1933, p. 13). Accordingly, Fosshage and Loew (1987b) credit Jung with being among the " . . . first in proposing that the meaning of a dream is apparent on its manifest level. The dream is valid as it appears and is neither censored nor disguised. Only the conscious position may resist the 'truth' of the dream" (p. 248). Even so, Jung did not take the next step of getting inside the dreamer's world.

Many contemporary theorists and clinicians speak about the importance of studying the dream phenomena in and of themselves, and yet the waking person and therapist are inevitably outside the domain of the dreamer (cf. Gendlin, 1977). Lowy (1942) described how the therapist's intuition might help sense what may be present inside the world of the dreamer. May (Caligor & May, 1968) emphasized the importance of the phenomenological meaning of the dream but still relied on the interpretations of an external therapist. Perhaps the approach of Boss (1957, 1963, 1977) is closest to the phenomenological method in emphasizing what is occurring in the actual dream itself.

The Distinctive Data of the Waking Person

With perhaps the notable exception of the experiential approach, virtually all dream approaches look at the dream from the perspective of the waking person. As indicated in Figure 2, this perspective cannot access the dream experiencing; nevertheless, it is the only perspective that can provide the waking person's associations and thoughts about the dream and her knowledge of dream meanings, symbols, and interpretations.

From the perspective of the waking person, the dream is distorted, unreal, and irrational. When we apply the norms and standards of waking life, dreams are weird, bizarre, delusional, and hallucinatory. "Dreams partake of the nature of hallucinations in so far as the dreamer appears to see and hear what is not actually present to his senses" (Stout, 1899, p. 414). The dreamer does things that are impossibly unrealistic when we apply the criteria of waking life. Consider " . . . the dreamer taking actions that would normally be impossible, such as flying, breathing under water, walking through fires, and moving heavy objects" (Corriere et al., 1980, p. 37). No doubt about it, dreams are irrational:

> . . . dream images often are especially irrational in that they are not subject to physical or time limitations and they frequently depict creatures not now found in the world of nature. For example, dreams are common of humans flying without wings or falling from great heights without injury. (Mattoon, 1984, p. 34)

These unreal and irrational features become the data to be worked with from the perspective of the waking person. When you are in the dream it is quite understandable that the printing press must be kept going if the ship is to stay afloat. But when you are awake, that piece of the dream stands out as absurd, as unique, as something to be dealt with in dream work:

> . . . He unties me, and shows me how to steer. I grab the wheel and then he tells me the secret of the ship. There is a printing press that must be kept going if the ship is to stay afloat, and ink and paper must be fed constantly into this press as I turn the wheel. . . . What is

unique in this dream is the unusual detail about a "printing press that
must be kept going if the ship is to stay afloat." (Rossi, 1985, p. 24)

If we apply the norms and standards of the waking world, then
some of the feelings you have in dreams are distorted, inappropriate,
weird, and "pathological." From the perspective of the waking world,
you are showing evidence of problems in the area of feelings. If you
notice feces on your leg in the dream, the norms and standards of the
waking world say that you should feel disgust or repulsion or some
sort of similar feeling. If you feel amusement, that is evidence of
"affective discrepancy" (Bonime, 1962, p. 114). If you were naked
among a group of strangers in "real" life, they would look at you in
astonishment or ridicule or outrage. If, however, the strangers in the
dream look at you in indifference, then that is evidence of something
wrong, unreal, a perplexing contradiction:

> In the typical dream it never happens that the clothing which causes
> one so much embarrassment is objected to or so much as noticed by
> the onlookers. On the contrary, they adopt indifferent or (as I observed
> in one particularly clear dream) solemn and stiff expressions of face.
> . . . The embarrassment of the dreamer and the indifference of the
> onlookers offer us, when taken together, a contradiction of the kind
> that is so common in dreams. It would after all be more in keeping
> with the dreamer's feelings if strangers looked at him in astonishment
> and derision or with indignation. (Freud, 1900, p. 243)

Indeed, whole chunks or the dream qualify as distorted and irrational
when we switch from the perspective of the dreamer to the perspective of the waking person.

*The experiential answer to why the dream is indeed distorted,
unreal, and irrational from the perspective of the waking person.*
According to the experiential approach, when you are dreaming, the
center of I-ness has moved out of the waking operating personality
and has entered into the qualitatively different deeper personality
(Figure 3). What is more, relationships between the operating and
deeper personality are almost always disintegrative. That is, the operating personality avoids the deeper potentials, blocks them, distrusts
them, fears and hates them, keeps safe distance from them (Mahrer,
1989a). Accordingly, from the perspective of the waking, operating
personality, what is deeper is anything but welcomed and friendly,
precious and wondrous. Instead, what you do as the deeper personal-

ity, as the dreamer, and what occurs in the deeper dream world are seen as irrational, dangerous, alien, bizarre. It is the qualitative shift back into the conscious, waking, operating personality that endows the dream with its unusual nature:

> That which seems absurd, bizarre, or meaningless in dreams only seems so from the older more established points of view and attitudes that still dominate the conscious mind. (Rossi, 1985, p. 15)

> The world of dreams appears as dissociated only in comparison with the world of conscious thought, in relation to the world of logical reality. But why assume and take for granted that the world of dreams wants to be compared with, and related to, the world of reality and realistic thinking? The contrary is much more probable. The world of dreams is a world apart. (Lowy 1942, p. 56)

You are not at all the same person when you shift out of the dreaming deeper personality into the waking operating personality who has such disintegrative relations toward the deeper personality. This is our explanation for the waking person seeing the dream as distorted, unreal, and irrational. But most theories of dreaming hold to a quite different explanation.

Most theories assume that the dreamer is the same personality but with reduced controls. What are the essential differences between the dreaming state and the awake state? This has been flagged as a crucial question:

> Not until we have succeeded in making a fundamental distinction between the waking and dreaming state of human existence, can we claim to have contributed anything of worth to the understanding of dreaming in itself. (Boss, 1977, p. 175)

Boss assumes a single personality that can be in a waking state or in the dream state:

> But waking and dreaming . . . are modes of existing of one and the same individual human being. One's waking and dreaming belong always and exclusively to one as an individual human existence. And although waking and dreaming are different, they are equally autochthonous conditions or states of one and the same human existence. (1977, p. 185)

This is the widely accepted view. In both the waking and dreaming states you are essentially the same person, the same personality:

> Dreaming and waking are not separate states of consciousness . . . while we are sleeping we have the very same affective and cognitive drives and abilities we have during the day. The dreamer and the waking person are the same. (Corriere et al., 1980, p. 27)

Then how may such theories explain why dreams appear unreal and irrational? If you are the same person when you are dreaming, then the explanation is that when you sleep and dream there is a reduction in conscious controls. This is the ancient explanation, and it is the explanation used in most contemporary theories. According to Plato, when you dream your ordinary waking defenses relax, rational reasoning processes are less vigilant, and therefore you are vulnerable to animal passions that account for the distortion, unreality, and irrationality of dreams. In the fourth century A.D., Gregory described how in sleep the intellect relaxes, allowing all sorts of absurd and bizarre sensory impressions. Aristotle likewise held that vigilant awareness is reduced in sleep so that tiny inner and outer stimuli can assume distortedly heightened proportions:

> Impulses occurring in the daytime, if they are not very great and powerful, pass unnoticed because of greater waking impulses. But in the time of sleep the opposite takes place; for then small impulses seem to be great. This is clear from what often happens in sleep; men think that it is lightning and thundering, when there are only faint echos in their ears, and that they are enjoying honey and sweet flavors, when only a drop of phlegm is slipping down their throats, and that they are walking through fire and are tremendously hot, when there is only a slight heating about certain parts. (Wolff, 1952, p. 17)

In academic circles of the early 1900s, the same idea was maintained essentially intact (e.g., Woodworth, 1929), and virtually every contemporary dream theory accepts some version of this idea. During the waking day, cognitive mechanisms prevail, whereas in sleep the cognitive mechanisms weaken and affective drives prevail, thus accounting for the bizarreness of dreams:

> During the day the cognitive drive overwhelms the affective drive. . . . We make sense by having thoughts instead of "having sensation." At

night this changes—the cognitive drive weakens while the affective drive begins to ascend, making our ways of being symbolic seem bizarre. (Corriere et al., 1980, p. 28)

In psychoanalytic theory, there is likewise the same idea of a reduction in conscious controls, reality-testing mechanisms, and executive cognitive controls (Monroe, 1955); in dreaming, " . . . the censorship of the ego is off guard, the critical control of the self as custodian of awareness is eliminated" (Fromm-Reichmann, 1958, p. 162), and the reduced awareness accounts for the absurdity of dreams:

> The basic assumption which we have offered . . . is that dreams represent what a person thinks and feels or hallucinatory acts while awareness and censorship are dormant. From this concept it follows that the type of mental operation and the means of expression used by the sleeper in his dreams are explained by the state of reduced awareness of the sleeper per se. (Fromm-Reichmann, 1958, p. 169)

Because the conscious controls are reduced, the unconscious impulses and wishes can intrude, but because there is still a residual measure of control and vigilance (Ullman, 1961), the unconscious impulses and wishes occur in a form that is distorted:

> We may therefore suppose that dreams are given their shape in individual human beings by the operation of two psychical forces (or we may describe them as currents or systems); and that one of these forces constructs the wish which is expressed by the dream, while the other exercises a censorship upon this dream-wish and, by the use of that censorship, forcibly brings about a distortion in the expression of the wish. (Freud, 1900, pp. 143–144).

The censorship of the dreaming person works to protect the person from the anxiety that would occur if the unconscious impulses and wishes were to appear in their pure form:

> We can plainly see the purpose for which the censorship exercises its office and brings about the distortion of dreams: it does so *in order to prevent the generation of anxiety or other forms of distressing affect.* (Freud, 1900, p. 267)

Accordingly, it is understandable that dreams would tend to be relatively free of feelings, especially bad feelings such as anxiety "and other forms of painful affect." Freud finds dreams as lacking in such feelings, evidence to the working of the defensive system on the presumption that the dreaming person is essentially the selfsame waking personality:

> A dream is in general poorer in affect than the psychical material from the manipulation of which it has proceeded. . . . It might be said that the dream-work brings about a *suppression of affects*. (Freud, 1900, p. 467)

This model can be stretched to account for apparent exceptions. For example, if the censorship protects the dreaming person against anxiety and does so by disguising unconscious impulses and wishes, how may we explain dreams of the death of a loved one? Using this model, Freud accounts for such monstrous dreams by saying that (a) the wish is so unexpected by the censor that it slips by through sheer bold audaciousness, and (b) the wish often hides itself behind some genuine concern for the loved one in the day's residue:

> There must be special factors at work to make this event possible, and I believe that the occurrence of these dreams is facilitated by two such factors. Firstly, there is no wish that seems more remote from us than this one: "we couldn't even dream"—so we believe—of wishing such a thing. For this reason the dream-censorship is not armed to meet such a monstrosity. . . . Secondly, in this case the repressed and unsuspected wish is particularly often met half-way by a residue from the previous day in the form of a *worry* about the safety of the person concerned . . . while the wish can disguise itself behind the worry that has become active during the day. (Freud, 1900, pp. 266–267)

Dreams will be distorted, unreal, and irrational because the dreaming person has sufficient residual controls to prevent the unconscious impulses and wishes from reaching the person in pure form. It follows that if there were no unconscious impulses and wishes, no discharging of these drives, then there would seem to be no basis for the dream disguise. This is the argument advanced by Greenberg (1987), who concludes that the idea of dream disguise is therefore not needed:

> . . . the evidence for drive discharge in dreams has not been confirmed by studies of REM sleep and REM deprivation. The idea of disguise derives from the notion that it is necessary to hide the meaning of the dream in order to conceal the forbidden drives that seek expression.

Without the concept of drive discharge, the idea of disguise is no longer necessary. (p. 49)

It also follows that as the person is in the process of awakening, the standard array of defenses are once again in place, and what had been able to penetrate the reduced defensive structure must be sealed off and pushed back down. Otherwise, that repressed material will tend to endanger the awakening person and may even intrude into the waking person's life (Leveton, 1961). Accordingly, the psychoanalytic theory counts upon a re-repressive mechanism in the process of awakening.

Yet the underlying theme across just about every contemporary theory is the ancient idea that the dreaming personality is the waking personality with reduced controls.

Data that are distinctive to the perspective of the waking person. When we move into the perspective of the waking person, distinctive data include the waking person's thoughts and ideas and associations from and about the dream (Figure 2). Only the waking person can say that this part of the dream reminds her of this or that and provide a series of such thoughts and ideas and associations. A second class of distinctive data consists of the waking person's knowledge of dream meanings and symbols and interpretations. Only the waking person can apply this knowledge to dreams and say that this a castration dream or that this is an archetype of the earth mother or that here is an authority symbol or that the dream indicates sibling rivalry or that this is a termination dream.

The Distinctive Perspective of the Therapist

The therapist can look at the dream itself and also at the way in which the patient talks about the dream. These two vantage points outfit the therapist with distinctive kinds of data about the dream.

In many ways, the therapist is in a very special role, one that has a distinguished history of at least a few thousand years. The therapist is supposed to have special knowledge about dreams and what they mean, and the therapist is supposed to have clinical acumen in discerning inferences about the patient and applying them to dreams. The therapist fulfills the role of the high priest and grand wizard of dreams (Mahrer, Dessaulles, Gervaize, & Nadler, 1987). From within this role, the "psychoanalyst" offers the "interpretation" of the meaning of the dream:

. . . the patient had a version of what his dream meant—however fragmentary, incomplete, and unspoken—but it was a version that could only be maintained by ignoring large chunks of evidence. The version suggested by the analyst's interpretation encompasses more of the evidence and, when the timing and relationships are right—the patient not too anxious or resistant—he can hear and use the new version suggested by the analyst's interpretation. (Breger, 1980, pp. 10–11)

The therapist provides the patient with the benefit of the therapist's impressions about the meaning of the dream, even if this perhaps lends an air of suggestion to the patient's understanding of the dream:

I give him the benefit of my guesses and opinions. If, in doing this, I should open the door to so-called "suggestion," I see no occasion for regret; it is well-known that we are susceptible only to those suggestions with which we are already in accord. (Jung, 1933, p. 65)

With or without the robes of office, the therapist fulfills a special role that requires knowledge beyond that of the patient. Accordingly, the therapist has distinctive access to at least four classes of data unavailable to the waking patient and certainly unavailable to the dreamer.

Knowledge of dream meanings, symbols, and interpretations. The therapist is supposed to have special knowledge of dream meanings, symbols, and interpretations. Accordingly, the therapist's meanings and symbols and interpretations of the dream are quite different from those available to the patient.

The therapist understands the symbolic interpretive meaning of a "semi-oriental" woman in the dream (cf. Henderson, 1980), or a journey down a river, or one object becoming another, or a horse that gives birth to a snake, or visiting the place where you lived as a child. These are all mysterious things that are known by the therapist because the therapist has extensive knowledge of what dreams mean, of their symbolic significance, of how to interpret them. The therapist brings an extensive knowledge of every field of understanding that bears upon the dream:

The interpreter, especially one who has been trained as a Jungian analyst, can be expected to have greater knowledge of myths, cultural and religious customs, and historical events. (Mattoon, 1984, p. 54)

Freud relied upon a study of the patient's stream of associative thoughts, starting from the dream, complemented by his own knowledge of the symbolic interpretive meaning of dreams:

We are thus obliged, in dealing with those elements of the dream-content which must be recognized as symbolic, to adopt a combined technique, which on the one hand rests on the dreamer's associations while on the other hand the interpreter fills the gaps from the interpreter's knowledge of symbols. (Freud, 1900, p. 353)

While the patient may have some knowledge of dream meanings, symbols, and interpretations, the therapist's is deeper and more extensive, for it comes from the perspective of the therapist, not that of the waking person or dreamer.

Therapist's associations and thoughts about the dream. The therapist's associations and thoughts may occur as the patient is telling the dream. They may also occur later on in the session, in a later session, or even in between sessions:

[The associations] . . . of the therapist occur while the patient is recounting his dream and after that. He associates, as does the patient, in the same session and also in later sessions. The analyst may also have useful associations to a patient's dream under a variety of circumstances after the patient has left the office. . . . An association may occur in an academic setting or at a psychiatric meeting or in the course of reading or discussing psychiatry. (Bonime, 1962, p. 16)

If the dream includes a steep cliff, the therapist may think, "Her close friend was killed when the car in which she was a passenger plunged over the side of a cliff," and thereby the therapist may offer this personal association to the patient: "The interpreter may also offer a personal association which the dreamer could have made but which did not come to mind" (Mattoon, 1984, p. 60). If the dream setting includes Parisian stores, the therapist thinks, "These Parisian stores are those in the picture in my waiting room, and therefore the dream indicates the patient's unconscious reactions to therapy." The therapist's own associations and thoughts about the dream are an invaluable source of data for the therapist, and are presumed to be helpful for the patient:

> The analyst can seriously convey that: "I don't know what your dream means and you don't know what your dream means, but we can work on it together. . . . We both become engaged in associative activity. I may see connections of an association of yours with something you've told me about yourself earlier. I may get a clue about something in your dream by recalling a personal life experience or something in a movie, a play, a book, or another person's life. My linkages may sound way off the mark to you, but at the same time trigger an illuminating thought or memory of your own." (Bonime, 1986, p. 15)

Inferences from the patient's associations and thoughts about the dream. If the patient does not associate to or have thoughts about something in the dream that the therapist regards as important, the therapist takes note of the omission and draws inferences from this (Whitman, 1980). When the patient hits a block in the flow of associative thoughts, the therapist notes this and draws inferences. Everything about the patient's flow of associations is material from which the therapist draws inferences.

The therapist is keenly aware of themes in the patient's flow of associative thoughts and draws inferences from themes of penis envy or sibling rivalry or masochism or regression or death wishes. The patient's associations and thoughts provide the material from which the therapist draws meaningful and important inferences.

Inferences from the patient's condition or state. The therapist can also draw inferences from the patient's psychopathology, emotional state, mental condition, psychodiagnosis, ego strength, defenses, everything about the patient's condition and state. On the basis of these inferences, the therapist can determine what to interpret in the dream, when and how to interpret it (Werman, 1978). The patient's pathological state enables the therapist to understand why the rooms are so small in the dream or why there are so few human beings in this series of dreams or why there is so little movement. The same dream will have quite different meanings depending on whether the patient is hebephrenic or a slow learner, enuretic or an incest survivor, a borderline psychotic or hypertensive, in the beginning, middle, or termination phase of treatment.

THE MOST USEFUL DATA
FOR DREAM WORK

You can get qualitatively distinct data from the perspective of the dreamer or the awake person or the therapist. Choose whichever perspective makes best sense to you and offers the kind of data you value. Because we value the dream experiencing, we choose the perspective of the dreamer. The other two perspectives cannot provide our data.

However, selecting one or more of the three perspectives is not enough to determine the actual data you will use in dream work. Each of the three perspectives will provide its own general kinds of data. But now you must make a specific selection of what data to use. What are the kinds of data that are useful in doing dream work? If you have a dream or a series of dreams, how do you go about deciding what parts of the dreams to use?

The Contents of the Dream Itself

You can choose useful data from the dream itself rather than from the relation between this and other dreams, or from the patient's thoughts and ideas and associations, or from an application of other clinical information to the dream. Yet even in getting useful data from the contents of the dream itself there are choices.

The dream as a whole. In this approach the dream is seen as a single package, and what you get from the dream is based upon the whole dream, generally the plot or story or featured event. On this basis you can say that this is a birth dream, or that it is a dream of sexual fulfillment or an anxiety dream. You can either make sense of the entire dream at a single stroke or decipher the parts and reassemble these into a single overall meaning for the whole dream:

> The first of these procedures considers the content of the dream as a whole and seeks to replace it by another content which is intelligible and in certain respects analogous to the original one. . . . The second of the two popular methods of interpreting dreams . . . might be described as the "decoding" method, since it treats dreams as a kind of cryptography in which each sign can be translated into another sign having a known meaning, in accordance with a fixed key. (Freud, 1900, pp. 96–97)

Freud however, did not value the dream as a whole: " . . . what we must take as the object of our attention is not the dream as a whole but the separate portions of its content." (Freud, 1900, p. 103). His arguments against using the dream as a whole rest on the two principles that . . . we should disregard the apparent coherence between a dream's constituents as an unessential illusion, and that we should trace back the origin of each of its elements on its own account. A dream is a conglomerate which, for purposes of investigation, must be broken up once more into fragments. (Freud, 1900, p. 449)

Nevertheless, some approaches are impressed by the apparent coherence and accept as the useful data the dream as a whole. Our approach declines these data.

Selected elements from the dream. One of the most popular ways of choosing the important data is to select particular elements from the dream. However, this brings up a number of problems in how you go about selecting the elements you want to use as your useful data.

In just about any dream, the first problem is how large or how small the element is to be. If you are held captive in a compound with other people, surrounded by a tall fence and guarded by soldiers with dogs, commanded by a short captain in a white coat, you have a choice of larger elements (e.g., military situation) or smaller elements (e.g., white coat). In actual practice, this is a knotty problem. Not only do approaches differ widely, but even for a given therapist the size of the selected element varies a great deal.

A second problem is how many elements are to be selected. Do you use one element or ten? On what basis do you select whatever number you use for this dream? A third problem is just how to go about selecting an element from all the elements in the dream. In the following dream, Henderson selects one element as central. See if you can predict which one is selected:

"My Dad smelt a smell of burning and we went in and there was a small flame that came from a match Dad had dropped. The flame danced like the fairies. My Mummy was very worried because the house might get burned, and you don't get anything back if the house burned down." The central event in this dream is the fire seen by Christopher as a fairy flame. (Henderson, 1980, p. 380)

The dream included lots of elements, both large and small. Would you have selected the patient's seeing the fire as a fairy flame? Or would you have selected the match Dad had dropped, or the house burning down, or not getting anything if the house burned down, or other elements?

Another problem is whether to select the elements on the basis of what the patient seems to regard as an important element or on the basis of what the therapist regards as the important element. There are choices galore if you add together all the elements the patient identifies plus all the elements the therapist wants to add to the pot.

Freud adds yet another consideration which upsets the whole apple cart: the elements that seem important in the dream are probably not the important ones at all. Perhaps the truly important element in the above dream is that the parents and Christopher "went in" to a room in the house, or Daddy "dropping" something. The apparently important elements are probably not the important ones to select:

> It could be seen that the elements which stand out as the principal components of the manifest content of the dream are far from playing the same part in the dream-thoughts. And, as a corollary, the converse of this assertion can be affirmed: what is clearly the essence of the dream-thoughts need not be represented in the dream at all. The dream is, as it were, differently centered from the dream-thoughts—its content has different elements as its central point. (Freud, 1900, p. 305)

A final problem, with two interrelated parts, is one of the most challenging aspects of relying upon elements of the ream: One part is whether you select an element with or without the situational context as given in the dream. The other is whether an element you select is to be made sense of in the dream situational context or in the context of the way in which you used other elements from the dream. Let us consider the above dream. Will you select the element of the little flame dancing like fairies? If you do, would the meaning of the flame dancing like the fairies depend on whether the situational context is a match dropped by your father that might burn down the house? Suppose that the little flame dancing like the fairies was in a dream context in which you are visiting an angel in a cave, and the angel hands you a gift of your very own, a tiny flame "dancing like the fairies." Do you take into account the situational context in making sense of the element? Now suppose that you select the element of the match dropped by your father. If that is an element indicating your father's inclination to destroy the family, then does the meaning of the little flame dancing like the fairies vary depending on whether the situational context is merely going into a room and seeing the tiny flame, or whether it is Daddy's impulse to destroy the family? The problem of using or not using the situational context, and the problem of what situational context, if any, to use, constitutes a most perplexing problem indeed.

Jung and Perls add even further complications to this problem of the element with or without the situational context. Consider a dream in which a train is racing along the tracks and you are horrified to see that a horse is on the tracks, the train smashes into and kills the horse, and then, further down the tracks, you see your mother who is also killed by the train. Contrast this with a dream in which your mother steps down from a train and presents you with a wonderful gift of a horse of your very own. Jung depends upon the dream context so that the former dream yields meaningful elements that would have altogether different meanings if they occurred in the latter dream:

> We must therefore look more closely into the meaning of the outstanding symbols, "mother" and "horse." These figures must be equivalent one to the other, for they both do the same thing: they commit suicide. (Jung, 1933, p. 24)

On the other hand, Perls chooses an element sometimes with and sometimes without the situational context. If there is a train in the dream, Perls may easily select that and have the patient simply be a train quite independent of the dream context:

> F: . . . So you can play the train. "I'm a train . . . "
> C: I'm a train and I'm going somewhere, but it's nowhere. It has direction—
> F: *I* have direction.
> C: I have direction. I have *enormous* direction. . . . (Perls, 1969, p. 98)

Quite aside from all these problems, most approaches rely heavily on the use of selected elements from the dream. In the experiential approach, we use these only as linkages from the dream to recent situations and incidents in the life of the person. They are not our useful data.

Unusual features of the dream. Suppose, for example, that there is something genuinely absurd, strange, or unique in the dream. You actually fly or the heavens open up or bathtubs sing in a chorus or there are people with three heads. These unusual features may be taken as indicating the person's possibilities for an emerging individuality:

That which is unique, strange, or intensely idiosyncratic in a dream is an essence of individuality. It is an expression of original psychological experience, and, as such, is the raw material out of which new patterns of awareness may develop. (Rossi, 1985, p. 25)

On the other hand, the sheer absurdity may be used to indicate the person's own absurd attitudes and relationships in waking life:

Still another characteristic of a dream image may be its absurdity; an absurd dream image may indicate that the dreamer is doing something nonsensical in waking life. For example, if someone dreams of wearing an incongruous combination of clothing, the ridiculous image may suggest that there is something absurd in an attitude of the dreamer. (Mattoon, 1984, pp. 104–105)

In any case, the data are whatever the patient and especially the therapist regard as unusual features of the dream. It may consist of another figure whom you know is really another you, another representation of yourself (Rossi, 1985). It may be lucid dreaming, in which you are aware that you are dreaming, and you may even have the sense of determining what is to happen next (e.g., Garfield, 1976, 1977; Green, 1968; Rossi, 1985). It may consist of the dreamer being in two places simultaneously, such as both inside and outside the huge whale. It may include some figure or object transforming into another.

Moments of peak feeling. In the experiential approach, the important part of the dream is when the dreamer's feeling is strongest. The feeling may be good or it might be bad, a feeling of anxiety or exhilaration, awe or tension, peacefulness or chaos, joy or fright. The feeling may be intensely powerful or only moderate.

There is always some moment when the feeling is strongest. It may seem that some dreams have no feeling to speak of. It may seem that in some dreams the feeling is at its peak throughout most of the dream:

The dynamic of expression in dreaming ranges from dreams in which there is no outward display of the dreamer's feelings or thoughts, to dreams in which the expression is so prolonged and complete that it dominates the dream. (Corriere, Karle, Woldenberg, & Hart, 1980, p. 44)

It may seem this way, but in most dreams there is some moment when the feeling reaches its peak. This moment is precious because our theory of dreaming tells us that, of all the places in the dream, the dream experiencing is most apparent, is most easily discovered, comes closest to the surface in the moment when the feeling is strongest.

Throughout the dream there are all sorts of scenes and situations and occurrences. Most approaches see all of this as expressions of deeper processes, as symbolic meanings, as pictoralized inner thoughts wherein " . . . a colourless and abstract expression in the dream-thought being exchanged for a pictorial and concrete one. . . . A dream-thought is unusable so long as it is expressed in an abstract form; but when it has been transformed into pictorial language" (Freud, 1900, pp. 339–340). "Dreaming is sleep thinking. However, it is not thinking in words but in visuomotor imagery" (Piatrowski, 1986, p. 47). However, in the experiential approach, most of what is present in the dream is a panoply of situational contexts within which the dream experiencing can occur. When the feeling reaches its peak, we hold that the experiencing is closest to direct open expression and that what is occurring at that moment offers the best possible gateway into the experiencing.

In the moment of peak feeling, the important data include everything occurring inside the dreamer—the dreamer's feelings and emotions and affects, thoughts and ideas and notions, visualized other scenes and recollections, puzzlements and confusions—and everything occurring outside and around the dreamer—the situational context, all the actions and interactions, the relationships, the props and scenery, the words and physical postures.

The Relation of This Dream to Other Dreams

We obtain our useful data from this dream alone. But many approaches get useful data from how this dream relates to other dreams, from a whole series of dreams, from its recurrence, from considering it as a common or initial dream.

Initial dreams. In psychoanalytic approaches especially, beginning therapy is a significant life event for the patient, and the initial dream is therefore especially useful for revealing the patient's feelings and attitudes toward therapy and the therapist.

Jung see initial dreams as especially revealing, not because they tell about therapy and the therapist, but because the patient is naive about therapy and dreams, and therefore the dream is considered marked by transparency. In any case, the initial dream is useful because it is the initial dream, and that in itself bestows a special usefulness.

Common dreams. There are some dreams that are quite commonly dreamed by lots of people, and are therefore taken as having the same meaning or significance for everyone. Freud believed that these dreams came from the same sources in each person:

> . . . there are a certain number of dreams which almost everyone has dreamt alike and which we are accustomed to assume must have the same meaning for everyone . . . they presumably arise from the same sources in every case . . . (Freud, 1900, p. 241)

I am aware of the common dreams that Freud identified and of the psychoanalytic meaning he attributed to each of these dreams. Because I use two peaks of feeling as containing the most useful data, and because I open up the experiencing in those moments of peak feeling, I quietly presumed that the experiential and psychoanalytic uses of these common dreams would differ. Instead, what impresses me is the commonality in the experiencings from the same common dream across different patients and the similarity between our dream experiencings and Freud's psychoanalytic interpretations.

For example, there are common dreams of missing an appointment, being late for the meeting, forgetting about meeting the person at the airport, noticing that it is now five hours after the exam was supposed to begin. As you realize the awful truth, you feel guilty, surprised, scared, embarrassed, worried. The common dream experiencing is the secret delight of saying no, the wickedness of not doing it, I didn't want to do it anyway, sweet defiance and rebelliousness, the joy of sticking it to the other person, a sense of nasty devilishness.

There is the common dream in which you are naked, or partly naked, in public, in a crowd or group, and these other people are not naked. While these other people do not notice you, you are filled with a pronounced sense of embarrassment and shame. "We are only concerned here, however, with those dreams of being naked in which one does feel shame and embarrassment and tries to escape or hide, and is then overcome by a strange inhibition which prevents one from moving . . ." (Freud, 1900, p. 242). The dream experiencing almost uniformly is that of exhibiting oneself, of daring to show, of exposing oneself, being bad, violating the rules.

There is a common dream of being pursued by an enemy, someone out to get you, to hurt or harm you. You are trying to get away from the pursuer, but you are unsuccessful. Your legs are like concrete or you are simply too slow or something slows you down or stops you. Although the other person does not reach you, you are certain that you will be caught and that something awful is going to happen to you. You are scared, frightened. The dream experiencing is that of being caught, reached, gotten to, being vulnerable, giving in, being passive.

There are common dreams in which you are terrified by the monster, demented thing, grotesque animal, vicious attacker. Between you and the monster is a penetrable barrier such as a door or a window or a screen. All your attention is riveted on the demented thing on the other side of the barrier. The dream experiencing is that of being wild, monstrous, powerful, primitive, out of control, violently assaultive.

There are other common dreams, but the practical point is that the commonness of these dreams may well be a bit of useful information for the dream experiencing or psychoanalytic meaning.

Recurrent and childhood dreams. Many approaches get useful data about a dream by labeling it as a recurrent one or as a dream that you had in childhood. The experiential approach declines to regard either as especially useful data.

A dream, in order to qualify as recurring, should be quite similar each time, even to the point of containing virtually the same details. It is not sufficient to say that the dreams involve general themes of trying to contact someone or being in social gatherings or going on journeys or being in some alien locale.

What useful data are provided by the sheer recurrence of dreams? One answer (Langs, 1980) is that the recurrence indicates that the patient senses problems in the transference or countertransference nature of the relationship with the therapist:

There is a relationship here between such dreams and countertransference. The patient is indicating unconsciously that she has been previously exposed to assaults and threats of this kind from the therapist—and others. The repetition may be connected to recurrent and similar day residues (adaptive contexts), and to fixity in the patient's unconscious perceptions and fantasies. The repetitive dream may imply a stalemated situation involving both the therapist's countertransferences and the patient's responses to them. (p. 351)

Accordingly, the same recurrent dream will have differing specific meanings depending on what is occurring in the patient's immediate life:

The repetitive dream also demonstrates that the same manifest content may carry different unconscious fantasies and perceptions, depending on the prevailing adaptive stimulus . . . distinctly different latent contents within virtually identical manifest material. (Langs, 1980, p. 351)

For others, the sheer recurrence is taken as signifying a trauma: "Repetitive dreams have very commonly been associated with traumatic experiences and are practically a symptomalogical constant in traumatic neuroses" (Bonime, 1962, p. 41). For Jung, the recurrent dream may indicate an earlier trauma that has not been worked through and assimilated, or it may signify a persistent compensatory function, or it may anticipate an important development in the person's psyche:

Jung mentioned three possible alternative purposes that may be served by recurring dreams. The first, compensation, differs from the compensatory function of a single dream only in its persistence and, hence, emphasis on a continuing defect in the dreamer's conscious attitude. . . . A second type of recurring dream is the "traumatic dream": the trauma has been assimilated, the dream ceases to occur. A third type of recurring dream may anticipate an important development in the dreamer's psyche. (Mattoon, 1984, p. 84)

In the Gestalt approach, a recurrent dream may be taken to indicate a persistent need that the patient has not recognized, confronted, met, and provided for:

. . . dream work calls attention to those needs in the individual which have not been met because they have not been recognized. So the need fulfillment pattern is interrupted, and as a consequence we have recurrent dreams, often nightmarish in quality, which will continue to clutter up the dreamer's sleeping field until they are confronted. (Fantz, 1987, p. 193)

The same use is often made of dreams that are recalled from childhood. Like recurrent dreams, they are taken to indicate some important childhood event, usually a trauma; " . . . the childhood dreams which the adult remembers are distinguished from other dreams in that they are the record of a lasting experience, usually a trauma that has left its traces on the mind" (Wolff, 1952, p. 90).

Dreams in series. The useful data are taken as a whole series of dreams, perhaps three or six or twenty or more. Using dreams in this way is around four thousand years old:

The oldest dream series that I have been able to find appears in the Gilgamesh epic of the Babylonians, which was composed before the Bible, probably around 2000 B.C. (Wolff, 1952, p. 100)

Among contemporary approaches, it is perhaps the Jungian that places most importance on using a series of dreams:

. . . I attach little importance to the interpretation of single dreams. With a series of dreams we can have more confidence in our interpretations, for the later dreams correct the mistakes we have made in handling those that went before. We are also better able, in the dream series, to recognize the important contents and basic themes. . . . (Jung, 1933, p. 15)

In using a series of dreams, one looks for motifs, themes, a continuing story, changes in themes:

Sometimes, a recurring motif takes different forms that reflect various facets of a situation, problem, or personality characteristic in the dreamer's life. For example, one dreamer reported a water motif in 26 dreams extending over a period of two months. Jung saw the series as illustrating the continuity of the unconscious and indicating how the motifs could be interpreted by comparing their various forms and the dream situations in which they occurred. . . . (Mattoon, 1984, p. 88)

The idea is that a series of dreams more clearly reveals some underlying general theme, although each series must be approached within some framework that tells you what kind of theme to look for. Jung looked for themes about the continuity of the unconscious, whereas Velikovsky studied a series of Freud's dreams to emerge with a psychoanalytic theme that they signify " . . . his inner struggle for unhampered advancement" (1941, p. 490).

Thoughts, Ideas, and Associations

In other approaches perhaps the most common source of useful data consists of the thoughts, ideas, and associations to and from the dream. There are two ways of getting these data, and each furnishes you with different kinds of useful data.

Departing from the dream and proceeding on to other topics. In psychoanalytic/psychodynamic approaches, the dream is regarded as largely the product of unconscious processes or dream thoughts rather than the conscious ego. Accordingly, the meaning of the dream is revealed by studying the patient's flow of thoughts, ideas, and associations that start from the dream and quickly depart to other topics:

> . . . dreams may be of great importance by setting off a train of fantasy which can be directed partly by consciousness but which honors the inner reality of the unconscious. (Henderson, 1980, p. 376)

The patient's thoughts, ideas, and associations can start from any place in the dream, from small items to the dream as a whole:

> The greatest source of help . . . is the patient's own associations to the dream. Before a therapist makes any attempt to interpret a patient's dream, the patient should be asked for his associations to the dream as a whole, to its various parts, and to single items in it which seem to warrant special attention. (Fromm-Reichmann, 1958, p. 171)

While the useful data lie in the actual stream of associations, the astute therapist can also gain useful data from the parts of the dream that are bypassed as the patient starts from the dream into lines of free association:

> A patient reported to his analyst the following dream: "I was driving along a road and there were two farm houses. One was a small one and one was a large one in the background. I drove up to the small one and found out that it had been completely redone inside and outside. I was very pleased." During supervision it was pointed out . . . that

the large farmhouse was completely untouched and unmentioned in
the patient's associations and that this paralleled the patient's unwill-
ingness to go into large areas of his personality. . . . (Whitman, 1980,
p. 49)

The standard procedure uses the patient's stream of thoughts,
ideas, and associations, starting from the dream (e.g., the farm
house) and immediately proceeding to other topics: "My wife talks a
lot about farms and missing where she grew up, and wanting to move
to a farm way out. She never seems to stop mentioning something
once she gets it in her head. My mother used to be that way before
she . . . she got real sick. . . . I miss my mother, I mean the way she
was before . . . " The first thing that comes to the patient's mind has
already departed from the farm house in the dream, and everything
that follows takes the patient further and further away from the farm
house.

Like the patient's flow of associations, the therapist's flow starts
from the dream and proceeds off in its own direction (Bonime, 1962;
Mattoon, 1984). Even more distant from the dream, the therapist's
flow may have as its starting point something that the patient says in
her stream of thoughts.

Centering on the dream element itself. In some approaches, the
associative stream is to stay centered on the selected dream element. If
we start with a farmer in the dream, everything the patient says is to
be in relation to that farmer. In the Jungian approach, the flow may
include a rather broad compass, yet all focused on or from the element in the dream:

> In the case of a human figure, for example, the relevant associations
> would include the dreamer's perception of it as a male or female, its
> name, occupation, interest and personality characteristics, the role it
> plays in the dreamer's life, and any of the dreamer's specific experi-
> ences in which the figure has played a part. Elaborations might include
> like-named figures in the dreamer's life, attitudes toward any of the
> facets or perceived characteristics associated to the figure, and the
> significance to the dreamer of the recounted experiences. (Mattoon,
> 1984, p. 56)

The Jungian therapist stays with the dream itself, for the dream is
to be understood for what it is, not as a disguise:

Freud insisted that the meaning of the dream lies in the latent dream thoughts, which can be discovered only by the process of free association to the images. Jung, on the other hand, adhered to the interpretation of the manifest content—the images themselves—because, he insisted, the dream is not a disguise. (Mattoon, 1984, p. 5)

Accordingly, the Jungian therapist focuses on the dream element in applying the patient's and therapist's fund of thoughts and ideas. In other words, the Jungian therapist would accept the initial association, but subsequent associations offer virtually nothing once they depart from the dream element itself:

In Jungian analysis, as in Freudian analysis, the first thing we ask the patient is what he associates to the dream. I consider it highly important to take the very first thing he associates spontaneously as authentic rather than associations that have been subsequently qualified and thereby falsified . . . the continuing use of free associations is not encouraged by the Jungian analyst, however, because elaboration forms a series of associations that leads away from the dream content. (Henderson, 1980, pp. 369–370)

One of the outstanding characteristics of Boss's Daseinsanalytic dream approach is this emphasis on staying with the dream element. It is this characteristic that allows Boss to refer to his approach as phenomenological. "Our new dream theory can be called a phenomenological approach . . . since it keeps strictly to the actual phenomena of dreaming" (1977, p. 27). Just focus more and more on the dream element itself:

Above all, he needs the seemingly simple, yet extremely rare, ability to see, clearly and accurately, what is there, before his eyes. To those who possess or manage to acquire this phenomenological vision most dreams will reveal very directly the dreamer's existential condition. (Stern, 1977, p. xiii)

Boss takes pains to distinguish this procedure from the psychoanalytic stream of associations away from the dream, and even from Jung's application of a broad swath of thoughts, ideas, and associations to the selected dream element:

The patient was exhorted to give a more precise account of what she had experienced while dreaming, but no more than that. Nowhere in the process of phenomenological analysis was there a need for any "free association" or "amplification," in the Jungian sense of introducing myths and legends with similar content. The patient was simply required to adhere strictly to those events and entities which she had visualized and immediately experienced during the dreaming period. She was told to describe them ever more precisely. . . . (Boss, 1977, p. 104)

But this emphasis on the dream element itself is not confined to Boss and Jung. In many psychoanalytic/psychodynamic schools, there is a similar controversy between those who stay with the "manifest" content of the dream and those who use the stream of associations away from the dream to uncover the "latent" meaning. Many psychoanalytic/psychodynamic dream theorists and clinicians prefer the manifest content and use the patient's thoughts, ideas, and associations as they bear more or less directly upon the manifest dream element itself (Erickson, 1954; Fairbairn, 1951; Fosshage, 1983, 1987; Greenberg, 1987; Greenberg & Pearlman, 1980; Kohut, 1977). Indeed, in a survey of psychoanalytic journals, Warner (1987) was struck by the preponderance of psychoanalytic writers who preferred to use the manifest content rather than the classical line of free associations away from the dream and supposedly toward the latent dream meaning.

Information About the Patient

In order to work on a dream, is it important to get information about the patient himself? Does the useful data include information about the patient's clinical condition, current life situation, what is happening in therapy? In the experiential approach, the answer is no. In many other approaches, the answer is yes.

Clinical condition and current life situation. In many approaches, the useful data include the patient's clinical condition. The idea is that an apparently similar dream will vary in its meaning depending on whether the patient is a simple neurotic or a chronic schizophrenic, whether the patient is entering into the throes of a blatant psychosis or is in a state or remission, whether the diagnosis is hebephrenia or personality disorder.

Even more widely accepted is the importance of knowing the patient's current life situation. Dreams may well remain essentially incomprehensible until the therapist knows about the person's waking life so that " . . . knowledge of what was currently important in the dreamer's waking life made the dreams readily comprehensible" (Greenberg & Pearlman, 1980, p. 87). Many approaches consider knowledge of the current life situation essential for dream work:

> Whatever the problematic conscious situation, it constellates in the unconscious certain contents which then appear in the dream . . . it is essential for the interpreter to know the conscious situation. . . . (Mattoon, 1984, p. 76)

The meaning of the dream is brought to light when you know that the patient is going to celebrate her eightieth birthday this Sunday, or that he is dying of cancer, or that she is four weeks from the delivery of the baby, or that he is in the midst of a scandal that certainly will result in his having to resign his public office. The meaning of the following dream becomes clear to the therapist who knows that the dream occurred on the evening of the patient's brother's birthday, a brother who is four years younger than the patient:

> "Had moved into a new house—at 73 Lewis (childhood house)—had cut through floor of kitchen and put stairs into cellar, stairs had been brought in sections which folded into each other, so were quite compact. Then assembled them in kitchen—my parents there—father wondered how stairs got in and I explained. Try to figure out the best place to put table." It does not take much imagination to see a four-year-old boy wondering about the secrets of pregnancy and birth. . . . (Greenberg & Pearlman, 1980, p. 90)

What is occurring in therapy. Psychoanalytic/psychodynamic approaches are perhaps foremost in elevating therapy into a preeminent event in the patient's life. It makes sense, therefore, that what is occurring in therapy is quite useful data in dream work. For example, the meaning of a dream will vary quite a bit depending upon whether the patient is starting therapy or has been in therapy for some time. For Jung, a dream in which you have sex with a "loved one" has one meaning when a patient is just starting therapy and quite a different meaning if the person has had extensive therapy:

> Different stages of therapy require varying interpretations of the same dream images, according to Jung, because of the changing requirements of the dreamer's psychological development. An explicit sexual image, such as the dreamer's having sexual intercourse with a loved one, for example, may be interpreted as a wish for that experience if the dream occurs early in therapy, when a dreamer's sexual impulses

may be still under repression. Later, when the dreamer's sexual impulses have been brought into consciousness, the same interpretation could result in arresting personality development. (Mattoon, 1984, p. 156)

It is standard psychoanalytic/psychodynamic practice to make sense of the dream in the light of the therapist's impressions of the nature of the relationship between patient and therapist. Depending on the nature, depth, and stage of the working alliance, transference, and countertransference, the same dream will tend to be given substantially different meanings. Even further, the useful data include casual remarks by the patient on merely entering the office, as well as whatever the patient talks about before recounting the dream. If the patient mentions something about the therapist, then the therapist tends to see the dream as elaborating further on the patient's feelings and attitudes toward the therapist:

> I reminded her that she had started the hour by telling me of her fear of accepting me as being like a friend—a fear of getting close to me. I therefore suggested that the crazy woman might represent myself. (Bonime, 1962, p. 74)

The experiential approach does not include any of this as useful data in dream work. We work with the dream itself and do not regard as useful such information about what is happening in therapy, or in the person's current life situation, not the therapist's impressions about the patient's clinical condition.

CHAPTER 5

Dream
Feelings

IN ORDER TO GET AT THE DREAM experiencing in moments of peak feeling, it is important to understand the way the experiential approach makes sense of the nature of the feeling in the dream. The purpose is to answer this question: How do we make sense of and use the nature of the peak feeling in the dream, i.e., whether the peak feeling is bad, very bad, or good?

The Topography of Personality:
Waking World, Dream World,
and Dream Feelings

When you are awake, the center of I-ness moves about in the operating domain (Figure 3). You experience whatever is present as "potentials for experiencing" in your operating domain. (These are indicated as OP 1–4 in Figure 3.) The center of I-ness may move from one operating potential to another, but it remains within the operating domain when you are awake. The topography also includes a deeper domain which contains potentials for experiencing, indicated as DP 5–8 in Figure 3.

Between the operating and deeper domains is a corridor, a kind of limbo in which the center of I-ness is not yet fully free of the operating domain nor fully contained within a deeper potential. Once the center of I-ness leaves the operating domain and enters into this corridor, the waking world is left behind and there are dreams. But the center of I-ness is still under the residual effect of the operating domain as the center of I-ness moves through this corridor toward the deeper potentials. Only when the center of I-ness leaves the corridor and enters into the deeper domain is the residual effect of the operating domain left behind.

According to this topographical model, dreaming occurs once the center of I-ness disengages from the operating domain. That is, a

101

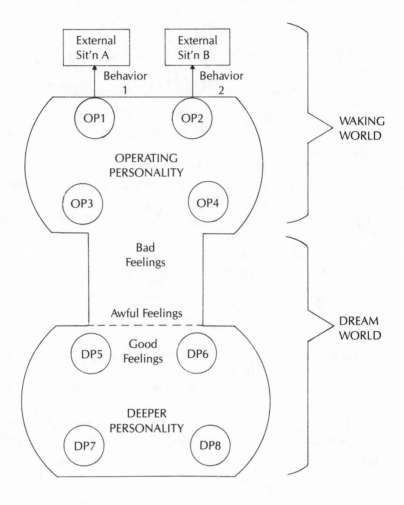

Figure 3. The Topography of Personality: Waking World, Dream World, and Dream Feelings

dream can occur when the center of I-ness has just left the operating domain and is just in the outer periphery of the deeper domain, or as the center of I-ness moves further away from the operating domain and is further along the corridor, when the center of I-ness has penetrated into the deeper personality (Figure 3). Given this model of the waking and dreaming worlds, we can answer the question of why feelings occur in dreams.

Why Feelings Occur in Dreams

In our approach there is a sharp distinction between the feeling and the experiencing. In Figure 3, an experiencing is indicated by one of the deeper potentials (e.g., DP 6) which may, for example, consist of the potential for experiencing soft and yielding passivity. In the existential-humanistic theory of personality, feelings occur in two ways. One involves the relationship between potentials. If the relationships are disintegrative, the feelings are bad ones: feelings of threat, tension, anxiety, dread, terror. If the relationships between operating potential 4 (e.g., toughness and firmness) and deeper potential 6 (e.g., soft and yielding passivity) are disintegrative, then the feelings will be bad ones. If, however, relationships are integrative, then the feelings will be good ones such as wholeness, oneness, peacefulness, tranquility, harmony. Relationships between the operating and deeper domains are almost always disintegrative, and therefore the feelings are almost always bad ones. The second way in which feelings occur is a function not of the relationships between potentials but rather as a function of the degree to which a given potential for experiencing is opened up, carried forward, expressed, entered into, allowed to occur. The more this occurs, the more the feelings are the good feelings of actualization, such as aliveness, vitality, excitement, vibrancy, pleasure, joy.

As the center of I-ness moves out of the operating domain and into the dream state, bad feelings will occur because of the disintegrative relationships between the operating domain and the deeper domain, for example, between the operating potential for toughness and firmness and the deeper potential for soft and yielding passivity. As the center of I-ness completes its journey and enters into the deeper potential, these disintegrative relationships are left behind, replaced with the good feelings of actualization. This is how and why feelings occur in dreams. This means that the feelings in the dream are the same kinds of feelings as occur in waking life, and that both waking and dream feelings can be explained in terms of relationships between potentials and the degree of actualization of a given potential.

Both waking and dream feelings are similar to one another and come about through the same principles. Freud likewise saw waking and dream feelings as similar:

> Our feeling tells us that an affect experienced in a dream is in no way inferior to one of equal intensity experienced in waking life; and

dreams insist with greater energy upon their right to be included among our real mental experiences in respect to their affective than in respect to their ideational content. In our waking state, however, we cannot in fact include them in this way, because we cannot make any psychical assessment of an affect unless it is linked to a piece of ideational material. (Freud, 1900, p. 460)

However, in psychoanalytic/psychodynamic approaches, the dreaming person is considered to be the waking person with reduced controls. Accordingly, it is understandable that dream feelings are commonly seen as a function of the patient's mental illness, psychodiagnosis, or pathological state (e.g., Kernberg, in Curtis & Sachs, 1976).

If we ask why a feeling occurs at this point in the dream, the experiential answer is that at this point in the dream the center of I-ness has come closest to the deeper potential, whether somewhere in the corridor or actually within the deeper potential. From the perspective of the waking person, it is often confusing that the peak feeling would occur at this particular point in the dream. If we apply the standards of the waking world, the moment of feeling should have occurred when she was nearly pierced by the laser shot from the enemy or when she managed to pilot the rocket ship through the narrow fissure between the mountain peaks. It should not have occurred when she is aware that one of her contact lenses has slipped a little. But this is an enigma only from the perspective of the waking person. Freud followed the same line of reasoning in explaining this apparent enigma, and held that the feeling is quite logical when seen in terms of the latent dream meaning:

This particular enigma of dream-life vanishes more suddenly, perhaps, and more completely than any other, as soon as we pass over from the manifest to the latent content of the dream. We need not bother about the enigma, since it no longer exists. Analysis shows us that the ideational material has undergone displacements and substitutions, whereas the affects have remained unaltered. (Freud, 1900, p. 460)

Not all psychoanalytic dream theorists share Freud's explanation. Monroe is representative of those who hold that the feeling is displaced from where it should occur in the dream because such displacement is merely another product of the defensive mechanisms.

Very often—indeed, typically—the real focus of the dream appears as a quite incidental element, and the apparent psychic intensity falls elsewhere. The major purpose of this lack of proper proportion, this displacement of affect, seems to be the familiar one of avoiding censorship. Appropriate feeling directly expressed would excite the dreamer to the waking point. The same intensity expressed about some sanctioned or trivial matter can be tolerated. (Monroe, 1955, p. 58)

Given our model of how and why dream feelings occur, we can now provide an explanation of why the peak feeling is bad or awful or good, and the uses of these peak dream feelings.

Bad Feelings

Bad feelings occur when the center of I-ness is emerging from the operating domain and is at the outer reaches of the deeper domain (Figure 3). The feelings are bad because of the disintegrative relationship of the operating domain with the deeper domain. These bad feelings signify that the operating domain is bothered by, wary of, distrustful toward, distancing, avoidant, threatened by the deeper dream potential.

It is as if the center of I-ness is in the zone where it is still bearing the residual disintegrative relation of the operating domain toward the deeper potential. Accordingly, the one who has and is responsible for the bad feeling is the conscious, waking, operating personality, and the bad feeling is the reaction of the conscious, waking, operating personality to the deeper potential.

If we use the vocabulary of psychoanalysis, the bad feeling is the reaction of the conscious person to the dream wish. In the following, Freud explains that the bad feeling is the reaction of the conscious personality (the "second instance") to the deeper process that gives rise to the dream wish (the "first instance"):

> . . . we can further say that distressing dreams do in fact contain something which is distressing to the *second* agency, but something which at the same time fulfills a wish on the part of the *first* agency. They are wishful dreams in so far as every dream arises from the first agency; the relation of the second agency towards dreams is of a *defensive* and not of a *creative* kind. (Freud, 1900, pp. 145–146)

It also follows that the bad feeling is not to be explained by the apparent circumstances of the dream. The bad feeling may occur at places where what is occurring in the dream does not seem to warrant a bad feeling and may not occur in places where ordinarily one would have a bad feeling. This is the position of experiential theory, and it is the position put forward by Freud:

> The anxiety that we feel in a dream is only apparently explained by the dream's content. . . . the anxiety in the dream is no better justified by the dream's content than, let us say, the anxiety in a phobia is justified by the idea to which the phobia relates. . . . the anxiety is only super-ficially attached to the idea that accompanies it; it originates from another source. (Freud, 1900, p. 161)

Even when the bad feeling occurs where one may ordinarily be expected to have a bad feeling, I share Freud's explanation that the bad feeling is the negative reaction of the conscious personality to the emerging deeper personality process. If the bad feeling occurs when the dreamer is face to face with a bird from whom he is protecting someone, it very well may be that the feared deeper personality process is contained in the bird:

> The interpretive hypothesis was offered that the bird was not an out-side force from which he was trying to protect her, but symbolized an *aspect of his own personality*, an attribute that it frightened him to observe. (Bonime, 1962, p. 116)

However, Freud also has another explanation for bad feelings in dreams, one I do not share. He sees these as the bad feelings accom-panying the childhood sources of whatever is present in the dreams. If you have dreams of flying or falling, and if your feeling is a bad one, Freud explains the bad feeling as one that occurred in childhood in relation to games involving flying and falling:

> . . . it is only the raw material of sensations contained in them which is always derived from the same source.
> The information provided by psycho-analyses forces me to conclude that these dreams, too, reproduce impressions of childhood; they re-late, that is, to games involving movement, which are extraordinarily attractive to children. . . . Childish romping, if I may use a word which commonly describes all such activities, is what is being repeated in dreams of flying, falling, giddiness and so on; while the pleasurable feelings attached to these experiences are transformed into anxiety. But, often enough, as every mother knows, romping among children actually ends in squabbling and tears. (Freud, 1900, p. 393)

While our explanation differs from this, it is consistent with the former one put forth by Freud, and involves the negative, disintegrative relationship of the operating personality to the deeper potential.

Awful Feelings

More than merely bad feelings, these are the peak moments of which nightmares are made: horror, terror, excruciating agony, utter anguish, absolute dread, sheer panic. What are the significance and use of these awful dream feelings?

The experiential answer is that these feelings occur at the point of absolute imminence of the deeper potential, where the sense of I-ness is on the verge of entering into the deeper potential. From the perspective of the operating domain, the catastrophically wrenching certainty is that the I-ness is going to be inside the deeper potential. The very existence of the operating personality is in wholesale danger of ending, of collapsing, of being invaded, engulfed, imploded by the terrible deeper potential. Quite literally, its identity, its very sense of self, will most certainly die. As Laing describes, the feeling of great terror occurs when the basic existential core is in absolute jeopardy:

> Few nightmares go so far as to call up anxieties about actual loss of identity, usually because most people, even in their dreams, still meet whatever dangers are to be encountered as persons who may be attacked or mutilated but whose basic existential core is not itself in jeopardy . . . one patient dreamt recurrently of a small black triangle which originated in a corner of his room and grew larger and larger until it seemed about to engulf him—whereupon he always awoke in great terror. (Laing, 1962, p. 54)

Bad feelings occur when the center of I-ness comes into the general vicinity of the deeper domain. Awful feelings occur when the center of I-ness is at the very mouth of the deeper potential (Figure 3). Accordingly, this model accommodates Freud's fond hope for such painful and terrifying dreams: " . . . it still remains possible that distressing dreams and anxiety-dreams, when they have been interpreted, may turn out to be fulfilments of wishes" (Freud, 1900, p. 135). One more tiny step and the center of I-ness will enter into the deeper potential and replace the awful feelings with quite pleasurable ones.

And herein lies the usefulness of such dreams. That is, the center of I-ness is so very close to the deeper potential that the deeper experiencing is already breathing on the person. Accordingly, the same dream experiencing will tend to be rather harder to find in dreams with mildly unpleasant feelings, and much easier to find in peak moments of awful feelings.

On the other hand, other approaches have different explanations and uses of dreams with such awful feelings. For example, Jung sees such dreams as containing messages that are merely difficult for the person to accept. In the following dream, Jung uses the dreamer's feeling of horror to indicate that her relationship with a man is really dead and gone, a notion which is difficult for her to accept:

> The following dream, which was offensive to the woman dreamer, is an example of what Jung meant: "A man unknown to the dreamer started to make love to her, suddenly was dead, and was taken into a cubicle. A woman who seemed to be a part of the dreamer followed the dead man into the cubicle. The dreamer stood outside, horrified because she knew that the other woman was having sex relations with the corpse." The corpse seemed to represent the impending death of the dreamer's relationship with a man in her waking life, and the shocking image galvanized her into accepting the end of the relationship which she had been trying to prolong . . . an image that offends the dreamer may be imparting a message that is difficult for the dreamer to accept. (Mattoon, 1984)

If we apply the experiential model to this dream, we would expect that the deeper dream experiencing is being rather openly played out in this moment of horror. Leaving aside the feeling of horror, the dreamer may be witnessing a woman ("who seemed to be part of the dreamer") having sex with a corpse. Just look at what she is doing! Perhaps the feeling of horror is the operating personality's reaction to the manifest imminence of having the experiencing of such wicked, lascivious, tabooed sexuality. Apparently, different explanations and uses of the feeling of horror allow for quite different explanations and uses of the dream.

But there are still other ways of explaining and using awful feelings in dreams. For example, Boss holds that a dream feeling of absolute dread is natural and understandable in particular kinds of persons already in a state of existential collapse. If the feeling of absolute dread occurs in a dream involving the threat of loss of hair, that is quite natural and understandable in persons already in such a state of dread:

Hair loss always brings with it . . . a certain *de facto* existential deterioration, which is often experienced as just that . . . only people whose entire existence is already pervaded by an abysmal dread of existential collapse have such a deadly fear of hair loss as the patient presently under discussion. . . . Of the little vitality remaining to a panic-stricken individual, a relatively large part resides in the hair on his head. That helps to explain why such a person, reduced to a narcissistic state, experiences hair loss as a catastrophe of the first order. (Boss, 1977, pp. 158–159)

Jones (1971) regards these nightmarish feelings as expressions of sexual impulses, especially incestuous impulses. Freud explains awful feelings as the accompaniment of masochistic tendencies which are in turn the product of dream distortion mechanisms against wish fulfillment:

There is a masochistic component in the sexual constitution of many people, which arises from the reversal of an aggressive, sadistic component into its opposite. . . . It will at once be seen that people of this kind can have counter-wish dreams and unpleasurable dreams, which are none the less wish-fulfilments since they satisfy their masochistic inclinations. (Freud, 1900, p. 159)

In our approach, awful feelings occur when the center of I-ness is on the brink of entering into the deeper potential, and the deeper experiencing is right at hand, expressed here in the peak moment.

Good Feelings

You can be dreaming while the center of I-ness is still dripping with the residual effects of the operating domain. Bad feelings occur when the center of I-ness is in the corridor, in the outer reaches of the operating domain. When you are having awful feelings, you are still in the general territory of the operating domain, but on the verge of the deeper potential. All of this changes dramatically when the center of I-ness penetrates into the deeper domain. You have just become a radically different person, the deeper personality, something you have rarely or ever achieved in the waking world. From within this deeper potential the entire world looks and is different, for the dreamer is now a qualitatively different person than the waking person.

Once the center of I-ness has entered into the deeper potential, there no longer is any basis for the bad or awful feelings brought about by the disintegrative relation of the operating domain toward the deeper domain. Now that the center of I-ness is wholly within the deeper potential, the bad or awful feelings are replaced by good feelings of excitement, vitality, energy, aliveness, vibrancy, joy, happiness, buoyancy, pleasure.

In terms of usefulness for dream work, the good feelings indicate that the experiencing is even more present and clearly manifest than in peak moments of awful feelings and especially of merely bad feelings. Typically the dreamer is openly carrying out the dream experiencing right here in what the dreamer is doing. In the experiential approach then, dreams of good feelings are relatively easy to understand and to use.

For Freud, good feelings in dreams were a perplexing enigma, perhaps mainly because in his theory the dreaming person is still the conscious waking person with reduced controls. Freud worked hard at explaining bad feelings in dreams apparently because there was such reluctance to accept his theory that dreams involve wish-fulfillments. But he seemed to have even more difficulty explaining good feelings.

He used a number of different lines of explanation for why the dream would include good feelings. In one, he believed that good feelings were the accompaniment of simple wishes in simple people. Much like children, these people were naive and pure, and therefore their simple dream wishes would be accompanied with good feelings (cf. Foulkes, 1982). A second explanation is that the good feeling in the dream comes from the good feeling that surrounded that activity in childhood. In childhood there are good feelings associated with being held up in the air by a loving parent, or standing with the head between the legs, seeing everything upside down, or being tucked into bed at night, or playing a trick on someone. When these occur as dream wishes, the good feelings of childhood may still be connected.

Freud's third line of explanation is that dream feelings may be as much a function of censoring mechanisms as everything else in the dream. Specifically, these mechanisms may well convert the bad feeling into an apparent good feeling. Accordingly, if you have a dream in which there is a feeling of affection toward someone, it may be that the mechanisms converted a real feeling of disaffection and defamation into the disguised feeling of affection:

> If my dream was distorted in this respect from its latent content—and distorted into its opposite—then the affection that was manifest in the dream served the purpose of this distortion. In other words, distortion

was shown in this case to be deliberate and to be a means of *dissimula-tion*. My dream thoughts had contained a slander against R.; and, in order that I might not notice this, what appeared in the dream was the opposite, a feeling of affection for him (Freud, 1900, p. 141)

Freud has created a situation in which a good feeling is really a bad feeling in disguise, and a bad feeling is really a good feeling in disguise, or the good feeling is really a good feeling because the childhood associated feeling was good, or the wish is good and the person a simple one having a simple wish. My impression is that Freud had a somewhat difficult time making sense of the good feelings in dreams. The major underlying difference between the Freudian and the experiential viewpoints is that Freud saw the dreaming person as the waking person with reduced controls, in which case it is rather hard to make sense of good feelings, given the psychoanalytic picture of the nature of unconscious processes. On the other hand, in the experiential approach, the center of I-ness has entered into the deeper potential, the whole basis for bad feelings is left behind, and the whole basis for good feelings is now present.

Why the Experiencing Is So Hard to Find and Why the Dream Is Such a Puzzlement

Dreams have always been a captivating puzzlement. Our way of making sense of them is about at the level that it was around two or four thousand years ago. The general question is why dreams are so puzzling; the specific question is why the experiencing is still so hard to find, even when the person studies the moment of peak feelings. There are five answers to this specific question.

One is that dreams are always going to be puzzling until you get inside the perspective of the dreamer. But suppose you do enter into the peak moment, why are dreams still so puzzling? Why is the dream experiencing still so hard to find? Why isn't the dream experiencing right here on the surface, conspicuous?

A second reason is that the experiencing may be housed within the dreamer or within another figure or object in the peak moment (see Chapter 6). Even if you go into the peak moment, it is hard to locate the dream experiencing.

A third reason is that the dream experiencing is masked by the dream feeling. The dream experiencing is closest, best found, in the moment of peak feeling. The trouble is that what is occurring is the peak feeling, which grabs all the dreamer's attention.

The fourth reason is that the operating domain does not like the deeper dream experiencing and does not want to know the dream experiencing. Because you, the ordinary operating domain, avoid the dream experiencing, Perls (1969, p. 124) can say the key to grasping the deeper dream process is through seeing what is avoided.

The fifth reason is that the dreamer, the center of I-ness, is generally not yet undergoing the dream experiencing. The dreamer is merely in the close vicinity of the deeper experiencing.

Only when the center of I-ness enters wholly into the deeper domain is the influence of the operating domain essentially left behind. Accordingly, in most dreams there is some residual influence of the operating domain. Freud also noted that in most dreams the content represented both the conscious operating personality (he referred to these as the waking thoughts) and the deeper domain:

> . . . not everything contained in a dream is derived from the dream-thoughts, but that contributions to its content may be made by a psychical function which is indistinguishable from our waking thoughts. (Freud, 1900, p. 489)

There is one special kind of dream where the dream experiencing is easier to find, where it is right on the surface. This is the dream in which the center of I-ness has entered into the heart of the deeper potential (Figure 3). In this kind of dream, as will be described in Chapter 6, the dreamer is the one who is housing the experiencing, is the main character, the experiential agent, and the feeling is a good one. These dreams are special. They are not so puzzling, for the experiencing is right here on the surface, interlaced with the good feeling.

With the exception of this special kind of dreams, dreams are entitled to be puzzling and hard to understand until you enter into the moment of peak feeling and allow yourself to undergo the dream experiencing.

We are now at the point where we identify the moment of peak feeling and enter into what is occurring in that moment, i.e., into the dream world.

CHAPTER 6

How to Reenter
the Dream

So far, the person has come into the session, recounted the dream, and identified the feelinged moments in recent events connected to the dream. In Figure 1, we have completed step 2.2. The next job is to get back into the dream. Whether you are a therapist working with a patient or a person working on your own dream, the aim is to reenter the dream world (Means, Palmadier, Wilson, Hickey, Hess-Homeier, & Hickey, 1986; Williams, 1980). Specifically this means identifying, clarifying and filling in the exact moment of peak feeling (step 3.1, Figure 1) and then entering into that peak moment (step 3.2) so that you are now living and existing and ready for the experiencing in the context of that peak moment.

IDENTIFYING WHERE THE MOMENT OF
PEAK FEELING IS

The first step is to identify where the moment of peak feeling is. For patients working with an experiential therapist the eyes of both therapist and patient have been closed from the beginning of the session. So too should the person working on her own dream have her eyes closed. All the attention should be poured into the dream itself.

Begin by selecting one of the two peaks of feeling. Either one will do, although sometimes one is more compelling and you can begin with that one. You will stay with that peak until you attain the dream experiencing (Chapter 9). That is, you identify where that moment of peak feeling is, then you clarify and fill in what is occurring in that moment of peak feeling, then you enter into that peak moment, and you remain in that moment until you open up the dream experiencing. When you have accomplished that, you then repeat the procedure with the other peak moment of feeling.

Begin by putting together the bits and pieces from the recording into an organized picture of the situation when the feeling is strongest. Nothing new has to be added. All we work with is what has already been recounted in the telling of the dream. Begin with the feeling as the anchor point. Given this feeling, the instructions invite the person to assemble the bits and pieces that comprise the moment of peak feeling:

T: The strongest feeling here is being scared (or being lost and alone, or daring, or tense, or being dazzled and captivated). Just describe what is happening when the feeling is like this. You already said a lot of things about the dream and this part. When you're having this feeling, what is going on, both outside you and inside you? Just tell what is happening when the feeling is strongest. Is this all right? Are you ready to do this? I will try and help, but you have to do most of the work. Is this OK?

Sometimes the work is easy. You can easily put together the pieces and bits from what you already recounted of the dream. Here are some examples:

Pt: It's when I am at the elevator, and the elevator doors open, sort of slowly, and there inside is this little girl, just standing. She's looking right at me, right into my eyes. The doors are open maybe two feet but that is enough. That's when I'm scared . . .

Pt: It's when I'm in the terminal and I hear this voice over the loudspeaker, and she says for me to return the parcels to the counter. That's when I get damned mad and I fling them. I'm really mad. I fling them over everyone's heads and I walk away.

Pt: The strongest feeling is when this blond woman is skating on the pond or lake. The sun was out and there were thousands watching her and she was great. She spun around and she was wonderful. We all watched her and I was dazzled. That's the strongest feeling.

More often, however, the person is vague and mixed up about what is occurring in the peak moment. It takes work to assemble the parts. It is relatively easy to know the nature of the feeling and the bits and pieces have been given, but typically they are disconnected from an organized picture of the peak moment. After the opening instructions the patient says:

Pt: I'm scared. I am scared, and there is this big penthouse and it's open and there's lots of flowers. (Start with the feeling)

T: You're scared, right. Scared. About something. What?

Pt: Scared of falling. I'm scared of falling. Something about a guy with a big hat wanting me to leave and I didn't know how I got there. (Things are fragmented, disconnected. We do not know what fits together or how they fit together. So we trust the feeling.)

T: And you're scared, maybe scared about falling. Something's happening when the feeling is strongest, the being scared, maybe scared of falling.

Pt: There are lots of leaves, and flowers, and some guy wants to dance with me, and the floor.

T: The floor, something about the floor? Is this when you are scared of falling? (She then fills in the scene in the moment of peak feeling.)

Pt: I'm right up against lots of flowers and there is this hole in the floor. That's when! I'm kneeling or something in this hole in the floor and there are these flowers and leaves and things all around and I'm reaching for something, and the hole is deep, goes down far and I don't know how far and I'm scared I'm going to fall down the hole. That's it.

It almost seems as if the components of the peak moment are disconnected, and the strong feeling is left hanging all by itself. Here is a feeling, and here are disconnected bits and pieces, none of which seem to relate to the feeling. Only when you put them together will the feeling make sense and will you know what is occurring in the peak moment.

T: So the main feeling is embarrassment, you feel ashamed or squeamish or something.

Pt: Yeah, and I'm in bed, and there's this older man and something about clothes, clothes on the floor. (There is more. This does not tell us about what is going on.)

T: Just fill in where you are and what is happening when the feeling of embarrassment is here. An older man and clothes, on the floor.

Pt: They're my clothes, and there's a table, and I think I treated him like a servant, and there was a girl. (Here are disconnected pieces. How do they go together around the peak feeling?)

T: And this feeling of embarrassment, ashamed. You are ashamed and embarrassed about something.

Pt: I'm in bed with this girl, and her father walks in, and he said that he had my clothes pressed. I was going to marry his daughter, and I left my clothes outside the bedroom on a table . . .

T: (It is all coming together around the feeling, so use the feeling even more.) And the feeling of embarrassment, you're ashamed about something? Being in bed with the daughter?

Pt: No, the clothes were all washed and pressed and I felt embarrassed that I
  treated him like a servant.
T: Oh. OK, I see.

When the circumstances are disorganized, take plenty of time to
assemble what is occurring in the peak moment. Just use the bits and
pieces from the recounted dream. You do not have to find new elements. Yet it is sometimes an effort to organize these bits and pieces.
Go slowly and work bit by bit. If you are working with your own
dream, make sure that you take it a little at a time. If you are a
therapist, you can try and help by adding your own guesses but make
sure you use the bits and pieces from the recounted dream.

You are not looking for any more than just what is happening in
the moment of peak feeling, using what you have in the recounted
dream. But sometimes you will have surprises. You know that the
feeling is being tense and worried, and you are frantically thinking of
how to get away. As you begin to piece together what is happening,
something new pops up:

Pt: I know I'm on this escalator, and I am watched. There is a bunch of
  people and they look at me funny, especially this older woman in a fur
  coat. She's with a kid. There is light, lots of light. It's bright. I have
  come here to buy something for the house. Seems like I did something.
  I went on a ride like in a carnival or a circus or something. I'm going
  up the elevator. (Shrieks) I am naked! I have nothing on! I just remembered!!

Pt: I am just a little boy and I peed. I peed in bed. When I woke up I thought
  for a second that I really peed. I didn't. Somehow the covers were like a
  tent. I remember that I had played with some toy soldiers. I just peed.
  There was a big bed. It is really big, and it is dark, but there is a light
  or some light under the covers here. I have pajamas on, and I remember letting go and out it came. I felt funny. Sort of not bad. How can I
  say. Like it was fun somehow. Wait! Oh I remember! My cousin was in
  bed with me! I peed on her! And she's sleeping the whole time! I forgot
  all about that! I forgot. Oh that's awful, an awful thing to do!

You have now identified where the moment of feeling is. But we are
not yet ready to enter into the peak moment, for there usually are all
sorts of bits and pieces that are vague and hazy. The rest of this step
of identifying the peak moment (step 3.1, Figure 1) is to clarify and
fill in these missing or vague elements.

CLARIFYING AND FILLING IN THE
MOMENT OF PEAK FEELING

The moment of peak feeling is just a moment. It is brief. If we are going to clarify and fill in what is occurring in this brief moment, the person has to freeze it. This is the art of attending to the dream and thereby putting it on hold:

> . . . with our attention we can hold the images of the dream in the same way we hold the images of the world. . . . The art of the dreamer is the art of attention. (Castaneda, 1977, p. 265)

Once you hold the peak moment, the aim is to clarify it, fill in what is missing, make a little clearer what is vague. You can get a little more detail by asking what the little dog looks like, or you can fill in broad strokes by inquiring just where the dreamer is when he is looking at his watch. Let us pick up with the dreamer in bed with the girl, when the father is there with the clothes, and let us see if we can clarify and fill in more of the features of the peak moment:

T: Oh. OK. I see . . . when the father walks in, I can't tell what he looks like and the clothes, are they in the room or what? Can we try and fill in some of this? I'm vague, and maybe you are too.

Pt: I don't know where the clothes are, but somehow I just know that they're all washed and pressed. Maybe they're somewhere in the room. He is a little old man with a little moustache, a thin man, and he's the father of this girl.

T: I picture him about ten feet away or so.

Pt: About that. He's standing by the door, and the room is a big room, Spanish-like. It seems open, like there are big archways all over. But I can't see what's out there. It's like a big place, not quite like a home. I don't know.

T: Now I'm turning to the girl. Can you see her and what it's like here on the bed?

Pt: She's a woman, maybe in her late twenties and she is sitting up in bed, and she's comfortable. I think we are going to be married. She seems comfortable about being with me. She's got long dark hair, black, and she's comfortable about her father walking in. She's wearing a nightgown and sitting up, and I'm on pillows and lying down and seeing the father.

T: And you're feeling embarrassed.

Pt: Yeah. He's so deferential to me, like I'm some special person, a king or royalty. That's the thing. I didn't want him to have my clothes pressed, and he's done it himself. I think he went and washed them himself and he pressed them, and he is acting just like a servant. She's not that way. She's an equal, but he's like a servant, all deferential with me.

T: Nobody's saying anything?

Pt: No, he said that he had my clothes pressed, and I knew that he had done it himself. He said that. That's all he said. Like a servant.

All you do is to start with the peak feeling and fill in what is missing or vague:

T: You're scared you're going to fall down the hole, and you're kneeling or something, and the hole is deep. There are all sorts of leaves and flowers around. But I can't get the physical posture. You are leaning over?

Pt: I think I'm on my knees, and I'm leaning over this hole and I'm reaching for something, a flower, I think.

T: I'm seeing the opening, the hole as maybe three or four feet across . . .

Pt: Oh no, it's big. It's round and at least eight or ten feet or even bigger.

T: Oh!

Pt: I'm leaning way over, and trying to get at some flower. There are lots of flowers, but there's one I'm after. There is a lot of greenery around the hole, lots of leaves and shrubbery and things all around the hole.

T: And you're afraid of falling? Are you in danger?

Pt: Not really, but the floor is slippery, and there are so many people, and they're dancing, and this guy wants to dance with me, and I'm afraid that someone'll dance and bump me and I'll fall.

T: How far down will you fall?

Pt: About six feet or so.

T: What? I thought it would be miles!

Pt: There's soft leather furniture and I wouldn't even hurt myself, but I'm still scared of falling. It's all open downstairs, and there are people there too. Probably no one'd even notice me down there, but I'm still afraid. I think I'm afraid just of falling and losing my . . . not killing myself or anything, just going over too far and maybe being pushed by someone and just falling.

Keep going until you have a reasonably clear picture of what is occurring in the peak moment. The more details the better. Just make sure that you leave somewhat vague what wants to remain somewhat vague in the above moment:

T: And this fellow with the big hat, he wants you to leave. Is he here with you?

Pt: I don't know. (Pause) I can't find him. I don't know. (That is all right. But something else pops up.). . . . But I am wearing a workout suit, like a leotard, and it is way too big on me.

T: I never even thought about what you're wearing. Hmm. Loose, too big. Is this making it hard? Maybe falling?

Pt: No, but I am wearing something. They are all dressed in gowns and it's formal. I'm a little ridiculous, but I'm mainly scared that I'm going to fall down.

Clarifying and filling in the moment of peak feeling can sometimes lead to surprises. These may be from the way some bit of the peak moment fits in, or they may come from something quite new that we uncover in trying to organize what is happening in the peak moment. Here is one surprise as we work on a peak moment in which the dreamer and his companion jump on top of a wooden fence:

Pt: There were bad cowboys in the shack over there, and this pretty lady, she's dressed in cowboy stuff, and has guns. I do too. We have to jump on this tall wooden fence, and then we'll jump down and attack them. We both jump and she makes it on top. I jump but I have one leg on one side and the other down.

T: And she's facing you.

Pt: She's about three feet away; we can touch. She's looking at me and I'm with one left on one side and the other on the other and I'm really embarrassed 'cause I can't just swing over and get down.

T: (Puzzled) Are you stuck here, like on a nail?

Pt: No, I'm feeling really funny about the position I'm in. Maybe cause she can jump up and I can't. No, oh! (Laughs) I got nothing on! (Hard laughter) You know chaps, I think they call them. My prick and balls are hanging out! I got nothing covering them! (Hard laughter) No wonder I'm embarrassed!

Despite clarifications, you are at this point still more or less outside the peak moment, a waking, conscious person who is recollecting something about that peak moment. You must still actually take the step of entering into the peak moment.

ENTERING INTO THE DREAMER IN THE MOMENT OF PEAK FEELING

What completes the job of bringing the person into the peak moment is to enter into the dreamer in the moment of peak feeling. Whether you are the therapist or working on your own dream, the aim is to enter into the very being of the dreamer in the moment of peak feeling.

Seeing if the Person is Ready and Willing

If the person is ready and willing, then the therapist can show what to do and how to do it. The person has the choice of going ahead or not. Almost every patient will agree to this on almost every dream. But the point is that the person has the choice. The therapist invites the person's readiness and willingness by saying something along the following lines:

T: Are you ready and willing to go back into that moment when the feeling was strong in the dream? We know what is going on and what is happening. Now it is up to you to get back inside the person you were in that moment. You will have the same feeling and you will be living in that moment. I will show you what to do and how to do it, but you are the one who can do it. If you are ready and willing, then we can start. If you are not ready and willing, then we won't do it. What do you think?

When the peak feeling is a bad one, it is not so easy to enter into the dreamer. You need the person's commitment, and therefore you must emphasize readiness, willingness, and choice:

T: It means being in the dark and going down the cellar steps, and sensing or feeling the breathing. Remember? Now that is very terrifying. We have to do it if we are going to get back into the moment when the feeling is strongest. But the feeling is terrifying. I will understand if you decline. But I hope you don't. What do you think?

If you are a therapist, and the patient agrees, then there are methods to be used. If you are working with your own dreams, and you are ready and willing, then you will use the same methods. In either case, it is the person who does the actual work of leaving the perspective of the one who has been here in the office, talking about the peak moment, and of becoming the dreamer, living and being in the peak moment.

Getting Inside the Dreamer

You are actively and voluntarily to get inside the dreamer in this peak moment. Take the dreamer's place. Feel what the dreamer is feeling. Assume the posture of the dreamer. Literally be the dreamer.

Whatever the dreamer is doing, you do it. Whatever is being done to the dreamer, let it be done to you. Whoever and whatever the dreamer is, that is who and what you are to be.

This is what the therapist tells the patient to do. If the person has any questions about what to do and how to do it, the therapist answers those. Once the person begins, the therapist joins in. It is as if the therapist plays the part of the person who is cordially welcoming being the dreamer: "As soon as you start, I will join along with you. We both can get inside the dreamer. There's room."

As the patient begins, make sure that it is done correctly. For example, make sure that everything is spoken in the present tense, and that the dreamer says it aloud, directly to the other person. The moment of peak feeling was when the dreamer was in the huge bathtub, and the patient has just agreed to enter into being the dreamer. Notice how the therapist is right alongside the dreamer, a ready and willing part of the person:

Pt: There was this big bathtub. It was white, and I was inside.
T: Well maybe you were inside it, but I am right here inside this big white tub right here. Here I am inside it, right now.
Pt: It's huge. You get four people inside. The sides come above my head. It's really big.
T: Right. So here I am down here. This is really something here.
Pt: And I'm with this guy and I think we are looking at one another . . .
T: Listen, it helps if we can talk directly to this guy. Say it out loud like you're saying it directly to him.
Pt: And I'm looking at you and this is the hard part 'cause you and I are in this tub and you are a quadriplegic and you're blind and we are lying naked in this tub and I'm a doctor and I'm preventing complications or something and I'm doing physiotherapy with you and I don't know how to tell you that I don't love you and I really want to get out of the tub but the sides are so big and slippery and I've resigned myself to being here and doing all these things for you.
T: And now I have feelings.
Pt: I am over you, above you, and I'm looking at your eyes and you can't see me, and the way you look at me. You're just totally helpless. . . . I can't leave you this way. . . . I'm afraid . . . to say that I don't love you and I want to get away. (She begins to cry.)

The big change is being inside the dreamer and fitting oneself to what the dreamer is thinking and doing. In the peak moment, the dreamer is sitting in the audience, feeling infuriated. Her chief research assistant is giving a presentation and is doing a terrible job.

The therapist explains how the person must get inside the dreamer, and the person begins:

Pt: Well, I'm sitting in this small room, and Sally is at the board. The peculiar thing is that I am some sort of researcher, doing research, not at a hospital, more in industry. I don't know what kind of research. Something like airplane engines, designing rockets, that sort of thing. And I think I have a large group of people working for me. Well, here we are in a room at the place, and there are some visitors here. They are here to visit my lab and to hear of the work we are doing. I am sitting sort of at the rear, maybe a few feet behind the others. I am in a simple chair and I have a pad with me to take notes. My attention is on Sally, who is my chief research assistant, and I am proud of the work she is doing. But the strange thing is that I am also thinking about how they must think of me because I am mad as hell at what Sally is doing. She's going on and on about the kind of work she wants to do herself, and it is just wild. She's getting all excited about native people! She's drawing crazy things on the board about their pelvises and how childraising varies with the size of little holes in the bones! It is absurd, and I am wondering what they all must be thinking. I want to ring her neck!

T: And are you saying anything? What are you doing?

Pt: Just getting more and more infuriated. I am furious.

T: With lots of thoughts!

Pt: About what she is doing and mainly what these visitors must think of me and my lab. They are from foreign countries and they are on a tour of the labs. They're all scientists and they are, well, they are trying to be polite, and they're not doing anything. They're quiet, but I'm furious and I'm just thinking how they must be feeling about me. I'll be a laughingstock. I think they'll think of me as absolutely ridiculous!

Getting Inside the Encompassing Peak Moment

You can help enter into the dreamer in the moment of peak feeling by being in the encompassing situational context. The dreamer is always in some scene, some surroundings, and the aim is to make these present and real, immediate, alive, and seen from the perspective of the dreamer. We know what is occurring during the peak moment. The task is to be undergoing all of this in and from the perspective of the dreamer.

In actual work, blend getting inside the encompassing peak moment with getting inside the dreamer. It is artificial to try and separate them. Here the therapist and patient are combining the two, but the emphasis is on getting inside the encompassing peak moment:

T: All right, so let's be in the moment. You are now the dreamer, and you are scared as hell when you look over your shoulder and she is gaining on you.

Pt: She is just marching along and I can barely move.

T: What's it like, barely moving?

Pt: My legs are heavy. It's like walking in water. Heavy. I can barely move. I'm moving but so slowly.

T: OK. I'm moving slowly, can hardly move.

Pt: I feel drugged. But my thoughts are racing and I'm scared as hell that she's going to get me. It's like walking in water and sand.

T: But we're not in sand or water.

Pt: It's ground. And there are bushes and I can barely get through the bushes. They're not thick, and they're just up to my waist. I have no idea why she's after me. But she's the enemy. Like I did something. I don't know. And there's no one else around. Open ground. And it's a little dark, not much. And there aren't even many bushes, just here and there. The ground is solid and I should be able to get away but I'm so slow. I feel like I'm her target or her enemy or something, and I look around and there's no place to hide. Not from her.

T: She's marching along, after you.

Pt: Like a soldier.

T: Describe a little about her.

Pt: She's big and strong and marching along. Nothing's going to stop her. She's really sure of herself. She's after me all right, and she's gaining on me.

T: I see her about 30 feet away. Am I even close?

Pt: No, she's only about eight feet from me.

T: Oh! That close?

Pt: She's practically right on me!

T: And then the hatchet or axe or something. She maybe can actually throw it at you?

Pt: It's in her hand but down by her side. She's not on me yet. In another second or two. Then she'll kill me. There's no hope at all! It's all over! I may as well give in! She's going to kill me and that's that!

Once the person knows what to do and how to do it, most of the work can be done by the person himself. Here is the patient being in bed with the daughter, and the father has come into the bedroom to let the dreamer know that the dreamer's clothes have been washed and pressed:

Pt: At first I feel squeamish about his coming in when his daughter and I are in bed. But the strongest feeling is my being embarrassed that he is so deferential.

T: OK, so make it real, like you are really in bed and all of this is happening. You really are the man in the bed and all of this is happening right now. Insert yourself into the dreamer and see what it is all like through the dreamer's eyes.

Pt: She's sitting up right here, to my right. Sort of cross-legged. I am a man who's going to marry her. Well, it's not damn certain, but probably. She is solid, beautiful. I'm naked. The covers are over me, and this dapper old gentleman comes in and just about bows. Your clothes are ready. I'd been a little concerned about whether I flung them around last night. This place is quite open. Maybe like a huge resort. Or maybe it is his estate. Thank you for my clothes. I say nothing, really, but he says that my clothes are washed and pressed. I think she and I just loved to make love, and instead of being offended, even if I am going to marry her, well, he is gracious and very deferential. I'm aware of the physical structure of the room, how open it is, with no doors at all, just domed and curved openings and very broad ones.

So far, I have carved up the process into three steps. First the person is to identify where the moment of peak feeling is, then the person clarifies and fills in what is occurring in the moment of peak feeling, and finally the person enters into the peak moment from the perspective of the dreamer. However, it is common that everything occurs almost at once instead of in three steps. In the following, the patient starts by telling about a part of the dream that seems to hold a peak moment. It is not at all clear where the peak moment is, but it is rather clear that she is already caught up in the dream, living in the dream as if it is real and immediate:

Pt: There is something hiding in some leaves. It is a snake, very white, like a cobra. Its head is larger. A big snake. I am scared a bit. It is about four or five feet long. I see its head first. It is aware of me. Then it tries to escape. I am scared, afraid it will attack me. The snake goes out of the room. Suddenly it is behind me. I can't escape it! Shit! What am I going to do? It's just there beside me, and it comes up my legs. It curls up my back, all gathered there on my back. Then it starts to bite me more than once. I'm going to die. I think I can get the snake off of me, and I have to do it slowly and hold its head away from me, and I do it very slowly. Then I got its head out in front of me very slowly, and then it escapes and goes into the kitchen, away.

It is all so very real, yet where is the peak feeling? Notice how we move back and forth between trying to identify where the peak feeling is and trying to clarify and fill in what is occurring in the peak moment:

T: And the feeling. When is it strongest?

Pt: My feeling is strongest when the snake is on my back and I was scared I was going to die. It's all curled up on me, and it's big, about five or six inches in diameter.

T: It's big and all white and it's the feeling that I'm going to die. It's already bitten me.

Pt: It just started biting me. Little bites, just little ones. I think, "It will kill you." It's a cobra, and I think I'm going to die. I don't like snakes, especially big ones.

T: It's biting me. I'm going to die, but the bites are just little ones.

Pt: Just little ones, pressure bites, just the pressure of the teeth, just into the skin, pressure not enough to get the venom into my blood.

T: Oh! Whew! So far the venom hasn't punctured my skin and into my blood. So far!

Pt: No. It might. I'm scared it might, but now it doesn't. But I'm scared it would.

T: (Aware that all of this is confined to the immediate vicinity of the snake's "teeth") And it's on my back. I can't tell if I'm standing or where I am or what I'm doing. Help me.

Pt: It's heavy on my back. I feel the heaviness.

T: Oh! Lying down? (This is new.)

Pt: I'm lying down on a bed. Have a coat on, and the snake came up my leg and under the coat. I have no clothes on under the coat. It's on my skin, my back. Like it's almost making love to you. It's warm and heavy.

T: It's warm and heavy and little bites. Why the hell doesn't it bite, really bite?

Pt: I don't know. I don't know! It wants room, wants a place on my, maybe it likes me! It's touching, up close, right on me . . . tender. . . . It's . . . it's making love to me!!

The goal is to get into the dream world, to enter into the peak moment. To do this the person has to locate where the moment of peak feeling is, clarify and fill in what is occurring in this peak moment, and get inside the perspective of the dreamer in the peak moment. Typically this occurs in a sequence, but there are lots of occasions where they just go together. Yet, at the end, the person is the dreamer in the moment of peak feeling.

SOME SPECIAL PROBLEMS

The person starts from outside the dreamer and then enters into the dreamer in the peak moment of feelings. When you think of it, this is quite a change. It can be accomplished, but sometimes it is not so easy, and you may face some special problems.

Getting Swept into the Dream

We want the person to get back into being the dreamer in the moment of peak feeling, and we count on the person's directing her attention onto the features of the peak moment. A number of studies report what therapists have already known, namely that when persons put their attention onto their dreams and talk about them in some detail, the dreams may become alive and real (Cartwright, Tipton, & Wicklund, 1980; Fiss & Litchman, 1976; Greenberg & Pearlman, 1975b). There are occasions where the person is swept wholesale into the dream, which can pose problems.

One of the problems resides in the therapist who stays behind, does not join the person in being the dreamer, and is bothered by the person's radical shift into being the dreamer. This is not the person's problem, but the therapist's. The therapist is supposed to welcome getting inside the dreamer and to be able to do this more easily than the person. If the dreamer is a savage beast bent on stalking her prey, and if the patient enters into this dreamer, the problem comes when the therapist stays behind and has all sorts of scary thoughts: "She is crazy! She flipped! My God, what if she doesn't come out of it? What am I going to do? She's gone too far!!" The way to solve this problem is to insure that it rarely occurs. (Incidentally, here is one problem that the person who works alone can avoid.)

Aside from the therapist's reluctance, what do we do when the person enters all the way into the dreamer in the peak scene, when the person is now wholly the dreamer and is existing wholly in the dream scene? To begin with, this is rare. I come across this once a year or so. Most every person can get back into the dream enough to make it quite real. But being swept into the dream is far beyond that. In the peak moment, he is knocked down by a large rafter that falls from the castle ceiling, and his mother rushes down the stairs because of the noise. The rafter hurts him, and he yells at his mother in the peak moment. Returning to that instant, he pauses, and then falls completely into being the dreamer. His voice becomes rather eerie, sounding just like a little boy of around 10 or 12, at first hurtfully furious and then crying. It is exceedingly real:

Pt: Why did you come down? (He is really mad at her.) You don't care about me? MY LEG HURTS! WHAT DO YOU CARE! I HATE YOU! Get up in your kitchen and do whatever you do. You never cared about me. You never did. You never would have had me at all if your baby didn't die!! (Here he cracks into hard crying. He is referring to a miscarriage that happened two years before he was conceived.)

The problem with such a wholesale entry into the dreamer and the peak moment is that the person drifts into other material, or becomes absolutely frozen by the bad feeling in the peak moment, or dilates the peak moment and drifts away. Therefore we cannot get at the dream experiencing.

What can the therapist do under these conditions? I have found that it works to let the dreamer do what he wishes, and then I suggest that we can perhaps now get back to this peak moment. After the dreamer had fallen into hard racking crying, and all of this subsided, the therapist says:

T: (Quietly) I would like to do something, but only if it is all right with you. I'll tell you what it is, and you decide. . . . I want to go back to where you are yelling at your mother. But this time, your mother and you are in this strange place, like a castle. You are exploring it together, and you yell at her because she is so stupid that you know she will some-how make it worse. You yell at her to just stay the hell away, that you'll take care of it yourself. Is this all right? No?

Pt: I know she'll just fuck it up. My leg is killing me and you'll make it worse. You are awful. Just stay away will you! Just get the hell away from me! I'LL TAKE CARE OF IT MYSELF!!

Occasionally, entering into the dreamer plunges the person into a state of being so powerfully gripped by the very bad feeling that he is quite frozen. Sometimes we cannot proceed with uncovering the dream experiencing. In the peak moment, the dreamer is hanging from an open elevator and a large screeching vulture digs its claws into his chest and is about to decimate his face. The feeling is terror. When he reenters into the dreamer in the peak, the terror fills him so completely and intensely that he is totally paralyzed:

Pt: Oh . . . oh . . . oh . . . (Hard breathing) Unnh . . . uunnnh . . . (Groans that are tough and short and hard) Aaaaw . . . (whimperings that seem propelled from inside)

When this happens, the therapist can try and make sure that the dreamer does not leave the peak moment until the paralyzing terror subsides just a bit. There is an important difference between being paralyzed in terror and remaining in the peak moment and having the strong feeling of terror.

Sometimes the person is swept so far into the dreamer and the dream scene that the very flow of the dreamer's activated thoughts removes her from the dream peak moment:

T: And the feeling is strongest when you're squatting on the bottle with the opening about three inches or so, and you're pissing, and you can hear the pee hitting the bottle, and the feeling is relief, actual wonderful relief.
Pt: My skirt is hiding the bottle, but it feels so good that I really don't care to hide it, or even if I miss any around the edges. At least it's being open. If I keep up the exercises it will be good. But I am too old to be doing this. I have no family and I have nowhere to belong. Maybe I am wearing all my clothes. It is like a protection all around me, a barrier between me and the world, but a soft one like a pillow, friendly and nurturing. It welcomes you to sleep and bundles around you like a friend the whole night. Just lovely sleep.

The flow of thoughts carries her away from the dream scene, so the therapist brings her back into the dream scene when the flow of thoughts subsides:

T: And such a great relief when all that piss sizzles in the bottle. Ah! Wonderful.
Pt: Just squatting here, but I am, and lots of pee is coming out. I think I'm filling the whole bottle. There really is a lot of pee, a lot. And it may be filling the bottle. Damn, it feels good.

One of the special problems is when the person is so fully swept into the dreamer that we cannot move toward the dream experiencing. But this is only one the special problems.

Backing Away from the Peak Moment

The waking person has excellent reasons for backing away from being the dreamer in the peak moment. One is that the operating personality has disintegratively fearful and avoidant relations toward the dream experiencing. Second, the waking personality is simply not going to sacrifice the center of I-ness to the deeper personality. Accordingly, it is understandable that many persons will, on occasion, back away from entering into the dreamer in the peak moment.

An exceedingly common way of bolting away from the peak moment is to select some aspect of the peak moment and to "talk about" it. Here are some patients doing this, starting with something from the peak moment:

Pt: . . . and that's the way I feel a lot. I mean that I try to say no or I object, and it means nothing. No one pays attention. I felt good in the dream, but ordinarily I just feel . . . impotent!

Pt: I have the same theme in lots of dreams lately. I'm being aggressive to someone. A sister or my husband or Ruth or someone. All my dreams lately . . .

Pt: I know what started that. I was starting to tell Joe about the way he never makes supper, and he put his hand over my mouth. It was funny. I tried to talk and he kept putting his hand over my mouth. It's the same thing like hitting her on the head with the spoon in the dream.

Pt: I know what it means. I have a lot of sibling rivalry. She is thinking of going to law school, and I got all funny about that. I want to be the family pet, and I have competed with her all my life . . .

Pt: We used to do something like that when we were kids. At the table. We'd sit next to each other and we'd start hitting each other. Not hitting, pushing. Mom would get mad at us. And we'd blame the other one all the time . . .

After any of these "backing away" ploys, the therapist again offers the patient the choice of going back:

T: Right! Now are you ready to go back into the peak moment in the dream? It means you'll have to let go of having memories like that. Good memories. But it means staying in the peak and letting yourself be here, right in the peak. Living here and being here. What do you think? Ready? Yes? No?

Many patients use these ploys as soon as we begin to attend to the dream and to locate the peak feeling. For example, the person backs away by means of a stream of talkings about this or that, and then the next this or that.

T: All right. Now are you ready to look for when the feeling was strongest? OK? . . . From the dream, it sounded like, well, you said it was when your son drives up in that car that is shaped like an old-fashioned sewing machine, and he starts running around like someone is chasing him, and that Chinese man appears in the doorway. The feeling is strongest somewhere in there. Can you begin to find when the feeling is strongest somewhere in this?

Pt: It's the strangest thing, the car. He poops around in this big old-fashioned sewing machine. A big one, and he uses the treadle, and the damned thing moves along pretty fast, but it is big like a car. I never had anything like that, but I remember my grandmother used to have one, and I have been thinking of her lately, I mean since Stella (her daughter) had her baby. It's hard for me to get used to being a grandmother. I'm still pretty trim, but I know that I smoke too much, and I know I drink and it's not good for me . . .

We still do not know when the moment of peak feeling is. So we invite the person to return to the identifying of that moment:

T: That is some fascinating car. You really are a creative dreamer. I was wondering about the fuel. But we have work to do. We have to try and figure out when the feeling was strongest and I thought maybe it was when the Chinese guy appears. No?

Pt: It's when David starts running around. I thought someone was trying to catch him. He is running everywhere, and he's just running.

T: So when is the feeling strongest, that moment?

Pt: He is running like wild. He's running in circles on the sidewalk. That's when I'm worried that something's really wrong. Like he's frantic. Out of his mind maybe . . . yeah, that's it.

Sometimes the person will back away as we are getting close to the actual peak moment in the dream:

Pt: It's when I slice off this little girl's arm. She is holding the noodle and I take this big knife and just slice off her whole arm. Like there's nothing to it.

T: It's when you slice it off.

Pt: Yeah. God, that's awful. I felt like I wanted that noodle. Like it was mine and she had no right to it. I was mad. Not at the slicing, just that I wanted the noodle. My God, that's heartless! No feeling! I was cold and heartless! How could anyone do anything like that? Oooh! I never am that way! I don't do anything like that! Even when I snapped a piece of rubber in Billy's eye I felt awful, and I never . . . I'm not like that. Cruel. That's the way my father was. He was heartless sometimes.

Instead of backing away, we try to locate the peak moment and enter into the dreamer:

T: Yeah, it sure is heartless. Right. Now, is it OK to get back into that moment a little? I know it's kind of repulsive, but are you ready to describe more of what is happening in that moment? Like where it's all happening and what she is doing when the slicing happens?

Pt: Well, she is holding the noodle in her right hand and she's got it behind her back, sort of daring me to try to get it. Then I just slice off the whole arm. Whoosh! I'm feeling mad, just like challenged. It is mine! Actually it feels good. Like I'm getting it. I don't even know if I take the noodle. I'm just mad at her!

Backing away from the peak moment is understandable, and it must be welcomed gracefully as you return to the peak moment and to entering into the dreamer.

There is another way that effectively blocks the person from entering into the dreamer and the peak moment. It consists of backing into a sleep-like state. The patient may be silent for a minute or so, may snore, may fall into dream-like, hypnogogic reveries, images, fantasies. Here is the patient after she began to identify and to clarify what was occurring in the peak moment in which she arose after the concert and was putting on her coat:

Pt: . . . and I knew I was the only one, but I was scared of what was happening and I had to leave, so I am getting up and I knew that I had to leave . . . my coat . . . I have my coat on . . . (long silence of about 35 seconds) . . . the water is warm . . . my feet are in the mud and . . . (20 seconds) . . . she's standing by the door . . . (then, with a jerk). . . . I think I feel asleep! I saw a bunch of little girls running along a corridor, and one turned to me and asked if I had my tennis racket, and I remember some girls playing volley ball. I was watching!

For some patients, this is a relatively common way of dealing with entering into the peak moment. They often go asleep and dream. In so doing, the person is not entering into the peak moment. If you are working on dreams alone, there will be minutes like this. When you awake, I suggest that you try reentering the peak moment and make sure that you are always talking. If the person is working with a therapist, then the therapist should give the person instructions when she has awakened from the sleep state: "If you are ready, let's go back into the peak moment, and just keep talking and describing. Be there. Enter into the peak moment all the way. Don't let yourself have long silences and pauses. If you sense yourself getting drowsy, keep your attention fixed on the peak moment. OK? Yes? No?" I allow the patient to slide into the sleep-dream state. I do not stop the person. But when she awakes I invite her to try again without giving in to the sleep-dream state.

Sometimes you will back away from the peak moment, and sometimes you will get wholly swept into the dream. But even if these problems occur, you can identify where the moment of peak feeling is, you can clarify and fill in what is happening in the peak moment, and you can enter into the dreamer in the moment of peak feeling.

ENTERING FURTHER INTO BOTH THE DREAMER AND THE OTHER AGENT

Once you are in the peak moment, you are ready to search around for the dream experiencing. This means that you are to enter further and deeper into the dreamer, and you are to enter further and deeper into the other agent in the peak moment.

Either the Dreamer or the Other Agent May Contain the Dream Experiencing

We are looking for the dream experiencing. Our theory allows the dream experiencing to be contained within the dreamer or within some other figure or object or agent in the peak moment. Just to be safe, it makes sense to try out both. That is, try illuminating the dreamer, and then try illuminating the other agent in the peak moment.

It is an old idea, and one that is held in many dream approaches, that what you are looking for may be contained in the dreamer or in someone or something else in the dream:

> For example, in the case of a dream involving grief, a dream character other than the dreamer is represented as crying during the dream but when the dreamer awakens he finds his pillow soaked, indicating that he himself has actually been crying. . . . It is evident that the dreamer in this type of dream is able to avoid the affect by displacing it onto another person who acts as his proxy in this regard. (Levitan, 1980, p. 226)

It is standard practice for Perls (1969) and Gestalt therapists to consider the other figure or object as the "projected" part of the personality. Jung also accepted the idea that in some dreams the important meaning was expressed in the other person, not in the dreamer. If the dream indicates a "latent psychosis," the process may be manifested by the other person rather than the dreamer:

> After about two weeks the patient brought a dream from which he had awakened in a panic: He was in a building empty of other people, and eventually made his way to a gigantic room. In the center of it was an idiot child of about two years, sitting on a chamber pot, smearing himself with feces. Jung did not interpret the dream to the patient; he saw it as indicating a latent psychosis for which the dreamer's apparent supranormality was compensating. (Mattoon, 1984, p. 151)

In many approaches, the important deeper process or meaning may be shown or carried in the other agent. Bonime (1962) reports the following dream from a patient: "I see a bird approaching. It hovers in mid-air, directly above the group of people below us and, because of our elevation, it is just at my eye level. The bird has a cold, cruel, inhuman eye that frightens me" (p. 116). This bird is understood by Bonime as the manifestation of something the patient feared to see in himself, " . . . an attribute that it frightened him to observe" (p. 116); " . . . the dream threatened to expose to him that he was not one of God's noblemen, a protector of women, above the common crowd, but instead a rather 'cold, cruel, inhuman,' predatory sort of bird" (p. 117).

In the following dream, Boss regards the other figure, the nurse, as manifesting the deeper personality process of grown-up womanliness:

> A twenty-year old woman dreamed that she was sitting in a perambulator. She was still a small child in the dream, although the pram had already become somewhat too small for her. A young, healthy nurse, about twenty years old, was pushing the pram up a hill. The nurse asked the dreamer to get out of the pram and to walk on her own feet. The dreamer refused, kicking and screaming. The nurse took the dreamer out of the pram, cut off her head and her limbs, buried the parts in the ground, and walked off. (1963, p. 266)

Peak Moments in Which the Experiencing Tends to Lie Within the Dreamer

There are some dreams where the experiencing tends to lie within the dreamer. We will describe three kinds of peak moments where the likelihood is pretty good that this is the case.

The dreamer is the main character, and the feeling is good. In these dreams, the feeling is a good one, and the dreamer is the main character. That is, the dreamer is usually carrying out the main action and behavior. As the main character, the dreamer is the "center of gravity" in that he is more aware of and centered upon his self, his actions, his thoughts and ideas. There generally is another person with whom the dreamer is interacting, but it is clearly the dreamer who is initiating the action and carrying it out as the main character. In the peak, the feeling is good as the dreamer is adjusting the fingers of the fellow whose hand he is shaking (see Appendix; "Shaking the hand, and the name is scratched out"):

Pt: Well, he is commenting to the other guy, some guy, earlier, that, some-
    thing like he knew me. But I am moving his fingers and I am using my
    left hand to move them, and I'm getting a firmer handshake.
T: Ha! Moving his fingers with the left hand.
Pt: Yeah, and I'm doing it, moving them. I'm arranging his fingers and mine
    so I can get a firmer handshake.
T: And there is a feeling here, doing this.
Pt: I like that. I'm moving his fingers, and I'm getting a firm grip. It feels
    good. It's a neat feeling, nice feeling. I like this.

In these good-feelinged dreams, it is often rather clear that the dreamer is the main character, carrying out the action, with the other people more in the role of background, part of the situation:

Pt: I have this microphone thing, even though there are only about a dozen
    people at the meeting, around the table. I'm walking around and I'm
    funny! I am making them laugh. I'm explaining how we can buy the
    grain elevators in the town, but I'm cracking jokes and they're grinning
    and laughing. I'm with them. I got the audience in the palm of my
    hand and I'm just funny.

The dreamer is the main character, and the feeling is bad. A large proportion of dreams are those where the feeling is unpleasant and the dreamer is the main character, the important one, the one from whom the action flows. The dreamer is generally the one who contains the dream experiencing; often he is the only character. Here is one such peak:

Pt: It's moonlight, and I'm skating on this lake. I can hear the music kind of,
    and there is some wind. I'm skating, and the ice is all right. But I am
    scared. I'm hustling along and I know that it's like something is going

to explode. I'm not even sure why I'm skating, to get away maybe. I'm going fast and if I don't watch carefully there'll be something. I'll get a mushy spot and there'll be an explosion, a little mine or something. But I don't know where it will be or even if it will be. I'm just skating along hard and fast, and the lake is vast. It's moonlight. I'm not frightened, just watching and worried. Well, I'm scared a little. I don't even think what might happen exactly . . .

In many dreams, the dreamer is interacting with others, but it becomes clear that the dreamer is the main character. We are in one peak of the dream, "The wino, the tough guys, and the hurt hand," and the dreamer emerges as the main character:

Pt: . . . and there are these four guys, and they look tough. They're wearing black jackets, leather. They're just waiting there. On the corner. The rest of the street seems deserted. They look real tough, like they're going to beat us up. I'm scared for myself, really worried. I'm scared they're going to beat me up. So I invent an excuse and I get the hell out of there.

T: So I got this bad feeling like these bozos are damned well going to beat me up, and my insides are all scary. Now when is my feeling strongest?

Pt: When I decide to beat the hell out of there, and I gave some sort of excuse and just run like hell, I really beat it out of there. I'm scared shitless and my little legs are churning and I'm thinking that's no place for me. Out! Just get away. Any excuse, flimsy, just get the hell away and fast!

The difficult dreams are those in which there is a genuine back-and-forth interaction. The dreamer is doing things, and the other person is doing things. In these dreams it is best to open up both the dreamer and the other person, even though it seems that the dreamer is probably the main character. In the peak, an adolescent intrudes into the dreamer's car, sits next to the dreamer, and starts fumbling around, as if trying to get money. Then the dreamer is aware, with an unpleasant feeling, that his pants are down to his knees, and the intruder is touching the dreamer's bare buttocks:

Pt: I'm thinking of pushing him away. Get out of here. But I just think it and I don't say anything.

T: So here you are, not saying anything. Just letting him do it.

Pt: I say nothing. I got my left hand on the wheel, and I could use my left hand to push him off, but I don't. So he's got his left hand under me and he's grabbing my ass.

T: He's grabbing my ass, and squeezing, sort of squeezing.

Pt: I think he's after the wallet, and I know that he'll never get the wallet cause it's scrunched inside my pants.

T: You're fishing around in the wrong place, kid.

Pt: And he keeps grabbing at me, but I know I'm in a vulnerable position here. Cramped in behind the wheel, and my pants are down, and I know, I'm afraid that he's going to grab my penis and pull it, and I'm so exposed. My damned hand's on the wheel and I'm doing nothing with my other hand. I'm just asking for it. I mean, anyone can see if they walked by. I'm exposed.

T: Oh God, hello everyone, it's just little old me.

Pt: I can't tell if my penis is out or if I got shorts on, but I'm not resisting. No, just sitting here. Damn. And I know that he'll grab my penis. My little cock is just exposed, like I am . . . oh Christ! This is so embarrassing!

In the above peak, the dreamer is interacting with the young fellow, and the dreamer is taken as the main character even though the young fellow is the active one, the one initiating and carrying out the behavior.

One step further and we have a special subclass of peaks in which the dreamer is the main character, but the dreamer is quite clearly the receiver of action, the passive object of action that is initiated and carried out by the situation. In these peaks, the dreamer is not the initiator or one who carries out the action. It is the situation that is active. Yet the dreamer is still the main character, the one who houses the dream experiencing. It is the dreamer who is the "center of gravity," exceedingly aware of himself and of his immediate thoughts. It is interesting that in this subclass the dreamer is the passive one, the accommodator, the pliable one, the one who takes in, who receives, and it is the situation which provides the demand or press. Here is an example as the person is entering into a peak ("Moving into the dirty apartment, and holding onto the car"):

Pt: . . . we are going for a drive, and I'm standing, holding onto something. I'm outside the vehicle. I think it's a car. We're going along, and there is this river or waterfall surging over the top of a cliff. The water and the wind is so strong that I'm almost pulled off of the car. The river is overflowing as if a lake is filled up and overflowing. It's a very wild scene, and very frightening and strange.

The attention is directed toward the situation, the wind and water and wildness and force. Also, there is a fair measure of attention on what the dreamer is doing as he is aware of merely trying to clutch onto the car:

Pt: Just a lot of water, and everything's rushing. The wind. I'm barely hanging on.

T: The way I'm in it, the car or something is moving along and the water is all around, and I'm clutching, trying to hold on.

Pt: I think the car's moving. Think so. The water is rushing. It's not at me yet, but it's sweeping all around, real high and hard, and the wind's hard, blowing, and I can barely hang on. It's pulling at me, blowing me back, away from the car. I know I can't hang on.

T: Oh oh!

Pt: I don't even know how I'm holding onto the car or something, but I know it's going to blow me away and the water's all around. I'll never hang on! Maybe a few seconds or so and that's all . . .

While the dreamer is the main character and the situation is the active one, the possibility is always there that the dream experiencing may be contained in the wind and the water, so make sure that you try out both possibilities.

In many of these dreams, the dreamer is doing nothing, and action is occurring somewhere else in the peak. Nevertheless, the dreamer is the main character, the center of gravity. For example, the dreamer has a new motorcycle, parks it in a large metal container in this huge parking lot. Then, in the peak, he returns and watches as a massive truck picks up three or four of the metal containers:

Pt: There are thousands of cars around and I see the truck lift up that container . . .

T: I'm standing fairly close . . .

Pt: No, I see it far away, too far to do anything. I just stand here and watch, feeling like I can't believe it! There are so many cars, and it's lifting that container in the air and pulling away. Just pulling away. My bike! It's got my bike, and I think maybe I can run, but can't. No way! I know I can't catch it. It's taking away my new bike!

Do not ignore the other agent, for example, the truck that is lifting up the container; however, in these peaks the experiencing tends to lie within the dreamer.

Situation is static, and the feeling is bad. In these peaks, nothing is going on. There is essentially no movement, no action, no relating, no interacting. If you were to see a picture of the peak moment, you would have virtually no idea of what might be going on. Indeed, the only avenue into what is occurring is through the thoughts and feelings of the dreamer.

In the peak, the feeling is bad, and the dreamer is sitting alone in a car. It is night. No one is around. It is in a desert, with the sky clear and no sounds. The more the patient and therapist fill in the surroundings, the more sterile the scene becomes. Nothing is happening. The only way to know what is occurring is to go into the dreamer's thoughts and feelings:

Pt: I don't know what to do. I'm a salesman and I got all my catalogues in the back seat, and I don't have it anymore. No drive, no nothing. I don't even have any thoughts. I don't know where I am or how I got here or nothing, and I really don't even know where I want to go. I still don't know where home is, and even if I did I don't care about going there. It's like everything is stopped, it's all over with. What's the use?

T: Well, that's a shitty feeling.

Pt: I don't know what to do! What's the use anyway? I'm so damned alone here! It's all over. I have no place to go. I might as well just give up . . .

Now we have some idea of what is going on, for the dreamer's thoughts and feelings are the best avenue of illumination in these dreams. Often the dreamer may be with another person or some creature or object, yet the situation is nevertheless static. One such peak ("The wino, the tough guys, and the hurt hand") occurs in a hospital room where the dreamer is visiting his friend Walter. Yet nothing is occurring:

Pt: His hand is hurt. We're in this room. I'm standing, and just standing here. Walter's there. I think he's on the bed, sitting. I'm just standing. I don't know what I'm looking at. Not Walter. But I know he's there and his hand is bandaged . . . It's a regular hospital room. No one else's there.

T: Sounds quiet. No one talking.

Pt: No talking. I'm about six feet from where he is.

T: And you're having some kind of feeling. You say it is a feeling of guilt.

Pt: His hand is all bandaged, and he's sitting there. I know he'll be going soon. I guess he's OK 'cause I thought those guys really banged up his hand.

T: But he's ready to leave.

Pt: They could have broken his hand with a crowbar or something. I don't know. Maybe they didn't. He's OK though.

T: You hope so.

Pt: I feel guilty 'cause I didn't help him at all. I don't even know what I'm doing in the hospital. I think they beat Walter up and I didn't do nothing. I don't know why I'm here. I feel bad, like I should be apologizing. Jesus, it's my fault. I ran away. I just ran away and they banged up his hand. They may have cracked it, and I feel rotten!

In these kinds of static, bad-feelinged dreams, it is likely that the dreamer houses the experiencing, rather than the dream experiencing being housed in the other figure.

Peak Moments in Which the Experiencing Tends to Lie Within the Other Agent

There are several kinds of peak moments where the other figure is the main character, the one housing the experiencing, and therefore the one you enter into in arriving at the experiencing.

Compelling other is main character, and the feeling is very bad. In these dreams, there are several characteristics that are usually found together:

(a) The feeling is very bad, generally one of terror that grips and immobilizes the dreamer.

(b) There is something about the other figure that is horrifying. It is demented, crazed, violently assaultive, ferocious, dangerous, uncivilized, uncontrolled, grotesque, twisted.

(c) Virtually all the dreamer's awareness and attention are poured onto that other figure so that it is seen with heightened clarity, distinctiveness, and vividness (cf. Freud, 1900, 330-1). It is as if the dreamer's center of gravity or self-awareness is drained from the dreamer and is poured onto that compelling other figure so that the dreamer is much more aware of the other figure's body, posture, looks, features, apparel, even its intentions and thoughts.

(d) The other figure is the main character, the active one, the initiator, the doer, while the dreamer is much more static, frozen, unmoving. Something awful is about to happen, is quite imminent, but it has not yet taken place.

(e) Between the dreamer and the compelling other figure is some kind of penetrable barrier such as door, window, screen, fence or bush.

Here are two such peak moments, described by two patients entering further and further into the peak scenes as they illuminate more and more of the compelling other figure:

Pt: I know it's going to get me! I'm alone inside this shaky old cabin. Just one room, and it's not solid. I am just scared stiff because he's outside. I'm standing by the door. It's shut, but I know he can get in! I know it! I can't see him, but I know he's crazy! He's huge! Fills the whole doorway! Oh God! He's growling and making animal noises. Growling. He wants to get in! I hear him scratching at the door and I'm all alone. He's got a huge head and body. Like a bear, a monster, a crazed monster. He's moving slowly out there and I know he's going to get in!

Pt: I'm in the apartment and I'm scared to death 'cause I'm by the window or patio door or something, and there's this thing on the patio. We're way up in the air, but he's just outside, weaving back and forth. Not drunk. Crazy, and drugged. Powerful. He could smash it in any time he wanted to. There's some lace, but he can see me, and it's when he looks at me, my eyes. God! I could die. He's out of his mind, and he's, just crazy! I know he's gonna smash the window. Nothing can stop him! He's not even thinking, just a maniac, weaving slowly back and forth, and he looks! God, that look in his eye! Scares the hell out of me! Freezes me up. I know I'm going to die!

In most dreams like this, the experiencing is housed within the other agent, and therefore you should enter further and further into these compelling other agents.

 The dreamer is a removed observer, and the feeling is good or bad. In these peak moments, the dreamer is removed from what is occurring, an external observer, not participating. Under these conditions, make sure that you enter further into what the dreamer is observing. Perhaps the easiest kind is where the dreamer is not in the scene at all, is a totally removed observer, and there is only one other agent. In this peak, the dreamer is watching a large snake wriggle out of its skin. The dreamer is watching as if she is not a part of this, just observing but not really there. The feeling is one of a kind of awe, as if she is watching something quite personal and quite special. There is no awareness of who she is or what she is or what she is doing there. It most likely is that the snake houses the experiencing.

 There are also peaks in which the dreamer is in the scene, but as a mere observer. When the dreamer is observing a single other agent, it is quite likely that the experiencing lies within that other agent:

Pt: I'm standing with a bunch of others, maybe four or five others, and we're on this ski slope. The sun is bright and the sky is blue. We're all looking up. There's this guy, a Chinese fellow, and he's up in the air.

He's doing twists and turns! Like ballet or acrobatics or something, twists and loops, going upside down and just great! He's almost flying or gliding or something. He's got a helmet on and the sun glistens. But the main thing is his acrobatics. I am just amazed, watching him up in the air. It is incredible!

Sometimes several figures are observed. The dreamer is removed and observing, and the focus is the interaction among the observed figures. Usually, one of the observed figures emerges as the main character to be entered into and illuminated further:

Pt: Then this big heavyweight fighter, the one with the huge upper body, square looking, in the middle of the first round, he suddenly stopped, looked really intent at the opponent, straight at him for maybe two seconds, and then he slammed the other guy really hard, with a right. The other guy just crumpled. I could hear the blow, it was so fast and devastating. And the other fellow just sagged and ended up sort of nestled on the canvas by his feet. I was amazed. The high point is when this guy slammed him with this one blow, and I saw that, and heard it . . .
T: One of them is the one you see more, and . . .
Pt: Yeah, he blew him right away. The worst part was that look on his face. Just staring at him. It seemed like a long time, and then the blow. I saw it. I heard it. Smash! Bang!

The other is the main character, and the feeling is good or bad. In these dreams especially, it is helpful to enter into both the dreamer and the other figure, for either can house the dream experiencing. Always be open to the possibility that the other may be the main character, the one who contains the dream experiencing. Here is the patient's description of the peak moment: "More people come in and they get the knife away from me, and now I don't have the knife anymore. There are a whole bunch of those guys. Now I'm going to get it because they'll kill me." The patient describes a little more of this peak, and then continues to reveal the other interactor as the main character:

Pt: My heart is really pumping.
T: Oh oh, I am scared, really scared. Yeah, my heart is racing.
Pt: They have the knife, and I'm at their mercy.
T: They have the knife, someone does, one of those guys, and I have thoughts, I'm at their mercy.

Pt: They're standing up, and they're to my left. There are about eight guys. Maybe ten or twelve. The only weapon is the knife.

T: There's the knife. That's it.

Pt: The guy who has the knife, he has curly hair, and he's stocky and very strong. The couple of guys that I knifed are on the dirt floor. He's aware of them, and he looks at me. He's glaring at me 'cause he knows I knifed them. I have good reason to be scared, they are going to kill me.

T: Oh God, I'm seeing that guy and he knows, he knows. And it looks like I am going to be killed. I am!

Pt: That guy with the knife. I know I could die. He has the knife. He's got big arms. Right now he looks, he plays with the knife, back and forth, and he's glaring at me. He looks like, he's just about to say something to me. He's made up his mind! He's the leader and he's going to make me pay for what I did!

Increasingly, it begins to appear that the other figure is the main character, the one to be entered into further.

Sometimes the relationship is devoid of action, of any overt interaction. Yet progressively entering into both the dreamer and the other person can reveal that the other person is the main character. Here is the patient entering increasingly into the peak ("Shaking the hand, and my name was scratched out"):

Pt: It is a party, and I am handed this thing by Peter. He was definitely in charge and oozing graciousness. He shows me this little brochure. I guess he thought there was something about me. I look through it and there was maybe a word or two about me. Maybe my name was listed and scratched out. I didn't like that, maybe said something or maybe something I said was scratched out. I felt intruded upon, but I knew that it was his house. He may not have been mad at me. I don't know why he scratched it out.

T: But there was some reason for his scratching it out, and this is what's happening.

Pt: Well, really, nothing is happening. I'm just looking at this flyer. Looking at it, and noticing that my name or something about me, referring to me, is scratched out.

T: Scratched out, scratched, scratched?

Pt: There's like a black pencil, pen, stroked it out. Really prominent. I'm seeing that.

T: I'm looking at it, and, now I'm starting to be aware of what's around me. People? And I'm standing. Standing up?

Pt: Well, I'm looking at it, looking at my scratched-out name. I think he did it. I'm sitting, just sitting in a deep stuffed chair, and just looking at the flyer, about some professional thing. He is sitting down too, nearby. I am seeing the flyer, and also I'm kind of aware of him. He is the one who scratched out my name. I know that. I know he did it, maybe 'cause I intruded. I walked through his house earlier, and so he scratched out my name. (And now a new wrinkle:) I wasn't really invited to this party. I wasn't. He scratched out my name, and I think it was an announcement of a meeting or something or proceedings of one. He scratched it out with a black pencil or a pen . . .

What a difficult peak to fathom. There doesn't appear to be much interaction at all between the dreamer and Peter. Peter oozed graciousness as he handed the brochure to the dreamer, and the dreamer notices that his name has been scratched out. Peter and the dreamer are not carrying out mutual actions that are conspicuous. Yet the more the person tells about the scene, the more Peter becomes clearly etched in terms of his manner, even the little behaviors of giving the dreamer the brochure, and in terms of Peter having scratched out the dreamer's name with a black pencil or pen. Even in this "impure" example of dreams in which the other interactor may be the main character, we want to enter further into this other agent.

In this chapter you were shown how to identify and clarify the peak moment (step 3.1, Figure 1) and then enter into it (step 3.2, Figure 1). The culmination is to open up the dream experiencing (step 3.3); the methods for doing this are presented in Chapter 9.

CHAPTER 7

What Dreams
Can Provide

WHAT ARE THE MAIN THINGS you can get from dreams? One of the lessons of this chapter is that there are lots of quite different things you can get from dreams.

MESSAGES FROM ALIEN SOURCES

You can consider the dream as a message from some alien source. For thousands of years dreams have been accepted as messages from the gods. "In early times, the dream was considered a divine incubation, a conjuration of the god who gave advice and healing" (Wolff, 1952, p. 16). Although not every dream was seen as a message from a god, and not everyone was regarded as a proper message receiver, there were always some special people who were given these divine messages: "While the imagination of sleep naturally occurs in a like and equivalent manner for all, some, not all, share by means of their dreams in some more Divine manifestations" (Gregory of Nyassa, 4th century A.D., in Wolff, 1952, p. 24).

Dream approaches of today do not ordinarily speak of divine manifestations or dreams as messages from God, but the idea is still around. We ask some unspecified alien source to allow us to have a dream, perhaps even a dream that will provide an answer to some important question or problem. Some dreams are still seen as quite special in a way that smacks of a divine source. Binswanger (1967) described this ancient use of dreams and then appeared to draw upon this source of meaning in making sense of certain kinds of dreams, such as one in which an eagle swoops down upon a goose and breaks its neck.

Today we may accept dreams as messages from alien sources that are more in fashion. For example, the dream may be a message from the kidney or pancreas or the state of cerebrospinal fluid:

As an example of a dream that identified an organic illness in a specific part of the body, Jung mentioned a dream that had been reported by a patient of Dr. T. M. Davie: Someone beside me kept on asking me something about oiling some machinery. Milk was suggested as the best lubricant. Apparently I thought that oozy slime was preferable. Then the pond was drained, and amid the slime there were two extinct animals. One was a mastodon. I forget what the other one was. . . . Jung . . . had no hesitation in saying that it indicated some organic disturbance, and that the illness was not primarily a psychological one. The . . . pond (which was drained) he interpreted as the damming-up of the cerebrospinal fluid circulation. (Mattoon, 1984, p. 152)

Or the alien source may be some other person, so that your dream really belongs to that other person rather than you:

[There is] . . . the possibility of someone dreaming another person's dream. . . . Jung sometimes found it possible to recognize this phenomenon because the "other person's dream" was an exceptionally strange one among those of the dreamer. . . . The basic criterion I have found useful for identifying "another person's dream" is that the dream can be interpreted best in relation to a person other than the dreamer. (Mattoon, 1984, p. 91)

Even further, your dream may come from a whole community or nation, perhaps entire cultures going back many generations; " . . . Jung recognized that occasionally an archetypal dream has collective significance, that is, it reflects the psychic state of an entire nation or group of nations" (Mattoon, 1984, p. 73).

As long as we are not quite sure where dreams come from, and as long as we are impressed that some source accounts for the dream's mystery and exuberant creativity (Byles, 1962; Krippner, 1980; Rycroft, 1979; Ullman, 1965), it is understandable that we take very seriously what happens in dreams. Primitive or aboriginal cultures may sometimes be a little more willing than we are to consider the mystical sources of dreams:

Why should he mistrust what he sees in dreams more than what he sees with his eyes open? He would be even more inclined to believe in the former because of the mystical origin of these data, which makes them all the more valuable and reliable. There is nothing about which one can feel more sure than about things revealed in dreams. (Lévy-Bruhl, 1923, p. 101)

It is both an ancient and a current idea that dreams might contain messages from alien sources, with the specific nature of these alien sources covering a wider compass than we might like to acknowledge.

RESOLUTIONS OF PERSONAL PROBLEMS AND PROPHECIES OF THE FUTURE

There is another family of uses whereby what you get from dreams are solutions to your personal problems, indications of how you should be and behave, and prophecies of your destiny, fate or future.

The dream provides the answer to the question you put to it. For several thousand years, people have asked their dreams to provide answers to personal questions and then searched their dreams for the answers. In ancient times the dreamer had to ask whether this particular dream was an answer dream or a message from the gods or a prophecy of the future:

> The Egyptians divided dreams into three categories: (1) unsolicited dreams in which the gods appealed to man's conscience, demanding repentance, pity, etc.; (2) warning dreams, in which the gods warned the dreamer of dangers ahead; and (3) dreams which were answers to questions put by the dreamer before the gods. (Wolff, 1952, pp. 10–11)

In some contemporary approaches, one still puts a question to the dream. Should I write a letter to my brother after all these years? Should I be less demanding of my daughter and give her more freedom? What can I do about all this fighting at work? Since the valuable characteristic of the dream is that it can provide an answer, I can examine my dreams to see what the answer might be (e.g., Davé, 1979; de Becker, 1968; Delaney, 1981; Faraday, 1974; Morris, 1985; Williams, 1980).

The dream performs the function of healing, regulating, balancing, adapting, integrating, working-through. The very process of dreaming may set things back in proper order; " . . . the dream is a function of a self-healing balancing process" (Whitmont, 1987, p.

53). If the unexpected death of a loved one wrenched you apart, left you decimated and broken, then dreams allow for a process of heal- ing, resolution, working through the grief and the agonized reac- tions, inner self-healing, resolution of the problem, adaptive dis- charge of tension. Many therapists from many approaches use dreams in this way, including many who follow psychoanalytic ap- proaches (Atwood & Stolorow, 1984; Baylor & Deslauriers, 1987; Bonime & Bonime, 1987; Breger, 1967; De Monchaux, 1978; Evans, 1983; Fosshage, 1983, 1987a, 1987b; French & Fromm, 1964; Glucksman & Warner, 1987; Greenberg & Pearlman, 1980; Jones, 1962, 1980; Kohut, 1977; May, 1975; Morris, 1985; Rossi, 1985; Stolorow & Atwood, 1982; Trosman, 1963; Van Bork, 1982; Winson, 1985).

Within the history of psychoanalytic approaches, Greenberg (1987) credits Maeder (1916) with playing a major role in moving away from using the dream to uncover psychoanalytic primary pro- cess material and toward using the dream as revealing " . . . the dreamer's efforts at adaptation to current emotional problems and the direction that might be taken in waking life" (Greenberg, 1987, p. 45). Indeed, it is this emphasis upon the dream's ego-adaptive and working-through functions that characterizes the departure from the classical Freudian use of dreams; " . . . post-Freudian theorists stress the ego's adaptive or working-through function in dreams, which accounts for some of the major differences in the clinical practice of dream interpretation" (Fosshage & Loew, 1987b, p. 245).

This use of dreams is relatively popular in research wherein the aim is to examine the idea that dreams offer adaptation and working- through of recent stressful experiences (Breger, Hunter, & Lane, 1971; Cartwright, Kasniak, Borowitz, & Kling, 1972; De Koninck, 1987; De Koninck & Koulack, 1975; Foulkes & Rechtschaffen, 1964; Sirois-Berliss & De Koninck, 1982). Accordingly, some re- searchers confirm that dreams show how the person is struggling and coping with problems and working toward solutions of those prob- lems. "The dream thus portrays problems and also the dreamer's efforts at coping with these problems" (Greenberg, 1987, p. 49). "In these dream series, one could see continuing attempts at solutions, even though unsuccessful. . . . They may show a process of grap- pling with a problem, and then the finding of a solution . . . " (Greenberg & Pearlman, 1980, pp. 90, 94). Both clinicians and researchers see the dream and dreaming as efforts at coping and coming to terms with personal issues.

The issues may not be limited to stressful personal problems. Those who understand dreams as neurological and physiological processes of thinking and cognition can make sense of dreams as the adaptive processing of new information (data, events) with what has been internally stored in the long-term memory bank (Bjerre, 1936; Crick & Mitchison, 1983; Fiss & Litchman, 1976; Hernandez-Peon, 1965; Lowy, 1942; Palombo, 1976, 1978, 1985).

The dream shows you what actions to carry out, and how you could and should be. This way of using dreams also enjoys a long and distinguished history. It has been quite popular in ancient, primitive, and aboriginal cultures for the dream to be seen as telling you how you could and should be and behave. In discussing how to use dreams in this manner, Wolff quotes from Lowie (1935):

> If a Zulu dreams that his friend attempts to take his life, he immediately breaks the relationship with him. . . . The Crow Indians receive through their dreams advice about medicine. . . . Dreams indicate the good places for hunting. . . . They also indicate the right time for planting. . . . Military actions are inspired by dreams. (Wolff, 1952, p. 7)

Biblical dreams are regarded as telling the person what actions are to be carried out; for example, to leave the country in which he is living and return to the country of his birth:

> In another type of dream man receives clues for action, as did Jacob in his dream of an angel (Genesis 31:11): "And the angel of God said unto me in the dream, Jacob: And I said, Here I am . . . And he said . . . now arise, get thee out from this land, and return unto the land of thy nativity." The dreamer experiences a calling in his dream, and a command. (Wolff, 1952, p.13)

The dreamer may feel obliged to carry out the actions that were carried out in the dream. "If I dream of doing something with my boyfriend I ask him in real life if we could go to this certain place and I try to do everything we did in the dream" (Greenleaf, 1973, p. 221). When the dream contains some object or event, then some would suggest that you behave so as to bring about that object or event in your waking life (Stewart, 1953). If the dream includes a rock garden, then build a rock garden. If the dream includes a song or poem, then express that song or poem in your waking life.

These actions and behaviors are blended into the kind of person that you could and should be. Accordingly, in contemporary dream approaches, the dream shows you what part of your personality is avoided and missing and should be expressed more. "To me, a dream is an existential message of what part of your personality is missing, and in the dream you can clearly see how you avoid" (Perls, 1969, p. 129). It shows you are lacking your aggressive or compassionate or sexual side. In this way, the dream can be used to point toward the direction of change you can pursue (cf. Gendlin, 1986). Jung used some dreams in this way. For example, he interpreted one of his own dreams as indicating that his direction of personal change might well mean the abandonment of his heroic idealism:

> The dream showed that the attitude embodied by Siegfried, the hero, no longer suited me. Therefore, it had to be killed . . . my heroic idealism had to be abandoned, for there are higher things than the ego's will, and to these one must bow. (Jung, in Mattoon, 1984, p. 61)

When you follow this path, the dream is used in a more or less direct and straightforward way, as a portrayal of the way you could and should be, as well as the actions and behaviors you could and should carry out.

The dream is an arena in which substantive personal change can and does occur. In this way of using dreams, what is special is that the dream is an arena in which substantive personal change can or actually does occur. It is much more than merely being in a somewhat different state when you are sleeping. There are at least three ways in which such personal change occurs in dreams.

In one way, the person undergoes a substantive change in the dream itself. These are special dreams in which the person actually becomes a substantially different kind of person. Actual changes are occurring in the dreaming itself, and dreaming is the arena in which personal change is immediately ongoing:

> In dreams we witness something more than mere wishes: we experience dreams reflecting our psychological state and the process of change taking place in it . . . The constructive or synthetic approach to dreams can be clearly stated: dreaming is an indigenous process of psychological growth, change, and transformation" (Rossi, 1972, p. 142).

Such special dreams are called "transformative" by Corriere, Karle, Woldenberg, and Hart (1980). Interestingly, the bulk of the changing process is held as occurring in the course of the dream itself rather than afterward when the therapist and patient talk together about the dream.

In a second way, change occurs when the person becomes aware that he is dreaming. The person settles further into this state of awareness and can even set about directing what is to occur in the course of the dream action. If you are being threatened by a monster-demon, you can exert a force of will and overcome your opponent, winning over, destroying or taming the monster-demon (cf. Edel, 1982). This way of using dreams to effect change is known as lucid dreaming, and is described by Boss (1977), Casteneda (1972), Corriere, Karle, Woldenberg, and Hart (1980), Delaney (1981), Fox (1962), Garfield (1977), Rossi (1985), Stewart (1969), and Whiteman (1961); interestingly, Garfield (1984) shows how children can also be instructed to do lucid dreaming. When the person uses this awareness of being in a dream state, the avenue of change is along the lines of heightened awareness, greater ego strength, heightened self-control and strength of will.

Finally, personal change can occur in dreams where you are in interaction with another figure who is you. That other figure may look exactly as you do now or as you did some time ago. Or the other figure may bear little or no resemblance to you whatsoever, yet you still know that the other figure is you. Change is said to occur as you engage with that other you, as you actually interact and relate with that other self who is you. When this occurs in the right way, the desirable change is one of further ego differentiation, an achieving of higher levels of self-awareness. This way of using dreams is described and discussed by Casteneda (1977) and by Rossi (1985).

One of the distinguishing features of this particular use of dreams is that the actual process of change occurs in the dream itself. More specifically, the waking personality is said to undergo change when any of these kinds of change processes can be said to occur in the dream.

The dream is a prophecy of the future. For thousands of years we have used dreams to foretell what is going to happen to the person, to tell one's destiny or fate, to offer premonitions of upcoming events. One ancient theory holds that everything in and of the world is connected with everything else, so that changes in one part are correspondingly connected with changes in others. With just a few additional terms having to do with current theories of time warping and relativity, this ancient theory is present in contemporary theorizing:

> Synesius of Cyrene (370–413 A.D.) started from Aristotle's emanation theory of images. He combined this concept with the ancient one of one united world organism in which everything had its correspondences, an idea which was revived throughout the Middle Ages. For instance, happenings in the stellar system and the Zodiac set up corresponding vibrations in the soul; dreams therefore allow divination. (Wolff, 1952, p. 25)

Accordingly, some dreams may be understood as prophecying the future. For Artemidorus there were the ordinary dreams dealing with present matters ("insomnium"), and there were dreams that forecast events ("somnium") (Wolff, 1952). Contemporary theories likewise accept prophetic dreams. In the psychoanalytic approach, some dreams may be seen as premonitions of new phases of development:

> One could quote countless examples of dreams and fantasies which represent, at one and the same time, both a return to analytically accessible stages of development and premonitions of a new phase which cannot be reduced in the same way. (Caruso, 1964, p. 144)

In the Jungian approach, some dreams are likewise acknowledged as looking to the future, as providing a kind of preview of what the unconscious may hold in store. They are called "prospective dreams." "The prospective function . . . is an anticipation in the unconscious of future conscious achievements, something like a preliminary exercise or sketch, or a plan roughed out in advance" (Jung, 1974, p. 41). Other Jungian dreams are regarded as providing direct prophecies, foretelling such destinies or fates as an imminent plunge into psychosis or a future suicidal depression or a heroic achievement or a return to healthy functioning. Such dreams are special and, in the Jungian approach, come from a special part of the unconscious:

> Unlike a non-archetypal dream, which usually focuses on the dreamer's immediate psychic situation, an archetypal dream may be concerned with the "fate" of the dreamer. The dream seems to come from a "different level" of the unconscious. (Mattoon, 1984, p. 65)

In all of these ways, the dream can help you to develop and change, can resolve your problems, prophesy what is to come, heal and work through difficulties. But there are still other things to get from dreams.

INFORMATION ABOUT THE NATURE AND
CONTENT OF PERSONALITY

Dreams are used to provide information about your personality, to tell about the kind of person you are. This is a popular package of things to get from dreams, but even within this large family there are different smaller packages of ways of using dreams.

The dream gives information about problems, personality characteristics, and "psychodynamics." The dream can be used to get information about the kinds of problems you have, about your personality characteristics, your conflicts and "psychodynamics" (e.g., Piatrowski, 1986; Spanjaard, 1969). Most of this is about the more or less surface personality, the "self" you refer to when you talk about your "self."

Because this useful information can be obtained from dreams, dreams may be helpful to counselors and psychotherapists who focus on the more conscious, surface, behavioral, short-term issues of their clients (cf. Merrill & Cary, 1975), and even to psychoanalytic therapists who seek information about the problems of the waking personality rather than information about supposedly deep-seated, unconscious impulses:

> Considering the hidden wish or the forbidden impulse as too constricted a framework, Horney herself, following in the tradition of Adler, saw in dreams a symbolic extension of the problems and adaptive maneuvers characteristic of the waking state. (Ullman, 1962, p. xi; cf. Adler, 1938; Ansbacher & Ansbacher, 1956; Krippner, 1980)

This way of using dreams provides you with information about what you conceal and hide from yourself. The idea is that the dream gets around your tendency to conceal and hide. "By examining your dreams rather than avoiding them, crucial concealed knowledge will be revealed and you can begin to understand how the hidden facts of your personality affect your waking life" (Morris, 1985, p. 4). Understand your dreams and you understand the intrapsychic conflicts, for " . . . dreams are visuomotor dramatization of dreamers' intrapsychic conflicts" (Piatrowski, 1986, p. 60). The dream tells about the kinds of feelings, affects, and emotions you have, but of which you may be unaware (Bonime, 1962), and how the kind of person you are has affected the way you interact and relate to people. By using dreams in this way, the therapist can help the patient " . . . to open his eyes to the fact that, ever since childhood, he had allowed others to step on him, mistreat him, push him around, not only physically as in his dreaming, but in regard to his whole emotional life as well" (Boss, 1977, p. 111). Here is how the dream reveals the "psychodynamics" that are concealed.

Often what is concealed by or from the patient is likewise consciously or unconsciously concealed from the therapist, but it will nonetheless be revealed in dreams:

> In psychotherapy, a somewhat more common type of dream carrying life-or-death significance is one that reveals a patient's suicidal thoughts which have been concealed from the therapist. Such a revelation may help to guide the conduct of therapy. Dreams, such as those revealing suicidal thoughts, and others carrying less dramatic information, which may be consciously withheld by the patient, demonstrate that dreams are sources of specific information for the therapist. (Mattoon, 1984, p. 3)

Accordingly, the dream provides information about your personal problems, your personality characteristics, and your psychodynamics. Most of this information you are essentially unaware of or cannot or will not put into words, and almost all of this information is about the more or less functional and surface part of your personality.

The dream gives information about the patient's attitudes and feelings toward therapy and the therapist. Psychoanalytic approaches are preeminent in treating therapy as perhaps the most significant enterprise in the person's life, and the therapist as perhaps the most significant person in the patient's world. If therapy and the therapist are so very important, then it is understandable that the dream is used to provide information on the patient's attitudes and feelings toward therapy and the therapist. Fromm-Reichmann (1958) puts this simply and representatively:

. . . while under intensive psychotherapy, dreams are frequently used
by the sleeper as a means of conveying something to the therapist
which the patient has been incapable of conveying while awake. All
the . . . implications in the doctor-patient relationship . . . may also
be reflected or represented in the dreams of every patient under treatment. (p. 163)

Sometimes the therapist occurs directly in the dream; sometimes
there are figures who are seen as representing the therapist. Gillman
(1980) says that the former occurs in about 9 percent of psychoana-
lyses, and the latter in 80 percent. In either case, the dream is used to
show the more or less hidden attitudes and feelings toward the therapist and therapy, in therapeutic work with adults and also with children (Jokipaltio, 1982). Some even see the presence and meaning of
the therapist or therapist-like figure in the dream as reflecting a little
helpful input from the therapist (Hall, 1984; Langs, 1980, 1982;
Little, 1951; Spero, 1984). The therapist will then appear in dreams
when the therapist's "inappropriate needs" intrude into the therapist-
patient interaction or when the patient seeks more or less inappropriate gratification from the therapist:

Such circumstances, in which the therapist's inappropriate needs are
being directly gratified are often, in my experience, evocative of
dreams in which the therapist appears directly. Similarly, such dreams
often occur when the patient is experiencing needs for direct and
inappropriate gratification from the therapist . . . the manifest appearance of the therapist in a dream of a patient, then, calls for a
detailed examination of the unconscious therapeutic interaction, and
often signals the presence of pathological inputs from both patient and
therapist. (Langs, 1980, p. 365)

Others see the appearance of the therapist as the patient's effort to
emphasize the therapist as a real person to disguise transference memories:

In these dreams the patient thrusts the analyst forward as a real person
to avoid the anxiety of the deepening transference neurosis. The patient's dream momentarily insists on the reality of the analyst in order
to repress those memories that are reappearing as transference feelings.
(Gillman, 1980, p. 34)

Still the basic idea is that the therapist's or therapist-like figure's occurrence in the dream is a reflection of the patient's feelings and attitudes toward the therapist or therapy and indicates something of the patient-therapist relationship, alliance, and transference (e.g., Angyal, 1965; Gillman, 1980; Gitelson, 1952; Martin, 1982).

Dreams that occur in the beginning of therapy are especially rich in information about the patient's feelings and attitudes toward therapy and the therapist (Waldhorn, 1967). What information is provided if the therapist actually appears in the first dream after starting therapy? One view holds that this indicates either severe psychopathology or a poor analyst-patient fit:

> Several authors have supported the view that if the analyst appears undisguised in the first dream of an analysis, the prognosis is unfavorable, there is a poor fit between analyst and patient, or there is severe psychopathology. Rapaport . . . supports Gitelson's view that either the analyst is in reality too much like a significant figure of the past or the transference is so eroticized that there is no "as if" between the analyst and the past. (Gillman, 1980, p. 30)

But the typical strategy is simply to see dreams early in therapy as showing the patient's feelings and attitudes toward starting therapy, and this holds whether or not the therapist actually occurs in the dream.

The dream may show that the patient must try and take charge of the therapy:

> . . . she brought to the first session the following dream: I got in a tramcar and walked straight through to the driver's platform, turned the driver off and drove the car myself. I put it to her that the tram was the treatment and I was the driver, and she felt the situation to be one in which she was in my power, as she had once been in her father's; and this she could not tolerate. Only if she could take complete charge of the analysis and run it herself, could she go on with it. (Guntrip, 1969, p. 295)

Or the initial dream may indicate how scared he is of the therapist:

> In an anxiety dream, which one patient experienced shortly after starting analysis, he is fearfully swimming away from a shark in a swimming pool. The dream reflects the patient's frantic efforts to get out of range of the analyst. (Bonime, 1962, p. 3)

Or the initial dream may portray the patient's need to be distinctive and different from friends who likewise are in therapy:

> He brought to the first session a dream that he had had the previous night. "I was at an ice-skating rink. All the skaters were going around in a circle. I was skating in a circle too, but I was going in the opposite direction. I was having a good time." The interpretive hypothesis was suggested to him that he had finally entered into analysis like many of his friends, but that he was still trying to maintain his special status, as represented by his skating in a different direction from the rest of the crowd. (Bonime, 1962, p. 125)

Because they occur early in therapy, dreams are used to provide information about therapy and the therapist, whether or not there are direct connections to the therapist and therapy. At the other end, dreams that occur in and near termination are likewise used to provide information about the patient's feelings and attitudes toward terminating therapy. Typically, these are dreams involving long trips or death or birth or indications that the therapeutic goals have been attained or signs of healthy ego functioning and resolution of the transference neurosis (Cavenar & Nash, 1976; Cavenar & Spaulding, 1978; Rosenthal, 1978). Whether the dreams are at the beginning or the end of therapy, whether or not the therapist occurs directly or indirectly in the dream, this use of dreams gains information about the person's feelings and attitudes toward therapy and the therapist.

The dream gives information about the psychodiagnosis and psychopathological condition. Most therapists think in terms of categories of psychodiagnosis, degrees and types of psychopathology. Dreams are a helpful way of providing information about the patient's psychodiagnosis and psychopathological condition. You can then label the patient as having some sort of neurosis or psychosis or the latest kind of personality disorder, or even a psychosomatic illness such as ulcerative colitis or bronchial asthma conditions (Bressler & Mizrachi, 1978a, 1978b; Mindell, 1982; Warnes, 1982). You can tell whether the patient is hebephrenic, schizophrenic or asthenic, or even moving from one subclass to another. For example, consider a dream in which the dreamer is driving a truck very carefully and cautiously and then, later in the dream, drives the truck at a recklessly fast clip. Such a dream gives information about the patient moving from the depressive to the manic phase of the manic-depressive psychosis:

Only a transition from a depressive to a manic mood is analogous to this patient's abrupt leap from a sort of obedient self-control, learned in his small town, to mad recklessness. No similar dreaming behavior has ever come to my attention, which did not originate in someone who was manic-depressive in his waking life. (Boss, 1977, p. 121)

Dreams may even be used in diagnosing latent psychoses, in which case the therapist must decide what to do with this important diagnostic information. One action is to withhold the information from the patient and bring treatment to a close before the psychosis "erupts":

Jung did not interpret the dream to the patient; he saw it as indicating a latent psychosis for which the dreamer's apparent supranormality was compensating. The sessions were continued but only until Jung could find an acceptable pretext for ending the analysis. The man had no subsequent severe difficulties but Jung was convinced that if the analysis had continued, the psychosis would have surfaced. (Mattoon, 1984, p. 151)

Dreams are used to provide information on the psychodiagnostic and psychopathological condition by noting the various kinds of special indicators, signs, and symptoms. For example, one supposed sign of a psychosis is when the patient shows "inappropriate affect" or "affective discrepancy", i.e., when the patient has one feeling, emotion, or affect where normally some other should be occurring. This can be evidenced in dreams when the dreamer does not feel fear in a situation where normally one should be scared: "I was in a street and there were bullets flying in all directions. I walked along in the midst of the bullets and I was not at all frightened" (Bonime, 1962, p. 114), and then, later in the dream: "I looked down and there were feces on my leg. I felt slightly amused . . . " (p. 114). The idea is that dreams can be used to diagnose psychopathological conditions using the same symptoms, signs, and indicators as for waking persons.

It is therefore understandable that researchers would be drawn toward studying persons diagnosed with all sorts of mental diseases and psychopathological conditions to see ways in which their dreams differed from one another (Beck & Ward, 1961; Hauri, 1976; Kramer, Whitman, Baldridge, & Lansky, 1966; Kramer, Whitman, Baldridge, & Ornstein, 1968, 1970; Langs, 1966; Miller, 1969; Okuma, Sunami, Fukama, Takeo, & Motoike, 1970; Van de Castle & Holloway, 1971).

The dream gives information about unconscious and repressed instincts, impulses, and wishes. This is perhaps the juiciest and most arcanely mystical kind of information the dream can offer. It is also one of the most ancient uses of dreams to provide information on the most deeply hidden shadow side of personality, the netherworld of alien and primitive instincts. Once human beings were seen as having a personality with its own underside, its own deeper nature, then dreams were valued as telling us something of that mysterious shadow side.

Plato says that dreams can reveal the unconscious, uncivilized wild beast in you, your most primitive animal nature:

> Plato, in his *Republic*, lets Socrates state that dreams reveal man's desires: "I mean those (desires) which are awake when the reasoning and human and ruling power is asleep; then the wild beast within us, gorged with meat or drink, starts up . . . goes forth to satisfy his desires." And: "In all of us, even in good men, there is a lawless, wild beast nature, which peers out in sleep." . . . the dream portrays the unconscious mind that is antithetical to the conscious one. (Wolff, 1952, p. 16)

Cicero continued this same line of thinking. The dream can provide information on the nature of the wild beast in you, on inclinations to carry out acts that the waking person would loathe as monstrous outrages:

> Marcus Tullius Cicero (106–43 B.C.), the orator and politician, also made an inquiry into dreams following the concepts of Plato. He agreed with Plato that the dream releases the wild beast in man. "If it were an institution of nature that men when they sleep really did the things they dream about . . . they would otherwise while dreaming perpetrate more outrages than madmen." (Wolff, 1952, p. 19)

By the fourth century, the notion of the deeper bestial nature was already refined and elaborated into unconscious psychological drives. As an example, Wolff describes the theory of Gregory:

> Dreams also reflect the stimuli of drives, especially that of sex. Allied to the drives are impulses such as anger, and all those "with which brute life was armed for self-preservation," — namely, the passions. Plato's concept of "man's wild-beast nature which peers out in sleep" now receives a psychologic interpretation. (Wolff, 1952, p. 25)

Here is an ancient picture of human personality in terms of an unconscious netherworld of deeply hidden alien stimuli and drives, a distinctly psychological nature of primitive animal instincts and impulses, predominantly sexual and aggressive. This theory and use of dreams flourished throughout the centuries, and reached its pinnacle of refinement through Freud's creative genius. In its oversimplified form, therefore, the dream gives information about unconscious and repressed instincts, impulses, and wishes:

> . . . Thus its content was the fulfilment of a wish and its motive was a wish. . . . When the work of interpretation has been completed, we perceive that a dream is the fulfilment of a wish. (Freud, 1900, pp. 119, 121)

Both Freud and Jung saw the dream as providing information about unconscious and repressed instincts, impulses, and wishes, although they had somewhat different ideas about the nature of these instincts, impulses, and wishes. Whereas Freud was drawn toward a brilliantly inventive study of the various mechanisms used in the dream to deal with these instincts, impulses, and wishes, Jung concentrated more on their nature and content. Nevertheless, the cornerstone of Freud's use of dreams rested upon a given set of unconscious and repressed wishes, and these are more or less still accepted today. "After all, Freud built his psychology of the dream around this concept . . . most analysts still subscribe to this view" (Eisenstein, 1980, p. 326). Perhaps the most substantive modification is from the object relations school, wherein some dreams are acknowledged as providing information on classical psychoanalytic wishes and impulses, and other dreams are seen as giving information on object relations wishes and impulses (Kohut, 1977):

> Kohut . . . cites the case of a woman who came to him for a second analysis. During the third year of her analysis she dreamed she was standing over a toilet urinating and was vaguely aware that someone was watching her from behind. Kohut states that the patient had had many similar dreams with a female analyst, and that this woman had repeatedly interpreted the dreams as the patient wanting a penis and wanting to urinate standing up like a male. Kohut, by contrast, pointed out that a more basic wish was to extract herself from a damaging relationship with a bizarre, emotionally shallow mother and to turn toward a more down-to-earth practical father. . . . (Whitman, 1980, p. 48)

Many approaches answer the question of what to get from dreams by valuing the information that dreams provide on the nature and content of personality, specifically on (a) unconscious and repressed instincts, impulses, and wishes, (b) the psychodiagnosis and psychopathological condition, (c) the patient's attitudes and feelings toward therapy and the therapist, and (d) the patient's problems, personality characteristics, and psychodynamics.

ENTRY INTO BEING THE DREAM EXPERIENCING

In the experiential approach, what we get from dreams is the opportunity to "be" the dream experiencing. You can actually disengage from your ordinary, operating personality, get inside the deeper dream experiencing, grasp and sense and be this deeper experiencing. The way to know the deeper experiencing is by getting inside and being the dream experiencing; likewise, getting inside and being the dream experiencing means that you are grasping and undergoing its nature and content.

If we ask what other dream approaches are somewhat similar, the closest answer is the functional approach of Corriere, Karle, Woldenberg, and Hart (1980; cf. Corriere, Hart, Karle, Binder, Gold, & Woldenberg, 1977; Karle, Corriere, Hart, & Woldenberg, 1980), and the Daseinsanalytic approach of Boss (1957, 1963, 1977; Boss & Kenny, 1987). In both of these approaches, there is an emphasis on what the person is actually undergoing in the dream, on what is being experienced, on the dream as offering the kinds of phenomena to which the person is experientially open. The Gestalt approach is also in the same general family. Different from the experiential, the functional, and the Daseinsanalytic approaches, Gestalt places less emphasis on what the experiencing may be in the actual dream itself. Rather, Gestalt emphasizes the dreams as comprised of projected parts of one's personality so that the person may reown these projected parts by entering into and being whatever parts appear in the dream.

On the other hand, this way of using dreams is quite different from the other ways discussed above. Using the dreams as an entry into being the dream experiencing is a far cry from using the dream as something that contains messages from alien sources. Nor is the dream valued as providing resolutions of personal problems or prophecies of the future. Nor do we get personality information from dreams.

There is a sharp distinction between using a dream to enter into the very being of the dream experiencing and, on the other hand, using the dream as a source of interesting and important clinical information. To begin with, when the intent is to use the dream to get information about the person's psychodiagnosis or psychopathology, the person will not undergo the experiencing that is present in the peak. Seeking information about a woman's psychodynamics around sabotaging her marriage in order to please her critical mother will mean that she will not enter into whatever dream experiencing lies in the peak moments. Even with regard to unconscious and repressed instincts, impulses, and wishes, the posture of obtaining sheer information insures that there will be no entering into the dream experiencing. There is a world of difference between nodding in agreement that you would like to own your mother and do away with your father and, on the other hand, the experiencing of sex with your mother.

The pursuit of information about the nature and content of personality will also fail to enable the person to enter into and be the dream experiencing. Nor will whatever information you obtain be the precise content of the dream experiencing. The person and the therapist can spend hours or years gathering information about unconscious impulses and ways of coping with repressed tendencies toward infant sexuality, problems around domination and the patient's attitudes toward a forced termination of a ten-year psychoanalysis, and yet they will neither identify nor enter into any experiencing contained in any peak of any dream.

Our way of using dreams is also quite apart from the various ways of valuing dreams for their ability to resolve problems and prophesy the future. It seems clear that entering into and being a dream experiencing is dissimilar from using the dream to answer some personal question, to provide a prophecy of the future, to regulate personality or work through some problem, or to tell you how you could and should be. Nor is our way of using dreams similar to using dreams as an arena in which personal change is to occur, to undergo a transformation process, to be aware of being in a dream, to direct how the dream is to progress, or to engage in an interaction with another figure who is also you. All of these are quite different from experiential dream work in which you actually enter inside whatever dream experiencing is here, live and exist and undergo the being of this dream experiencing.

Here, then, are several answers to the question of what to get from dreams. Each answer is distinctive. There are clinicians who subscribe to each of these ways of using dreams, and there are clinicians who like to believe that they use all or most of these ways of using dreams. These therapists feel that they lose something if they cannot combine all these uses, or if they cannot pick and choose from among all of them. For example, since psychoanalysis seems to get some things from dreams and the experiential approach seems to get something else, then it is supposedly worthwhile to combine the two approaches to get even more from dreams:

> . . . therapeutic dream work involves the double working of the dream. The therapist and patient shift from experiential work to analytic work and back to experiential. . . . Certain patients' pathologies may require an analytic focus to build ego consciousness and reflectivity. For example, schizophrenic patients whose thinking is weak need grounding in causal thinking and understanding of their personal processes. Some obsessively defensive schizoid patients whose identifications are entirely within the analytic mode must experience the experiential mode in order to begin to grow out of the schizoid vacuum. (Bauer, 1985, p. 23)

In the experiential approach, there is no place or meaning for terms such as the patient's "pathology," "ego consciousness," "schizophrenia," "weak thinking," "obsessively defensive schizoid patient," or "schizoid vacuum." Nor is there any place for combining or alternating quite different conceptual approaches to human beings and dream work (Mahrer, 1989b). While a few of the uses of dreams may be combined, most of them cannot. Assuredly, what the experiential approach gets from dreams is almost uniformly different from and uncombinable with what other approaches get from dreams.

CHAPTER 8

Ways of Working
With Dreams

CHAPTER 7 DESCRIBED MANY OF the different things that dreams can provide, especially when you take into account the many approaches to dreams. The main purpose of this chapter is to describe the various ways of working with dreams to obtain what dreams can provide. I have organized these into five ways that are used in most dream approaches, including an introduction to the way that is used in the experiential approach. Chapter 9 gives a fuller description of the experiential way of working with dreams to discover the dream experiencing.

In addition to presenting the various ways of working with dreams, this chapter also answers two related questions: Whatever way you use, how can you be reasonably confident in what you get from the dream? And, what kinds of dreams are regarded as very important in the various approaches?

METHODS OF DREAM WORK

Get the Symbolic Meanings of the Elements, and
Reinsert Them into the Dream Context

If you are swimming under water and an eel slithers by your leg, and then you are atop a mountain, observing a raven fall dead from the sky, how can you use this dream to get a message from alien sources, or to get a resolution of personal problems and prophesies of the future, or to get information about the nature and content of personality? One method is to see the dream as made up of symbols, to know the meaning of the symbols, and to organize these symbolic meanings. In most of our current approaches, and for thousands of years, swimming has been symbolic of something else. So too is being under water. There are lots of symbolic meanings of slithering eels, mountains, being on top of a mountain, birds, dead birds, dead birds falling from the sky. In order to get what you seek from dreams by seeing the dream as made up of symbols and giving meaning to these symbols, you have to go through several steps, and each step involves decisions and options.

Figure out how to divide the dream into elements that are to have symbolic meanings. The first step is to divide the dream into elements and to select particular ones as having symbolic meaning. This is far from a simple step. Will you use the whole dream or a series of dreams as the unit? Will you take the whole dream as one big symbol and call it a birth dream or a termination dream or a dream symbolizing the flowering of sexuality? Most approaches do not take the whole dream as one grand symbolic unit. Instead they divide the dream into elements and then identify some as having symbolic meaning.

It is quite a problem to divide a dream into elements, for the dream does not come ready-made in units. You must do this. Suppose that in the dream you are visiting a friend in a hospital. You are sitting in a chair and your friend is reading with the lamp turned on. There are flowers in the room. Your friend is there for medical tests because of chest pains, and then the nurse comes in to inquire if he has taken the pills. You are aware that visiting hours will be over soon, and you excuse yourself and exit. How do you divide the dream into parts, and which of these will be given symbolic meanings?

Would you select the reading lamp as a part that may have a symbolic meaning? If you do select the lamp, then how do you select the aspect or characteristic that has symbolic meaning? Do you select the element on the basis of its being a decorative lamp or a floor lamp or a table lamp or a contemporary lamp or an oil lamp? If you identify the element as an oil lamp, not just a lamp, then is that enough, or is the key aspect the light that it casts ahead into the future, or its being an old style lamp that is out of date, or its decorative value, or its relative ineffectiveness as a light source, or something else?:

> . . . a symbol can have, for the same dreamer at the same time, multiple meanings which are all facets of the same central truth. The symbolic meaning of an oil lamp, for example, could be found in its light, which it casts ahead into the future; its age, which suggests the past; its aesthetic value as a decorative object; its ineffectiveness in comparison with electric light fixtures; and its belonging to a particular person in the dreamer's life. . . . (Mattoon, 1984, p. 98)

Or should we divide up the phrase "oil lamp" so that one part is "oil" and the other part is "lamp"? It is quite respectable to parse a word or phrase and use each part for its own symbolic meaning. We do it today, and we have done it for thousands of years:

> Symbolism may even draw upon the characteristics of language which, like a rebus, is translated into images. A famous example was Aristandros' interpretation of Alexander's dream before the siege of Tyre. Alexander had dreamt of a satyr (Greek: satyros). Aristandros said that satyros contained the elements sa and tyros, sa meaning in Greek "your," and tyros being the name of the city he wanted to conquor. Thus the dream told him Tyros will be yours, expressing a prophesy. (Wolff, 1952, p. 22)

If the dream is going to tell you something about psychodynamics or give you information about interesting unconscious instincts, and you are going to get this by understanding the symbolic meaning of what occurs in the dream, then you are going to have to figure out the elements of the dream, and then decide that this one is symbolic and that one is not. This first step is full of options and decisions.

Get the symbolic meaning for each of the elements. Once you select out the oil lamp and the satyr and a few other parts of the dream as symbols, then you have to figure out the symbolic meaning of each element. If the satyr had prominent features of a horse, the horse would symbolize a loved woman, but so would a mirror or a ship. At least this would be the symbolic meaning according to the system worked out by Artemidorus a few thousand years ago:

> Artemidorus assumes that the dream images are symbols of thoughts and that "those who are skilled in interpretation discern their wishes through the veil of symbols." If the dreamer "is in love with some woman, he will not see the object of his passion, but instead a horse, or a mirror, or a ship, or a sea, or a female animal, or a woman's garment, or some other thing which may represent a woman symbolically." (Wolff, 1952, pp. 21–22)

Systems of symbolic meanings are very old and very rich. You have your choice of many systems, new or old. Among contemporary systems, one may choose a Jungian approach or a Freudian approach, an object relations approach, one of a whole number of variations on Freud's approach, or the many symbolic systems bearing little or no relation to Freudian or Jungian symbolic schemas. What is even more disconcerting, even within any given system or approach there are lots of different principles for arriving at the more or less accepted symbolic meanings.

For example, the symbolic meaning may be derived from some idiomatic expression or colloquial word use or some other feature of language. Losing teeth in a dream has had a long, distinguished, and extremely varied history of symbolic meanings. If we apply the idioms of Freud's Austrian vocabulary, losing teeth symbolizes masturbation. "Freud was convinced that the loss of teeth in dreams should be 'interpreted' as a 'masturbatory symbol,' simply because in the Viennese dialect of his patients, the phrase 'rip one out' (*einen ausreissen*) was reserved to describe onanism" (Boss, 1977, p. 129). In the same way, hundreds of idiomatic phrases and colloquial expressions enable you to go from the dream part to its symbolic meaning.

Another way to get symbolic meanings is to have a few large meanings that include just about everything that a dream part can mean. Let us say that nearly every dream tells us about the patient's attitudes and feelings about therapy and the therapist. That narrows the possible meanings quite a bit. Then we can say that lots of dream figures stand for the therapist or "analyst": a parent, judge, policeman, head of state, God, any omniscient figure, a prominent historical personage. Whatever happens in the dream is then taken as indicating something about what is happening in therapy. If a dream journey is coming to an end, it symbolizes something about therapy. If you are naked in front of someone clothed, it tells something about therapy. If you are in water and the waves get so big that you are scared of being overwhelmed, it tells something about therapy:

> I was at a beach and in the water, bathing. The waves were small, and I waded in deeper and was enjoying myself. Then the waves began to get bigger and bigger and I kept bathing, but I was worried. I wasn't sure I'd be able to keep from being overwhelmed. . . . The interpretive hypothesis was suggested that the prospect of "wading in deeper" to look at his true feelings was very frightening to him. He was afraid of the emotions he might find welling up in himself, afraid that he might be overwhelmed by his feelings. (Bonime, 1962, pp. 125–126)

The few large meanings may have to do with therapy or with whatever you believe are the basic personality processes. If you believe that a large proportion of dreams symbolize sexuality, then you can provide explanations of how this particular dream part symbolizes the sexual impulse. Accordingly, in dreams where you are unable to move, the inhibited movement symbolizes the sexual impulse. These are dreams in which, for example, you are anxious as you are trying to reach the airplane or train that is leaving, or you are trying to escape from the enemy who is after you, and you just cannot move rapidly or perhaps even at all:

> Thus the "not being able to do something" in this dream was a way of expressing a contradiction—a "no"— . . . Thus the sensation of the inhibition of a movement represents a *conflict of will.* . . . When, therefore, the sensation of inhibition is linked with anxiety in a dream, it must be a question of an act of volition which was at one time capable of generating libido—that is, it must be a question of a sexual impulse. (Freud, 1900, pp. 337–8)

In the same way, the symbolic meaning of dream parts is easy to figure out if everything symbolizes the person's basic conflict between getting too close and being too far away, or the fundamental relationship with God, or the polarity between maleness and femaleness, or independence and dependence, or any other large categories of symbolic meanings.

Once you hold to a few large categories of symbolic meanings, the meaning of a dream part can be discerned simply because of its actual form and shape. If sex is a useful large category, then things in dreams may be symbols of sex if they resemble penises, vaginas, and the sexual act itself. We then can proclaim that " . . . sticks, canes, and snakes may stand for the male organ" (Fromm-Reichmann, 1958, p. 164), and we can get the symbolic meaning of the female organ:

> Boxes, cases, chests, cupboards and ovens represent the uterus . . . and also hollow objects, ships, and vessels of all kinds . . . Rooms in dreams are usually women . . . if the various ways in and out of them are represented, this interpretation is scarcely open to doubt. (Freud, 1900, p. 354)

There are other ways of going from this dream element to that symbolic meaning, but each requires some important basic schema of dream symbols.

Reinsert the symbolic meanings into the context of the dream The essential final step is to put these symbolic meanings back into the context of the dream. The symbolic meanings must be understood within the dream context, if only because each dream element may have several symbolic meanings: "They frequently have more than one or even several meanings, and as with Chinese script, the correct interpretation can only be arrived at on each occasion from the context" (Freud, 1900, p. 353; cf. Rycroft, 1962).

If a particular element in a dream, for instance "yawning," is taken as symbolizing "boredom," then the meaning of the dream comes from reinserting "boredom" in the original dream context. Then the dream means that the patient is bored with his wife and presumably with his marriage:

> In the first dreams of the series under consideration, "he is trying to help the child of his sister to pronounce the name of the dreamer's wife, Maria. He says, 'Mari-ah, ah (like yawning). The family members protest this joke." Jung interpreted the episode to mean that the man was bored with his wife and, presumably, with his marriage, hence the yawning. (Mattoon, 1984, pp. 89–90)

Even if you get the symbolic meanings of a fair number of elements, the overall meaning of the dream is provided by the dream context. Here is a dream where symbolic meanings are obtained for seven elements that are italicized by me from the original text:

> I am *cold* and *starved*. I go into a *restaurant* hoping to get some warmth, but it is freezing in there. The *server* serves three *other people* before me even though I was there first, and he gives me the *leftovers*. I am hurt and angry, but I eat the *crumbs* anyway. I think maybe I should leave but I am afraid that there may not be any other restaurants open. Crumbs are better than nothing. I notice that I am wearing *diapers*, and I think to myself that if it weren't for the diapers, I would get better service. (Weiss, 1986, p. 70)

The symbolic meanings of these seven elements are as follows. "Restaurant" symbolizes her marriage. "Server" is a symbol for her husband. "Other people" stand for her husband's three children. "Crumbs" or "leftovers" symbolize food and attention the husband provides for the dogs. "Cold" symbolizes the lack of warmth in their relationship. "Starved" signifies being starved for love, affection, and warmth, and "diaper" symbolizes her childish, helpless nature, her wanting to be taken care of. Putting these symbolic meanings back into the dream, the context allows for the following meaning:

You are starving for affection and warmth but settle for crumbs from your husband, letting him put his children ahead of you, because you are afraid that you won't find anything else. You also tell yourself that if you can stop acting helpless and childlike, you may get better treatment from him. (Weiss, 1986, p. 76)

So here is one common way of getting what you want from dreams: You start by presuming that the dream contains symbols; then you decide which elements of the dream to use and attach symbolic meanings to these selected parts; finally, you reinsert these symbolic meanings back into the dream context and arrive at your overall meaning.

Get the "Essential Distinguishing Characteristics" of the Elements and Reinsert Them into the Dream Context

Except for one important feature this way of getting something valuable from dreams is quite similar to the first one. Instead of looking for the symbolic meaning of some element, you get the meaning from the element itself. That is, you stay with that particular element and try and grasp its distinguishing essence or characteristic. If your dream includes a table made of planks of wood or an ink well or a cello, you get the meanings by probing into these elements rather than following a chain of connections leading elsewhere:

. . . we must keep as close as possible to the dream images themselves. When a person has dreamed of a deal table, little is accomplished by his associating it with his writing desk which is not made of deal. The dream refers expressly to a deal table . . . . (Jung, 1933, p. 13)

Instead of regarding the deal table or ink well or cello as disguising or hiding some meaning, this way of getting meaning from the element holds that the meaning lies right in the element itself. "Its intent is to reveal rather than conceal . . . not as subterfuges and disguises. . . ." (Ullman, 1962b, p. ix). If the dream includes an authoritative male, then the meaning lies right before you. All you have to do is to presume that " . . . each dream figure's attributes reflect the dreamer's feelings, thoughts, and intentions regarding the type of person that the dream figure represents (male, female, old, young, and so forth)" (Piatrowski, 1986, p. 60).

Perhaps the leading proponent of getting the meaning from what is right here in the dream image is Medard Boss (1957, 1963, 1977), who has waged a protracted battle against the psychoanalytic methods of symbolization and free association as the way to get the important things from dreams. Boss encompasses his method within a phenomenological foundation and asserts that the method of extracting the essential distinguishing characteristic is more objective and rigorous:

> The phenomenological approach . . . strives to avoid exclusively "logical" conclusions and to adhere instead entirely to factually observable things, aiming to penetrate their significances and contexts with ever greater refinement and precision, until the very essence of them is fully recognized. (Boss, 1977, p. 3)

As with the first method, you begin by selecting the elements whose essential qualities you will seek. Once you have selected the elements, the task is to identify their distinguishing essential characteristic. That yields the meaning. If a person dreams of a jungle, the meaning of jungle is " . . . a dark, untouched region of nature, teeming with plant and animal life, and barely permitting access" (1977, p. 39). Get at the meaning of a snake by defining the essence of snakes: " . . . one peculiarity that sets them apart from mankind is their cold-bloodedness . . . snakes can be extremely dangerous to unprotected humans. They spring out of a hole in the earth without warning to capture their prey, and their winding movement is unpredictable, therefore frightening" (1977, p. 40). What is the meaning of a bird? It indicates flight: " . . . flight is the most striking characteristic of birds as birds" (1977, p. 115). The essence of teeth is " . . . catching hold of, of grasping, of seizing something" (Boss, 1963, p. 267). "Teeth serve in a very specific realm of man's relation to his world, namely, the realm associated with seizing, gripping, capturing, assimilating, and gaining dominion over things" (Boss, 1977, p. 130). If a person dreams of the Persian king Cyrus, the essence is power: "It is the Persian king Cyrus, one of the most powerful monarchs of the ancient world. . . . In his waking life, the patient had had only an extremely distant relationship to the exercize of power; in his dream, however, he came in close contact with that faculty in the person of Cyrus" (1977, p. 93). Whiteness " . . . connotes purity, innocence, and cool distance" (1977, p. 102). If the dream contains an exuberant, unkempt beard, the essential distinguishing characteristic is that of masculinity: " . . . the wild, exuberant growth [signifies] something vital, inherently masculine . . . " (1977, p. 65). What is the essence of eating a hot dog?

There is nothing easier, of course, than to make the dreamed hot dog out to be a Freudian "symbol" for the male member . . . the process of eating a hot dog constitutes an assimilation of something fleshy and animal-like, rather than something bloodless from the vegetable kingdom. (Boss, 1977, pp. 79–80)

As with the first method, you begin by selecting out particular elements as the ones whose meanings you wish to extract, and then you get the overall meaning by reinserting the interpreted element back into the dream context. For example, here is a dream in which a woman and her companion witness an accident:

One or two motorcycle riders lay on the ground. One body was an amorphous mass, dark and round; its head lay to one side, separated from it. Then I saw a second man's head (or was it the same one?) that had been severed right down the middle. All of the anatomical structures along the wound were displayed in exact textbook fashion. I woke up very disturbed after that. (Boss, 1977, p. 77)

Boss selects "motorcycling men" as the meaningful element. The essential distinguising characteristic he describes as "powerful masculine physicality." Then, reinserting this meaning back into the dream context, Boss comes up with the meaning of the dream:

Does it become clear to you now in your waking existence, for instance, that your relations with the men you encounter are confined to a distant, rational, dead formalism, wherein the entire realm of powerful masculine physicality is perceived as merely a dead, amorphous mass? (1977, p. 79)

Here, then, is a second way of getting the answer to a personal question that you put to the dream or information about the individual's inner personality characteristics or mental illness.

Get the Patient's Thoughts and Ideas Starting from Selected Parts of the Dream

In the above two methods, attention was mainly on some element in the dream itself, and there was very little input from the patient. In the present method, the attention shifts radically away from the dream element and to a series of thoughts and ideas of the person right now, starting from the dream element and proceeding directly to other topics. In psychoanalytic dream work this is called "free association."

What part of the dream do you start from? You can start from any part of the dream whatsoever. The patient may select some part or the therapist may select some part. The patient may select one part, give thoughts and ideas starting from that part, and then go back and select one or several other parts. The therapist may then use the patient's thoughts and ideas from that one or several parts, or the therapist may draw the patient's attention to a few other parts as a launching pad for still other series of thoughts and ideas.

You may also start from the thoughts and ideas you had after you awakened from the dream. For example, if you awake and then have thoughts about disliking the dream, or about this dream being unusual because it was in color, or about the fact that your feet feel cold just like in the dream, then these thoughts and the thoughts and ideas starting from these thoughts are useful data:

> . . . the judgements which are passed upon the dream as it is remembered *after waking* and the feelings which are aroused by the reproduction of such a dream, form part, to a great extent, of the latent content of the dream and are to be included in its interpretation. (Freud, 1900, p. 445)

Some therapists include the patient's thoughts and ideas about the dream as a whole, such as the patient's thoughts and ideas of the meaning and interpretation of the dream: "The analyst . . . may employ a direct stimulus such as, 'What do you think the dream means?'" (Bonime, 1962, p. 26). On the other hand, others who follow a modified psychoanalytic approach would decline starting from here:

> The practice of asking the patient her impression of the dream, her thoughts about it, or what she believes it to mean . . . to intellectualize and speculate about her own dreams, [is] an effort that is bound to be defensive. (Langs, 1980, p. 359).

The train of thoughts and ideas will be quite different if the patient starts from this or that part of the dream, if the patient has one train or ten. The starting point makes a big difference.

The role of patient and therapist in identifying and giving meaning to the particular thought or idea. Someone is going to identify which particular thought or idea in the whole train is important and what it means. If there is an exuberant fellow in the dream, the patient may note that this fellow is just too happy to be real, that his friend Jackie was like that and committed suicide, that suicide takes more guts than the patient has, and that even his wife looks down on him as a pleasant follower. Ordinarily it is the therapist who picks out the important thought or idea and then provides the meaning. For example, the therapist might select the thought about suicide and then go on to make sense of this thought: "It was important . . . to pursue the hypothesis that he might be entertaining suicidal impulses" (Bonime, 1962, p. 305).

Other times it may be the patient who has the determining hand in deciding which thought is important and what meaning to give to that thought. In the following, the patient selects the initial thought and provides the meaning:

> Another time the same dreamer told me a short dream which was almost reminiscent of the technique of a rebus. He dreamt that *his uncle gave him a kiss in an automobile.* He went on at once to give me the interpretation, which I myself would never have guessed: namely that it meant auto-eroticism. (Freud, 1900, pp. 408–9)

The patient's thoughts and ideas are commonly taken as providing broad hints about meaning. When the patient starts with his sitting on his mother's lap in the dream, his thoughts and ideas may contain almost direct hints about being a child again, and both patient and the therapist will be inclined to find meaning in the area of the patient's "regressive tendencies." In actual practice, therefore, there is usually a blurred distinction between the stream of associations and the attributed meaning and between the contributions of patient and therapist.

It becomes even more complicated when the present method is mixed with that of symbolic meaning and; in fact, frequently it is hard to differentiate the two. If a dream includes chickens and the patient's ensuing thoughts and ideas have to do with eating chickens, the therapist's mode of listening to and making sense of the thoughts and ideas may blend symbolic meanings and meanings intrinsic to what the patient is saying. In the following, Jung tends to stay with the symbolic meaning of chickens, and to place less weight on the patient's thoughts and ideas about chickens:

In the dream, he has four chickens. In spite of his efforts to contain them, they escape. . . . The dreamer's associations to the chickens were limited to eating them. Jung saw them as panicky, dumb creatures, "an excellent simile for fragmentary tendencies repressed or never come across by us," that is, the chickens are an excellent simile for the dreamer's erotic feelings. (Mattoon, 1984, p. 90)

In his discussion of this issue, Freud distinguished between relying on symbolic meanings of the dream element and relying on the meaning obtained from the patient's ensuing thoughts and ideas. In contrast to Jung, he leaned toward the latter:

. . . I should like to utter an express warning against over-estimating the importance of symbols in dream-interpretation, against restricting the work of translating dreams merely to translating symbols and against abandoning the technique of making use of the dreamer's associations. The two techniques of dream-interpretation must be complementary to each other; but both in practice and in theory the first place continues to be held by the procedure which I began by describing and which attributes a decisive significance to the comments made by the dreamer, while the translation of symbols, as I have explained it, is also at our disposal as an auxiliary method. (Freud, 1900, pp. 359–60)

What remains unresolved is the extent to which symbolic interpretation also enters into the therapist's getting meaning from the patient's stream of thoughts and ideas.

In any case, this method relies upon the patient's thoughts starting from the dream. From these you can discern the answer to the question you put to the dream, or some notion of the nature of the underlying problems, or indications of unconscious impulses and tendencies.

Be the Dream Elements as Projections of Yourself

In this method, virtually everything that comprises the dream is considered a grand externalization, a projection of your own personality or self. In order to reown that projected part, to take back that externalized part into your personality, you are to "be" that dream element.

Virtually all dream elements are considered projections of yourself. In many approaches, certain elements of the dream are seen as perhaps housing or expressing something of your own personality.

For instance, your own personality process may be manifested in the vulture or the salesman or the captain of the steamer. In the experiential approach, the dream experiencing can be housed within the dreamer or within some other figure in the peak moment (see Chapter 6). Likewise, in the Jungian approach, each figure may be a personification of the person's own personality:

> The whole dream-work is essentially subjective, and a dream is a theatre in which the dreamer is himself the scene, the player, the prompter, the producer, the author, the public, and the critic. . . . Such an interpretation . . . conceives all the figures in the dream as personified features of the dreamer's own personality. (Jung, 1974, p. 52)

In one version of the psychoanalytic approach, it is also understood that the patient's personality processes may be manifested in other dream figures, maybe even three simultaneously:

> " . . . in a crucial dream a patient was represented as three distinct individuals. . . . One individual was clearly and unmodifiably the patient; a second was a friend of his, a photographer; and a third was another friend who had committed suicide. Each symbolized a distinct attribute of the patient . . . his depressive, self-destructive tendency; his self-observant aspect; and his commitment to recovery. (Bonime, 1962, pp. 4–5)

In the Daseinsanalytic approach also, a dream figure may be understood as the expression of the patient's own personality. A powerfully built man may be " . . . the potential in your own existence for vital, masculine behavior" (Boss, 1977, p. 84). The rationale is that " . . . such potentialities not yet realized in waking life are usually met with, in these dreams, in the guise of 'others' with whom the dreamer fails to identify, and in the enactment of events in which he fails to participate" (Stern, 1977, p. xviii).

In many approaches there is some use of the idea that a dream figure may be seen as the expression, manifestation, externalization, or projection of the person's own personality process. In its purest form, however, this method requires that virtually every dream element be considered a projection of the dreamer. "I believe we are all fractionalized. We are divided. We are split up in many parts, and the beauty of working with a dream is that in a dream every part—not only every person, but every part is yourself" (Perls, 1969, p. 95).

Reown the projected parts by being the dream elements. What is this method designed to get from dreams? The method is not especially designed to get messages from alien sources or to provide prophesies of the future. It offers no answers to questions that are put to it. Nor is the method designed to provide information about problems or personality characteristics or psychodynamics, about attitudes and feelings toward therapy and therapist, about psychodiagnosis and psychopathology, about unconscious and repressed instincts, impulses, and wishes. The method is designed to enable the person to bring that alienated part back into the fold, to take back the projection, to reown the part of personality that was externalized. Of all the things that the various approaches get from dreams, this is closest to the experiential use, in which the dream is used as a grand means of entering into and being the dream experiencing. In the Gestalt approach, it would be stated somewhat differently:

> Every image in the dream, whether human, animal, vegetable or mineral, is taken to represent an alienated portion of the self. By reexperiencing and retelling the dream over again in the present tense, from the standpoint of each image, the patient can begin to reclaim those alienated fragments, accept them, live with them, and express them more appropriately. (Enright, 1970, p. 121)

The goal is to reclaim and reown those projected parts by being them:

> If you are pursued by an ogre in a dream, and you *become* the ogre, the nightmare disappears. You re-own the energy that is invested in the demon. Then the power of the ogre is no longer outside, alienated, but inside where you can use it. (Perls, 1969, p. 178)

Each part of the dream is a likely candidate as a projected part; there are explicit rules regarding which part to be. Nevertheless, the method consists of literally being, carrying out, and taking the role of the dream part: "Perls' main method for dealing with dreams entailed having the patient role-play, and speak for, each of the various symbols within the dream" (Shaffer, 1978, p. 90). If the dream includes a whale, Perls says, "If you were this whale, what kind of existence would you lead, and what would you do with Jim? . . . now play the whale again. This time, try to identify with the whale and play the whale. Get up and play the whale. . . . " (Perls, 1969, pp. 127–128).

While "being the whale" is popularly identified with the Gestalt approach, the practice of being and acting as the figures and objects of the dream is ancient and widespread. So too is the idea that somehow the whale is connected to you, and acting as the whale is somehow sensible. It is a simple and straightforward procedure, useful and helpful for adults and even for children (Jacobs, 1982).

Enter into the Underlying Dream Experiencing in the Moment of Peak Feeling

In the experiential approach, the valuable thing about a dream is that you can get inside and "be" the experiencing that is contained in the dream. How do you do this? Getting back into the peak moment is the first step. The next step is to insinuate yourself deeper and deeper into this peak moment until you begin to undergo the underlying experiencing. The method is complete when you are being this dream experiencing.

None of the other methods can do the job. None of the other methods enables you to disengage from your ordinary operating domain and enter into the dream experiencing, nor can these other methods enable you to grasp, have, undergo the dream experiencing. Most of the other methods involve the patient and therapist standing outside the dream, trying to interpret what the dream means. From outside the dream you are unable to get inside the peak moment, unable to get down into the experiencing. "Interpretation, the rationalizing of symbols, distances us from the dream, whereas actualizing or reexperiencing the dream brings us closer to it" (Williams, 1980, p. 15).

Freud relied on symbolic meanings and free associations to grasp meaning from dreams. Jung used just about any method that seemed to promise to open up the dream meaning, hoping that somehow he would find a way for the dream to speak to him (Greene, 1979). Yet he always stayed outside the dream, always observing it, always seeking its meaning. To get what we want from the dream, this does not work. Indeed, none of these "outside" methods will work.

Ways of making symbolic sense of the dream and dream elements are of little use to us. You can engage in endless talk about penis images and castration symbols, archetypes and amplifications, earth mothers and regressive symbolization. You can figure out all of the essential distinguishing characteristics of teeth and white fur, gnomes and snakes. You can have hundreds of ways of obtaining thoughts and ideas about and from the dream. When all of this is over with, you will still be outside the dream, arriving at some meaning or other. You will not have entered into the dream experiencing. We have undertaken the basic shift into the dream experiencing. "This basic shift frees us from the need to figure out what the symbols mean" (Corriere et al., 1980, p. 12).

What about the method in which the person is to "be" (act as, get the feel of being, take the role of) each element in the dream? This method has been most refined and described by Perls (1969). There are at least two reasons why this method will not provide what we want, although it bears a familial kinship. One is that our aim is to enter into the *single, main experiencing* housed within the dreamer or other figure in the moment of peak feeling. In Perls' approach, the person is to "be" any or all of the elements in the entire dream. This means that, if the dream may be said to include 10 or 30 or so elements, the person will "be" any or all of these elements. While we go directly to the dreamer and other agent in the peak moment, someone following the Gestalt approach may never get to these figures; in fact, she would probably be pursuing lots of other elements, and would rarely if ever arrive at our dream experiencing.

A second reason is that our aim is the dream experiencing *in the context of the peak moment*. The context of the dream is absolutely essential to uncovering and being the dream experiencing. In the peak moment I am a policeman who is watching my drunken old father urinate on a lamp post, and there are lots of people around who know he is my father and are just waiting to see if I am going to arrest him or let him go. In the experiential method, the person will enter into the policeman or the father in the context of this peak moment. In Perls' method, the strong tendency is to have the patient be the policeman and the father, with considerably less emphasis on the situational context. Accordingly, the crucial context of the peak moment is seriously diluted.

Our method differs from that of being each of the dream elements as projections of the self and even more from the other methods of deriving meaning from dreams. There are additional variations and modifications, but these are the five major methods for getting what you value from dreams. Inevitably and understandably, each of these methods will give you something different about the dream.

HOW TO BE REASONABLY CONFIDENT IN WHAT YOU GET FROM THE DREAM

How can you be reasonably confident that you got what you think you got from the dream? What can you do to get something in which you can have reasonable confidence? There are two different actions implied in these questions. One involves doing something in actual dream work; the other, occurring outside dream work, consists of checking on the method you use, studying and doing research on the method itself.

SEE IF OTHERS GET THE SAME THING
FROM THE DREAM

Generally this means that you arrive at something from the dream, and then someone else confirms that he would have gotten the same thing or, more rigorously, works independently on the dream and arrives at the same thing you do. Then you are entitled to be more confident that the dreamer is in the throes of a transference relationship, or is headed for a psychotic breakdown, or has deep-seated identifications with the hated father, or is experiencing a weakening in obsessive defenses—or whatever you get from this dream. Of course, the confirming therapist should share your ideas on what to get from dreams in general. If the two of you differ, then this way will not be very helpful.

It would seem reasonable to test the soundness of the method by seeing if others applying the same method come up with the same thing you do. The idea is to assemble some information about a patient and a dream, present it to a number of therapists, and see if they tend to come up with similar or different things from the dream. In one of the most careful uses of this procedure, Fosshage and Loew (1987a) provided a number of therapists with information from a single patient, including a series of verbatim dreams, a summary of the patient's stated reasons for starting therapy, information about the patient's case history, course of therapy, and extratherapy life, and some associations to each of the dreams. The therapists all shared the same general psychoanalytic orientation. The conclusions confirm what most other such attempts have found, namely that what you get thing from a dream is virtually a matter of individual creative artistry: " . . . psychoanalysts usually perceive, understand, and interpret dreams quite differently, depending on their particular theoretical orientation and clinical approach to dreams" (Fosshage, 1987a, p. 23).

The moral is that you must be careful in seeing if others come up with the same thing you do. First, be careful by using others who share your approach to dreams; otherwise you will tend to have differences that tell you little or nothing about whether you are using the method properly. In addition, some methods call for a more or less "blind" study of the dream itself, whereas others call for a therapist and patient working together in order to uncover such data as a stream of thoughts and ideas. This means that if you rely on data from the dream itself, and if you present the dream to colleagues who share your approach, and then if your colleagues corroborate what you got from the dream, you can have some added confidence in your method and in what you got.

You also can invite colleagues to go over an audiotape or videotape of a dream work session. At each little step, your colleagues may indicate whether they confirm or disconfirm what you did and what you are getting. I use this procedure on the presumption that the experiential method should yield the same dream experiencing regardless of therapist. When several experiential therapists follow a given audiotape or videotape step by step, they should be able to confirm that the therapist is following the method properly, and they should be able to confirm or disconfirm the dream experiencing.

Finally, there is the special case of common dreams. I am referring to dreams that most therapists regard as common (see Chapter 4), where prominent therapists from different approaches have been impressed with the similarities in what they get from these common dreams, and where you have worked with these dreams and likewise found pretty much the same thing. I am impressed that when I work with these common dreams, not only do I end up with the same dream experiencing, but my dream experiencing is very similar to what others get from these dreams even if their approach and language system differ from mine.

For example, there is the common dream in which the dreamer is suddenly aware of being late for an appointment, having missed the test, forgotten the meeting. You are surprised and guilty that it is 5:00 and the test was at 3:00, or your aunt was due at the airport at 3:00 and now it is 5:00. This common dream has been made sense of in several different approaches, and the theme has to do with missing the appointment, resisting or not wanting to attend the meeting or take the test. Each approach drapes its own vocabulary over this common theme, yet there is a persistent underlying commonality that adds a measure of confidence.

All in all, you can gain some confidence in whatever you get from dreams by seeing if others get the same thing. You should, however, be careful in selecting colleagues with the same dream approach. Also, it must be clear that this procedure is of little help to the therapist in the actual session. Only in between sessions can the therapist check with others to see if they get the same thing from this dream.

It Is Virtually Impossible to Have
Justified Confidence in the Interpreted
Meaning of a Dream

The most popular way of getting something from the dream is to arrive at an interpreted meaning. I contend that, no matter what method or system or approach you use, it is virtually impossible to have justified confidence in the interpreted meaning of a dream.

Choosing the dream elements to be interpreted. Here is a rather short and simple dream. "I storm into the burning house to search for my parents. I find them in the bedroom, but it's too late. The flaming walls collapse on us. There is no escape from the fiery death for all of us! That's when I wake up screaming" (Boss, 1977, p. 112). In order to interpret the meaning of the dream, you must choose which dream elements to interpret, and it is extremely difficult to have justified confidence in whatever choice you make.

The reason for the lack of confidence is that there are no sound guidelines for telling you:

(a) How many elements to interpret. Do you select one (fiery death?) or four (burning house, parents, no escape, bedroom?) or more?
(b) Which elements to choose once you have settled on a number, say three. Do you choose burning house, parents, and bedroom, or would you prefer searching for my parents, flaming walls collapse on us, and waking up screaming?
(c) Whichever ones you choose, how large or how small the package of each element is to be. Is the element to be "flaming walls" all by itself, or is the element to be "flaming walls collapsing," or is it still further enlarged into "flaming walls collapsing on us"? Or should the element be very small, and consist only of "flames"?

These choices are exceedingly important, not only because they determine the nature and content of the interpretation, but also because the elements you do and do not interpret play a very large hand in helping to shape the final overall dream interpretation.

Boss chose two elements, not one or three or five. If he had chosen one or four, the overall interpretation would have been altered drastically. Can you guess which two he chose? He selected "burning up" and "parents" within the context of the elements that were thereby left uninterpreted. Boss interprets "burning up" as the ending of something, and "parents" as signifying parental relationships. Accordingly, the dream is given the interpreted meaning of indicating " . . . the 'burning up' of your parents *as* parents, i.e. as human beings existing as mothering or fathering relationships to you . . . " (Boss, 1977, p. 113).

Sometimes the sheer size of the element can be a vexing package of problems. In a short dream, the dreamer is holding an umbrella, and the umbrella is black and conservative, but it has holes in it and is practically unusable. What attracts the dreamer's attention is the gold handle and the noise of the wind ripping the umbrella. If you are going to give interpreted meaning, what is the size of the element? Do you take the whole package of "umbrella"? Do you emphasize the enfolding, protective aspect of the umbrella, the handle that you are grasping, or the pointed end? Do you select "black, conservative umbrella" or "an umbrella that has holes in it and is practically unusable"? What about the sheer word "umbrella" and its possible parsing into "Ella," his sister-in-law-, and "umbrage" toward her? Do you choose the gold handle or some other larger or smaller piece? Element size is a difficult problem indeed.

The choice of how many, what size, and which elements is not designed to provide a solid sense of confidence. What is more, the eventual interpreted meaning varies considerably with your selection at this initial step.

Going from the dream element to an interpreted meaning is a highly personal, creatively artistic achievement. Once you have chosen the actual dream elements to be given interpretive meaning, the journey from each element to whatever interpretive meaning you assign to it is so convoluted, so filled with choices, that the enterprise qualifies as a highly personal, creatively artistic achievement. Here are five considerations that entitle you to have very low confidence in whatever interpreted meaning you attribute to the dream elements:

(1) You have to decide whether the interpreted meaning is personal or is universal or is some sort of combination of personal and universal.

If you select a cow as something to be interpreted, do you get the meaning from the supposedly universal meaning of cow, or do you work with that person's personal experience and meaning of cow, or do you somehow combine the two? Is it helpful or not helpful to know that the patient is a member of the committee on women (C.O.W.) or that her young daughter just returned from a day at a farm with the rest of her class, full of stories about cows? You get one interpretive meaning from a personal perspective and a different one from a universal perspective.

There is little or no problem if you see all dream symbols as universal or, on the other hand, as quite personal: "Dream symbols arise out of the specific life history of each individual, and it is only from the individual's life history that we can derive the meaning of his dream symbols" (Bonime, 1962, p. 32). The problem comes when you hold that some meanings are universal and some are personal, and perhaps some are a little of both.

Freud used both universal meanings and meanings derived from personal thoughts, ideas, and experiences of the patients. These two lines of interpretive meaning are quite different:

> Freud observed that symbols of a more or less universal nature are employed by the dream or other unconscious manifestations, and that they must be interpreted as such apart from the particular associations and experiences of the individual. (Monroe, 1955, p. 61)

Jung likewise differentiated the two sources of meaning and noted that some dream symbols " . . . are not the exclusive property of the dreamer, but are instead a common human heritage" (Corriere, Karle, Woldenberg, & Hart, 1980, p. 71). This means the interpreter must have knowledge of several fields in order to give a universal meaning to a cow or a cross or entwining snakes:

> The interpreter looks for amplifications in mythology, history of religions, archeology, the practices of preliterate peoples, alchemical treatises, and indeed "all branches of human sciences." . . . The archetypal parallels usually are supplied from the interpreter's store of knowledge or from information sought out during or between psychotherapy sessions. Discovering the relevant parallels may require extensive research. . . . (Mattoon, 1984, pp. 69–70)

The problem comes when you look at the snake in the dream and have to decide whether to use the universal meanings of snake or those coming from the personal life experience of this patient. This can be most disconcerting for the interpreter, who might otherwise interpret the snake as a phallic symbol but must consider that a more personal meaning may well apply:

> In many patients . . . a dream snake may not in any manner refer to the phallus. A woman patient . . . during her childhood, while walking with other children, might have overcome her fear of being bitten by snakes by picking one up. For this patient, a snake in a dream could symbolize courage, a courage utterly unrelated to sexuality. (Bonime, 1962, p. 37)

If a dream element can be interpreted personally or universally, is there any way of deciding whether this particular dream element is to be interpreted one way or the other? Jung says yes and identifies certain elements as having universal meanings. These include, for example, wise old men, a child hero, movement at tremendous speeds or for enormous distances, gross changes in bodily proportions, being inordinately large or small, or dying. Water is regarded as a universal symbol for the unconscious, " . . . and the sea as a relatively fixed symbol that 'signifies a collecting place where all psychic life originates, i.e. the collective unconscious' " (Mattoon, 1984, p. 88). What is more, Jung " . . . saw 'mother' and 'horse' as relatively fixed symbols, standing respectively for the origin of life and the animal life of the body" (Mattoon, 1984, p. 99).

Freud also identified certain dream elements as more suited to universal than personal meaning. These include houses, fires, hollow vessels, caves, sticks, tall buildings, loss of teeth, flying, steep inclines, ladders, and stairs.

An element may also be interpreted as a combination of personal and universal symbols. Binswanger (1967) regarded many dream elements as the product of the individual person's own personal input combined with such grand universal forces as Freud's id, Jung's collective unconscious, and Habelin's Universum. In the Jungian approach, these combined elements were known as "natural symbols." "A natural symbol could occur in a dream of anyone anywhere in the world, and it could carry either a relatively fixed or an individual meaning" (Mattoon, 1984, p. 99). If your approach sees "fire" as having both a universal meaning and a personal meaning, then whatever symbolic meaning you give to "fire" may be modified depending on personal information about the patient. If you regard the patient as enuretic, then perhaps the fire in the dream " . . . can be understood to stand for the passion which this boy expresses in his behavior and enuresis" (Henderson, 1980, p. 381).

If the dreamer is bitten on a heel by a snake and is instantly paralyzed, and if you wish to combine both universal and personal meanings, which of the many universal meanings do you use? Do you use psychoanalytic symbolic meanings of snake and heel? Do you use the meanings of being bitten on the heel by a snake as given in the Hindu culture or Babylonian mythology or a famous painting or the Bible? If you also include personal life experience, do you select the patient's medical condition, the hole in his sock, mother's pampering when he was a child, or his sexual attraction to feet? Jung arrives at a very particular interpretation by combining one specific universal meaning and two personal ones:

> [The army officer with a pain in his left heel] . . . dreamed after he had been in analysis for some time, that "he was bitten on the heel by the snake and instantly paralyzed." Jung assumed that the dreamer probably had learned at some time of the Biblical story of the serpent who was made the enemy of women and her offspring, with the decree, "You shall bruise his heel" (Genesis 3:15). The relation of the injured heel to the mother in the Genesis story had its parallel in the dreamer's history: He had been pampered and, hence, weakened by his mother: indirectly, therefore, she had lamed him. . . . Thus, amplifications supply the essential fact that is missing in the officer's dream: A woman was the agent of his paralysis. (Mattoon, 1984, pp. 70–71)

It is hardly confidence-inspiring to face the almost bewildering choice of whether to select your interpretive meanings from the universal realm or the personal realm or from some kind of combination of the two.

(2) Everything can easily be regarded as a symbol for something else, so that you can never really know when and where to stop.

If you dream of a key or a stick or a snake, one system tells us that they stand for penises plain and simple. Jung treats penis as itself a symbol for the power of healing and fertility. Phallic symbols " . . . are supposed to stand for the membrum virile and nothing more. Psychologically speaking, the membrum is itself . . . a symbolic image whose wider content cannot be easily determined. [it refers to] the creative mana, the power of healing and fertility, 'that which is unusually potent'" (Jung, 1933, p. 23; cf. Hall, 1962). Is the snake a penis or the power of healing or fertility or what? If snake stands for penis, and penis stands for something else, where do we stop? Whatever element you start with, it is symbolic of X which itself is symbolic of Y, and the chain may go anywhere.

(3) There are dozens of choices of which system or subsystem or combination of systems to use in arriving at an interpreted meaning.

The problem is not so much which large-scale system of interpretation to use, although that is hard enough. The more perplexing problem is what variation or subsystem you choose from those proposed by, for example, Binswanger, Bonime, Cayce, Caligor, Castaneda, Corriere and his colleagues, Ellis, Fairbairn and the object relationists, Faraday, Fosshage, French and Fromm, Garfield, Green, Hall, Langs, Mendel, Perls, Rossi, Ullman, and many others.

This problem is immeasurably compounded when you seek to combine several interpretive systems (Mahrer, 1989b). Suppose that you are drawn toward psychoanalytic, Jungian, Daseinsanalytic, and Gestalt systems. If you are working with a pond in the dream, on what basis do you combine these four approaches to arrive at some meaning of the pond? If you like the idea of switching from one system to another, on what basis do you switch from this system with this element to that system with that element? All in all, the use and combination of several subsystems are hardly designed to leave you with a solid sense of confidence in whatever interpretive meaning you might artistically create.

(4) There is a confounding interactional effect between the system of interpretive meaning and the element choice, so that even with the same interpretive system you can easily end up with quite different interpreted meanings for what appears to be the same element.

If you have a dream of a key being inserted into a lock, do you have two elements or just one? If you have two elements of key and lock, then if the key stands for penis and the lock stands for vagina, then the key entering the lock would seem to be interpreted as intercourse. On the other hand, if you see key and lock as two sides of a single unit or as opposite parts of a single whole, then the key entering the lock has the meaning of the union of opposites, unlocking a secret, or opening a door to success (Mattoon, 1984).

If your interpretive system has one meaning for snake, a different meaning for idol of worship, and a third meaning for mythological creatures, you will have trouble deciding in which category to put the following element: "There is this huge golden statue, about twenty feet high. It's a serpent, with wings, and everyone is bowing down to it." Is the element a snake, an idol of worship, a mythological creature, or something else?

In one of Jung's well-known self-interpreted dreams, he defines an element as "Siegfried," and then gives an interpreted meaning to that element: "Siegfried . . . represents what the Germans want to achieve, heroically to impose their will, have their own way. . . . " (Jung, in Mattoon, 1984, p. 61). Jung then interprets his dream to indicate that he is to abandon his heroic idealism in favor of higher things. In sharp contrast, Fodor (1971) redefines the element as the two words "Sieg" and "fried," taken as standing for "Sigmund" and "Freud." The ensuing different interpretive meaning is in regard to Jung's death wish toward Freud; " . . . he wanted to step into Freud's place without delay and owe him nothing" (Fodor, in Mattoon, 1984, p. 61). The interpretive system determines what elements to select and how to define the elements, and that choice in turn plays a large hand in determining the nature and content of the interpretive meaning.

(5) Any given dream element may have multiple interpretive meanings even within the same system, so how do you make your choice of which meaning to attach to the element?

Loss of teeth has all sorts of interpretive meanings, such as loss of ego structure (Henderson, 1980) or loss of " . . . our grasping, apprehending relation to the world" (Boss, 1977, p. 131). Or consider "flying": in an Adlerian approach, it symbolizes superiority and domination over others (Adler, 1974); one classical psychoanalytic meaning is that of a sexual wish; the Jungian meaning has to do with freedom from restriction (Jung, 1933); Stekel regarded flying as symbolizing death (Gutheil, 1974); and Ellis (1911) lists a whole series of other meanings. If you are flying and lose your teeth, you have a very wide choice of available meanings.

Even within the same system of interpretation, most elements have sets of different meanings. Going down a stairway is taken as indicating the sexual act or entering deeper into one's unconscious. The color red may have the meaning of blood, passion, a warning, or basic energy force. Drinking can mean physical pleasure or purification. The act of drinking a glass of tomato juice as you walk down stairs can be interpreted as a warning against seeking to purify yourself through probing into your unconscious psychodynamics, or it can mean that the sexual act expresses passionate physical pleasure, or it can be a warning against the dangers of the physical sex act for your immunological system.

The problem becomes even more complicated if you have to take into account all sorts of information about the patient and the patient's own personal life experience. For example, you may hold that the same dream elements, and perhaps even the same entire dream, will have different meanings depending on whether the dreamer is young or old:

> Jung stated that two men, one young, one old, brought him essentially the same dream: "A company of young men are riding on horseback across a wide field. The dreamer is in the lead and jumps across a ditch of water, just clearing it. The others fall into the ditch." The image is that of the dreamer's overcoming an obstacle that defeats others. For the young man, who was cautious and introverted, the dream indicated possibilities in life which he was not realizing. For the old man, who was an invalid and did not follow medical instructions, the dream seemed to mean that he had an illusion of his capacities, far above that was true for his age and situation. (Mattoon, 1984, pp. 76–77)

It is challenging enough to choose the dream elements you wish to interpret. It is essentially confidence-shattering to go from those selected dream elements to a set of interpreted meanings. The even more awesome problem is that you are not done. You still have to construct some sort of final, overall interpretive meaning for the dream as a whole.

Constructing the final, overall interpretive meaning is even more personal and artistically creative. Arriving at a single interpretation is a matter of putting together just about anything and everything that seems to relate to this dream:

> The manifest dream can be fully understood only after the patient's associations to it are combined with what the analyst himself can contribute from his knowledge of the patient beforehand as well as from his clinical experience, theoretical background and familiarity with symbols. (Sloane, 1975, p. 62)

It is very difficult to confidently organize two to six interpretive meanings into a single overall interpretation. Once you take into account the personal circumstances of this particular patient, you are in the realm of the virtually impossible. This was the conclusion of a five-year continuing workshop among a group of psychoanalysts:

Zane and Eckhardt reported on the results of a dream symposium that was carried on, over a five year period, by members of the American Academy of Psychoanalysis. Zane's evaluation of the symposium begins with the eyebrow-raising remarks: "Nothing seems more important for our field than to confront the recurrent finding in our workshop over its five year existence that regarding the same dream psychoanalysts derived very different meanings, took very different approaches, and had striking difficulties in communicating with each other, and that our divergencies actually increased when, in addition to the manifest dream, we provided clinical material about the dreamer and his therapy. . . . " (Boss, 1977, p. 4)

"Unless we can resolve the unsettling phenomenon of irreconcilable difference in response to the same dream disclosed in our workshops, I find that qualified psychoanalysts will continue to give highly individual responses to the same dream. . . . " (Boss, 1977, pp. 4, 6)

This challenge was carried out under conditions designed to strengthen confidence in the obtained overall interpretation. The therapists shared the same dream approach, agreed to participate in the venture, and probably tried to be rather careful in arriving at an overall interpretation because it was going to be compared with the overall interpretation of others. Little wonder that both therapists and patients who rely on interpretation can easily be drowned in an ocean of uncertainty:

This leads to mutual suspicion that the analysis has not been sufficiently "objective," and to justifiable distrust on the part of the layman who is only too ready to imagine that all interpretations have been invented by the psychoanalyst. (Boss, 1977, p. 147)

Let us start with a short dream:

"I am walking along 34th street. I come to a group of people waiting in line for hot dogs, especially good hot dogs. I feel 'Oh boy!' and I look forward to it. I found soon, though, that I am actually in a queue waiting for a bus. The discovery gives me a feeling of disappointment." (Bonime, 1962, p. 112)

Bonime gets interpreted meaning from the patient's associations to three elements. "The patient's immediate association with the locale was the analyst's office. With the hot dog he associated penis, and with the bus he had the connections of 'going somewhere, getting somewhere'" (Bonime, 1962, p. 112). How do you arrive at an over-all meaning of the dream using these three interpreted elements? Would you say that the dream means the patient is competing with other patients for the therapist's penis, but that he is disappointed and so he is inclined to go somewhere else? Would you say that it means the patient first was like other patients in seeking the analyst's penis, and is disappointed that in reality he is embarking on a differ-ent kind of journey? Even with the three interpreted elements, putting everything together into an interpreted meaning is an act of personal creativity. Here is the way Bonime puts it all together:

> The interpretive hypothesis was offered that the dream . . . indicated a happy anticipation of seducing the analyst; this was represented in strictly homoerotic terms by his hoping to get the analyst's penis (hot dog), but in broader terms it signified his desire to make a personal conquest of the analyst. (Bonime, 1962, p. 112)

Most approaches rely on some way of interpreting the meaning of dreams; however this very process precludes confidence in the inter-preted meaning. Under these conditions, as may be expected, confi-dence levels are usually inflated, as the threat of unconfidence must be countered by the confidence of authority.

Rely on the Recurrence of a Motif in a Series of Dreams

One way of increasing confidence in whatever you get from dreams is to use a series of several dreams and to look for a recurrent motif. We use a variation of this method when we look for the common experiencing in two peak moments of feeling in the same overall dream. Generally, however, the dreams are from different evenings. Hall (1966) recommends using dreams that occur over a short series of two or three nights, while others prefer a longer series of dreams occurring over weeks or months.

How do you identify a recurrent motif? Jones (1962) describes a method used by Hall whereby you start with one dream whose mean-ing is conspicuously self-evident and then look for corroboration in the other dreams of the series:

> Often the meaning of one dream is self-evident and illuminates a major conflict like a spotlight shooting its beam into the darkness. Armed with the hypothesis drawn from a spotlight dream, the other dreams of

the series are scrutinized for projections of the same basic conflict. If a number of dreams of an individual fit in with the same interpretation, this interpretation is felt to be corroborated and is assigned to the dream series. (p. 95)

Jung, in a somewhat different way, used the recurrent theme from earlier dreams to help illuminate the meaning of the present dream and then he verified the correctness of his interpretation of this dream by noting the changing theme in subsequent dreams:

Jung seemed to consider the dreams preceding a given dream to be part of its amplification, especially if motifs recurred. He used dreams following the given dream as tests of verification to confirm or correct an interpretation. . . . A correct interpretation can change the content of subsequent dreams by contributing to psychological development. An incorrect interpretation can have a comparable effect by eliciting a dream that corrects the invalid interpretation. (Mattoon, 1984, pp. 81, 91; cf. Hall, 1982, 1983)

In looking for the recurrent theme, you face the problem of how to tell whether the same motif is continuing, whether a new motif is present or, as some studies suggest (e.g., Trosman, Rechtschaffen, Offenkrantz, & Wolpert, 1960), several motifs come and go in cyclical fashion. In any case, the sense of confidence comes from identifying or verifying or corroborating a recurrent motif in a series of dreams.

Rely on the Actual Occurrence of a Common Experiencing in Both Moments of Peak Feeling

In the experiential approach, confidence comes from (a) actually undergoing the experiencing (b) that is common to both peak moments. In one step, confidence comes when you actually have the experiencing, when bodily sensations come alive. You can feel tearfulness or your head gets dizzy or there is a pounding in your heart or your legs start to tremble or there is a tingling excitement in your chest. Your body lets you know that some experiencing is going on. This is the first step in gaining a sense of confidence that you are on the right track.

The second step is to find a commonality in the experiencings that are present in the moments of peak feeling in the dream. Look for the experiencings in one peak. Then find the experiencings in the second peak. When you find a commonality in the experiencings across the two peaks, you are entitled to have a sense of confidence in the nature of the experiencing. Something almost magical happens when you go to the second peak, work at extracting the experiencings, and are impressed by the occurrence of a common experiencing. It gives you a sense of faith in the method and in the designated nature of the dream experiencing.

The relationship between peak moments or scenes or episodes of the same dream. In the experiential approach, the idea is that the same experiencing is present in the several moments of peak feeling in a dream. There may be some variation in the nature of the peak feeling so that it may be bad in one and good in another. There may also be variation in who is the main character, the one who houses the experiencing. But there is a single experiencing to be found, and the commonality provides the sense of confidence.

Others have also studied the relationships between the parts or episodes of a single overall dream. However, we think in terms of peak moments of feeling, whereas others use the whole episodes or scenes or tandem subdreams. Also, it should be clear that we look for experiencing, whereas other approaches look for all sorts of other things such as surface characteristics or manifest content or latent unconscious meanings. Nevertheless, the overall concern is the relationship between the various parts of a dream. Finally, there is a difference in what is accepted as a single overall dream. If you wake up with a dream, fall back asleep and have another dream, I tend to accept these as part of a single dream, although I am much less inclined to do so if you are deliberately awakened or if the two awakenings are separated by five or more hours.

In general, there are clinicians and researchers who share a concern with the issue of the relationships between parts of the same dream, but there is quite a difference in what is identified as a part (episode, scene, peak moment, etc.), in what is seen as perhaps similar or different or related in some way (e.g., experiencing, manifest or latent content), and even in the unit of what is called the dream (e.g., a single dream versus several dreams interspersed by periods of awakening). Nevertheless, the general conclusion seems to be that " . . . when a dream has several scenes that can usually be best understood as varying ways to describe the same central idea" (Edinger, 1972, p. 23). Studies (Cipolli, Baroncini, Fagioli, Fumai, & Salzarulo, 1987; Dement & Wolpert, 1958; Kramer, Hlasny, Jacobs, &

Ruth, 1976; Kramer, Whitman, Baldridge, & Lansky, 1964; Offenkrantz & Rechtschaffen, 1963; Rechtschaffen, Vogel & Shaikun, 1963) report consistencies in various kinds of themes, in dream thoughts, and in manifest content over dreams in the same evening. Summarizing research on this issue, Jones (1970, p. 49) concludes that a fair number of studies report some commonality over scenes and episodes of a single dream and over dreams of a single evening.

Clinicians have traditionally accepted the idea of a commonality between the different parts of a dream and have used ingenious ways of discerning the commonality. For example, Fenichel (1953) tells of a dream in which, in one episode, a large woman is trying to crawl through a doorway that is too cramped for her and, in another episode, some flowers are too small to be inserted into a vase. The commonality is held as lying in the similar theme beneath the apparent opposites, so that the two episodes " . . . could mean the same thing . . . both feelings were very likely concerned with the same unconscious ideas. . . . The giant woman's crawling through the door is a duplication of the vase and flower motif, only here the state of affairs is reversed; the *big* body must go through the *small* opening" (1953, pp. 162, 165).

Even within the same approach, clinicians are free to rely or not to rely on the supposed commonality. For example, Jung did rely on commonalities, but other Jungian analysts are less convinced:

> . . . the dreams of one night are assumed by many dream interpreters to focus on one theme. This is a useful hypothesis in interpretation, but it has not been demonstrated empirically, to my knowledge. (Mattoon, 1984, p. 82)

In the experiential approach, we are not concerned with the order or sequence of the two moments of peak feelings. But many clinical theorists and researchers have probed into the larger question: Beyond a mere commonality, what is the specific relationship between a first and a second episode or scene or subdream?

One answer is that the two episodes express the same theme or meaning, with the first one a little more vague, indirect, and distorted, and the second more distinct and specific. This was Jung's position: "The two dreams make nearly the same assertion, but, as is usually the case, the second is more specific" (1933, p. 25). Freud had a similar view of the relationship between the earlier and later episodes or dreams:

The content of all dreams that occur during the same night forms part of the same whole. . . . In interpreting dreams consisting of several main sections or, in general, dreams occuring during the same night, the possibility should not be overlooked that separate and successive dreams of this kind may have the same meaning, and may be giving expression to the same impulses in different material. If so, the first of these homologous dreams to occur is often the more distorted and timid, while the succeeding one will be more confident and distinct. (Freud, 1900, pp. 333–4)

A second answer is that the first episode is the earlier version of the theme and the second represents a more recent version: "They represent the same wish or motif. The first is the earlier or more primitive; the second is the latter or more recent transformation" (Fenichel, 1953, p. 165).

A third answer is that the two episodes constitute a single train of thought with the first episode as the subordinate clause and the second episode as the principal clause or, in deference to the mechanisms of dream distortion, reversing the two so that the conclusion is in the first episode and the premises are in the second episode:

Suppose the dream-thoughts run like this: "Since this was so and so, such and such was bound to happen." Then the commoner method of representation would be to introduce the dependent clause as an introductory dream and to add the principal clause as the main dream. If I have interpreted aright, the temporal sequence may be reversed. But the more extensive part of the dream always corresponds to the principal clause. (Freud, 1900, p. 315)

Quite a common technique of dream-distortion consists in representing the outcome of an event or the conclusion of a train of thought at the beginning of a dream and of placing at its end the premises on which the conclusion was based or the causes which led to the event. Anyone who fails to bear in mind this technical method adopted by dream-distortion will be quite at a loss when confronted with the task of intrepreting a dream. (Freud, 1900, p.328)

A fourth answer is exemplified in Jung's use of the episodes or scenes as that of a single unfolding story. Jung interprets each episode separately and then weaves the sequential interpretations together along the lines of a story. For example, in the first episode, the patient returns to the humble village where he grew up and a villager criticizes him for seldom visiting. Jung interprets this episode as indicating that he is turning his back on his humble beginnings: "'You forget how far down you began'" (Jung, 1954, p. 141). In the second episode, a train goes faster and faster until the rear coaches are derailed. Jung interprets this episode as indicating the ominous consequences of his frantic urgency to achieve and get ahead. Jung puts these two interpretations together into a story comprised of two episodes or scenes:

> It is obvious that, at the present phase of his life, the patient has reached the highest point of his career: the strain of the long ascent from his lowly origin has exhausted his strength. He should have rested content with his achievements, but instead of that his ambition drives him on and on, and up and up into an atmosphere that is too thin for him and to which he is not accustomed. Therefore his neurosis comes upon him as a warning. (p. 142)

The relationships of the first and second episodes or dreams are interesting, and they may or may not add to the sense of confidence in what you get from the sequence. What is more important here is that, regardless of sequence, you can get a measure of confidence in the commonality across the several episodes or scenes or dreams. In the experiential approach, this commonality is so important that we only work with dreams of multiple peaks, and it is essential to gain a sense of confidence in the experiencing that is common to both peak moments.

In general, you can have a measure of confidence when you look for some commonality or theme or motif over a few peak moments or episodes or scenes, and perhaps even over a series of dreams from several days or weeks or longer. You might gain some confidence in your approach by seeing if others get the same thing that you get from the dreams, but this way is quite slippery and is not of much help when you are actually engaged in dream work. On the other hand, if you look for the interpreted meaning of the dream, there is precious little to provide a sense of confidence in whatever interpreted meaning you come up with.

VERY IMPORTANT DREAMS

A few thousand years ago, an occasional dream was hailed as very important because it came from the gods. We still hail some dreams as very important; in fact, what we get from dreams and how we get it depend on whether the dream is special according to the particular approach being used.

Archetypal Dreams

Ancients divided dreams into ordinary personal ones and special ones that came from the gods. In the Jungian approach, ordinary dreams come from the personal unconscious and special ones come from the "collective unconscious." These special dreams are characterized by archetypal material:

> Thus we speak on the one hand of a personal and on the other of a collective unconscious, which lies at a deeper level and is further removed from consciousness than the personal unconscious. The "big" or "meaningful" dreams come from this deeper level . . . these archetypal products are no longer concerned with personal experiences but with general ideas, whose chief significance lies in their intrinsic meaning and not in any personal experience and its associations. (Jung, 1974, p. 77)

These very important dreams include such archetypal material as a wise old man, a "shadow" figure, the "animus" or "anima," primordial or earth mother, special cosmic qualities such as spatial or temporal infinity, flying through space at great speeds, being the earth or sun or planet. These dreams indicate that the person has gone beyond the personal self or ego, has achieved a deeper or higher level of individuation and development:

> [Archetypal dreams occur] . . . when the dreamer has integrated much of the personal unconscious and is in the advanced stages of the individuation process. Then his dreams begin to reflect his wider consciousness of objective interests and the world at large, perhaps philosophical or religious problems, such as the contemplation of death, rather than the limited world of the ego. (Mattoon, 1984, p. 68)

Split-Self Dreams

In this category of very important dreams there is another figure who is also you. You may merely sense the presence of another figure whom you know is also you, a figure who may be adjacent yet whom you do not actually see. You may be a removed observer of another figure who looks just like you or may bear little or no physical resemblance, although you know that figure is you. These "split-self" dreams may be seen as occurring in stages, with the final stage one in which you are actually engaged in an interaction with that other self. "The final stage . . . was usually ushered in by a dream that many of us have had at one time or another, in which one is looking at oneself sleeping in bed" (Castaneda, 1977, p. 269).

There are two ways in which such dreams are regarded as very important. Boss (1959) considers such dreams as indicating a seriously pathological state of ego splitting that occurs in schizophrenia or organic psychoses. On the other hand, Rossi (1985) regards such dreams as signifying the emergence of a new side of personality, the achievement of a higher plane of ego development, individuation, ego awareness, and self-reflection:

> . . . the dreamer sees himself in the dream as if from the perspective of an outside observer. This outside perspective is actually a visual representation of the dreamer involved in a process of self-reflection. It is only with the introduction of self-reflection that one can begin to see one's self and take an active stance in facilitating psychological growth. (p. 28)

These dreams signify the emergence of another side of our nature, and this is a "critical change in personality":

> The existence of two or more levels of awareness within the same dream is another indication that we are undergoing a critical change in personality; we are breaking out of the old to experience other sides of our nature that are emerging as the new. (Rossi, 1985, p. 16)

Lucid Dreams

In lucid dreams what is important is not the mere content of the dream, but rather the way in which you become aware that you are dreaming and may even proceed to controlling the direction of what happens in the dream. Yet the basic feature is that " . . . the dreamer knows he is dreaming and feeling fully conscious in the dream itself" (Tart, 1969, p. 1). Once you have achieved this state, you can be especially aware of and attentive to what is occurring, how the other persons are being, what is being said by you and others (Casteneda, 1972; Delaney, 1981). Then you can take control of what is occurring and can direct what is to happen, take charge of the action, vanquish the bad and befriend the good, have a large determining hand in what happens (Castaneda, 1972; Delaney, 1981; Eliade, 1960; Faraday, 1972, 1974; Fox, 1962; Garfield, 1974; Green, 1968; Ouspensky, 1962; Stewart, 1954, 1969; Tart, 1970; Whiteman, 1961). When " . . . a dreamer purposefully decides to intervene into the dream events . . . (it signifies) an astounding strength of will while dreaming" (Boss, 1977, p. 184), the achievement of heightened awareness, ego strength, executive control, ego development, individuation, ability to take charge of your own waking self and your world (Castaneda, 1977; Corriere et al., 1980; Evans-Wentz, 1967; Rossi, 1972).

Transformative Dreams

These dreams are characterized by particular changes that occur either within a single dream or over a series of dreams. While others have described the characteristics of such dreams, they have perhaps been most extensively described, discussed, and identified as "transformative" by Corriere, Karle, Woldenberg, and Hart (1980). The simplest kind of transformation is from one figure or object into another (Rossi, 1985), such as an ape spontaneously transforming into a sailor or the young bartender transforming into your old uncle. However, Corriere and his coworkers also identify four dimensions of transformation, with one consisting of dreams that move from content that is confusing, mixed up, symbolic and distorted, to those in which the content is realistic, clear, and nonsymbolic. A second is from dreams without feeling to those in which there is full feeling expression. A third dimension is from dreams devoid of human beings and human contact to those marked by human interaction (cf. Stern, 1977). Finally, the dream transforms from those in which the dreamer is a mere observer, passive and removed, to dreams in which the dreamer is active, an initiator of action and interaction. These changes are taken as indications of significant transformations at the deepest levels of personality and of personality development.

The Experiential Model of Depth of Dreams

In the experiential approach, the closest we come to "very important dreams" are those in which the dreamer is the main character who houses the experiencing and the feeling is genuinely good. These dreams are special because they show that the person is ready for that experiencing to be a part of her ordinary operating domain and therefore to be and behave from that experiencing in the everyday world. However, the occurrence of these dreams makes no difference in the steps of dream work, except to suggest that the steps ought to proceed a little more easily.

Shallow, intermediate, and deep dreams. The model of depth of dreams is given in Figure 4. As indicated in this figure, dreams occur once the center of I-ness leaves the operating domain and enters into the realm of the deeper domain. We can then distinguish different kinds of dreams and identify some as shallow, as intermediate, or as deep.

Shallow dreams are those in which the center of I-ness has just emerged from the operating domain, is still in the vicinity of the operating domain, and is only in the outer periphery of the deeper

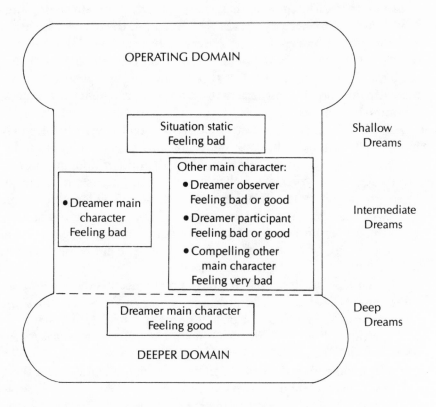

Figure 4. The Experiential Model of Depth of Dreams

domain. Being so close to the operating domain, the feeling is bad because of the bad (disintegrative, distancing) relationship of the operating toward the deeper potential. Because the center of I-ness is so far away from the deeper potential, there is little or no action or movement. The deeper dream experiencing is not doing anything, is not carrying out anything.

What do these shallow dreams look like? There is essentially no action, no movement, either by the dreamer or by others. The situation is static, fixed, unmoving. The feeling is bad. It is not one of terror or catastrophic fear, just ordinary unpleasant feelings. Finally, these dreams are characterized by the dreamer's thoughts, ideas, perceptions, ruminations.

At the other extreme, once the center of I-ness has entered down into the actual bowels of the dream experiencing, the feelings come from the dream experiencing rather than from the bad disintegrative relationship of the operating domain toward the deeper domain. No longer is that disintegrative relationship exerting its effect. In addition, when the center of I-ness is wholly within the deeper potential, it is the person himself or herself who is the experiential agent. No longer is the experiencing housed in some other figure or object. No longer is the experiencing externalized. The feeling is generally good, typically the good feeling of actualization, viz., excitement, aliveness, vibrancy.

All other dreams are intermediate. For instance, the dreamer may be the main character because the center of I-ness is sufficiently distant from the operating domain to allow the deeper domain to carry out its action; however, the feeling remains bad because the center of I-ness is in that intermediate zone which is still vulnerable to the effects of the disintegrative relationship of the operating domain toward the deeper potential and has yet to enter into the deeper domain where it is free of these negative disintegrative relationships. This is one kind of dream in the intermediate zone.

In other intermediate dreams, the main character is the other figure rather than the dreamer because the center of I-ness is still some distance from the heart of the deeper domain. The dreamer may only be a removed observer of the other main character (Figure 4). A step deeper in this intermediate zone and the dreamer may be an interactive participant with the other figure as the main character. In these two cases, the feeling may be bad or good.

There is a special case when the other figure is the main character and the center of I-ness is extremely close to the deeper domain, on the verge of entering it. The other figure will be "compelling" because it is as if the center of I-ness is almost assimilating into that other figure. Just a tiny bit further and the center of I-ness will actually be inside the compelling other figure. The feeling will be very bad— heightened threat, fear, terror, chaos, collapse—because this is the state most feared by the operating domain. It is the state of collapse, death, total loss of its soul, i.e., the center of I-ness.

In the experiential model, some dreams are shallow, some intermediate, and some deep. In terms of allowing us to grasp the deeper dream experiencing, all dreams are important. However, in terms of sheer change in state, the deep dream is qualitatively distinctive and therefore very special.

It is interesting that there is so little overlap between our "deep" dreams and those regarded as very important in other approaches. Perhaps the main exception is the impressive similarity between what we regard as deep dreams and what are regarded as transformative dreams in the functional approach (Corriere et al., 1980).

Lucid dreams are an enigmatic case (Castaneda, 1972; Delaney, 1981; Garfield, 1974; Evans-Wentz, 1967; Rossi, 1985; Stewart, 1954, 1969; Tart, 1969). To begin with, I have rarely come across such dreams in my own personal dream work or in the dreams of my patients, so I have no solid basis for placing them in the schema. My tendency is to consider lucid dreams as at the lighter level of intermediate dreams in which the dreamer is a removed observer. This way of regarding lucid dreams is similar to that of Arlow and Brenner (1964), in whose psychoanalytic approach lucid dreams indicate that the ego has not undergone regression but has instead retained its more conscious reality-testing functions, and to that of Freud, who discusses the dreamer having the thought, "After all, it's only a dream":

[The thought] is aimed at reducing the importance of what has just been experienced and at making it possible to tolerate what is to follow. It serves to lull a particular agency to sleep which would have every reason at that moment to bestir itself and forbid the continuance of the dream—or the scene. . . . It is too late to suppress [the dream] and accordingly the censorship uses these words to meet the anxiety or the distressing feeling aroused by it. (Freud, 1900, 488–9)

Changes in depth of dreams within a single dream and over a series of different dreams. My impression is that within a single dream the two peaks either are at the same level or vary by one level; in no dream is one peak shallow and the other deep. This impression was exemplified in a soft clinical study of 70 dreams brought to me by 20 patients (Mahrer, 1987a). I randomized the two peak moments in each dream so that I had 140 peak moments which were then placed into the model of depth of dreams. When I examined the relationships between each pair of peak moments in terms of the six categories of dreams in Figure 4, I found that (a) some pairs of peak moments were both at the shallow level, some were both at the intermediate level, and some were both at the deep level; (b) some pairs of peak moments included both intermediate and shallow, and some included both intermediate and deep; and (c) there were no pairs between shallow and deep levels. I had no information on which of the two peaks came first, partly because in a fair proportion of these dreams the patient likewise was unsure of the order.

On the other hand, both the experiential theory of dreaming and the pragmatics of experiential dream work suggest that there ought to be a predictable direction over a series of dreams involving a single dream experiencing (cf. Hall & Nordby, 1972). If a series of dreams does involve a single deeper experiencing, the direction should be toward deep dreams. That is, if a dream or a number of dreams dealing with the same deeper potential is at the shallow or intermediate level, subsequent dreams should be at the deep level.

There are some conditions, however. One is that you are looking at a series of dreams involving the same deeper potential. If you remember dreams every other day for a month or so, it is likely that the dreams will include two to four or so different deeper potentials. The change from shallow or intermediate to deep is only in regard to the same deeper potential. A second condition is that the initial dreams are at the shallow or intermediate level. The third and most important condition is that dream work enables the person to get inside and "be" the dream experiencing. When you undergo the steps of dream work, you are increasing the integrative relationships between the operating and deeper potential. As this occurs, as the deeper potential and the operating domain have more integrated, more friendly relationships, it will be easier for the center of I-ness to move down into the deeper potential.

In other words, effective dream work will have an effect on subsequent dreams. The net effect will be that of moving from shallow to intermediate to deeper dreams in which the dreamer is the main character and the feeling is good. Boss likewise understands that effective therapeutic work will show itself in the nature of subsequent dreams:

> [Dreams] show that in concrete cases, the content of the dreaming experience is an excellent indicator of the effectiveness — or failure — of Daseinsanalytic treatment. Whenever therapy is having little or no effect, the dream entities, and the dreamer's attitude toward them, usually undergo little or no alteration. (Boss, 1977, p. 142)

There is a final direction of change. This occurs in persons whose dream work is soundly effective so that the deeper dream experiencing becomes genuinely a part of the operating domain. When this marvelous change occurs, a new, even deeper potential will begin appearing in dreams. In other words, these will begin to show new dream experiencings. Contrast this, for example, with the Adlerian position, in which persons who approach optimal functioning are expected to have fewer dreams: "We should expect, therefore, that the more the individual goal agrees with reality, the less a person dreams; and we find that it is so. Very courageous people dream rarely for they deal adequately with their situation in the daytime" (Ansbacher & Ansbacher, 1956, p. 359), a position that prompted Jones (1970) to wonder if Adler remembered many of his dreams: "We must suspect that Adler did not remember many of his dreams, for he repeatedly spoke of dreams, and of dreaming, in prejudiced ways" (p. 78).

The main purpose of this chapter is to describe the various ways of working with dreams. In the next chapter we concentrate on the experiential methods.

CHAPTER 9

How to Discover the Dream Experiencing

THE PURPOSE OF THIS CHAPTER is to show you how to attain the dream experiencing. This means that you have the experiencing, you undergo it, you are reached and touched by it. Virtually everything you do in dream work swings around this chapter since everything you have done so far is aimed toward getting the dream experiencing, and everything that follows is based on the dream experiencing.

THE METHODS OF ATTAINING THE DREAM EXPERIENCING

You can use any of the four methods described below, but, as we will see, the nature of the peak moment will call for one or two especially. After introducing the methods I will provide some guidelines and illustrations of when and how to use each of them.

(1) Be the Dreamer and Penetrate
Through the Bad Feeling

I recommend using this method when the peak feeling is bad or very bad, mildly discomforting or so threatening that you are blasted awake. It does not matter whether the main character is the dreamer or the other figure, or whether you have trouble identifying who the main character is.

This method consists of penetrating through the bad feeling and exposing yourself to whatever the bad feeling is about or hides. It means having the bad feeling more and more, penetrating into its very nature until you have the experiencing about which you are having the feeling. The feeling is like a corridor through which you pass to arrive at the experiencing, at something that is going to happen, at the underlying experiencing of what is occurring right now.

The difficult part of this method is exposing yourself to the bad feeling. If you are scared or guilty, then you will be feeling it more, gripped more and more by the bad feeling, opening more of yourself to the feeling. This adds a new dimension to the bad feeling, for now you are coming closer and closer to that about which you have the bad feeling. The net result is that the unpleasantness of the feeling increases manifold as you penetrate down into and open up the nature and content of the bad feeling and its underlying experiencing.

In the peak moment, you are on snowshoes in the mountain snow, trying to get away from the feared pursuer, and your legs become heavy. You slow down and then collapse. Here he comes. You are scared. As you enter into this peak moment and allow yourself to be filled with the scary feeling, you are confronted with questions. What are you scared of? Why are you so scared? What are you scared is going to happen? The more you open up the nature of the scared feeling, the more you can ask these questions about the opened-up aspect of the scary feeling, and the closer you come to the dream experiencing.

In the peak moment, you are filled with guilt as you realize that you put the wrong needle into your brother-in-law's arm. Instead of a sterile needle, you inadvertently used one that was infected with a fatal disease. Allow yourself to have the guilty feeling. Be even more guilty. What are you so guilty about? What is the meaning or significance of the act about which you are filled with justified guilt? What is going to happen that entitles you to the guilt? The answers bring you closer and closer to the experiencing.

(2) Describe the Scene From Outside the Dreamer and the Bad Feeling

Like the first method, this one is used when the feeling is bad. Bad feelings have a way of locking you in, keeping you filled with the bad feeling so that you have no freedom of movement to get into the experiencing. Once you are filled with fear or fright or worry, you will tend to be frozen in and by this bad feeling. In the first method you go even deeper into the bad feeling until it dumps you into the underlying experiencing. In the present method you simply disengage from the dreamer entirely.

The method consists of being in the scene, staying in the peak moment, but no longer as the dreamer. Situate yourself at some distance from the dreamer and the other figures in the peak moment. Pretend that you are an invisible, nonparticipating observer of what is happening here in the scene. This maneuver extracts you from the grip of the bad feeling. You are no longer feeling frightened or worried or any other kind of bad feeling. You are still in the scene, watching, seeing, able to describe what is happening, but you are now in a new posture, a new position.

In this new position, you can describe what is happening, and your description can now engage you in what each figure is doing. As you describe the dreamer and the other figures, be exceedingly open to the experiencing in the figure you are describing. As you describe what each figure is doing, how the figure is being, what is going on inside the figure, you will be coming closer and closer to the experiencing.

In the scene with the dreamer on snowshoes, you are free to describe the dreamer and the pursuer. One of these may be the main character, the one housing the experiencing. Yet, being outside the dreamer, you are also free of the dreamer's scary feeling. Accordingly, you are free to describe what you see until you are gripped with an experiencing: "He is trying to get away from the other fellow. He is maybe 20 feet from him and then he slows down. He is unable to move fast any more. He is going to be overtaken. The other guy is going to get him. He is just there. He stops! He stops and the other guy is going to get him. He just lets it happen! He didn't get away!"

Make sure that you describe both figures, especially when you are not certain which one is the main character. You can say, "That other guy is after him, just pursuing him. He is mad at the guy and going to get him. He is really out to get him, and he is working at it. When the other guy slows down and practically stops, he can get him. He is coming closer and closer and is practically on him. Yes, he is just about to get him and reach him and maybe beat him or grab him or do something!"

The more you can extract yourself from the bad feeling, the easier it is to describe what is there before you in a sort of "good form," a form that is a good-feelinged experiencing. The dreamer may be gripped with guilt as he injects the needle in the brother-in-law's arm, but the bad feeling is bracketed as he describes what is happening from the vantage point of a third person in the scene: "The person is sticking the fellow with a needle. It's going to kill the fellow. He is just killing him! He is injecting him with something and it's going to kill him! He's killing the other guy. He's just killing him! My God! That's awful! Or something! That sure as hell gets rid of the brother-in-law!"

(3) Be the Other Figure

Use this method when there is some other figure in addition to the dreamer. The "figure" may be another person, an animal or object, a dog or a gorilla or a snake, a burning bush or a tornado or a flying saucer. The important thing is that there is another figure in the peak moment, a fair possibility that this other figure may be the main character. In some dreams it seems rather clear that the other figure is indeed the main character. In other dreams it seems that the dreamer is probably the main character. As long as you think that perhaps the other figure may be the main character, it is safe to use this method.

It does not matter whether the feeling is good or bad. Be the other figure regardless of feeling. Interestingly, when the feeling is bad, being the other figure is an effective way of bracketing the bad feeling, for once you enter into the other figure, you have essentially disengaged from the dreamer's bad feeling.

The method consists of getting inside the skin of the other figure in this peak moment. You are to be this other figure, to see through his eyes, to carry out what he is carrying out, to have his thoughts and ideas and feelings. As you do this, you will experience something. That is what we want.

In the dream, you had very bad feelings as you were unable to get away from the pursuer on snowshoes. Suppose that you allowed yourself to get inside the skin of the pursuer, to feel what it is like to be after the dreamer and to see that he is slowing down and now you are going to get him. Here is your chance. "I've been after him and I'm going to get him now, and then I will be right on him! I can pounce on him and thrash him or kill him! I caught up with him! I got him!" In so doing, there is some experiencing welling up in you. That is the goal.

As in the Gestalt method, you are to be the other figure and to allow yourself to be reached and affected by the experiencing. Unlike the Gestalt approach, you are to be the other figure or object in the peak moment, whereas in the Gestalt approach you are to be the other figures and objects throughout the whole dream. Secondly, you are to be this other figure within the specific peak moment, whereas in the Gestalt approach there is much more room merely to be the other figure or object in general.

(4) Be the Dreamer and Have the Experiencing Connected With the Good Feeling

Use this method when the feeling is a good one and when there are fair prospects that the dreamer is the main character. Any kind of good feeling will do as long as it is quite clearly a pleasant feeling. The dreamer may be doing anything at all as long as there is some reasonable prospect that the dreamer is the main character.

Carrying out this method means that you are to start with the good feeling and then open it up so that you are undergoing that about which you are having the good feeling. There is always some experiencing connected with the good feeling. Have the good feeling and allow yourself to dilate it so as to include the connected experiencing. Suppose that you are feeling very excited and pleased, joyous and alive, and you are having these good feelings as you are doing a complicated jump in a figure skating competition in front of thousands of spectators in the arena. You are up in the air, twisting and turning, and you land perfectly on the ice. Dilating the good feeling allows you to undergo what it is like to perform the wonderful feat, to be so very accomplished, to perform in front of all these people. Here is the undergoing of the experiencing.

These are the four methods. They are options, for in many peak moments you can use several of these methods. Each method will enable you to attain the experiencing so you are free to use any method(s) that seem appropriate. The following guidelines will help you to use these methods carefully and well.

GUIDELINES FOR USING THE METHODS OF ATTAINING THE DREAM EXPERIENCING

These guidelines show you how to use the method for getting at the dream experiencing. They come into play once you enter into the peak moment.

Use the Methods That Fit What Is Occurring in the Peak Moment

Each of the four methods is called for by some characteristic of the peak moment. For example, use the method of penetrating down through the bad feeling only when there is a bad feeling. Use the method of being the other figure only when there is another figure. If there is another figure and the feeling is bad, you might use both of these methods. As you become skilled in going from the peak moment to the use of one or two of the methods, you will carry this out smoothly and naturally, with little thinking. But for now let us do some thinking about the nature of the peak moment and the kinds of methods that fit. Here are some characteristic features of the peak moment and the methods that are fitting for each:

If the feeling is bad, then you can be the dreamer and penetrate through the bad feeling (method 1), you can describe the scene from outside the dreamer and the bad feeling (method 2), and you might also be the other figure (method 3) if there is some other figure who might qualify as a main carrier. It pays to use a few of these appropriate methods when the feeling is bad.

If the dreamer is the only figure in the peak moment, and if the feeling is bad, you can describe the scene outside the dreamer and the bad feeling (method 2), or you can be the dreamer and penetrate through the bad feeling (method 1). If the dreamer is the only figure and the feeling is good, you can be the dreamer and have the experiencing connected with the good feeling (method 4).

In most peaks, the dreamer and another figure are interacting, and either may be the main character. You may be the other figure (method 3). If the feeling is bad, you can be the dreamer and penetrate through the bad feeling (method 1). You can also describe the scene from outside the dreamer and the bad feeling (method 2). If the feeling is good, you can be the dreamer and have the experiencing connected with the good feeling (method 4). The final condition is when the dreamer is a removed observer, only witnessing the peak moment without participating. You can be the other figure (method 3). If there are two other figures, this means being one and then being the other.

It sounds complicated but it isn't when you learn to attend to whether the feeling is good or bad, whether the dreamer is the only figure or there is an interaction, or whether the dreamer is a removed observer. These distinguishing peak characteristics go easily with appropriate methods.

In almost every peak scene it is both quite natural and conservative to use several methods even if you end up with two different experiencings. That is just fine.

Really Be and Behave in the Peak Moment

As you use one of the methods, let yourself really be and behave in the peak moment as if it were real, as if you were really in the scene. When you behave, carry forward the behavior as if it were really taking place in the immediate live scene. Say all the words in the present tense, for then it is occurring right here and right now. When you behave, do it within this present moment. When you interact, interact directly with and toward the other figure or object. When you penetrate through the bad feeling, make the opened-up feeling absolutely real. When you are being the other figure, truly be inside the other figure and then carry out the actions of the other figure as if they were real. When you are the dreamer with good feeling, be wholly in this peak moment and dilate the good feeling so as to have the connected experiencing that is real. Even when you describe the scene from outside the dreamer and the bad feeling, allow what is occurring before you to be as real as can be.

The experiencing will occur, will grip you and fill you, only when you are really being and behaving in the peak moment. Looked at the other way, when you use a proper and fitting method and you allow yourself to be and behave in the real scene, you will be gripped and filled by the experiencing.

Keep Going Until the Bodily Sensations Are New and Strong

The experiencing is present when you have bodily sensations that are new and relatively strong. You will have a chill down your back, stomach muscles will clench up, tears will be ready, there may be a shooting pain in your shoulder or a dizziness in the head, you will feel warm and sweaty, there will be a trembling in the hands or feet or arms or legs, your chest will feel tight, your heart will beat faster, your skin will itch, there will be sexual sensations, your legs will get heavy. The bodily sensation is not the experiencing, but it signals that the experiencing is here. If there are no bodily sensations, then keep going until they appear.

When you are working on your own dream, you will know when the bodily sensations are new and strong. When you are the therapist, you will know because there will be new and strong bodily sensations in your own body. Every time the patient talks, let those words be as if they are coming in and through you: "When he goes I will miss him. He'll be going soon and I don't want him to go. . . . I just feel like I'll miss him so, 'cause we all love him. . . . He's my grampa and there's no reason to leave; . . . I think, I guess if he leaves he'll never come back. . . . " With these final words something new happens in the body. Both therapist and patient may have similar bodily sensations of getting ready for crying, with puffiness in the eyes and cheeks. These sensations just appeared, palpable and quite present. This means the experiencing is right at hand.

At this point you experience something that is most likely new.

One of the most consistent guidelines is that (a) from the beginning you will have a predetermining hint about the nature of the experiencing, and (b) you will almost always be mistaken. You may sense that the dream probably has to do with loss, or expressing anger, or protecting yourself against hurt. I regard these easy hypotheses as the work of the operating domain, trying to make its own sense of the dream. These prejudgments are interesting, common, and almost always off the mark. This same distrust is found in some of the interpretive approaches, where the person is warned not to pay much attention to these easy premature interpretations:

> If one thinks one has the whole meaning of it straight away it is almost certain that the real meaning remains concealed. The interpretation of a dream then involves a search for those areas of unconscious activity in which the psyche may reveal more of its secret workings than is ordinarily perceived in waking consciousness. (Henderson, 1980, p. 377)

Indeed, if the therapist or patient have a premature expectation of the meaning, that alone is grounds for suspicion:

> . . . Jung warned that any interpretation that meets the expectations of the interpreter or dreamer should be regarded with suspicion, because such an interpretation is presumptuous and does not overcome the dissociation between conscious and unconscious. (Mattoon, 1984, pp. 96–97)

It is the operating domain that describes the dream as a castration dream, a dream of rebirth, a dream signaling the termination of therapy or, in the experiential vocabulary, the experiencing of anger, caring, or closeness. In terms of actually arriving at the experiencings, these are little more than the irrelevant sputterings of the ordinary operating domain's thought processes. Once you actually undergo the dream experiencing, the actual experiencing will typically have nothing to do with these premature thoughts and ideas about the dream experiencing.

In the actual work of attaining the dream experiencing, you will be mainly engaged in being in the peak moment. The earlier thoughts about the dream ("it is the experiencing of anger") will have been replaced with the work of being in the dream peak. When you do attain the experiencing, it will indeed be new and different, but you will neither be thinking or feeling, "This is new and different."

But it will be. The experiencing you attain will be sensed as new and different because it will invade you rather suddenly. Here you are in the peak moment, lowering yourself into the main character. Right at this moment you may well be experiencing something, and then the dream experiencing fills you. Here is a new experiencing of being cheeky and forward, pushing and aggressive, or of being silly and a little wacky, unpredictable and outlandish. It was not there a moment before. Now that it is here, it is new.

After Attaining the Experiencing in One Peak, Repeat the Process With the Other Peak

When you are done with the work in one peak, you can describe the experiencing. You can say that the experiencing is that of rage and explosive frustration; or bursting through, getting it done; or softness and tenderness, loving, gentleness. Now that you can describe the experiencing in one peak, start all over again with the second peak. That is, identify where the moment of peak feeling is in this scene. Then clarify and fill in what is happening in the scene. Finally, use a few of the methods to attain the experiencing, and you can describe what this second experiencing is like. Essentially you are repeating the whole process in working with the second peak.

No matter how confident you may be with the experiencing from one peak, work with the second peak anyhow. For one thing, it gives you a good habit to follow in dreams where you are not all that confident from using one peak. Secondly, working with one peak may give you a couple of different experiencings, and you need the second peak to see which one is common to both. Third, no matter how confident you may be from the first peak, the second one will almost always combine with the first so as to add something new or highlight some unforeseen commonality. In other words, you need the experiencings from both peaks to describe what the experiencing is.

Some dreams have three peaks, and you have a choice of using two of three peaks. I prefer using the two peaks that have the most pronounced feeling in peak moments that are the most vivid and detailed. This is generally not much of a problem because three-peak dreams are not very common, and typically one of the peaks has a more muted feeling in a more diffuse peak moment.

ILLUSTRATIONS OF HOW TO USE THE METHODS
TO ATTAIN THE DREAM EXPERIENCING

Chapter 6 showed you how to get inside the peak scene so that you are living and being in this scene at least to some extent. Here we will illustrate how to use the methods to get at the experiencing. The illustrations are taken from work with patients, but the methods are used in the same way if you work with your own dreams. Accordingly, the illustrations are for both therapists and persons working on their dreams independently.

The illustrations are organized into categories such as "when the dreamer is the main character and the feeling is good." However, when you are doing dream work you do not have to think, "in this peak the dreamer is the main character and the feeling is good, therefore I will use the method in which I get inside the dreamer and open up the good feeling." Instead, once you are living and being in the peak scene, you will almost naturally use the appropriate methods.

When the Dreamer Is the Main Character and the
Feeling Is Good, Open Up the Good Feeling

In these cases the simplest and most natural method is for the person to get inside the dreamer and to amplify or dilate the good feeling so as to undergo the experiencing to which the good feeling is connected. When you clarify and enter into the scene, you will start to have the good feeling once again, and you will be living and existing in the peak moment. Once you are in the scene, the key to the experiencing is through the good feeling.

Start with that good feeling and go to what it is connected to, both "inside" and "outside." If the good feeling is one of being excited and on edge, happily expectant, then the experiencing occurs when we open up what it is connected to inside. The therapist asks, "What do you feel so good about? What's happening that is making you feel so excited? What is so good and exciting in all this?" She says, "It's mine, it's all mine! I made it! It's really mine!" These words define the experiencing. We can also start with the feeling and see what it is connected to "outside." So she says, "The nurse is coming with my baby. I'm going to see her, my baby, my very own baby!"

In the peak moment ("Flying the airplane, and piloting the plane on the ground"), the dreamer is having delightful feelings. We pick up what the patient is saying as he is describing the peak moment in detail:

Pt: The sun shines off the wing, little glints of sunshine, and there's a stripe. It's a classy looking plane. Clean. The white looks great, and I feel excited. I really feel good. (He is concentrating mostly on the details of the scene and also the nature of the good feeling. Now we are ready to go further. The therapist is in the dreamer's perspective, and is sharing the good feeling. We can open up the good feeling to get at what the good feeling is connected to.)

T: You really appreciate this piece of machinery.

Pt: It's a thing of beauty. Sure I do.

T: But you are happy! I mean you're almost on cloud nine here. You're kind of exhilarated and you love this. What the hell's so pleasing about all this?

Pt: I'm driving this beauty! Here, right here in traffic. I can maneuver it. Well I'm doing it slowly, but I'm doing it! It's downtown, and I think it's noon, and there are lots of people. I'm really doing a job. This corner is hard to do and I had to take it easy, go slow, and I'm doing a good job!

The therapist has new, pleasant feelings in her body. She is also experiencing something, something real and viable. She is undergoing something. We can describe the nature of this new experiencing as the sense of being capable of handling it well, of doing a rather special thing, of being responsibly in charge and carrying it off. These words describe the experiencing in one peak of the dream.

Once you are in the peak scene, having the good feeling, keep going until you have something new, until you have some kind of experiencing. It spins off the nature of the good feeling.

In the peak moment, the feeling is pleasant relief. She had walked toward church, placed a bag of her clothes along the path, and continued to church. In the peak moment she has not yet entered the church. Instead, she decides to go back along the path and fetch her bag. In the moment of decision she has this nice feeling of relief. We can remain inside the dreamer, start with the good feeling of relief, and see what kind of experiencing we arrive at:

T: It's a great feeling. Relief. I finally made a decision. That's it . . . no, no. Relief that I decided to do what I wanted to do—take off for a while.

Pt: I hated going to church and I realized that I didn't have to.

T: Ah! So the good feeling, relief, that's when you realize you can avoid the rotten church. It's about the church.

Pt: Well, I got my belongings in a bag, a dress, lots of things. I'm running away from home.

T: So maybe it's relief about finally leaving home, it's leaving home, and the church isn't such a . . .

Pt: Fuck it! I'm not going to listen to them say more, my father and my mother! What the fuck! (Laughs) It's supposed to be my duty to go to church and pray! Pray to God! Let them all follow the rules! Not me!!

Here we have arrived at an experiencing of independent rebelliousness, defiance, getting away and being free, saying no.

Pursue what the good feeling is connected to. Here is a good feeling. What is it coming from? In the peak moment, she is running along a causeway that gradually submerges under water, with increasing obstacles. Yet the feeling is wonderful. She describes it as a wonderful feeling of confidence. Notice how she opens up the feeling until the experiencing occurs:

T: Yeah, confidence. Here you are, running. Now there's water over your ankles, right? And there are all sorts of impediments, dips, things. It should be hard as hell to run. But you! You're still barreling along. And you feel good!! How do you get off feeling confident?

Pt: Sure, the path is crumbling, but I'm going to do it. It's all under control, and I'm moving ahead rapidly. I'm flying along. I can cope, and I feel quite sure. I got a feeling of freedom, just joy, 'cause everything's fine, the path's leading me on. I'm going on like a ball of energy moving on. Even if something else comes up, I feel that, shit, here's another damned obstacle and I'm going to do it, no strain!

At this point, the therapist is having a sense of exploding self-confidence, a sense of being able to handle obstacles, an energetic ball of energy. This is the experiencing.

In these peaks, the only person is the dreamer and, since the feeling is good, it is natural to stay with the dreamer. If the dreamer is the main character and the feeling is good, use this method even if the dreamer is interacting with another figure. You are always free to be that other figure and see what experiencing you get by doing so.

In the peak ("Maniac with the knife, and controlling the maniac"), she is in the midst of a group of people who are terrified by a fellow with a knife. After he has threatened to kill them, she starts talking to him and, when the feeling is strongest, he is no longer a terrifying person. Instead, he is whimpering, crying like a pathetic little boy. Notice how her opening of the good feeling attains the experiencing, and how the good feeling is connected to both inside and outside elements:

Pt: . . . I can't believe it, that it worked. I feel great, power, a feeling of power. It worked. I brought him back. I have him in my control. I established contact with him. The other people are still scared. I got him. I hooked him. They're relying on me to make it right.

All of this points toward an experiencing while describing what the good feeling is connected to, both inside (power, control) and outside. Maybe the experiencing involves the fellow with the knife (power and control over him) or perhaps the other people in the group (they are scared and relying on her to make it right).

T: And you do have him in control, so you're doing it, and they can all rely on you.

Pt: I'm pretending that I really care. I'm being warm, trying to diffuse him. It's working! I can do it! I can tone this guy down! I don't believe it! He's just a run-of-the-mill guy and I'm more competent! I can take care of him!

As therapist I feel something now, something beyond a mere good feeling. I am actually experiencing a sense of power and control over him, a competent taking charge of him.

The final illustrations come from both peaks of a dream ("Cupping the woman's breast, and the tiny mines explode"). In one peak, he is lying down with a woman and places his hand on her breast:

Pt: I cup her breast and I feel warmth, wonderful warmth. We're head to head. She's wonderful, so different from me, and all of this is so, shouldn't happen, like we've slid into another life. She's on her elbows, and we are, our bodies are overlapping. We're directly opposite one another, lying on the grass, and both on our stomachs.

T: And the feeling is wonderful, wonderful warm. What makes it so wonderful? And the warm is good. In what way? (The therapist is searching for the inner part of what the feeling is connected to. But the patient opens up much more until the experiencing happens.)

Pt: I'm amazed when my hand reaches out and touches her. It's so lovely, and she's so lovely, like you radiate happiness, like you're the goddess of loveliness. I'm surprised! I'm doing something unconventional! Acted on impulse! Just reached out! Impulsively! Like a comedian! I feel so . . . playful!

Now we can identify an experiencing of delightful spontaneous impulsiveness coming not only from the inner side of the good feeling, but also from what the dreamer is doing and the way he is doing it. Something quite new happens when he opens up the inner part of the feeling until there is an actual experiencing of surprise and impulsivity and playfulness. Something quite new also happens when he clarifies the outer aspect wherein his hand just reaches out and touches her breast. Both the inside and outside faces of the good feeling open up the experiencing of impulsiveness, spontaneity, being outrageously playful.

The other peak moment in this dream also includes a good feeling. The dreamer notices a small mound of brass casings in the driveway of his home. The mines are tiny, and had been there for years " . . . but they never exploded. Maybe no one drove over them. I get some large stones and drop them on the mines and, holy shit, it explodes! It blows up!" We start with the exciting feeling of "holy shit" and proceed to open up its inner and outer aspects so that the experiencing comes forth:

T: Holy shit? What the hell is so "holy shit" about doing this? You're blowing up mines!
Pt: Yeah! I'm blowing them up! I got these stones and I'm dropping them on the mines. I feel a little wacky, little out of control and it's just fun! I'm doing a crazy thing! I feel like a silly kid! (He makes a kind of chortling noise.)

Here is an experiencing that may be described as "being a little wacky, out of control, silly and crazy."

When the Situation Is Static and the Feeling Is Bad, Penetrate Through the Bad Feeling

In these peaks there is virtually no motion, no action, movement, interaction. The situation is static. If you were a removed observer, you would have practically no clues as to the experiencing. The only clues are inside the dreamer's head. We can get at the experiencing by penetrating through the bad feeling. Ask what the person is scared of, bothered about, guilty of, what is going to happen that is so awful. Open up the bad thoughts and feelings until you have some bodily sensations. What you are undergoing, signaled by the bodily sensations, is the experiencing.

In the peak, there have been some strange goings-on in a large corporation that is somehow a hospital. A man has just been wheeled away on a stretcher and, in the peak, the dreamer is alone in the hallway. Clarification of the peak shows that the dreamer is standing still, no one else is present. Everything is indeed static.

Pt: I'm scared.

T: I know. What are you scared of?

Pt: I don't know what move to make or what is possible.

T: So if you don't make the right move, something scary will happen? You have to make the right move, or something scary will happen. (We are penetrating the bad scary feeling, pointing in the right direction.)

Pt: I'd be done away with. I've been very naïve. I have evidence, my photographs. Part of the meeting. How can I get out? I really have no place here, and I'm implicated. I took pictures. I suggested that he not go.

T: So the fellow that's been wheeled away, he's the problem. And you really are implicated. It sounds like something may happen. You're scared that you are really in trouble.

Pt: I'm a witness that he really isn't himself.

T: Oh God! So you're in trouble. You really are in trouble. What are you scared of?

Pt: Something about their hushing people up, and their hushing up the president, the one they wheeled away. Something about mutilation. I'm terrified they're going to do it to me!! Get me! Mutilate me!

Now there are bodily sensations. With these sensations, the experiencing is that of being caught, mutilated, tortured. We arrived at this experiencing by penetrating through the feeling of being scared, by her filling in the circumstances and conditions of what she is so scared of. It is a matter of penetrative clarification of the nature of the bad feeling.

Start with the feeling. Invite the patient to detail the feeling so that its bad nature can be penetrated more and more. In the peak ("The fantastic skier and the dope shop"), the dreamer is in the "head" shop, walking slowly up a few stairs. There is no talk, no action or interaction. After describing the loud music, fluorescent lighting, the odors, we turn to the bad feeling.

T: The feeling is not good. You don't feel comfortable here. Can you describe that more?

Pt: It's not where I want to be. It's too strident and flashy, pretentious, phony. It pushes on me, like an overload on my senses. It's too showy. Too many demands. The loud music. It's all too much. It's too chintzy, too full of hype. Not my kind of place. It's not real.

T: OK, sounds like you just want to criticize the shop. Like it is just too much for you. I can't tell whether you're just going to walk out of here 'cause it is repulsive somehow, or you're going to let it invade you or something like that. Just what is the feeling like?

Pt: It's too much. Too flashy. Too many demands. I feel worried, worried.

T: Worried? Like something might happen to you?

Pt: (Very absorbed) Being like the store. Being like that. Being flashy and showy. Flashy and putting on a show, being something special. "Hey everybody, come and look at me!" That kind of flashy.

With these words, something strange happened in my body. My breathing became shallower and I felt something a little exciting. I was not having the uncomfortable feeling of the excessive stimuli of the shop. Instead, I was having the experiencing of giving in to the flashiness, being special, putting on a show. It was new and quite vibrant. We arrived at this experiencing by starting with the bad feeling and by penetrating down into it, and as the bad feeling involved aspects of the shop, we included these aspects in the further penetration of the bad feeling.

Very often the bad feeling is so solidly connected to the circumstances of the peak moment that you really wonder if there is any place further to go. There always is. You can always penetrate further into what is so awful about the peak moment. Consider a peak ("Moving into the dirty apartment, and holding onto the car") in which the dreamer is standing alone in an apartment. It is dirty and windowless, with nothing but a filthy mattress and a makeshift toilet in the middle of the room. He described his feelings, solidly connected with the apartment:

Pt: I feel like I'm at the bottom, worse than living in a slum. Like eating shit, like it's all over. The place is so dirty and slimy, like starting all over. It's a feeling of starting over with nothing. I have nothing. Being on skid row. Despair, I feel despair, and I'm looking at the mattress.

This is just the kind of feeling that fits the circumstances of this peak situation. Where do we go from here? Let the person go deeper:

T: This is terrible. But why is this so bad—for you? When you feel this, why is this so awful? You feel bad that it means starting all over, and having nothing, and here you are in this awful place. What is the underside of starting all over like this?

Pt: It's terrible. I'm alone (and now there are tears). So very alone, and just
    alone, and it's unfair (more tearfulness). What's the use. . . . There's
    no hope! Like an old bum! By myself . . .

Now we come to something new, the experiencing of hopelessness,
aloneness, being an old bum. When the patient cries, you have conspicuous bodily sensations. You know something is happening and
that the experiencing is right here.

Consider the peak where the dreamer ("He is mounting my dog,
and too far to walk") is standing at the base of a mountain, quite still.
Nothing is happening. By clarifying the peak it is shown that you are
negotiating how to walk over or around the mountain, considering
the snow and the terrain, and so on. The feeling is also defined.

Pt: . . . and I'm feeling sort of tired, I guess. I don't want to do it. It's a
    waste of time 'cause I'd have to walk all the way around. But I do want
    to get over the mountainside, but it seems like just so much trouble. I
    don't feel good. I don't like it, and I'm just not sure, I don't know.

You have a number of options. What is so bad about going and doing
it? Maybe it is just tiring, and you don't really have your heart in it?
Or would it be so awful if you just decided the hell with it? Is that so
awful? Or are you worried that you'll maybe just stand here until it's
too late — provided that you are doing the thing for some reason?

T: I'm not quite sure why the hell you'd want to go over or around the
   mountain anyhow . . .
Pt: I'm not sure.
T: Well, what's so awful about just slogging ahead? Is that going to mean
   something devastating? Or suppose you just decided to quit and not do
   it. Is that terrible? What's wrong?
Pt: I worry that I won't do it, or I'll start and then . . . I don't know. I feel
    like it's just too much for me. . . . It's not convenient . . . (There is a
    slow, kneading-like movement in the belly.) I'm afraid that, well, I
    don't like it.
T: Something's starting up in me here. It's not convenient. Maybe not going
   along the mountain? Is deciding that bad somehow?
Pt: I'm afraid I won't do it (a quivering sensation in the chest). The hell with
    it! I won't do anything!

With these words there is a palpable quivering sensation in the chest,
and the experiencing is that of saying no, refusing, saying the hell
with it.

When the dreamer is in a truly static situation and the peak feeling is bad, you have almost no option other than penetrating down into the bad feeling. Give the patient plenty of space to feel the increasingly bad underside. Look for what is so painful and unpleasant about this particular bad feeling. As you probe further into the bad feeling, your bodily sensations will tell you that right here something is happening. This signals the experiencing. Put it into words.

When the Dreamer Is a Removed Observer, Be the Other Figure

It is rather easy to identify peak moments where the dreamer is a removed observer, not really a part of the scene, more like someone sitting in the audience watching a play. When this is happening, the experiencing is housed within the other figure or figures. Accordingly, the best way of getting at the experiencing is by getting inside and being the other figure(s).

Tell the patient that she is to get inside the skin of the other figure. Provide explicit instructions on how to do this. Emphasize readiness and willingness.

This method is used for both good and bad feelings. If the feeling is good, it is relatively simple for the patient to enter into the other figure. However, when the feeling is bad, you need plenty of outside description of the setting and plenty of description of the other figure. Then, after sufficient description of what that other figure is like, is thinking and feeling, you can invite the patient to get inside that other figure.

When the peak feeling is a good one, the only hurdle is disengaging from the removed observer and getting inside the other figure. In the peak moment ("The fantastic skier, and the dope shop"), the dreamer is observing a skier doing acrobatics. The patient had described the scene in some detail and had already described the skier in sufficient detail to enter into the peak moment. After giving instructions for how to get inside and be the skier, the therapist invites the patient to describe even more of the skier, every detail, both inside and outside.

T: Let yourself see him closer now. Tell what you see and what you know he is thinking and doing. Move closer so you can describe everything.
Pt: It really is like ballet, the twists and turns, all in the air, like he's flying, gliding. There's such grace, graceful. He's so good, no effort, so easy for him. Doing it, just looping up and over so graceful and really skilled. It's so easy . . .

T: Can you sense what it is like for him to be doing this? Like being inside his body, like being him right now. Let yourself be inside him, right now, doing this. Do it, do it as if you're being this fellow. OK? Yes?

Pt: I'm so accomplished and practiced. It's so easy. Up in the air, lazily floating and up and up and now over . . . yes . . . (Here is where the bodily sensations arise.) . . . I'm a star. Performing. They are amazed, watching ballet in skis. Performing for them. They think I'm incredible . . .

Now the bodily sensations are present, and the good-feelinged experiencing is that of performing, putting on a show, being an accomplished performer.

In some scenes the dreamer is not wholly removed, but is nevertheless a somewhat removed observer who is having good feelings. The peak is from the dream, "Protecting the bone and holding the breasts." The dreamer and the dreamer's sister had just called their collie, who has a bone. Another dog comes by and the collie protects its bone, squares off against the other dog and the other dog ambles away. The feeling is a good one. After sufficient detailing of the scene, the therapist invites the patient to get inside the collie in this instant, to be the collie.

Pt: There is this dog in front of me. You're a little bigger than me but it's my bone. My bone, and you can't have my bone. It's mine. I have this bone in my jaws, see! Back off! It's mine. It's mine! Grrr! Letting you know! Get back! You better stay away! It's mine! Get the hell away! Grrr!

Now I feel shivers down my back and a tightening of the muscles in my upper back. The experiencing is a standing of my ground, confronting, staking out my territory, protecting what is mine.

When the feeling is bad, you tend to be anchored by the bad feeling. Make sure that you describe the other figure carefully, have all the instructions, and are quite ready and willing. In the peak ("The opponents are squaring off for the kill, and I throw the bomb to one of them"), the dreamer is a removed observer who sees two men engaged in a fight to the death. They are both crouched. One is much older. They fight by using a small black bag filled with something like sand. The bag is thrown back and forth in ritualistic fashion until one kills the other. It seems clear that the dreamer is much more drawn toward the younger man as the main character. However, the feeling is one of heightened anxiety and tension. After the patient provides plenty of detail about the scene and especially the younger combatant, the therapist gives the instructions:

T: Now you are to get inside the younger fellow, to see what it is like to have his thoughts and his feelings. It is as if you are in a crouch and you are squared off against the older fellow. But you are the younger one, not you. You take on his ability and his everything. You take on his thoughts and all his ideas. All the tension and worry that you had as you watched all of this is still there in the you who is watching. But now you leave all that behind and you go inside the fellow who is here, crouching, engaged in this ritualistic fight. You take on the sight of this fellow so that you see the older man. See him there, crouched right in front of you. . . . Now you can talk and feel and act. Take on the person who is engaged in this battle. Show what is happening in you.

Pt: I am going to kill him! I know killing! All I know is killing. I am going to kill him! I am superior. A MOVE! Grabbing him!! GOING TO KILL YOU! DIE! AAAAAhhhhh! Oh Oh.

It was a sudden burst of killing the other one, putting to death, primitive killing.

Sometimes it is very hard to be the other figure. It is almost as if the dreamer senses the experiencing about which the feeling is so bad. In one peak of the dream, "He is mounting my dog, and too far to walk," the removed dreamer is filled with a mixture of worry, frustration, and annoyance as a large animal, a combination mule and dog, is about to mount the dreamer's own smaller dog. The mule-dog is clearly and vividly seen, is the main character, and is described fully by the dreamer. Yet the dreamer is very reluctant to move into being the mule-dog when the therapist gives the invitation.

Pt: That's repulsive! I can't do that! It's an animal!

T: You can try it and see what happens. But if it is too bad, if you really do not want to, then you need not. It is your choice. You can try or you can decline.

Pt: Look what he's doing!

T: I know. I know. Would you prefer to leave it go?

Pt: Well, I'll try.

T: You can try until the feelings get too bad, then you can always stop.

Pt: (Pause) I have this huge upper body. Massive. And I have my paws around, I'm grabbing this lovely little dog. Mounting her . . . and . . . I feel powerful. Real powerful. And . . . I got this huge red prick . . . this huge prick . . . (The bad feelings are left behind now and there are bodily sensations starting.) . . . I want to . . . just shove it

in. I am big. Tough. I got this dog, just locked her . . . No one messes
with me! NO ONE! Oh! Shoving it in and in and again and again and
there and there and THERE . . . (Heavy and hard grunting noises.)

The therapist is filled with the experiencing of thrusting animal sexuality, macho bruteness and sexual strength.

In each of these illustrations, when the experiencing is housed
within the other figure, the dreamer is to disengage from the role of
removed observer and to enter into the other figure. If you are unsure
which other figure is the main character, it pays to try out both other
figures. Generally, however, one other figure is clearly the main character.

When There Is an Interaction Between the Dreamer and Other Figure(s), Use Several Methods

The above three kinds of dreams (dreamer is the main character
and the feeling is good; situation is static and the feeling is bad;
dreamer is a removed observer) are rather easily recognizable. The
trouble is that these three comprise less than half of the dream peaks.
In most dreams there is an interaction between the dreamer and
another figure or two. You cannot be certain whether the dreamer or
the other figure is the main character housing the experiencing, and
therefore it is not clear what method to use.

The solution is to try out a few appropriate methods. Try one
method with the dreamer as the main character and use another
method with the other figure as the main character. After all, you will
be selecting from only three methods, and the selection is essentially
made for you when you try out the dreamer or the other figure as the
main character.

In each of the following illustrations, the dreamer and other figure
are interacting, we are not certain which is the main character, and
the feeling is good or bad. In these peaks, you can arrive at the
experiencing by (a) being the other figure, (b) describing the scene
from outside the dreamer and the bad feeling, or (c) penetrating
through the bad feeling.

Being the other figure. In many peaks, you have a fairly good
guess that the other figure is the main character. Whether the peak
feeling is good or bad, the other figure is active and moving and is
seen rather clearly. As you clarify more and more of the other figure,

it often happens that you move closer into that other figure. The demarcation diffuses and you sense what the other figure is thinking and feeling and doing. It is as if you get a foretaste of what it is like to be the other figure. When that happens, take the next step and move into the other figure.

In one peak of the dream, "Flying the airplane, and driving the plane on the ground," the dreamer is in a small, two-seater airplane piloted by Katherine Hepburn. As the person describes more of what is occurring, it becomes evident that the dreamer is enthralled by her, mixed in with a feeling of moderate sexual excitement. It is a pretty day. Katherine Hepburn may be naked from the waist up, leaning away from the dreamer. As the patient and therapist enter into the peak and clarify what is happening, it seems that she is doing lazy loops with the plane, as if the plane is on automatic control yet the pilot also is controlling the loops. Katherine seems to be coy, even though she is naked above the waist. The patient is in love with her and yet they are not saying anything to one another. Katherine is piloting the plane without looking straight ahead. Then the patient seems to take the step into the other figure:

Pt: (Laughs) She's a little wild. I mean she's looping the plane but she's still in control, a good pilot I guess. . . . She's outrageous! I mean she has nothing on, and being a little crazy! Like she's going to seduce this guy (notice the wording) while the plane is going in big loops, going along . . .

T: So if we move over inside Katherine Hepburn, and kind of share in what she's doing and thinking and all, just slide over inside her own thoughts and feelings and what she's doing, go ahead.

Pt: Well, I'm sort of in charge of everything here, I mean the plane and things, and doing what I want, just like I want, everything that I want to, piloting the plane here, and being a little crazy, naked and all that, looping the plane, and sexing him up and being crazy but always in control!!

Here is where the bodily sensations arise, and the experiencing is being in control, and letting oneself be a little wild, crazy, impulsive, seductive, outrageous.

In one peak in another dream, the feeling is warm and friendly. The dreamer is in a restaurant made up of small shops and, in the peak, a woman walks by and gives him a friendly pat on the balls. As therapist and patient enter further into the peak, dialogue yields the following:

Pt: She just touches my balls and it feels good. . . . She has dark hair, pretty, and she looks at my body, friendly, says hello. . . . I'm surprised, have a warm feeling. Feel comfortable . . . it's like a greeting, like she's being familiar, sort of like a pat on the bum, that way, a love pat. . . . I'm not thinking of anything, just that she's patting me. . . . She has her hand on my balls, up and down again, for maybe three or four seconds . . . (Then he takes a step toward being inside the other figure.) . . . She's looking at me, a warm smile . . . touching me, smiling and pleasant, both feeling a little aroused, the look on her face . . . so easy for her . . .

T: So what she's thinking and feeling, what's going on inside her, you know, if we somehow share what's happening inside this woman, like getting inside her and sharing what she's doing and . . .

Pt: So easy just to walk up to this guy and touch him on the balls . . . and feel sexual and casual, real friendly, easy like . . . and to touch him up and down, yeah . . . just rub them, and with a friendly look . . .

What the patient is doing and saying, and the way he is saying it, allows an experiencing of free and easy sexual forwardness, seductiveness, being sexually friendly and open.

When the feeling is bad, it is not so easy to get out of being the dreamer and to get inside the other figure. When the feeling is *very* bad, it is even harder. In the peak ("Maniac with the knife, and controlling the maniac"), the dreamer is terrified of the fellow with the knife. He has just knifed a person in the room, and the rest of the group is frozen in fear. At the peak moment, the fellow has just run the knife lightly over the dreamer's neck, and she is in terror. "I'm just petrified 'cause I'm all alone here with him, they're all over there, and he's a lunatic. He looks crazy . . . scared that he will do something. I don't dare move a muscle . . . I'm scared shitless 'cause I know he can stab me any second. Just a tiny push and he'll stab my heart out. He's tired of being pushed by the group. . . . I can feel my heart pounding. God, I'm terrified." All of this and more comes out as she clarifies what is occurring in the peak moment. Already, she knows what is happening inside the fellow ("Just a tiny push and he'll stab my heart out. He's tired of being pushed by the group"). While we may not be able to get inside the fellow, we can try and open up his perspective enough to gain a sense of the experiencing. If the therapist and patient seem ready to move all the way into the other fellow, that is just fine. But if the heightened and intense bad feeling locks them in the dreamer, we can still lean heavily in the direction of the other fellow's inner perspective.

T: You can sense that he really can stab your heart out, just one tiny little push. He's already tired of being pushed by the group. Keep going. What else is he feeling? He may be a lunatic, but he's having stuff going on inside. What's happening inside him? What's going on inside him? Move closer inside him.

Pt: (Still frightened) He's really on edge here. One little thing can set him off. Bang! He'll do it! He will! Someone'll move or say something. That's all it takes! He's really got us! HE'S GOT US SO HE CAN DO ANYTHING. NO ONE'S GONNA MOVE AN INCH. HE'S IN CONTROL AND HE KNOWS IT!

The new bodily sensations release. The therapist is almost drawn into being inside the fellow, experiencing the sense of sheer control, having them all in his power.

If it seems that you can make the shift into being inside the other figure, the source and object of the very bad feeling, then do so. Otherwise, try and focus the patient's attention down inside the other figure's thoughts and feelings, ideas and intentions.

Even though the person is gripped by the very bad feeling, the leaning can be toward being within the other figure. Entering into the peak ("Slamming the intruder, and panicked about the gorilla") where he is fixated on the gorilla, the patient is already filled with the fear. Well into the scene, the patient says:

Pt: I'm scared to death it's going to break in! Here's this huge damned gorilla in our back yards! It's massive! . . . There's nothing anyone can do! It's huge! It must be 40 feet high! King Kong! Nothing's going to stop it!

T: You're seeing that damned thing. See it. Yes. It has thoughts and ideas. Nothing's going to stop it. Just see inside that gorilla.

Pt: It's standing inside Annie's yard, looking with those beady eyes. It just stops there, not moving, looking back over its shoulder. Stopped. Has that weird look on its face. It isn't scared of nothing!

T: Right! It doesn't have to be, and it sure as hell isn't scared!

Pt: It's just powerful! POWERFUL. It can do whatever it wants!

T: RIGHT.

Pt: It hasn't done anything yet. But it CAN. Anything it WANTS. It knows that no one's gonna mess with it. It's POWERFUL. DAMN. IT'S A POWERHOUSE! BOOM! BOOM! IT'S POWER!!!

Even though the patient has not fully entered into the gorilla, there is a sense of what is occurring inside the gorilla, and the experiencing is that of power—absolute, primitive, raw power. When the feeling is bad, even leaning can provide you with a sense of the experiencing going on within the other figure.

Describe the scene from outside the bad feeling. When there is an interaction between the dreamer and other figures and the feeling is bad, another method is to get around the bad feeling by standing off from the scene and describing what is occurring until the experiencing happens. Mainly, this method circumvents the bad feeling that ordinarily locks in the dreamer and prevents getting near the experiencing. If you can take another vantage point, then you are free of the bad feeling and you can undergo the experiencing.

Consider the peak in which the dreamer is a little girl, jumping up and down with her girlfriend on the bed. The dreamer gets inside the large nightgown of the girlfriend and jumps up and down until the dreamer is aware of her mother standing in the room. "I felt guilty. It was awful. . . . I didn't want her to know we were playing around like that. . . . It was just awful, knowing that she was there. . . . I felt terrible, just terrible, and I was caught. Like having cold water all over you." The therapist invites her to get into a more neutral vantage point:

T: If you could stand over here with me, in the room, just watching, I am going to try and describe what I see. Would you try and stand over here with me? We are about ten feet from the two ladies and the mother when all this is happening. Correct me if I'm wrong. There are these two girls, women, on the bed, and one is inside the nightgown of the other. I'm guessing that the one who got inside the nightgown is naked . . .

Pt: And they're giggling and jumping up and down and then mother comes in. (She is being almost matter-of-fact, with little of the bad feeling, yet a little wary.)

T: OK, go ahead. Keep describing, as if we are right here, watching, maybe invisible.

Pt: They are jumping up and down and silly. Silly. And then mother comes in, and the naked one, I guess the one that started it, she gets all uptight and feels funny because mother came in.

T: Wait a minute! How the hell do you know she feels funny? Maybe she does. But just describe what is going on in front of your eyes.

Pt: These two girls are giggling and jumping up and down. Actually they are naked and clowning and silly and inside one big nightgown.

T: Right. That sounds like fun. So far.

Pt: Yes. And a woman comes in. She's the mother. She catches them. They are being silly. It sounds like they are making a lot of noise. So the mother comes in. What they are doing is acting silly in front of mother. They are sort of being sexual. They are acting like little girls, except that they are, well, mature and I guess they are sexing each other up and doing it in front of . . . (she is laughing in half embarrassment) . . . showing it to mother! They're silly!

Perhaps it is understandable that she feels a bad feeling in connection with the experiencing of sexual silliness and openness, childish sexuality, exhibited freely and openly to mother.

The peak scene often includes a number of figures, any of whom may be the main character, and the feeling is bad. For example, in the peak of the dream, "The wino, the tough guys, and the hurt hand," the dreamer and his friend Walter are walking along a street until they see some tough guys ahead, at which point the dreamer is filled with a feeling of fear that these tough guys will beat them up, so the dreamer invents an excuse of having to go to work and leaves his friend. Is the main character the dreamer, the tough guys, or the friend Walter? As we enter into the peak moment, the patient is increasingly bound by the bad feeling, and he concentrates on how menacing the other guys are and how justified he is for bolting to work. The therapist then gives instructions:

T: Just pretend that you and I are standing nearby and watching and hearing all this. We see the two guys, Walter and his buddy, and we see the tough guys too. And we hear everything, everything the tough guys are saying and between Walter and his friend. Could you just describe what is happening for me? I want to see it through your eyes.

Pt: Walter and his buddy are walking, and I don't think Walter sees the tough guys. But the buddy does, and then the buddy says he has to get to work and he leaves. (From this vantage point, the dreamer is the buddy.)

T: How does he leave?

Pt: He runs away. He's scared. Actually he's just scared of getting beaten up, so he lies.

T: He lies?

Pt: He says he's gotta get to work. Walter doesn't see the tough guys there. They don't have knives or anything, but they're going to cream Walter.

T: Ha!

Pt: He's a coward.

T: Walter?

Pt: No! That guy is a coward. He is too chicken . . . he should tell his friend about the tough guys, but he doesn't. He just runs away. He's a sneaky little bastard who lets his buddy get creamed.

T: He sees trouble and then gets the hell away—forget about his buddy!

Pt: (The feelings are strong now.) Yeah! He saves his ass and lets his buddy be the fall guy, get beaten up! He saves his own ass! Walter's going to have the shit kicked out of him! (We both feel this.)

The experiencing is that of being a sneaky bastard, of the wicked inner pleasure of ducking out and leaving his buddy to be beaten up.

The patient is often uncertain about who the main character is, and is locked into having the bad feeling. Notice how the locking effect of the bad feeling is resolved by taking the new vantage point. Consider the peak moment in the dream, "Late for the wedding, and watching the nurses." The dreamer is a nurse, standing around at a nursing station while all the other nurses are busily rushing around. At the peak, one of the nurses says to her, "You are a nurse. Function." The dreamer is caught, confused and bewildered. She doesn't know what to do, and she is bothered. Should we try out the nurse as a main character, and then try out the other nurse who is speaking to her? While we remain in the dreamer's perspective, there is merely a deepening of the bad feeling of being unable to function, not helping, being new here, just generally feeling unpleasant. But if we stand to the side, we leave behind the dreamer's bad feeling, and this allows us to come closer to the experiencing that is crowded out by the bad feeling.

T: Now I'm off to the side here, watching the scene in front of me. I see a bunch of nurses, and they are all busy moving about efficiently. Something is up. But wait, I see one who is . . . could you come over here with me? Just come over here and describe what you see. Maybe it is different than what I see. You can concentrate on the new nurse there if you want.

Pt: That one is standing there, a little hunched over, maybe feeling left out, but there was an emergency, and the doctor buzzes off to take care and three nurses get to work, and everyone's busy and efficient . . .

T: Except . . .

Pt: That happens every so often on that ward. They got to move fast . . . but she's new. . . . She is almost in the way . . .

T: So everyone's doing their job, all but that new one. "Get away, dink! We got a job to do!"

Pt: Well, she's new here! She really is not helping. Everyone's hopping to it.

They have things to do, not waiting on her or attending to her even if she is new.

T: "Where's the coffee shop? Forget the emergency!"

Pt: She should either help or just get out of the way . . . I guess everyone's busy except her.

T: So what's she doing?

Pt: Nothing. Nothing at all. She's in the way! She's really just in the way. She could help!

T: But she isn't!

Pt: Not at all! No. She isn't helping at all . . .

I get a sense of almost excitement in my body as she is saying these words, almost wickedly. The experiencing in me is one of refusing, defying, staying away, saying no, not being involved.

Penetrate through the bad feeling. When you use this third option, the intensity of the bad feeling will increase until a point is reached where the experiencing emerges. As this happens, the bad feeling may either further increase in intensity or be replaced with the good feelings of sheer experiencing.

In the other peak of the dream, "Late for the wedding, and watching the nurses," the dreamer is to be married. She is skating on a large ice pond looking for her wedding party among a large number of wedding parties. She asks several people where her wedding party is, and she is panicked because she is quite late.

Pt: I'm scared! Where is my wedding? There are so many people, I can't find my wedding!

T: You're scared of what might happen. What is it? If you can't find it, then?

Pt: I'd miss it.

T: All right . . .

Pt: I'd miss my own wedding! I won't be there! (She is quite upset. Her voice is shrill and tight.)

T: Right. They won't go on without you.

Pt: (Still very tense and agitated) It's my own wedding and I'll miss it! All the preparations! I don't know which one it is and I'm skating around aimlessly . . .

T: (It is here that the therapist allows the experiencing of missing my own wedding to occur, free of the bad feeling.) OK, so I miss my wedding, I miss my own wedding. I guess I miss my wedding. Say, I forgot about all the preparations. Now that is getting serious. Missing the wedding—well, at least you have a wonderful excuse. You were ice skating. Hmmm, doesn't sound like such a dandy excuse. (Here is the point where the patient can sustain and even intensify the bad feeling, or she can lighten up and enjoy the sense of letting go of the wedding.)

Pt: (Abrupt hard burst of laughter) I wanted to get married!

T: Why, honeybunch, of course you did. That's why you were gracefully skating around . . . everyone understands, ha ha ha!

Pt: I don't even know who the husband is!!! (This cracks her up and she laughs heartily.)

T: What the hell's the difference? I mean, you miss one wedding, you miss 'em all!

Pt: (Still laughing) We should have just gone skating — whoever he is . . .

We are both undergoing the experiencing of staying away, not getting involved, saying no indirectly.

Sometimes the bad feeling is so gripping that the patient cannot leave go. The dreamer has been on a bus, where she found a whole pile of money. She stuffs some in her pocket but the bulk is left in a little box. She then walks off the bus, realizes she has left the box on the bus, and, with horror, sees the bus pull away. After entering into the peak, we begin penetrating into the feeling, and all the patient can say is how painfully dumbfounded she is standing here and watching the bus pull away. Over and over again she says, "All that money . . . I didn't even realize till it was too late. . . . I feel rotten, just rotten. . . . I don't know why I did that, just forgot. . . . "

Pt: . . . I left all that money on the bus and now it's gone. Just gone! I can't believe it! I don't know what to do!

T: Get a taxi and run after the bus! Stop it and get on it and rescue all the money. That box is mine!

Pt: I just walked off! Like I was in a trance! All that money!

T: Well, if you are going to walk off in trances you're going to leave a lot of little boxes of money on buses.

Pt: I wanted that money. It was mine!

T: How about screaming that so loud the bus driver hears you?

Pt: I don't know what to do!

T: You already did it, dummy! You walked off and left the money in the box!

Pt: DAMN!

T: WHAT THE HELL YOU SO MAD ABOUT?

Pt: I just left the money behind! I just let it go! My God! I just let it go!!

T: You sure as hell did!

The feeling was not good, yet that is as far as we got. Bodily sensations were up and had been for some time. The experiencing was that of giving it up, leaving it go, walking away from it.

Very often, penetrating the feeling means that you are on the verge of some sort of incident, some scene in which the feeling would be more intense. The description of the feeling sheds some forward light on the nature of this incident or scene. Consider the peak from the dream, "Surreptitious in the store, and avoiding one another." The dreamer is in a bookstore, nervously looking at a book of photographs of intercourse, and keenly aware of three or four neighbors who are in other sections of the store. As he clarifies the scene and enters into the peak moment, his feeling is connected to a fear that the neighbors might see him:

Pt: I'm so scared that someone'll see me. I feel vigilant, scared and . . . scared that someone'll just look up and see me. If they see me. . . . I don't know why I don't close the damned book and move around. But here I am. I know someone'll spot me. I feel like a sitting duck. I'm so aware. Like radar.

T: So it might be someone. Someone will suddenly be staring at you. Who?

Pt: Betty, one of them. Betty. She might. Oh God!

T: And? What'll happen?

Pt: She'll see me.

T: OK, so Betty spots you. Ha! Look there!

Pt: Oh God!

T: What? What?

Pt: I don't want her to see me!!

T: Why not? What is so damned awful about her looking up, seeing you there with the filthy book, and . . . what?

Pt: Oh no!

T: Oh no what?

Pt: That'd be terrible?

T: How?

Pt: She'll see me!

T: So what? So she sees you! So what?

Pt: That would be terrible!

T: Just 'cause she's watching you? She knows you're there? Why is this so damned awful? It is! But how?

Pt: I'd want to die! I'm exposed! They'll all be looking at me! They'd all see me! I'm here in this . . . looking at this porno book! They'll see me. God! That's awful!!

The imminent feared scene is one where he is holding this pornographic book and all of the neighbors are riveted on him, keenly aware that he is doing this bad thing. The experiencing is that of being found out, exposed, caught, seen.

Following the guidelines will provide you with some guesses about the nature of the experiencing in one peak moment. When you repeat this procedure with the second peak, you will have some guesses about the nature of the experiencing in that moment. You have now completed step 3.3 in Figure 1, i.e., you have opened up the dream experiencing in both peaks.

IDENTIFYING THE SINGLE COMMON
DREAM EXPERIENCING

The next step is to identify the single common experiencing from the two peaks. You have some words for each of the experiencings in the two peaks. If you and the patient look at the words, are there any commonalities?

Sometimes the two sets of words are virtually identical. Sometimes they overlap a little and you have to look for the commonality. Occasionally you will arrive at a couple of experiencings in a single peak. Then you go to the second peak. Whatever experiencing you get in the second peak will tend to be similar to one of the two experiencings in the first peak. In general, the idea is to look over the words you use to describe the experiencings, paying special attention to what is conspicuously common. That commonality identifies the dream experiencing.

The sense of confidence comes from blending the two experiencings. Sometimes the words are quite similar. In the dream, "Late for the wedding, and watching the nurses," the words used for one experiencing were: refusing, defying, staying away, saying no, not being involved. For the second peak the words were: staying away, not getting involved, saying no indirectly. It is relatively easy to identify an experiencing of saying no, staying away, not being involved. The two sets of words are so close that they are almost interchangeable. After describing the experiencing in the second peak, the therapist turns to the commonality:

T: When you were with the nurses, there was this same feeling, saying no, not doing it, just somehow not getting involved.
Pt: I'm just not going to do it.
T: Yeah, well it happens. I will not.
Pt: Some person! You can't make me . . . !

Usually, the two sets of words are not identical and you must locate the commonality. The actual words used to describe the experiencing in one peak ("Flying the airplane, and piloting the plane on the ground") were: sense of being capable, of handling it well, of doing a rather special thing, of being responsibly in charge and carrying it off. In the second peak the words were: being in control, letting oneself be a little wild, crazy, impulsive, seductive, outrageous.

T: So there's this feeling of being in control of things, and letting yourself be a little wild and impulsive, but within bounds.
Pt: I felt good!
T: Sure did. That's very much like what you ended up feeling in the other part of the dream. A feeling of being responsible and sort of still in control. In both of them, you like being in control all right, being in control and responsible even though you're doing something a little different, impulsive maybe.
Pt: I'm handling things OK. I can handle things!

Often you and the patient can work together in arriving at a way of describing the common experiencing. In the dream, "The fantastic skier, and the dope shop," the two sets of words were: (a) giving in to the flashiness, being special, putting on a show, and (b) performing, putting on a show, being an accomplished performer. After working on the second peak, the therapist says:

T: It seems like what we got to in the other one. Pretty much the same thing.
Pt: Yes. Yes.
T: It's the skier and the shop. They do it all, the lights and the signs.
Pt: Both flashy. Really flashy performances.
T: Yeah! Right!
Pt: Putting on a show.
T: Showy, right. That's a good way to put it, putting on a show.
Pt: The skier was putting on a better one, performing. I didn't care for the shop.
T: Arrogant kid. Performing, flashy, putting on a show.

Notice the common thread in the words used to describe the experiencings in the two peaks on the dream, "Cupping the woman's breast, and the tiny mines explode": (a) delightful spontaneous impulsiveness, a comicalness, spontaneity, being outrageously playful, and (b) being a little wacky, out of control, silly and crazy. Occasionally it is the patient who notices the common thread after getting the experiencing in the second peak:

Pt: I am feeling kind of silly and doing weird things. Breaking out. Playful. That's the same thing in the other part.

T: With the breast . . .
Pt: I felt the same way, kind of silly, and like it was all right.
T: Kind of silly, like it was all right being silly and wacky, a little.
Pt: Not wild, a little, a little wild, but having fun.
T: That's a good way to put it.
Pt: It feels good. It does.

In each of the above dreams, there was a single experiencing in each peak. Often, however, you may get two experiencings in the same peak; for example, you get one experiencing from one figure and a quite different experiencing from a second figure. Under these conditions, the words used to describe the experiencing in the other peak are very important in identifying the commonality. Consider the dream, "Maniac with the knife, and controlling the maniac." In one of the peaks, the experiencing identified by staying with the dreamer is described in these words: power and control over him, a competent taking charge of him. In the same peak, the words describing the experiencing in the other figure were: helpless, passive, like a little boy. When we turn to the other peak, the experiencing is described by these words: sheer control, having them all in his power. Now we can find the commonality:

Pt: Having them all in his control. That feeling, it's the same as in the first dream.
T: You ended up feeling that way, when you were with him, you had him crying.
Pt: It is the same.
T: A feeling of control, that feeling of power, control, being in charge.

Rarely it happens that the experiencings in the two peaks simply do not match. You probably made a mistake somewhere. Maybe you arrived at the wrong experiencing in one of the peaks. Maybe you got an experiencing from one figure and failed to get an experiencing from the other figure. In any case, you end up with two sets of words that do not match. This occurs in the dream, "He is mounting my dog, and too far to walk." In one peak we arrived at an experiencing described by these words: saying no, refusing, saying the hell with it. The words used to describe the experiencing in the second peak were: thrusting animal sexuality, macho bruteness, sexual strength. There is no fitting commonality unless you construct one by trying to jam together the two non-overlapping experiences. What do you do under these conditions? I give up:

T: They don't fit. Do you see how they fit? I don't.
Pt: No, they seem different.
T: Hmmm. I think we're stuck.
Pt: (Silence)
T: Yeah, let's give up.
Pt: All right.

In experiential therapy, we can go back to some other starting place in the session. If I am working on my own dream and cannot identify a commonality, I end the session. It is exceedingly rare, but it does occur. When I study these dreams in an effort to learn more about dream work, I find a number of possibilities. One is that there were three peaks in the dream, and the two I selected were not from a single deeper experiencing. A second possibility is that I used one figure in a peak while the other figure proved to be the one that housed the experiencing. A third is that the patient had one peak dream, woke up and recorded it, fell back asleep and had the second dream tapping a different experiencing. These are the usual three conclusions I have arrived at. Occasionally I am simply stuck and have no explanation whatsoever.

With such rare exceptions, you will rather easily identify a commonality in the words used to describe the experiencings in the two peaks, and thereby you have identified the dream experiencing. This is the precious jewel, the experiencing that is the basis for the rest of your work.

CHAPTER 10

How to Be the
Dream Experiencing

How do you get inside of the dream experiencing, disengage from the ordinary personality and enter into the radically new and different personality of the dream experiencing? The extent to which you allow this to happen is the extent to which you are undergoing a complete and wholesale transformation in your very person. Just as in the depth of dreams (Figure 4), disengaging from your everyday, continuing personality can occur a little bit or all the way. You have the possibility of disengaging completely from the everyday, continuing personality and undergoing a wholesale transformation into being the dream experiencing.

Whether or not you can "be" the dream experiencing a little bit or all the way, there are two special features to this very precious change. One is that you will feel more at home with this deeper potential, much more welcoming and friendly with it. The dream experiencing will become a part of what you are, as barriers between you and it are washed away. These radically changed good relationships are referred to as integration. The second feature is that you will be able to undergo this dream experiencing, to behave and act from it, to sense and feel what it is like to be this experiencing. This is referred to as actualization.

Being the dream experiencing is a radical achievement. Rarely if ever are you being the dream experiencing in your daily life, certainly not in an integrated way that feels good, peaceful, harmonious, easy, or in an actualized way that is full and complete, alive and vibrant, open and active. The purpose of this fourth step (Figure 1, p. 00) is to enable you to "be" this dream experiencing.

Being the dream experiencing requires a proper context, an appropriate situation. We use three contexts in a sequence. The first is the context of the peak moment in the dream. You have an opportunity to go back into this peak moment and "be" the experiencing in a way that provides a good measure of integration and actualization, i.e., so that you are the good form of the experiencing and so that you can be

238

the experiencing rather fully. Second, you have the opportunity to be the experiencing within the context of earlier scenes, moments, incidents in your life. Finally you have the opportunity to be the dream experiencing within the context of the recent life incidents connected to the dream, those you identified in the recording of the dream (step 2.2, Figure 1).

BEING THE EXPERIENCING
IN THE CONTEXT OF
THE DREAM PEAK MOMENT

The task is rather straightforward. You are to be the experiencing, fully and completely, pleasurably and enjoyably, in the peak moment. This means you are to have a good idea of what the experiencing is and enter back into and live within the peak moment. In the work so far, you came close enough to sense the dream experiencing, you touched it a little from the side, and you were touched a little by it. You felt the experiencing enough to be able to use some words to describe it. Now you are to go much further. You are to be the identified experiencing fully and completely. In the dream you did not. You may have had a strong feeling in the dream, but that feeling was not the experiencing. Now you are to have and be and undergo the full measure of the experiencing. What is more, you are to be the *good* form of this experiencing, the form that is free of any bad disintegrative feeling and is accompanied by the good feelings of being the experiencing fully. But above all, you are to be the deeper experiencing, to actively and forthrightly disengage from your own personality and enter wholesale into being the deeper experiencing.

Selecting the Peak Moment

Since you can only enter into one peak moment at a time, the first decision is to select one of the peaks. A few guidelines are helpful. (1) It is generally easier to select the most recent peak you worked on; (2) a peak in which the feeling was good rather than bad; and (3) a peak in which the experiencing was housed within the dreamer rather than in the other figure.

Is it sufficient to be the dream experiencing in just one peak moment or is it better to be the dream experiencing in both? Quite frequently, I use just one of the two peaks; however, using both peaks provides the patient with another opportunity to be the dream experiencing. You should select which peak you will use first and then use the other peak, although I do not do this consistently.

The Instructions

There are several parts to the instructions, and the therapist needs to take plenty of time for each. One part consists of describing enough of the peak scene to enable the patient to be in it again. The scene is to be made alive and real and immediately present. Tell the patient to sketch the scene by describing where she is, what is happening around her, what the mood is, what the physical features are. All this description is to be from inside the skin of the main character. Here is this part of the instructions for the patient who is to be experiencing one of the peaks from the dream, "Maniac with the knife, and controlling the maniac":

T: If you are ready and if it is all right, then you are to go back into that scene and be living real and alive in this moment. Just describe the scene like it's going on right now. It's this neighborhood meeting, and your husband isn't here for some reason, and there are all these mats around in this living room here, and Randy is here and all the neighbors. And now all the neighbors are too scared to do anything, and this guy that everyone was so scared of is sitting down in front of you. His hands are down and his body is relaxed. Just see him and describe everything, every little bit here . . .

Make sure the instructions include being inside the skin of the main character.

T: . . . See the guy, right here in front of you. Let yourself be inside the skin of the person you are in the dream here. You see him right here in front of you . . .

Being the main character is usually more difficult when the main character is another figure or an object. Suppose that you select the other peak of that dream. In this peak, the character housing the experiencing is the other fellow, the one with the knife. The instructions tell the patient to get inside this fellow and to describe everything that is happening in the scene so that it is alive and real:

T: If you are ready, then let yourself be inside the skin of this guy. You have the knife. And out through your eyes you can describe what is happening. You have just run the knife slowly down the neck of this woman

who is here. Feel it, and now you describe what is happening around
you, the people who are here, where you are, how they're all scared as
hell of you, and everything else to set the scene and make it all real, all
very real . . .

Sometimes it is rather easy for the patient to be the main character
and to set the scene from that vantage point. Often it is difficult,
especially if the patient is to be the other figure or object rather than
the dreamer. You can make it easier by giving the task a kind of
pretend quality.

T: Remember, all you're doing is pretending. You're not really this maniac
with the knife, and you're not really someone who does the mean and
awful things he does. Of course not! But you can pretend. You can play
the role of the guy with the knife, and who knows, if you do a good
job maybe they'll hire you for a few days. What the hell. then, afterwards, you can go back to being good old ordinary you, a basically
sweet and charming person who would never do what this guy with
the knife is doing. Oh no. Got it? Is this all right?

The second part of the instructions involves describing the experiencing. Describe the experiencing fully enough, within the context of
the peak moment, so that the patient has a clear picture of its nature
and is inclined to have a little of the experiencing even as you are
giving the instructions. Here is the therapist describing the experiencing in which the dreamer is talking to the fellow with the knife:

T: You are this person who feels a wonderful sense of control. I mean you
got this guy in your hands! You have this feeling of what it's like to be
in absolute control. You have to admit it, of all the people here, you're
the one who is dominating this little guy who used to have the knife
and scare the shit out of all the neighbors here. You are the one who is
doing it. So inhale this delightful feeling. I'm in control here! I'm the
one in charge! That's me!

The third part of the instructions invites the patient to "be" the
dreamer (or the other figure). You can also show the patient how to
do this, how to be inside the main character and to *be*, to undergo
this experiencing:

T: Your job is to let yourself be this woman, this particular woman, right
here with this fellow, and letting yourself feel this wonderful feeling of
control. Being in charge right now. You've got to be this woman and do

whatever you have to do to have the feeling. It means doing things. Saying and doing things. Here, I'll show you how to do it. One way. I'll be this woman and do what gives me this wonderful feeling: "That's right, little boy, just tell competent old momma here all those baddie feelings—'cause that way I get to have you in my power! I am the controlling one! You're reduced to being a friendly, sad little boy. And I did it! I did it! Take a look, everybody! See what I can do! There, there, little boy—ha ha ha—just you put your little head on my lap and go ahead and feel bad—'cause I am the boss, and I got you in my control."

Go ahead and talk to him. Talk to the other people. Pat the guy on his knee. Just let yourself celebrate this wonderful feeling of being in control, having the power, being in charge.

The final part of the instructions is to acknowledge the patient's wholesale readiness, willingness, and choice:

T: Is this all right? Are you clear on what to do? It is your choice. If you are ready and willing to do this, then go ahead. Do it till you really feel it. It means letting yourself do these things, letting yourself really feel this sense of controlling him. If you are ready, then take a few seconds and begin being this person in this scene here. OK?

Give these instructions in whatever way feels natural for you. The main thing is to include all the parts.

Helpful Guidelines

Once the patient agrees and starts to be the dream experiencing, there are some guidelines for carrying this through more easily. The first is limited to something the therapist can do. The other two guidelines are for both the therapist and the person who works on his own dreams.

Join the person in being the dream experiencing. Once the therapist finishes giving the instructions, the patient will be the dream experiencing in the peak moment. She will talk from and as the person in the peak moment. As a therapist you are to do the same thing. Allow yourself to be right here with the patient in the peak moment. See what the patient sees. When the patient talks, allow the words to be as if they are coming in and through you too. Join the person in saying and doing whatever she is saying and doing. As she is experiencing the sense of being in control, share in this. Add a little. Say something from this experiencing. When the patient says,

"There's nothing scary about this guy, I can handle him easily," you can say, "Right, I'm the boss here." This makes it easier for the patient to be the good form of the dream experiencing.

You can also be other parts of the patient. While the patient is rather fully being the dream experiencing, you may be the voice of other parts. Accordingly, the patient is truly and genuinely being the dream experiencing as she says, "There's nothing scary about this guy, I can handle him easily." Joining the patient may mean that you sense a little cautionary hesitancy. You give voice to this, saying, "Listen, are you sure? This is not your usual line of business you know!" The important point is that you are joining the dreamer and having friendly, close, loving, playful relationships with and as the controlling woman. Yet the overall guideline is for the therapist to join with the patient, both in being the dream experiencing and perhaps in speaking for the balance of what is occurring in the patient as she is being the dream experiencing.

Avoid the avoidances. The patient is engaging in an incredible accomplishment. She is to disengage from the ordinary personality and be the deeper dream experiencing. Furthermore, she is to undergo this remarkable and radical shift in a way that feels good. Some patients do this easily and well; some patients have a hard time. They avoid doing this by any means available. Once they begin to be the dream experiencing they may drift off into other topics, start to get a headache or to feel nauseous, pull out of the scene and talk about it, become tied up by anxiety, talk in an incoherent way, or withdraw into crying.

The solution is for the patient to avoid the avoidance. If the patient begins to be the dream experiencing and then drifts off into other topics, patient and therapist need to start over again and this time make sure that they do not drift off into other topics. If the patient avoids by pulling out of the scene and engaging in a safer "talking about it," then the therapist tells the patient to return to being the dream experiencing in the peak moment, to decline any tendencies to pull out of it. If the patient avoids by having a headache or feeling nauseous or starting to cry, then the patient is invited to return to the task and this time to bypass the headache, nausea, or tears. We are following the procedure of Corriere, et al. (1980):

> It's important (since he can cry so easily) that he maintain these feelings inside his body (not try to get rid of them in the shape of tears) . . . T: Say it without crying. (p. 171)

The patient may accept the instructions, enter back into the peak moment, start to be the dream experiencing, and then bolt away. She is being with the fellow, existing in the scene, and entering somewhat into being the experiencing of control and taking charge. There is an avoidant pause, and she says, "My sister could be that way. . . . She used to boss me around something fierce. . . . " This can have a somewhat shattering effect on the therapist who is well into the scene and is already being the dream experiencing. It is as if the patient has leapt out of the dream scene and reappeared in another dimension. From within the vantage point of the experiencing main character, the therapist invites the person back to work:

T: What! Here I am, being with this guy here, starting to have this feeling of taking charge of this guy, and suddenly you're off and talking about your sister! No fair! How about coming back? You stay here and be the person I know, the one who is in control of this guy. None of this running away. OK? And if you get any more inclinations to run away, don't do it! Is that all right? What do you think?

As soon as the patient starts avoiding, return her to work. You need no long explanations or justifications. Avoidances are to be avoided, and they are to be avoided by the patient who is ready and willing to do so.

Keep going until experiencing is real and strong and until there are new bodily sensations. This applies whether you are working on your own dream or working as a therapist on someone else's dream. Be the dream experiencing with vigor and loudness, amplitude and volume. Throw yourself into being the experiencing. Make it as real as can be. Act it out, belt it out. Do it with every fiber of your body. Be loud, Move your arms and legs. When you do all this, a point will be reached where you are really being the experiencing. When it happens you will have no thoughts like, "Now I am really being the dream experiencing." Instead, you will really be the dream experiencing.

This emphasis on fully being the dream character is found in other approaches, notably in Gestalt dream work, and also in the functional approach of Corriere, et al., (1980). If the main character is in the street eating chicken, and if the experiencing is that of devouring the chicken in an earthy manner, openly acknowledging the naïve gluttony, thoroughly enjoying doing all this, then the patient is to do it in such a way that the experiencing is real and strong:

P: That's true. But that was me coming out with the chicken into the street. T: Snap your arms forward.

P: . . . I did that 'cause I wanted to. (Yelling.) Just walked out the way I was. And I was standing there eating it before anybody said it was OK. I was standing there eating it. Munching it. I would feel it dripping down my face. And that's me. That's me. That's me. T: Say it strong. Snap it! P: That's me! That's me *inside*. I am so alive. I don't want to run away and hide! I don't want to explain anything! I don't have to stop!" (Corriere, et al., p. 174)

The criterion is that there be new bodily sensations. Of course, if you scream out words and move your arms there will be bodily sensations. But in addition there will be new bodily sensations that are coupled with truly being the dream experiencing. There will be bodily sensations of vibrancy, excitement, aliveness. There may be a felt tingliness inside your body, like a little light electricity, a lacing of aliveness and excitement. Your chest and head may feel lighter. Once the experiencing is real and strong there will be new bodily sensations. Keep going until these appear.

The therapist gives the instructions and the patient enters into the peak moment, is the main character, and is able to wallow and revel in being the dream experiencing. The therapist joins with the patient in being the dream experiencing, assists the patient in declining avoidances, and insures that patient and therapist keep going till the experiencing is real and strong and there are new bodily sensations.

Some Illustrations

The dream is, "Maniac with the knife, and controlling the maniac." The experiencing is a sense of power and control, being in charge. We are working with the peak scene in which the dreamer has achieved this control over the fellow with the knife. The therapist has given the instructions, the patient has agreed to be the experiencing, and now the patient steps into the role of the dreamer to carry out the experiencing.

Pt: (In a sort of lilting sing-song voice) So you see, sonny boy, I have diffused you. No more scaring the other people. Now just you tell Momma how the people were mean to you. Oh, you want someone to understand. Well, I understand. I have the skills. I am a professional understander.

T: (Delightfully) Shit! You got me patting his head, and we both love it.

Pt: There there there. Just sit there . . . damn, I'm good. I got you under my control little boy. I am basically an in-charge kid. I keep just about anything under control. Even you. I mean, you came in here like a herd of elephants, scaring everybody. And then I just waltzed in and took over and calmed you down, and now you're just this nice little boy, pouring your heart out to me, the little Momma.

T: Sort of like Napolean. I'm in complete charge of you, kid!

Pt: (Her voice rises and is much louder.) I want all you people to come and sit around this guy! That's right! Now everyone put your arms around him and looove himmmm! Tell him that you loooove himmm! That's right! Everyone do what I say!! I am the little Momma, and I'm in charge of everything!!!

T: EVERYTHING.

Pt: I'M POWERFUL! I REALLY AM IN CONTROL!

T: (With arms raised) I'M IN ABSOLUTE CONTROL. I GOT THE POW-ER.

Pt: I can handle anything, ANYTHING! (In the therapist is a new bodily feeling of giddiness.) WOW! (She breaks into a delightful laughter.) I GOT THE POWER! IT'S WONDERFUL!

T: WELL, WHAT THE HELL'S SO WONDERFUL ABOUT IT?

Pt: (Silly and happy) Everybody dance. Oh come on, little boy. Everything's going to be all right. Little Momma's in charge! There! See! Now everyone hold hands and do what I say!

T: Yes teacher!

Pt: This is marvellous!

She has achieved the state of being the experiencing, being it in a full actualized way, and being the good integrated form of the experiencing. This is what we want.

From the dream, "Late for the wedding, and watching the nurses," the commonality consisted of the experiencing of staying away, being free and out of things, not being involved or caught. In both peaks, the feelings were unpleasant and bothersome. That makes it a little difficult. In both peaks, the dreamer was the main character. That makes it a little easier. The therapist and patient select one of the peaks and the therapist gives the instructions:

T: So there's this feeling of staying away, of being free, staying out of things, not being involved, never letting yourself be caught. Ha ha ha. Now are you ready to really feel this? Just inhale it. You really feel this way. I'm going to get out of this thing here. I'm free, dammit! I'm not involved in any of this shit. I'm free!

It means going back into this scene here. Now you are a nurse, OK? And you're right here at the nurses' station, and there are all those nurses and even the doctor, running around like they are run by some battery, or charged up by electricity, and here you are, only this time you are a person who knows what it is like to stay away from all this. No one is going to get me involved. No way! I am free! I am free enough to do what I want. I am out of all this!

Are you ready to be this person? Just be this whole new person, with solid feelings of your own, and belt them out so that everyone can hear you and know what you are like and what you are expressing. Just go ahead. You can even talk to the three nurses and the doctor, if you can slow them down. Is this all right?

Pt: I'm not going to do it! No way! I refuse! Don't have to!

T: LOUDER!

Pt: (The level is higher now.) I'm staying out of this one. Shit! I get involved in everything. I let myself, and no more. NO more, baby. I'm getting off that train. You can all do your little jobs. Go ahead. I admire you. No I don't! I really don't. How about just saying fuck it! Let's all go get drunk. Say no! Just come away for a moment, for once in your life. Tell them no, no way. Just stay out of things for once. I'm going to stand here and watch you all. Mind if I just sit here and strip a banana and watch you all make complete fools of yourselves? Boy, I'll bet you love your vacations. They give you a chance to get away. Well, try just saying no once in a while. I can. No. No way. Hear me? Do you hear me? You're all too caught up in all that shit. I will see you! Have a great time you all! Enjoy yourselves! I'm quitting! I never quit anything in my life! All my lovers and husbands had to blast their way from me. But the worm has turned, baby. Good-bye! Good-bye!!

T: Hey, this is fantastic. Listen, do you think you can also enjoy yourself in the scene at the weddings, on the ice? Huh? What do you think? Would you? Please? Are you ready? (This is a rather abrupt switch to the other peak.)

Pt: Sure.

T: Great! So skate over to where all those hundreds of people are having weddings . . .

Pt: Ugh!

T: . . . yeah, and enjoy being this woman who revels in the sense of "I am free, I am staying away thank you, no way for this kid . . . "

Pt: Want to see a little free skating? I will do a little exhibit for you all. What do you say? I will miss my wedding? I can picture my mother and my grandmother. Oh Elizabeth will be pissed! Where is my granddaughter? I am over here, Grandma! No wedding today! I managed to catch myself just before another mistake. No! Listen! There are dozens of other weddings all around. I'm sure they will be pleased to have you. You're all dressed and ready for a wedding. Go have one! Not me! No way! I am free!

T: I am free! I am free! I am free as a bird on the wing, ta ta! (The therapist is swept into off-key singing, enjoying the sense of saying no.)

Pt: No thank you, Momma! Here is a deep bow as I sail around on my skates. I am skating around and lots of people are looking at me, a little diversion from all the weddings. I am skating by myself and I hope you all enjoy your weddings, and I'll be back for all the divorces. Hey! I really can say no!!!

This was new, for the words shot out: "Hey! I really can say no!!!" She meant it. It had the ring of truth, and she literally had the experiencing of not being involved, caught, being free, being able to stay out of things.

T: Damn! It feels easy. No, thank you.

Pt: (Very seriously, as if she is only now having this genuine thought) I can get married or not. Do what I want. Don't have to be caught in anyone's problems. Do this, do that. No, I really can be free.

Being the dream experiencing can be difficult when the peak feeling is especially unpleasant and the experiencing is more passive. The dream is "Surreptitious in the store, and avoiding one another," and the experiencing is described in these words: being found out, seen, caught, exposed. In both peaks the feelings were quite negative. For example, in one peak, the dreamer was in a bookstore, secretly riveted on a book of pornographic photographs. His neighbors were also in the bookstore, and the experiencing burst forth as the patient penetrated through the bad feeling to reach the underlying experiencing.

Pt: I got shivers! She looks up and, she's only about 10 feet away. She sees me and I'm trapped! I'm caught! I'm trapped here! She knows!

T: Exposed! Found out! They'll all know!

Pt: (Moans hard) Aawwohoh! Whew!!!

Going back and celebrating the dream experiencing means letting oneself undergo the appreciated, good form of the experiencing of being caught, found out, exposed, seen. The therapist gave the instructions, indicated that it was not going to be easy, and showed the patient how to be that experiencing in the peak scene:

T: . . . so go ahead and celebrate it. What the hell, if you're going to be the feeling of letting them see you, finally being caught, really exposed, then you may as well do it all the way, and have a festival. Just let it go. Is that all right? What do you think?

Pt: (He is quite willing to try.) Hi Betty! Well, here I am looking at my pornographic little books here, ha ha ha. Just a little naughty, wouldn't you say? Ha ha ha. Nothing special here . . . nope. (There is a sense of trying to cover up. The therapist has more of a floppy sense of being caught and exposed.)

T: Just being exposed here, Betty. . . . You say my prick and balls are hanging out? Really? Just out in mid air here? Oh my! I knew I had a little erection down there, but I thought it was inside my pants. It isn't? Ah well, I think I will just finger around here and see. What do you know—I am exposed!

Pt: Do you mind ripping off your dress so I can see your tits? I have thousands of photographs of lovely tits in my garage—no, in the vault under the garage. . . . You, ah, didn't know about the vault? That's cause I used to keep it hidden, but I guess that's all over with now. (His voice is getting louder and firmer.)

T: SO TELL THE PEOPLE! YOU PERVERT WHO IS NOW EXPOSED AND CAUGHT BY THE WHOLE DAMNED NEIGHBORHOOD!

Pt: (Burst of laughter) I would love to drop my pants and have nothing underneath. Putting on a show (sing-song style). Take a look at me. I am the neighborhood PERVERT! I fuck all the dogs and cats, and lust after the little girls and boys—and the big girls with the big titties. Take that look off your face, Betty, you look lusty and should be shocked. What? You too? You collect used condoms! You? Oh my God, we'll all have to get together and share our sexy secrets. Perverts Anonymous! Of Market Avenue!

The voice volume is loud and full. In allowing the patient's words to come through her, the therapist now had a new set of strong bodily sensations. These changes came along with a live and real experiencing of being caught, of being exposed, of being found out, and celebrating it.

At this point you, the dreamer, have succeeded in undergoing a radical change. You have entered into a deeper potential for experiencing, experienced what it is like to be this potential, behaved and acted as this deeper experiencing within the context of the dream peak. This is most likely an achievement beyond anything in your life. When you dream, you manage to leave the operating domain and to go at least part way toward the deeper domain—unless the dream is a genuinely deep one, in which case you enter into the deeper potential itself. But now you have been the deeper potential voluntarily, as the sense of I-ness that chose to be the deeper potential and to be and behave and experience from within the deeper potential. This is a precious and magnificent change. You are now ready for the next step.

BEING THE EXPERIENCING IN THE CONTEXT OF EARLIER LIFE SITUATIONS

If you are going to be the dream experiencing, what are the most useful contexts? One is the peak scene in the dream. Another is some scene or situation from your earlier life. First we have to locate some appropriate earlier life situation (step 4.2, Figure 1), and then you are to be the dream experiencing in that earlier life situation (step 4.3, Figure 1).

How and Why Earlier Life Situations Are Useful in Experiential Dream Work

Chapter 3 dealt with the connections between dreams and life situations occurring a day or so before the dream. We are now ready to address the issue of how and why earlier life situations are useful in experiential dream work.

Earlier life situations are useful contexts for being the dream experiencing. When you are living and existing in some earlier life scene, some situation from your past, you have another opportunity to be the dream experiencing, to be and behave and think and feel from within this dream experiencing. In addition to providing another context for being the dream experiencing, different kinds of earlier life situations offer different kinds of useful bonuses:

There are earlier life situations where the deeper experiencing did not occur at all; however, it might or should have occurred. You can return to these situations and provide yourself with an opportunity to be and behave as the dream experiencing.

In some earlier life situations the deeper experiencing occurred but in its bad form, with feelings that were painful, troublesome, racking. You can reenter these earlier life situations and be and behave as the good form of the dream experiencing.

There are earlier life situations in which the good form of the deeper experiencing occurred a little bit. It was slight, muted, and the behaviors were likewise mild and limited. When you go back into these life situations you can be the deeper experiencing much more fully, with behaviors that are new and more effective.

What about earlier life situations where you actually were the stout good form of the experiencing, where the experiencing was full and strong and accompanied with wonderful feelings? These are especially useful because you can so easily get back into these earlier life situations, and be and behave as the deeper experiencing. There are also a few added bonuses from these situations. One is that you have a chance to rediscover and regain an experiencing that was operating for a time during childhood and then receded into a deeper potential for two or three decades or so. A second bonus is the rediscovery of behaviors that opened up the experiencing earlier in life and are absent in your life today. These behaviors are precious and can be put to use (chapter 12).

Useful earlier life situations may be relatively recent or rather remote. While I prefer using earlier life situations from a long time ago, the time frame is wide open. Freud likewise used life events that occurred in the last few weeks or so and from infancy and childhood. "Freud observed that the dream materials were very likely to come from childhood as well as from the quite recent past, with relatively sparse representation of conscious memories in between" (Monroe, 1955, p. 52). "In most dreams . . . childhood experiences are directly repeated" (Fromm-Reichmann, 1958, p. 164). Fenichel (1953) echoes the same refrain: " . . . a proper dream always stood on two feet — in repressed infantile material and in current events" (p. 164). On occasion, however, Freud found that some of the in-between life events may be useful: "Dreams can select their material from any part of life, the dreamer's experience of the dream-day (the 'recent' impressions) with the earlier ones." (Freud, 1900, p. 169).

In contrast with most approaches, we may select earlier life situations from the period roughly approximated by a year or so before conception to several years after birth, situations in which the main players were parental figures rather than the actual infant. Our theory of human beings (Mahrer, 1989a) holds that the basic potentials were laid down in that period and consisted of the activated experiencings in the interrelating parental figures, especially in relation to the infant or infant-to-be. Accordingly, significant early life situations may involve mother and father clinging together as they tried all sorts of ways to conceive the infant-to-be, or the pregnant mother centering attention on the fetus and having little further use for her husband, or mother hating the newborn baby because he interferes with her youthful style of living. These "primitive" scenes feature the parents and others as the key figures, with the patient playing little or no role whatsoever.

This period is the bedrock of personality, the foundation of the basic potentials which comprise the patient. Occasional dreams will reach back to such early situations. With these precious exceptions, most of the early life scenes will be from early and later childhood, from adolescence and adulthood, or perhaps the last few years.

How dream work makes use of the past versus how the past is held as causing the dream. Occasionally, past scenes and situations are regarded as useful, but we do not consider the past as causing or as explaining dreams. In other approaches, notably the psychoanalytic, the past is held as causing the dream, as explaining the dream meaning.

Consider a childhood incident in which grandmother is reciting a prayer that she wants the patient to learn and to say each evening before he goes to sleep. We use that incident to enable the patient to be the dream experiencing. We hold that in that early incident the dream experiencing could or should have occurred, or started to occur a little bit, or occurred in a painful way. We do not hold that the early incident caused the events that occurred in the dream or the dream experiencing.

Dream work often dilates the memory of the early event. All you ordinarily remember is that your grandmother was the one who told you the prayer. The memory opens and closes with her telling you the prayer. When you engage in dream work, however, much more is recollected. You now remember that it occurred when you were staying at her home, and that the two of you were in her bed ready to go to sleep, and she recited her prayer. You pleased her when you added the final words to her prayer, and that is when she said the whole prayer over again and again, so that you could learn it all that night. You also remember how that brought the two of you close so that she then told you stories about your mother and father before you were born, and how delicious it felt to be so close to her. The partial memory dilates to include so much more.

Yet the early life situation is used primarily as a context for the patient to be the dream experiencing, and the connection between the dream and the past event is one of utility. In contrast, many approaches see the past as connected causally to the dream, so that the dream is this way because of those childhood events, or the meaning of this dream is given in those childhood incidents, or this happens in dreams because of those childhood situations. For Freud, childhood events caused, explained, and gave meaning to dreams. For example, dreams of flying or falling or floating are accounted for by childhood impressions from such situations as being a baby lifted above the parent's head, and childhood memories account for dreams in which the dreamer's nakedness is visible to a group of people who are themselves dressed and are innocently unaware that the dreamer is without clothes:

> . . . a memory of the dreamer's earliest childhood lies at the foundation of the dream. Only in our childhood was there a time when we were seen by our relatives, as well as by strange nurses, servants, and visitors, in a state of insufficient clothing, and at that time we were not ashamed of our clothing. (1950, p. 143)

Because trains of thought connect the dream to these childhood events, you can start from the dream and trace the associated connections back to their origin in childhood (Marmer, 1980). The meaning and explanation of the dream lie in the childhood sources of these important trains of thought:

> " . . . important trains of thought proceed which reach back into the earliest years of childhood . . . I should say that every dream is connected through its manifest content with recent experiences, while through its latent content it is connected with the most remote experiences" (Freud, 1950, p. 119).

In both the experiential and the psychoanalytic approaches, working with the dream includes going back to earlier life situations. However, we tend to use different earlier life situations than the psychoanalytic approach and to use them in different ways, for our aim is to use appropriate earlier life situations as useful contexts for being the dream experiencing. In contrast, the psychoanalytic approach tends to explain dreams in terms of earlier life situations, to regard these earlier life events as causally related to the dream.

We now turn to the matter of how to go from the dream to these earlier life situations. Only some approaches aim to find earlier life situations. Only a portion of psychoanalytic therapists do so. But for those who wish to uncover some useful earlier life situation, you need some method. In psychoanalysis the method is through associational thoughts:

One of the interesting features about these dreams is they all lead to associations of a primal scene. Through the analysis of these dreams and a careful sifting through of the associations, the patient and I were able to arrive at a reconstruction. Around Christmastime, when the patient was about a year and a half old, she was restless and awake and walked to her parents' bedroom to observe her parents in intercourse. Her father discovered her standing in the door, leapt from the bed wearing a nightshirt, his penis still erect and exposed, grabbed her by the right arm, and marched her off to bed stiffly, and told her to leave, shouting at her loudly. (Marmer, 1980, pp. 170–171)

In the experiential approach, we decline to use the person's train of associations. We rely either on the common features in the two peaks or on the dream experiencing.

Discovering Earlier Life Situations by Means of Common Features in the Peak Moments

We start by excluding the experiencing. Leaving that aside, what would you say are the common features in the two contexts, in the scenery and the general situations, the figures and their interactions? Take the common features that are more or less conspicuous. If both peaks take place in a bathroom, then a bathroom is a common feature. If one peak takes place in an elevator and the second takes place in a bathroom, then the commonality may be that of a small room. You may note that both peaks contain a person with a larger group, or two people doing something together like working on a project, or vehicles going at fast speeds, or a leader getting people to do something.

In the dream, "Maniac with the knife, and controlling the maniac," one of the peaks may be described as follows: a group of neighborhood people are scared and threatened, watching a fellow with a knife slowly running the knife over the neck of one member of the group. In the other peak, one person is sitting and talking to a fellow with the knife, and the neighborhood group is watching, scared and threatened. The common features may be described as a group of neighborhood people meeting in a home; they are rather scared and frightened, and they are watching two persons, one of whom is an outsider, a little odd, different, threatening.

Look for common features that are surface, manifest, easy, conspicuous. Simply scan the two peak scenes and see how they are rather similar. In one peak of the dream, "Late for the wedding, and watching the nurses," one person is on a very large pond, skating around, looking for her wedding party. There are lots of wedding parties on the pond, and she cannot locate hers. In the other peak the dreamer is a nurse who arrives at a nursing station on a hospital floor, and suddenly a doctor and some nurses are galvanized into action. One of these nurses tells her that she is a nurse too and she should function as a nurse. What similarities impress you from the two peaks? In both there is a group of people engaged in something, doing something (the nurses and doctor in one, and the wedding party in the other), and there is a solitary, somewhat removed other figure who is not part of the group.

In one peak ("Flying the airplane, and piloting the plane on the ground"), the dreamer and another person are in an airplane piloted by the other person who is flying loops while virtually turned away from the dreamer. In the other peak, the dreamer is driving an airplane on the ground, in city traffic, and doing a fairly good job. Simply at face value, what would you say are the common features in both? Perhaps you might say that in both some person is driving-piloting an airplane or large vehicle and is doing a rather surprisingly good job.

When you describe the commonality, pay attention to the similarity in locale and situation, and to the figures and what they are doing. In one peak, the dreamer is making a fire in the cave, where he lives. In the other peak, the dreamer has been swallowed by a whale, and he is checking his body, seeing if he is all right. Do you see a commonality in both locales and in the figures? The therapist puts the common features in this way: "There is a person, by himself, all alone, and his is in a special place, an enclosed special place."

You are on the right track if you find some way to identify the common features. It is not all that important that others might find other common features, and that others would likely use different words to identify the common features. In one peak of the dream, "Slamming the intruder, and panicked about the gorilla," the dreamer is beating a fellow who intruded into the house. The intruder simply came into the kitchen and turned on the oven, and the dreamer, enraged, started beating up the fellow who was being such an outrageous intruder. In the second peak, the dreamer's attention is riveted on a huge gorilla standing in a neighbor's yard. The dreamer is terrified that the gorilla will come into the dreamer's house and do damage. Our way of framing the common features is as follows: "In both there is a house, a home, and there is some other person, an intruder or possible intruder, and this other figure is able to cause trouble, to do something physical, damage."

But suppose you cannot find any common features without straining. If you work at it, you can always come up with something. You can identify something that is secondary ("Both took place in the daytime . . . in both there was a linoleum floor"), or you can be so very general as to be almost meaningless ("Both involved interpersonal relations . . . both were domestic"). If you run into trouble finding common features that make sense, what should you do? I find useful common features in almost every dream. However, one in every ten or twenty stumps me, and I know that I will have to strain to find some common features. When this happens, I use just one of the peaks, making sure that the words I use are general enough to apply to more than the peak moment. I describe the peak moment with words that fit and yet are not pinpointed to that peak.

In one dream, the dreamer is observing a dog protecting its bone against another dog, and the other dog just gave in and left. In the other peak, the dreamer is flirting with a woman, comes up behind her, reaches around, and holds her breasts. The scene is light-hearted and playful, and the whole family is present. The therapist found no immediate commonalities. You might think of the dog holding the bone and the dreamer holding the woman's breasts, but that simply did not ring true as a common feature. So the therapist stayed with one of the peaks and tried to describe it in somewhat general terms: "One person is flirting with another, and everyone is happy, and the family is around, and everything is kind of playful . . . "

The instructions. At this point, neither the therapist nor patient nor the person who works on her own dreams has some earlier life situation in mind. Maybe it is a little more accurate to say that the instructions will illuminate some earlier life situation that is different from whatever earlier life situation you perhaps are already thinking of. It is as if we are going to go on an adventure to discover some new recollection. The following instructions are for therapist and patient, but they also apply to the person working on her own dreams.

The therapist begins by getting the patient's readiness and willingness to undergo this next step. Tell the patient what we are seeking to accomplish so that the patient is fully apprized.

T: I want to go back into your past and see if we can locate some time that was something like what happened in the dream. What happened in the dream most likely happened some time earlier in your life. I want to look for this earlier time, but only you can find it. I can show you what to do, but you must be the one to do it, and then maybe we can find something earlier in your life that comes from the dream. Is this all right? Are you ready to try? What do you think?

If the patient agrees, then the therapist tells the patient to get ready by assuming the posture of being in the past. You can open the window quite wide by inviting the patient to be ready to be a child or an adolescent or a young adult:

T: Let yourself get ready to be a young child or in your teens or maybe a little older. You are a child, thinking like a child, being the child. Maybe you are an adolescent or maybe a little older. Your body is the body of a little kid or a little older. The way you think and how you feel, everything is a little kid or a little older maybe.

If you wish, you can select some more defined period in the patient's life. You might get the patient ready to see scenes from when he was a child, just a young boy of three or five or seven or ten or so. Fill in where he lived during this childhood period, who was in the family, what his school was like, some of his acquaintances. You may select his adolescence and get him ready by having him first see the neighborhood, his friends, what he liked doing then. You might even prepare him to see scenes involving his parents around the time of his conception or just a little earlier or later, scenes in which the parents were the major players.

Once the patient is ready, explain that you will be describing scenes in a general way, with bold strokes and in words used in describing the peaks. Explain that it is the work of the patient to find specific scenes, to be on the lookout for whatever images occur.

T: OK? Now I'm going to be describing situations and incidents. I will be saying words that came from the dream. As I say the words, you have to see whatever scenes and situations come to your mind. I'll be saying some general words, and you have to see whatever specific things appear. Almost without thinking, you will see things. It may be clear or maybe kind of vague. Either one is all right. It may be just a fleeting image or a thing that you see clearly and vividly and it stays here. It may be just a little piece, like a hand or a bathroom floor, or it may be a whole scene. But you will see something.

Let the patient know that he may be an integral part of the scene or that he may play no part whatsoever.

T: When I describe, you might be a part of what is going on, and it is happening to you. Or it might be that you see other people or things, and it has nothing to do with you. If I say that there are two people and they are playing ping-pong together, you might see it as one of the players, or you might see two other people playing, and you aren't even a part of the scene. So just let yourself be free, and just see what you see, either way. You may be a part of it or you may not.

What the patient sees may have a sensible connection with what the therapist is saying, or it may be apparently quite disconnected. It doesn't matter. Just use whatever appears:

T: Just see whatever you see, no matter what. Whatever you see, that is what you start describing. It may have no connection at all, just comes to you from out of nowhere. That's OK.

Tell the patient to start describing as soon as anything appears. It does not matter what is seen. Just indicate that something is here, and start describing:

T: . . . and as soon as you see something, anything at all, start talking. You can say, "I see something" or just "yes," but say something and then start describing whatever you see, anything at all. Am I clear? Know what to do? Are you ready?

Evoking the earlier life situation. The last part of the instructions consists of the therapist's describing the common features in the two peaks. Say these words as if they are indeed pointing toward some earlier life situation. You do not know precisely what that earlier event is, but you know there is one, and the words will point generally in its direction. Say the words slowly and carefully, say them again and again, and speak in a rather low and even tone of voice so that your words point toward the earlier event rather than drawing attention to you. Here is what the therapist says from the dream, "Maniac with the knife, and controlling the maniac":

T: There is a group of people, and they're in someone's home, and they're upset, scared and bothered by something, and they're watching a couple of people, two people, and one seems kind of odd, a little different . . . anything? . . .

Pt: I remember. My mother came home. Someone, I think my mother was away all night and someone brought her home, and she was drunk, on the front lawn, she was making a lot of noise. My Dad and I went out. All I remember is that Dad was screaming something about the neighbors, and Katkovsky's came out and just stood on their porch. I was scared as hell. She was so drunk and everyone saw her.

Once the patient remembers an earlier scene, fill it in so that it is locked in place, clarified and more fully remembered, alive and real and present. Do this by filling in the hazy or omitted parts, filling in the moment when the feeling is strongest, filling in the patient's thoughts:

T: The Katkovsky's are watching all this? They are on the porch seeing and hearing everything?

Pt: It was crazy! My Dad. He could have killed her. And Mom's really drunk. Dad's out of his mind. I've never seen him yelling, and his fists. I thought he'd hit her.

T: You have thoughts, and what are they? There are thoughts that he'd hit her, maybe. And more. Thoughts are in you.

Pt: I don't really know what I was thinking. About Mom and what she's doing, and Dad. I'm just crazy. I don't know what I'm feeling. Mom's drunk and the neighbors are watching and Dad's furious. I'm not crying or yelling. I'm not doing anything. I don't even know what's going on in me!

Sometimes the elicited memory will be one that has been buried since childhood. Following the instructions, the therapist recites the common features from the two peak moments from the dream, "Surreptitious in the store, and avoiding one another":

T: Ready? There is something dirty, pornographic, pictures that you shouldn't be looking at. Dirty pictures. Bad pictures. But very exciting. And people. Maybe just one or two, people that you don't want to know. You feel very funny about them seeing you.

Pt: I remember pictures, photographs. I remember one where a guy . . . my God I must have been just about five. A guy had his prick on a plate. A woman's sitting at a table with a fork and a knife and she's pretending to cut it up and eat it. Jesus! I was staying with my Aunt Helen and Uncle Steve, and I got the pictures from their bedroom. I took them from someplace in their bedroom. They had them somewhere in their room, I remember. They were in a drawer in their dresser. I poked around in their room and found them and I kept them. And I was looking at them in their bedroom. My God, I was lying on their bed and looking at the pictures. I haven't thought about that ever! Ha! That's the first time I even thought about that! It's hard to believe! What a memory! That's really strange! I don't think I've ever even thought about that!

Sometimes the memory is quite mundane, as illustrated when the therapist gives the common features from the dream, "Late for the wedding, and watching the nurses":

T: There is a group of people and they are doing something, and you are not really in the group, maybe even off a little separated. You ought to be participating, but you're not.
Pt: I just see the family, at the table. There's a lot of talk, everyone's, well, there's a lot of noise, as usual. And I'm not, well, I'm sitting like in a cocoon. I am there but not really. I don't say anything, and I just sort of sit there.
T: Kind of withdrawn like.
Pt: Yeah! I remember I used to, a lot, I mean I did this a lot. I'd look at my glass of milk and stare at it, and I pretend that I'm invisible. The noise, all the talk, I heard it, you know, but I didn't make out what they were saying. I'd do that a lot.

Very often, the elicited earlier situation will be near to a moment when the feeling was relatively strong. It takes a bit of work to fill in the scene so as to find the moment of strong feeling. Here is the therapist giving the common features from the dream, "Protecting the bone, and holding the breasts":

T: One person is flirting with another, and everyone is happy, and there are adults there, older people in the family.
Pt: Yeah, I was in elementary school, and I used to walk Carol home, and we came to the side door, and her mother asked me in.
T: What was that like?
Pt: OK, I guess. Well, I liked Carol, and I used to get kidded by the others 'cause I liked her.
T: But her mother isn't kidding you.
Pt: No. I never saw her. I mean this was the first time. She surprised me. I was nervous. (The feeling level is getting stronger.)
T: Yeah?

Pt: I think I went in. She asked me in! I was real nervous. I think there were people there, in the kitchen. I don't remember. But I really liked her. I had a crush on her.

T: What the hell is it like here in the kitchen with them?

Pt: She had black hair, like blue. It was something. I always wanted to touch her hair, but I didn't. And Carol sat at the table. And then I freaked out. She had a note in her hand. I sent her notes, trying to be clever. Not a love note. She had my note in her hand! I don't know what I said! She had my note! It was blue. I wrote it on blue paper, and there it was! I nearly died!

Almost without exception, the earlier scenes will come from childhood or later. But rarely you may evoke earlier scenes from what is called the primitive field (Mahrer, 1989a). Suppose that the common features include one or more people going away, far away, and never returning, with perhaps just a few remaining behind. Prepare the patient in the instructions, and then use these common features to evoke a memory from that primitive period:

T: I am going to describe some scene, and I need your help. I am going to describe something that maybe was going on while your mother was pregnant with you, or maybe even a year or so before. Can you get ready? Where are your mother and father then? What is going on in their lives? Remember? I mean, what do you know?

Pt: I think Dad was still in school in Hamilton, yeah, and Mom was still working. And, I know that Mom had a miscarriage about, maybe a couple of years before I was born. They lived in Hamilton, pretty close to my grandpa's.

T: OK, now what am I describing? Ready? Someone's going away, or lots of people are going away, far away. They probably won't be coming back, and some are left behind . . .

Pt: Grampa died of a heart attack or something. He died before I was born. I never saw him and my other grandparents, my mother's, they lived in Florida, and they died too, about the same time. I think they died the same time. Mom never talked about them. I don't even know how they died. Mom and Dad were only children, so they got a lot of money. That's when they bought the house where I grew up. They were wealthy. My mother's parents had some cleaning places, cleaners, I think five or six of them, and we inherited all the money.

What do you do if no memory is evoked? When this happens you can use the alternative method of discovering an earlier life situation by means of the dream experiencing. But it helps to keep note of the common features, for subsequent dreams typically will yield the same common features. It is as if a number of quite separate dreams point generally toward some early event. For example, the common features in a number of separate dreams consisted of something ominously large coming down on a person who is small and unable to get away. In each dream we found no early memory, and therefore moved over to using the dream experiencing. However, one dream, perhaps the fifth or sixth over a period of months, added the helpful right ingredient:

T: One person is sort of pressed down on, and can't breathe, and something big is weighting him down, something moving, something that is inhuman.

Now the patient recollects. It is as if the context becomes a little clearer now, and a memory emerges:

Pt: (In a low, incredulous voice) I don't know if it really happened. My mother's youngest sister, Dora, well, she had a friend stay at our place. She drank a lot. My mother and father talked about it, her drinking. She squatted on me, and I think I thought she was killing me. I don't know how she was in my bed, my room, she was killing me. She sat on my head and I couldn't breathe. I don't know what I did. . . . Her pussy! She, oh my God, I never . . . I think she wanted me to suck her off!! She was on my head and she must have wanted me to suck her off! This is crazy! I never thought about this! What is this? She was over me and scared the hell out of me, and she had something on. A dress or something. And I couldn't breathe. Hell, she was squatting on my face!

In these illustrations, you have discovered an earlier life situation by means of the common features in the two peaks. In this method, you do not use the dream experiencing, only the common physical features of the two peaks, the nature of the figures and perhaps something of their interaction. We now turn to the use of the dream experiencing to discover the earlier life situation.

Discovering Earlier Life Situations by Means of the Dream Experiencing

You can discover an earlier life situation by means of the common features of the two peaks. You can also use the dream experiencing to locate earlier life situations where the same kind of experiencing took place. This means that the two ways of finding earlier life situations will produce a somewhat different yield. You will get earlier events similar either in physical features or in experiencing. The chances are very good that you will get different earlier life situations from the two methods.

The instructions. Parts of the instructions are the same used in discovering the earlier life situation by means of the common features of the peaks. Begin by telling the patient what we are going to do, and seeing whether the patient is ready and willing. The instructions may be as follows:

T: I want to find some time in your life when you had the same kind of feeling. It might be a few years ago or maybe when you were very very young, really just a little child. But you had the same kind of feeling that you had in the dream. I'll show you what to do and how to do it, but the important thing is whether you are ready and whether this is all right. Yes? No?

Then you invite the patient to assume the posture of the past, as if the patient were living five years ago or ten years ago or as a young adult or adolescent or older child or baby:

T: All right, then let yourself be maybe just a little child. Here you are being a little child. Just a little child. Or maybe eight or ten or twelve years old. You're living where you live as a child, and you are a child.

The more you posture the patient in the past, the easier it is for the patient to discover scenes. You can help by framing in some particular period. Visualize the house where you lived when you were about five to ten years old. See the street. Remember your room. The more you fill in the mundane cornerstones of this period, the more the patient is already in this past period rather than being in the office, today, and trying to remember something that happened many years ago. Whether you are entering into the past through the dream experiencing or through the common features in the two peaks, you have the choice of leaving the past wide open or of using a defined period. In effect, the choice is between saying, "Let's find some earlier incident in your life," and "Let's go back to when your mother and father were separated and you were three to five years old, living with your father and his ladyfriend." You might wish to define a particular period because, for example, the recurrent dream began when she was 14, or the severe stuttering began when he was eight (Mahrer & Young, 1960), or he has no memories whatsoever of the soldiers breaking into the house and killing everyone else in the family when he was eight years old. In any case, you can either leave the window to the past wide open or you can predefine a particular time.

Next, tell the patient what you are going to do and what the patient is to do:

T: I am going to describe what you are feeling. As I describe what you are feeling, let yourself feel what I am describing. Just have the feeling. Then you will see something. It may be something you remember, or it may seem to come from nowhere. It may be just a little thing like a picture on the wall, or it may be a whole scene, with people doing things. Just as soon as you see something, you stop me. Say, "I see something," or just start describing what you see, what you think about, remember.

You may open up the past scenes by preparing the patient to see someone else who has that experiencing. It is easiest and most common when the dream experiencing occurs within the patient. But it may be someone else. You can open up the instructions in this way:

T: I am going to describe the feeling. It may be a feeling in you or it may be a feeling that is happening in someone else, anyone else. So get yourself ready to have the feeling in you or to let the feeling be in someone else, and you will see that other person.

It is very important that the patient uses whatever bits and pieces of imagery float by. It does not have to be a memory. It may be just a disconnected image of something that has no apparent connection to the scene or the words of the therapist. No matter what the therapist says in describing the experiencing, the patient will start to have some images. It may be helpful for the therapist to emphasize this:

T: When I describe the feeling, you will start to see something, some image. Mention whatever it is, no matter whether or not you think it has anything to do with the feeling. Just say that I see a toy gun or a bathroom floor or a bannister or my Dad's watch or a flash of my school yard, or anything else that jumps into your mind. Anything. As soon as you see something, mention it. OK?

Evoking the earlier life situation. Now that the patient is ready and postured, the therapist merely describes the dream experiencing, using the word "experiencing" or "feeling." Say the words slowly and carefully, describing the experiencing in the present tense. Say the words as if the patient were having this experiencing right now. Say the words over and over so that the patient is actually undergoing this experiencing. In the following, the therapist is working from the dream, "Flying the airplane, and driving the plane on the ground":

T: You feel what it is like to be in control, in control, you are in control. You are responsibly in charge, you have a sense of being capable and handling it well . . .

Pt: Yes . . . I remember. I remember I used to play soldiers. I had a collection of toy soldiers, and I used to play in my room, on the floor. I used to be the general, and I had favorite ways. I'd had a favorite, yeah, a soldier, three of them, and they were a team, and they would carry out missions. I loved this. . . . They were buddies and I used to put all the soldiers around and have them carry out missions. They'd attack the enemy, and they'd blow up enemy stuff. A team . . .

Now we can look for the moment when the dream experiencing occurred or started to occur. It is a matter of clarifying and filling in more of the details, and also of looking directly for the moment when the feeling was occurring:

T: On the floor, in the bedroom.

Pt: Yeah, and I'd use the bed, under the bed, and I had a box, a shoe box, from the closet. I turned it over and that was a fort. I'd put toilet paper on the fort.

T: Flat sheets.

Pt: Flat sheets, five or six of them.

T: And the best time, you know, when the feeling's best.

Pt: I hold these three buddies in my hand here and cup them and we'd be a real team. Us, we did it! It's the best. And I'm the boss! It's *my* team!

Usually the careful recitation of the dream experiencing is enough to evoke the scene. Sometimes it helps if the therapist gives a few examples. For example, the therapist is describing the dream experiencing as follows, and then mentions the images that come to mind:

T: . . . the feeling is risky, doing something kind of risky, and fun, exciting. Like sneaking out the window and on top of the roof. You know you shouldn't be here and it is exciting and scary like you can fall, and you're way above everyone, or you are with about two or three other girls and boys and you all decide to take off your clothes and look at each other . . .

Pt: I remember that Jan and I would play together in the ditch. It was a little trickle of water behind her house, and we weren't supposed to be there. We'd take off our shoes and walk in the water. It was slimy and yucky, and we always had fun together.

One memory often will lead to another, especially once the patient undergoes the dream experiencing in the particular scene:

T: Ah! Now there are a couple of you feeling this riskiness. We're not supposed to be here but it's fun.

Pt: Oh yeah. I think the worst thing we did, I remember. We'd go, they were building houses, new houses. We lived out in the country, and when we were little they were building houses there, out there, and we got caught by the police. We would build fires. My God, there was smoke and we'd got yelled at. We made a fire inside one of the places, crawled in, and we had matches, and we'd, shit, we could have burned the place down. We'd take twigs and things and make a little fire, it was in the summer, and we were little, and I guess someone saw the smoke and called the police, and we got yelled at. The police came to the top where we were and I was scared out of my mind. So was Jan. It was scary . . .

All by herself, she goes to still another memory of having the same experiencing:

Pt: . . . I remember all sorts of things like that, doing risky things. My brother and I, we used to, well, we'd take off all our clothes and we'd play together. I mean, we would stick things up our asses and do all sorts of things, and one day we got a lizard and put in my Mom and Dad's bed (giggles), and I used to steal things. Oh yeah! Gert and I stole all sorts of things from the corner store! We sure did! We never got caught!

The illustrations so far have been from childhood. But sometimes the window is wider open and you merely invite the person to have the experiencing within some scene that may have occurred anytime in the past. Or you might highlight the last five or ten years or so.

Having given such open instructions, the therapist then describes the experiencing from the dream, "Cupping the woman's breast, and the tiny mines explode":

T: You are feeling a little outrageous, outrageous, ha, a spontaneous impulsivity, a risky playfulness, risky playfulness. It feels just like this. Ah yes.

Pt: I saw these women walk into . . . (laughs hard) . . . it was the women's bathroom. But they were together, and they were wearing pants, I mean slacks, and they had short hair, and I thought they were guys! I never, it never entered my mind. (Laughs again) So I went right in and I got inside and saw all these women. I just stood there. Seemed like about five minutes. I got all flustered and ran out. (Laughs) I really thought they were men. I never even looked! It was at a restaurant in Montreal. I'd never been there! I think that happened a couple of years ago. (Laughter)

On the other hand, you might want to look at scenes from the "primitive field," that period from a year or so before conception to a few years after birth. In this case, the instructions prepare the patient to see parental figures during this period of time and to allow the description of the experiencing to illuminate one of these figures rather than the patient. Following the instructions, the therapist describes the experiencing:

T: . . . Someone feels free, really free and liberated, being on one's own, finally, free of the whole load, letting go of all of it . . .

Pt: Well, my Mom. She was doing everything. They had a big family, and everyone left. Grampa had this little grocery store and he was retired, and Mom ran the store. She was the middle sister. Her older brother Harry went away years ago, and Mom took care of the whole place, and she cleaned the house and made suppers for Gramma and Grampa and her sister Maude, and she was depressed and smoking and skinny, and then she met Dad and they fell in love. Betty made Mom leave. She dragged her away, and I guess that was the biggest change in Mom's life. That's when Mom started painting and she was good I guess. She still makes money at it, and she and Dad fell in love, and they lived with Betty and Len.

T: So you see your Mom feeling free, letting go of the whole load.

Pt: I can see her, young, and painting. By the lake, by the barn. She seems so happy. Thank God Betty got her out. I see Betty there too, and they really liked each other. Yeah, she escaped!

Now that you have found some earlier life situation, you are ready for the patient to "be" the dream experiencing in the context of that earlier life situation.

Being the Experiencing

The aim is for the patient to disengage from his operating, ordinary personality and to get inside of the dream experiencing within the context of the earlier life situation.

The instructions. When you have finished giving the instructions, the patient should be quite clear about what to do and how to do it, should have either agreed to go ahead or declined, and should be partially in the past situation or moment and partially being and behaving as the dream experiencing.

From the dream, "Surreptitious in the store, and avoiding one another," the therapist and patient elicited a past scene in which the five-year-old patient discovered some pornographic photographs in the bedroom of his aunt and uncle, and lay on the bed fascinated with the pictures. The therapist tells the patient what to do:

T: Now you are going to be a whole new personality, a little boy who can let himself be found out. Yeah! He can be seen. That's right. It is just fine to be caught. He can be exposed, right here. That is all right. Catch me. See me. That's fine. This is the kind of guy you are. Just let yourself be this fellow, this delightful kind of fellow. Inhale being this kind of kid, a special kind of kid.

Tell the patient that he must set aside the actual feelings and ways of behaving in the old scene. Instead, he or she is to be and behave as the dream experiencing. Here are the instructions from the earlier scene located from the dream, "Maniac with the knife, and controlling the maniac." In the earlier scene, she is a child hearing her father yell at her drunken mother while the neighbors are watching:

T: You know that it was awful, that you felt awful, that you just stood there and were tight and scared and your whole body was screaming inside. You're not crying and you're not yelling, but there's a lot of yelling around you and you are so aware of Dad and Mom and the Katkovsky's. . . . But this time you can set all that aside. This time you can get inside a whole new person, a person that you were in the dream. You can feel what it's like to be in control of things, to be fully in charge. There is a sense of domination in this here little girl. She is the boss, she can take charge of things.

The instructions are thoroughly open in telling the patient what to do, to aim at and try to accomplish, and how to accomplish it:

T: You can make it all as real as possible by being right here in the live scene. This means seeing your Mom, really looking at her, every detail, and it means seeing your Dad, watching that look on his face as he is yelling at your Mom, and it means your saying words, saying them out loud, and saying them to your Dad or to the Katkovsky's, directly, talking and saying the words right at them.

In many earlier situations, the dream experiencing was present in a muted way or accompanied by negative feelings. For example, in the dream, "Late for the wedding, and watching the nurses," we located a past scene in which the patient had the same experiencing of staying away, being free of things, out of things, not being involved or caught in things. The patient is a child, sitting at the table. There is lots of noise, and she withdraws into a cocoon of distance, staring at a glass of milk. The instructions show her how to be the good form of this experiencing, being it all the way, fully.

T: Let's be back here, at the table, at the same table here. Now you are a little girl at the table, and you are sitting here at the table. Your mother is here, right here, and she is talking. You are aware of them, mother and father and the others. Talk and noise, buzzing. It is just noise. Sounds. Nothing but sounds. Right here at the table.

And now you are slowly becoming a little girl who doesn't have to be a part of all this shit. Not me. Listen to all this noise! Just listen to it! You don't have to be a part of all this! No way. I am me. I am me! You are a person who doesn't have to get caught in all this. Stay away. Sure. You are free of all this. Listen, to tell the truth, you are not really a part of all this. Let it be. Remove yourself. So let yourself be free of this.

Essentially, the therapist is describing the same old experiencings of being removed and withdrawn, pulling inside herself. The difference is that the therapist is describing this in a good form, accompanied with good feelings, and the therapist invites the patient to do it and be it all the way.

Commonly, the past scene is one in which the patient houses the experiencing and is the one to carry out the experiencing, but there are also past scenes in which the person who is the experiential agent is someone other than the patient. Consider a dream in which the experiencing is being the intruder, the unwanted one who does not belong, and the located early scene is one in which the key figure is not you; it is your second cousin, Bobbie, who came to live with your family when his parents separated. He was dumped in with you and your sister for three years. It is Bobbie who houses the role of intruder in the early scene in which he is crying in his room. The instructions invite you to be Bobbie in carrying out the dream experiencing.

In situations and moments from the primitive field, the key figure typically is not you. If the dream experiencing is that of being the intruder, the key figure may be mother who is lower class and highly pregnant when she and your father have to get married. Father's family is prominent in the small town, and they insist on the marriage. In the scene, mother is at the wedding ceremony. The patient's job is to get inside the young bride in the wedding ceremony, to fully experience being the intruder.

In still other past situations and moments, the key figure may well be the other person in the interaction with the dreamer. The dream experiencing is that of being the tyrant, the cold authority who is removed and unreachable. The located early scene is one in which you are being scolded by your father. Everyone in your large family was scared of father, and all of you stayed away from him as much as possible. In the scene, you are terrified of him when he comes home late at night, drunk, and he begins interrogating you about whether you have taken out the garbage like he told you to. You are frightened to death as he screams at you. In being the dream experiencing, the instructions invite you to get inside the old man and to be the tyrannical, cold, removed authority.

The therapist helps the patient ease into being the other figure in the scene. This may take a little time and little extra help.

In showing the patient what to do and how to do it, the therapist may be the model, the exemplar. From the dream, "Surreptitious in the store, and avoiding one another," the early scene is one in which the patient is a child lying on his aunt and uncle's bed with the pornographic photographs:

T: Here, I'll show you what I mean. Give me a few seconds to be the kind of kid who can be exposed, seen, caught, found out. . . . "I'm lying on their bed! Their bed! And they can come in any time. Here they come!!! Oh hello Aunt Helen and Uncle Steve!!! Look what I found! I found these great dirty photographs! And I'm just a little boy! THEY GOT ME ALL SEXY! WOW! I LOVE THESE THINGS! I NEVER SAW ANYTHING LIKE THIS! WOW WOW WOW!!! ARE YOU GOING TO BEAT THE HELL OUT OF ME 'CAUSE I FOUND THEM? THEY ARE GREAT!!!" . . . Hey, I think I did pretty well. What about you?

In the early scene where the patient's Mom is drunk in the front yard, the therapist says;

T: And you are going to be a whole different kid, and you're going to be a kid who is the boss, who feels what it is like to be in charge, who takes charge, who is in control of things. Mind if I take a shot at it? It can go like this. . . . "All right, everyone, super-daughter is here now. No more yelling. I SAID NO MORE YELLING! MOM'S SLOSHED AND I'M TAKING CHARGE NOW. DAD, YOU GO OVER TO MOM AND YOU PICK HER UP. COME ON. THAT'S THE WAY. LET'S PICK HER UP AND DRAG THE OLD LADY INTO THE HOUSE. THEN I'M COMING OUT AND I'M GOING TO HAVE A LITTLE CONFAB HERE WITH ALL THE NEIGHBORS." . . . Oh, I like doing this. But that's me. You're the real one here. How about doing it your way?

No matter what the nature of the dream experiencing is, the therapist lets it occur in its good form. In the dream, "Late for the wedding, and watching the nurses," we elicited a past scene in which the patient had the experiencing of staying away, being free and out of things, not being involved or caught in things. In the scene, the dream experiencing occurred in its bad form. She had the painful experiencing of being hurtfully withdrawn, pulled away, lost, not belonging, not a part of the family, being a little crazy. As with all painful and hurtful experiencings, the therapist describes it in its good form. What is more, the therapist wallows in the experiencing, gives it full life, opens it up. The therapist celebrates the experiencing:

T: All right, I am going to be the little girl, sitting at the table, and being away from it all, being free of them, the family, not being involved in them and what they are doing to me.
Pt: I felt crazy.
T: Right.
Pt: Didn't even know what they were saying.
T: (Being the dream experiencing) I don't even know what the hell you are

saying! I am withdrawn from you all! So long everyone! Bye bye! I am becoming a withdrawn nut!

Pt: (Low chuckle)

T: You got a schizo kid here! I am withdrawn from you all! Distanced from you all! Living here in my own crazy little cocoon! Just a little beserk creature! I'm a complete weirdo! (She clucks.) A lunatic! Here is where it all starts. I am withdrawn from you all! And I have all sorts of private thoughts! Crazy thoughts. See me staring at my glass of milk? Separated from you all. I am not a part of the family. WITHDRAWN! Absolutely gone from you!

Pt: (Giggles)

The therapist gives the instructions as an external agent who tells the patient what to do and how to do it. Then, gradually, as the instructions invite the patient and therapist to be in the scene and to be the dream experiencing, it is as if the therapist and patient are together. The therapist begins to be in the scene and to be the dream experiencing. It makes it easier for the patient when the therapist shares in the dream experiencing, as if the therapist were a part of the patient, ready and willing to be the dream experiencing in the early scene.

The instructions have shown the patient what to do and how to do it. They culminate with the invitation to go ahead and be this experiencing in this moment. As always, it is up to the patient.

Some illustrations of being the experiencing in the context of earlier life situations. The main thing is for the patient to wallow in the good form of the experiencing, to be inside the very core of the experiencing, to live and exist as the experiencing.

The instructions define the immediate scene, define the experiencing, and invite the patient to be the experiencing in this scene. Then it is up to the patient, as illustrated in the scene where the patient is a young boy fascinated with these sexy photographs ("Surreptitious in the store, and avoiding one another"):

T: Then let's go back into that scene, only this time you are going to be a person who knows what it is like to be found out, seen, caught, exposed. This is the young boy that you are, your personality. But we have to go back to the scene. Describe it enough so that it is real again, and you are in the bedroom of your Aunt Helen and Uncle Steve. Remember? You poked around in their dresser and found those great photographs! There's this one of the guy with his prick on the plate and a woman, naked, sitting at a table with a fork and a knife, and you're lying on their bed, fascinated as hell with the pictures . . .

Pt: I think I'm more shocked by the pictures. I never saw anything like that. It was weird. I don't think I'm feeling sexy. I get twinges in my prick, I remember, but the thing, I was excited as hell, and scared maybe someone'd find me.

T: (Inviting the patient to be the dream experiencing) Now let yourself be a whole new kid, altogether different. You can enjoy being found out. You can be caught and it is just fine. You can actually enjoy being seen. They know! Sure they do! Let them know! Be open! You are exposed because you're open. Are you ready to be this fellow?

Pt: (A pause for about eight or ten seconds, then . . .) LOOK AT THESE PICTURES! THEY ARE FILTHY! HEY AUNT HELEN AND UN-CLE STEVE! WHERE THE HELL DID YOU GET THIS STUFF! COME ON IN HERE! Look at these! Where did you get them?

Once the patient is being the experiencing, the therapist opens it up even further, carries it further, joins with the experiencing and gives it voice:

T: For God's sakes, don't make so much noise! They'll hear you!

Pt: I WANT them to come in! EVERYBODY COME IN. I FOUND SOME-THING. I FOUND SOMETHING. LOOKEE WHAT I FOUND.

T: SEX STUFF. THE KID FOUND SEX STUFF. LOOK WHAT HE FOUND. EVERYBODY IN.

Pt: Here I am, lying on this bed, doing bad things . . .

T: And he can do bad things — like letting everyone know what he found!

Pt: There you are Aunt Helen. Hello Uncle Steve.

T: What am I doing on this bed with these pictures? GUESS!

Pt: You think I'm such a nice well-behaved kid.

T: WRONG! DEAD WRONG!

Pt: I looked around in your room. I did a bad thing . . .

T: AND IT WAS GREAT.

Pt: Yeah, I LOVED doing that. I steal all over in Mom and Dad's place, and I never got such a great find.

T: LOOK AT THESE PICTURES. I MEAN JUST TAKE A LOOK AT THEM!

Pt: And look at me! ON YOUR BED AND STEALING YOUR PIC-TURES. SOME KID HUH!

T: AIN'T I JUST WONDERFUL?

Pt: Hey, aunty, do you do this . . . do you two get like this?

T: NAKED AND WITH TITS AND PRICKS AND CAN I WATCH?

Pt: Can I show you my little weenie? It's so small! Can I have some pictures like this? Please! Huh! Boy do you look shocked. Don't worry, I'll tell Mom and Dad all about these dirty pictures that you got, hid, hid in the drawer. What? You got them from Mom and Dad? Oh!!

T: What's your favorite? WHAT DO YOU DO WITH THEM?

Pt: YEAH! DO YOU SCREW TO THEM? (Laughs)

T: Can I watch, please!

Pt: I hope you don't mind my poking around in your dresser, but I love poking around, and I'm starting to get real sexy, and I'm just a little boy. Nothing really great at my Mom and Dad's. But this is the find of a century! I bet you got more, right? You know I'm going to poke around, right? You want to follow me around and catch me all over the house? Can I watch you screwing? Oh please?

This fellow has wallowed in a sense of being openly and freely exposed, caught, found out. He yelled loud enough to attract his aunt and uncle, and then carried out the being and behaving as this dream experiencing. He gets the sense of what it is like to live out this dream experiencing. That is the aim.

Sometimes the dream experiencing is quite different from what the patient recalls being and experiencing in the earlier scene. ("Maniac with the knife, and controlling the maniac"):

T: OK, there's Mom. Drunk. Gassed out of her mind. And Dad is yelling, and the neighbors are seeing and hearing all of this, and the Katkovsky's are here, watching. . . . And now you are a whole new person. Oh you are a person who controls things, you are the little girl who is in charge. Take charge. Take over, kid. You are the one who can take charge of all this, and do it all your way. Here you are, just let it go . . . OK, your turn . . .

Pt: Hey, everybody! THAT'S ENOUGH!!! GO GET MOTHER AND TAKE HER IN THE HOUSE! DO IT! That's right! We'll deal with this mess inside! Now DO IT. AND YOU ALL! COME AND HELP. COME ON. MR. KATKOVSKY! GET YOUR ASS DOWN HERE AND HELP DAD GET MOM IN THE HOUSE! MRS. KATKOVSKY! YOU COME WITH ME AND WE'LL MAKE SURE EVERYTHING IS ALL RIGHT. I WANT TO PUT MOM TO BED! AND YOU ALL DO WHAT I SAY!!!

T: Listen to the little kid going! Who is this kid? She sounds like the boss!

Pt: I AM! I'M GOING TO TELL YOU ALL WHAT TO DO . . .

T: AND YOU'RE DAMNED WELL GOING TO DO WHAT I SAY.

Pt: I'M IN CHARGE NOW.

T: THAT'S THE ONLY WAY TO SHUT YOU UP.

Pt: AND OH BOY, YOU ARE GOING TO SHUT UP AND LISTEN TO ME.

T: ATTA GIRL! TELL 'EM WHAT TO DO!

Pt: (She is in high spirits now, and there is a giggle in her voice.) BOOM BOOM BOOM. I'M MARCHING OVER TO YOU DAD. NOW YOU LISTEN TO ME. STOP YOUR DAMNED YELLING. THAT DOES NO GOOD AND IT NEVER DID. IT ONLY MAKES THINGS WORSE. YOU ALWAYS YELLED FOR NOTHING. THAT'S WHY MOM'S DRUNK. SO STOP YOUR YELLING AND GO OVER TO MOM AND YOU JUST PICK HER UP. TAKE MOM IN THE HOUSE. I WILL TAKE CHARGE OF EVERYTHING.

T: GOOD. NOW YOU GOT THE RIGHT LOOK ON YOUR FACE OLD MAN. I'M IN CHARGE NOW.

Pt: IT'S TIME THAT I TOOK OVER THIS FUCKED UP FAMILY!

T: All right! Everyone ready? March!! One! Two! One! Two! I'm the sergeant around here. So everyone does what I say.

Pt: YEAH. 'CAUSE I SAY IT.

T: And what I say goes! GOT THAT?

Pt: So hop to it! AND BRING ALL THE NEIGHBORS TO MY HOUSE . . .

T: "MY" HOUSE! LISTEN TO THE KID!

Pt: . . . AND I'LL EXPLAIN EVERYTHING TO THEM.

T: I'll give the news bulletin, and let you all know what I want you to know . . .

Pt: 'CAUSE I'M THE BOSS.

T: RIGHT ON, BABY!

Being the dream experiencing may be quiet or, as in the above illustrations, loud. It must be full and saturated whether the noise level is quiet or loud. In addition, the dream experiencing is the good form of what actually started in the earlier scene. From the dream, "Late for the wedding, and watching the nurses," we evoked an earlier scene in which she is at the table, staring at the milk. Being the dream experiencing means entering fully into the sense of being free, out of things, not being involved or caught up. It can occur quietly:

Pt: My mother, everyone thinks of me as the little girl who was so sick, you know, a good girl now, and so talented. They like the way I draw and they praise me. So talented. They say how pretty I am, and such a talent! I think they are driving me crazy. No one even asks anything about me . . .

T: The kid's having private inside thoughts! She's existing in her own little world. Look at her at the table. She's like a kid from another planet.

Pt: I do have thoughts. My own inner thoughts. Momma, I am watching your nose go up and down from the side, you talk, and I can not hear what you say, like a television screen with the sound turned off. I am withdrawing (with a lilt and lift to the word)! I am going into my own world! Good-bye family!

T: Ooommmmm.

Pt: Inside myself. In my own little world here! I am me, all me. I am aware of my stomach when I breathe. I can listen to my thoughts. All inside myself here. Good-bye family! Enjoy yourself. I close my eyes and I am a little girl meditating. Yeah! You all are slowly suffocating me with your . . . trying to get me to be nice and talented and frail. I am not any of those things! I am a little girl with my own thoughts—and they are not the thoughts you think I have! I am not going to stay here at the table! I am going to float away! Light! Floating away! Here I am with my eyes closed at the table! Poppa would have a fit! Grampa would glare at the little girl! I don't give a damn! Aaaahhh! I am going away now. Please excuse me. And I walk away. I take little steps and walk away. I have freed myself. Good for me. I am a person. My own person. Thank you for letting me be in this family. But you cannot force me to be something you all want me to be. Thank you and enjoy yourself and I am floating away. I have my own friends, and we talk about our thoughts, and I am feeling light and floaty, just . . . light and I am floating so easily over the trees, light, and everything is so peaceful . . .

Frequently, the patient slides into other situations in which she had pieces and bits of that same experiencing, or even full measures of the dream experiencing. It is as if she has entered into a new part of her personality, and that opens up new memories that are apparently attached to this dream potential. We follow the experiencing into these new situations:

Pt: . . . and I am floating away. I have my own friends, and we talk about our thoughts, and I am feeling light and floaty, just . . . light and I am floating so easily over the trees, light, and everything is so peaceful . . .

T: Aaah, just floating around . . .

Pt: My Dad and Mom used to fight. They would fight. Bicker. They are in the kitchen, and I remember I used to stay there and feel all tight inside, and I remember I walked away and they both yelled at me and I got mad. I talked back and told them I hated their fighting and I got mad at them!

T: Great! Who needs them?

Pt: Who needs you? I don't go ahead and fight. . . . I used to go to my girlfriend Gloria and we talked about how our parents used to fight. I think that's when I turned to my friends. I liked them. I used to stay in my room and read. Just 'cause they were fighting all the time. I got away from them. I got away from them. I remember I wanted to go live with my . . . with Gloria's family. I actually asked her if I could live with her, and Gloria and I would talk about having our own place 'cause it was free of all that crap. I did get away. I stayed away from them. I did it.

Whether the patient finishes being the dream experiencing in the context of the past scene or goes on to other recollected past scenes, a point will be reached when she finishes. She has been the dream experiencing all the way, and this step of dream work is over.

BEING THE DREAM EXPERIENCING IN THE CONTEXT OF RECENT LIFE SITUATIONS

The goal of step 4 (Figure 1) is for the patient literally to be the dream experiencing. First we do this in the context of the peak moments in the dream (step 4.1), then in the context of the earlier life situations (step 4.3). Now we are ready to be the dream experiencing in the context of recent life situations (step 4.4).

Using the Recent Life Situations Obtained Earlier in the Session

Chapter 2 described how to record the dream and then to get two or three linkages or connections between the dream and incidents in your recent life a day or so prior to the dream. Chapter 3 described how to start with those incidents and to find the moment of strong feeling. Now you are ready to "be" the dream experiencing in these recent life situations.

There are at least two reasons for using these recent life situations. One is that we are moving closer and closer to being the dream experiencing in the real world outside this room where we are working (Chapter 12). The second is that our theory of dreaming holds that the linked recent life situations are extremely appropriate for the dream experiencing because it was exceedingly present. It may have occurred just a little bit, or it may have occurred painfully, or it may have been activated but not expressed. In any case, we are ready to use the recent life situations obtained earlier in the session.

In the dream, "Late for the wedding, and watching the nurses," one of the linkages came from "ice skates": "It was on a large pond. Everyone was on ice skates." A few days before the dream, she had called her ex-husband, and he had cavalierly mentioned that he and his new girlfriend had just returned from ice skating. That is when the feeling happened. She remembered how he had cleared everything out of their apartment, even taking her ice skates. That was the moment on the phone when she was hurt and crushed. A second linkage came from the following piece of the dream: "The doctor said that he was sorry, he didn't have time." The linkage was to the recent moment with her older brother, who was fixing her back porch. She had asked him to please finish fixing the steps because it was over a month and she wanted to use the steps. He snapped that he was sorry, he didn't have time, and she was frozen numb.

Sometimes the linked recent situations are quite ordinary, and the feelings are only moderate. In the dream, "Surreptitious in the store, and avoiding one another," one of the linkages was from a book of photographs. The day before, his wife asked him where the camera was, and he answered that he wasn't quite sure; he hadn't used the camera in a year or so. The feeling was a moderate lethargy. He was tired and didn't want to start looking for the camera. The other linkage was from the blonde girl who was in the photograph in the dream. She was very young, not terribly attractive, and she had blemishes on her face. Her face was the face of the girl at the corner store, the daughter of the owner. She was at the cash register yesterday when he purchased some frozen orange juice. The feeling was moderate as he remembered her as a toddler, and here she is handling the cash register. He felt old and stable and secure.

In the dream, "Maniac with the knife, and controlling the maniac," one of the linkages came from the mats: "There were mats, like gym mats, laid out in this living room so that people could sleep." The linkage was to the apartment of a fellow she had slept with a few days ago. He had a large loft, and one section had gym equipment: mats, a weight machine, and a fancy rowing machine. Her feeling was a mild disdain, for he was pudgy, and she kidded him about having the right "equipment" but not taking advantage of it. They laughed. A second linkage came from the part of the dream wherein a neighbor " . . . was explaining that the reason we were all sleeping there was that he had gotten into an argument with somebody and the guy had threatened to kill him and burn the neighborhood down. . . . " The "argument with somebody" connected with a recent argument she had with her sister. A few days before the dream, her sister had begun arguing with her. It started with her sister's accusing her of borrowing money and not paying it back and it went on to everything else. Her feeling was that of always being on the defensive with her sister.

The task is to be the dream experiencing in any of the recent situational contexts. In the dream, "Maniac with the knife, and controlling the maniac," the dream experiencing is that of power over the other person, sheer control over the other one. You can be this dream experiencing in the recent scene in the fellow's loft, where you are kidding him about his "equipment," or you can be the dream experiencing in the scene where you are arguing with your sister. You can select either one or you can use both. All we need is the recent scene and the explicit moment in the scene when there was some sort of feeling.

Being the Dream Experiencing in the
Recent Life Situation

Once again the therapist invites the patient to be the dream experiencing. This time, however, the context is much closer home, and therefore it is often more difficult for the patient to allow herself fully to be the dream experiencing. After all, the recent scene may have occurred within the last day or so, and we are inviting the patient to be a whole new and deeper experiencing in a radical redoing of who and what she is in this recent scene.

Starting from the dream, "Late for the wedding, and watching the nurses," the patient was able to be the dream experiencing of staying away, being free and out of entanglements, not being involved and caught, letting go. She was able to be this experiencing within the context of the peak moment in the dream. Then she was this dream experiencing in the early scene of being a child at the table, staring at the milk, and also in another childhood scene of telling her friend's family that she intended to move in with them. Now she has the opportunity to be this dream experiencing in the recent scene in which she is on the phone with ex-husband Harry, who tells her that he just returned from ice skating with his new girlfriend.

T: Remember a few days ago, talking with Harry on the phone? You called him. He mentioned something about just coming back from skating with his new girlfriend. Well, you've been divorced for almost two years. Suppose that you continue just being this person who feels what it's like to stay away from all this crap, who feels what it is like to be free and out of things, not being involved or caught in problems, not setting things up anymore. Who can be free. Just go ahead. Be this person for a while. What the hell would you do? Huh? You do it. OK? Yeah? No?

Pt: Well, I still like him.

T: Sure you do.

Pt: But I wouldn't call him. Bye Charlie! Enjoy yourself! I got my own life now and I don't need him. Good-bye! . . . I'd say, "Hey, what am I doing running after you? I shouldn't even be bothering you! Hang up! . . . " What the hell am I clutching after him? That's dumb!

T: Hey Charlie or Harry or whatever the hell your name is! What the hell am I doing clutching after you? That's dumb! I mean that is really dumb. I am an absolute ninny!

Pt: I'm just making myself miserable talking with this guy! And I did it to myself! Shit! I don't have to call him! That is dumb! And that crack about ice skating. Shit! I asked for it! I call up and practically tell you to hurt me. That is really dumb! Go lead your life, kiddo! I'm cutting the bonds! I'm letting you go!

T: Good-bye! So looong! Ta ta!

Pt: Enjoy yourself!

T: Now I think I'll hang up and cry my little heart out!

Pt: No way! (Here comes a precious shift in which she is now fully being the dream experiencing.) You're all right, Harry. . . . I don't have to call you up and get you to hurt me. . . . I did that to you all the time, didn't I? . . . I'm sorry. . . . I really am. You poor boy . . . it's all right. I feel so different now. Like I really can leave you . . . let you be alone. I don't know . . . I have my own life.

She sounds different and she is being different. She is being a person who can be free of hurtful entanglements, who can let go in ways that feel right and honest and internally wholesome. This is what we want.

When the patient is still being the dream experiencing in the earlier scene, the therapist can speak to this new and different person, inviting him to live and be in the recent situational context. From the dream, "Surreptitious in the store, and avoiding one another," the dream experiencing is that of being found out, exposed, open and transparent. The patient is fully being this experiencing in the earlier scene in the bedroom of the aunt and uncle. When this step finishes, the patient remains the new and different experiencing. The therapist addresses this new and different person and invites him to be in the recent scene at the corner grocery:

T: I like you. I think you are great. . . . Would you be willing to live in a scene that happened just a couple of days ago? Here's the scene. You are at the corner grocery. At the cash register is this young girl. You remember her when she was just a toddler, and now she is old enough to run the cash register. Can you imagine? Well, here you are, a person who loves to be seen, found out, caught, exposed, and you are this person now in the store. You are at the cash register, right? What are you going to do to get this delightful feeling? Will you let yourself?

Pt: Uh-huh. Sure.

T: Your turn . . .

Pt: You're supposed to be a tiny little girl! About this big! What happened to you? My God! Am I this old? I am an old man now. You are old—and I must be ancient! Yeah, I think that's what I was thinking, a little. I couldn't say that. Like an old crickety old man, a dirty old man. You'll probably think, your mother will tell you not to talk to old dirty men like me. Never can tell what they'll do. I want to go home and tell my wife. I was at the store and I got old. I am old! I feel old. I want to confess all kinds of things to you. I never tell you. I think 'cause I hate to admit that I'm old, really ancient. I feel old! God, do you feel old? Do you think about dying? I do. I wake up in the morning and I feel like crying 'cause I, our kids are grown and gone and my mother and dad are dead, and I feel like crying. I don't want to die! . . . Hell, I never talk to you anymore. You know why? 'Cause I'm ashamed at what I'm thinking! That's why! I'm afraid you'll laugh at me! You never feel like that. Do you?

He is truly being the experiencing of being seen, being exposed and open and transparent, and all starting from the recent life situation.

Let us turn to the dream, "Maniac with the knife, and controlling the maniac." The experiencing is that of being in charge, controlling, dominating, having this person in her hands. She has just finished being this experiencing in the early scene in which her mother had come home drunk and passed out on the front lawn. Now the therapist offers her a chance to be the dream experiencing in the context of the recent scene in which she is at the apartment of the fellow she had slept with, and she is kidding him about having the right "equipment" but not taking advantage of it:

T: You really enjoy this, don't you? I mean being the little kid who takes over, is in charge. Good for you. What about with Tom, in his apartment here? You can be cocky in kidding him about his "equipment," that he ought to take advantage of it. Fine. Now maybe you could let yourself get that great feeling of taking charge of good old Tom, being in control. Just be in control of the guy. Hi Tom, baby, just put your equipment in my hands, kiddo, and I'll show you what you can do with it . . .

Pt: (A little nervous giggle) Oh, I don't know. (She stops.)

T: (She flipped away from the dream experiencing and into her ordinary operating personality. It is always the patient's prerogative, even though the therapist, as the part of the patient, is ready and willing to go ahead.) Yes you can! Do it! Do it! Hell, you did it in the dream, and you did it on the front lawn with your mom and dad and the Katkovsky's. . . . Naw, don't. It's embarrassing, and a little scary. What the hell. You decide. You're the boss, and you will have to be the one to feel what it's like. Your decision.

Pt: I don't think . . . that's not me. I'd be acting! I don't do that with men.

T: (Being the other part who can) OK, OK already. I could. I know damned well I could. But all right. No. That's it. No. . . . Hell.

Pt: (Pause)

T: Will you please stop pausing! It's OK, don't do it. Just let me sulk a little here. It's only fair.

Pt: That'd be rude.

T: (Pause) Huh? What'd be rude? What are you talking about?

Pt: Bossing him around.

T: Right. Bossing him around would be rude. Ordering your old Poppa around was rude. Right. And taking charge on the front lawn was rude. Right. So forget it. Right?

Pt: I'm not that way with guys! I guess I'm not a dishrag, but I . . . well, I don't order them around. I've never done that. I don't even think I'd like it.

T: What the hell are you thinking of, picturing doing? I'm just picturing you being right here in his apartment and being this time a woman who has the feeling of being in control, taking charge, being the big boss. That's all.

Pt: You know what I'd like to do?

T: What?

Pt: I'd like to be like I was in the dream, but I know he wouldn't cooperate. I'd like to have him crying, down on his knees, crying!

T: Here we go! Look, it doesn't have to be real! Let's start here. Here he is, down on his knees, crying. Let's pretend. There he is, confessing all his frailties and uncertainties—which Tom of course would never do. But we got him doing it. Let's start here! Tom! Down on your knees! CRY! OK, kiddo, your turn.

Pt: (She blurts it out like an order.) Put your head between my legs!! SMELL IT. TAKE A WHIFF! You're never getting any sex from me until you start treating me nice! No more of your holier than thou shit! JUST WHO THE HELL DO YOU THINK YOU ARE!! No more running after you, you bastard! You come to me! You like my body? Seduce ME! DO WHAT I SAY! I WANT YOU TO SAY YOU'RE SORRY FOR HURTING ME! SAY YOU'RE SORRY! LOUDER! YOU MEAN IT!!! CRY YOU LITTLE BABY. MOMMA'S GOING TO MAKE IT ALL BETTER. SEE! YOU'RE A ROTTEN FUCK! FROM

NOW ON I WANT REAL FUCKING AND YOU'RE GOING TO DO IT MY WAY! MY WAY!!! I WANT REAL LOVE MAKING FROM YOU OR WE ARE THROUGH. STARTING TONIGHT! NO! STARTING NOW! (She is screeching, the words exploding in a rush. There is an almost exultant exhilaration in her words.)

T: WOW!

Pt: THAT'S NOT ME!

T: WHAT A DAMNED PITY!

Pt: (Coming down) I've never done anything like that.

Pt: What a damned pity.

Pt: Yes. Yes. It is a damned pity.

T: Well, it sure felt delicious.

Pt: It sure did.

The patient was rather reluctant to be the dream experiencing within the context of the recent scene. In the beginning of this example, the patient was already back into her old operating domain, whereas in the first two examples the patients were still wallowing around inside the dream experiencing. The therapist always gives the person the choice of whether or not to be the dream experiencing in the context of the recent scene. But it is especially important when the person is no longer in the dream experiencing. You must give that person a genuine choice. Otherwise being the dream experiencing in the recent scene will not work.

The radical and precious accomplishment of this step is that the patient is the dream experiencing, is inside and existing and experiencing as this potential. We accomplish this magnificent transformation by enabling the patient to be the dream experiencing within the context of the dream itself, within the context of connected early scenes, and within the context of recent life scenes and situations. We are now ready for the final step in the session.

CHAPTER 11

The Importance of
Being-Behavior Change

THE FINAL STEP OF THE SESSION is to experience what it can be like to be and behave as a new person. The final step gives you an opportunity to taste and sample what life could be like if you were to be and behave as the dream experiencing within the context of scenes and situations from the next few days or weeks or perhaps from now on. Here we discuss the importance of this final step in a session of experiential dream work.

THE VALUE AND SIGNIFICANCE OF
BEING-BEHAVIOR CHANGE

The directions of change through experiential dream work. When you began the experiential dream work session you were the person given at the left in Figure 5. The person you can become is given at the right. There are four directions of change.

One is toward increasingly integrated relationships between the dream potential (Deeper Dream Potential 2, Figure 5) and the ordinary person (Operating Potential 1, Figure 5). When relationships are "integrated," there are characteristic changes that tend to occur. Instead of disintegrative feelings such as anxiety, threat, feeling disconnected and in pieces (indicated by the two negative signs in the channel of relationships at the left in Figure 5), you will have integrative feelings such as internal harmony, oneness, peacefulness (indicated by the two positive signs in the channel of relationships at the right). Externalizations of the deeper potential (Externalized Deeper Potential 2, Figure 5) will tend to extinguish so that you will no longer have persons in your world who represent your own disintegrative deeper potentials. Nor will there be any "internalized" physical-bodily manifestations of the deeper potentials that have been pushed down and barricaded. Finally, there will be a decrease in former disintegrative behaviors (B2); these will tend to be replaced with integrative behaviors (B7). These changes comprise the increasingly integrated rela-

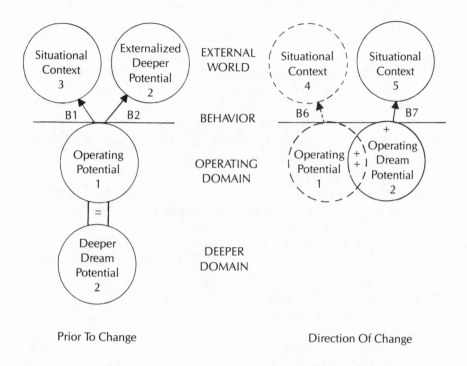

Prior To Change   Direction Of Change

Figure 5. The Direction of Change Through Experiential Dream Work

tionship between the new you, as the dream potential, and the former you, as the operating potential.

The second direction of change is that the deeper dream potential will become a part of the operating domain. In other words, the dream potential will become a solid part of the person that you are or, in still other words, you will become the dream potential. In Figure 5 this is indicated as the change from being outside of and beneath the operating domain, on the left, to being a part of the actual operating domain, on the right.

The third direction of change is called "actualization." It means that you now are the dream potential in the course of your actual living and being. You behave in new ways (B7) that provide for the experiencing of the dream potential and that construct and use new situations (Situational Context 5, Figure 5) in which the dream potential can be experienced. It also means that behaving on the basis of this dream potential and experiencing this dream potential are accompanied with good feelings of aliveness, excitement, and vitality.

These are indicated by the single positive sign at the top of operating dream potential 2, on the right in Figure 5.

Finally, the fourth direction of change is that the former operating potential (Operating Potential 1, Figure 5) will tend to extinguish. This is the risk of the other three directions of change. You may no longer "be" operating potential 1, may no longer experience this potential. It may simply go away. This risk is indicated by the dotted circle around operating potential 1 on the right in Figure 5, the dotted circle around situational context 4, and the dotted line indicating behavior 6. In other words, the old operating potential may well extinguish, and with it goes the former situational contexts and behaviors that construct and use the old situations. Instead of merely involving changes in your "responses" to situations, the risk is a far more sweeping one, in which your former operating personality, its behaviors, and its actual life situations no longer are present. Yet the risk is also that the operating potential will remain; if it does, it will be different, and it will be different because of the good integrative relationships between it and the dream potential. There will be new behaviors (B6) and it will occur in a new external world (Situational Context 4).

These directions of change point the way toward the ideal person, the optimal functioning (Mahrer, 1967, 1985a, 1986a, 1989a). At the end of every session you get a taste and a sample of what this direction of change can be like. This is why we refer to this final step as "being-behavioral change" rather than merely "behavior change." In effect, "being-behavioral change" refers to the change in who the patient is as well as how the patient behaves.

What part does the dream play in determining the directions of change? In the experiential approach, the dream gives us the deeper experiencing. Once we know the nature of the deeper experiencing, the directions of change are to provide for the integrated and actualized deeper experiencing.

Outside of the experiential approach, one common principle is that, if the dream is interpreted as indicating some unpleasant or dangerous process or event, changes are to be made in the imminent world so as to forestall and avoid the possibility of its occurrence. This is an ancient way of using dreams: "If a Zulu dreams that his friend attempts to take his life, he immediately breaks the relationship with him" (Wolff, 1952, p. 7). This same principle is used in many contemporary dream approaches. If you interpret the dream as indicating the possibility of an accident or illness, changes are in the direction of avoiding their occurrence:

> Premonitions of dangerous possibilities may render a dreamer more cautious and tend to prevent serious mistakes, such as accidents, infectious illness, and the like. (Henderson, 1980, p. 378)

In many approaches, the dream is used to give a picture of some developing psychopathology, and therefore the therapist guides or prescribes changes aimed at preventing the outbreak of the psychopathological process. If the dream is used to indicate the presence of a "latent psychosis," the therapist may then determine that the appropriate extratherapy change may be that of avoiding situations of "stress," or that there be a change in medication, or that the patient gain added "support," or that changes be made to increase the "reality foundation" in the patient's extratherapy world.

In the experiential approach, we figure out the kinds of possible behavioral changes after we get some idea of the nature of the dream experiencing, and the new behaviors are to serve the dream potential by providing for its experiencing. In many other dream approaches, in contrast, the therapist already has a good idea of the behaviors that are to change even before the dream session. For example, the patient is to behave in less depressed ways, or reduce the drinking of alcohol, or be more assertive. The predetermined changes are in whatever behaviors are considered part of the patient's "problem."

The culmination of experiential dream work is the patient's new-found choice and capability for being-behavioral change in the external world. When this final step is effective and successful, you can leave the session as a wholesale new person. You have a newfound capability of being and behaving in new and different ways in the external world, and a newfound choice of being and behaving in these new ways or not doing so. This is the culmination of our dream work. Our work ends here.

The culmination of experiential dream work is the successful and effective achievement of this being-behavioral change step. When the patient experiences what it is like to be and behave as the dream potential within the context of the external world, our work is over. If the dream reveals the experiencing of masculine power, then we seek to "realize" this potential:

The straight-laced young man who experienced the dramatic shift from weakness to power in the last example felt within this dream the reality of his masculinity for the first time; therefore his entire therapy was geared to its progressive realization in "cool, confident" steps. (Rossi, 1985, p. 16)

The goal is to be this experiencing from now on. Behavior is the means and the effect, but not the sole goal. That is, new behaviors lock you into the dream potential, and new behaviors also flow naturally out of your being the deeper potential. So the success of this step is your being and behaving as the deeper potential; it is not simply behavior change.

Yet all of this is occurring right here in the office. You are existing in scenes from tomorrow and next week, yet all of this is occurring here, with your eyes closed. It is as if the world of the future is brought into the immediately present office, or as if the immediately present office is extruded out into the future.

The emphasis is not merely on behavior change in the waking world. It is more than that. It is using the external world as the arena in which the patient can be and behave as the new dream experiencing:

We cannot dismiss the possibility that his waking existence may be open and responsive to much more diverse and richer world phenomena. This is especially likely if the analyst encourages the patient to begin to think about a possible relationship between the dreaming and waking life. (Boss, 1977, p. 41)

When this step is finished, the patient is actually being a person who is the dream experiencing, actually behaving in new ways, and actually existing in the imminently future world. If the session ends without going through this final step, the person is left in a limbo state. There are twitchings to be and behave in this new way in the imminent world out there, a lingering sense of incompleteness. A sliver of this ominous state is contained in the Huron Indians belief " . . . that if they have dreamed of something and have failed to carry it out, some misfortune which was mysteriously expressed in the dream will befall them" (Lévy-Bruhl, 1923, p. 116). The injunction is to undergo this final step of the session or suffer the consequences.

Actual being-behavioral change in the external world is a function of the patient's newfound choice and capability rather than the func-

tion of successful dream work. Most approaches to dream work salute actual changes in the external world as the responsible outcome or goal of effective and successful dream work by the therapist. The criterion is what happens in the actual external world between sessions or after the sessions are over. It is as if the therapist or researcher were to accompany the patient to see if actual changes did indeed occur. Corriere et al. (1980) are representative of most approaches in holding that the goal and mark of successful outcome are actual changes in the external world consequent to dream work:

> It is the way he or she responds to life following a psychotherapeutic session that will create change and lead to the transformation. If functional analysis doesn't move the person to new methods of behaving outside the therapy session, it becomes just another way of interpreting dreams. (p. 175)

In experiential work, the final step of each session is precious and important because it provides the person with a chance to be a whole new personality within scenes and situations from the imminent external world. When the patient leaves the session, he has a newfound choice and capability of actually behaving in new ways in the actual external world. It is as if he has actually been in the external world and carried out the new ways of being and behaving.

We hold and trust that this person's newfound choice and capability play a large hand in determining whether or not he will or will not carry out new behavior. Looked at the other way, the actual occurrence of new behavior in the external world is in part a function of the patient's own newfound choice and capability.

If you want being-behavioral change, you need explicit methods for bringing it about. You can be the dream potential from now on, and you can behave in all sorts of new ways. But according to the experiential approach they come about by using explicit methods.

Many dream approaches offer you a way of understanding the meaning of the dream. The idea is that if you understand the meaning of the dream, there should be changes in personality and subsequently in behavior. You do not need explicit methods of being-behavior change. I cannot agree with any part of this reasoning. Understanding the meaning of the dream tends to anchor you even more in the personality you are and is counter-effective to being the dream experiencing. Even more, I contend that significant behavior change will not occur automatically, and certainly not in behavior connected to the dream experiencing. You need an explicit package of methods for being-behavior change.

Nor are these methods those of merely talking to the patient about the sorts of being-behavioral changes she could or should make in her extratherapy world. When dream work is done, some therapists tell patients to think about ways of being different. For example, Boss interprets a patient's dream as indicating feminine possibilities and then proceeds to ask the patient to consider ways of opening up this feminine side in the actual external world:

> Could there be a task, for instance, faintly appealing to you and demanding of you as a waking person to bring to light the femininity not only of an external distant Latin word, but the feminine character traits of your own existence? In your waking states you have showed up to now only a decidedly masculine bearing. Has not the moment come when your own possibilities of feminine ways of relating toward that which you encounter have to be carried out? (Boss, 1977, p. 63)

Similarly, if the person works on his own dream, the idea is to see what the dream indicates and to think about behavior change:

> When you have found out what your dream refers to, and you have gotten a bodily sense of a growth direction and how you might want to change, it is time to devise ways of acting in a new way in accord with how you wish to change. (Gendlin, 1986, p. 176)

I do not believe that being-behavioral changes occur merely by seeing what the dream is taken to mean or by coupling this with thinking about ways to change. Talking to the patient about change does not work, nor does it work for the patient to talk in general about intended changes. If you value actual being-behavioral changes in the external world, you need explicit methods of bringing these about.

Neither the ordinary operating personality nor the external world wants being-behavioral change. This final step is precious and supremely important because it is just about the only way for the person to get a sample of what it can be like to be and behave as this dream experiencing and to carve out and live in an external world that fits the dream experiencing. The ordinary operating personality has worked long and hard to construct an external world that absolutely suits it. From the perspective of the dream experiencing, there is virtually no room for change. The ordinary operating personality has not welcomed the dream experiencing, and certainly has not constructed a world cordial to the dream experiencing. What all this means is that the dream experiencing faces an operating personality and an external world that are alien and unreceptive.

In practical terms, this means that when the person who is the ordinary operating personality faces the possibility of effecting being-behavioral changes in her current world, she will likely face a formidable blank wall. This is grim state of affairs. The ordinary operating domain might have some room for its own package of behavior changes, but these are quite different from whatever behavior changes might be entertained by the dream experiencing.

While the reluctance to change behavior is strong, the reluctance to change "being" is even stronger. The operating domain and its external world would do almost anything to prevent the shift into the dream experiencing. As long as the center of I-ness is inside the ordinary operating domain, the person is virtually unable to get out of this personality, get into and "be" the dream experiencing, and exist in an external world. The stable operating personality simply will not permit this.

In most dream approaches, what changes is the way you behave, but not the actual you, not who you are, not the operating potentials that comprise you. In most approaches, including psychoanalytic/psychodynamic approaches, there is a stable "you" or self that does the free association and gets insight from the interpretations, and then modifies its perceptions and attitudes and behaviors in the waking world; but this self is stable and safe from substantive change:

> Through the disciplined methodology of free association and interpretation, the individual can make this translation from the symbolic abstractions, and can be in a position then to correct the conceptual distortions of his waking consciousness and the concomitant distortions of his feelings, his attitudes, and his practices. (Bonime, 1962, p. 34)

This operating and functioning "you" or self or ego or operating personality will not permit substantial change in what it is. It will perhaps allow minor changes in its distal parts, perhaps even in carefully selected behaviors, but changes in its actual self are beyond limits.

If you are a therapist, this means you should follow the guidelines for selecting the methods of effecting being-behavior change, the scene and the actual behaviors. If you are a person working on your own dreams, it means that you also should follow the guidelines for selecting new behaviors and situations. Without these helpful guideline questions you will face a formidable blank wall.

Experiential being-behavioral change versus therapist-enhancing extratherapy changes. In our approach, the dream experiencing is the determinant of the being-behavioral changes. You can work toward these changes when you are an experiential therapist with a patient and when you use your own dreams. Indeed, one of the advantages of working on your own dreams is that you are free to obtain these kinds of changes. When you are a patient who is enveloped in any of the common therapist-patient relationships, it is unlikely that you can obtain these kinds of being-behavioral changes. Even worse, my thesis is that in virtually all therapeutic approaches the kinds of extratherapy changes that occur are limited mainly to those that enhance the role of the therapist and the therapist-patient role relationship.

I suggest that in virtually all approaches the relationship between therapist and patient limits the allowable changes to two classes. In one class, the changes work toward enhancing the role of the therapist in the patient's life and eliminating any competitors for the therapist's role. Suppose that the therapist plays the role of the omniscient one, the one with special knowledge, the one who truly understands the inner psychic structure of the patient's personality. In order to reinforce this role and to get rid of competitors, the extratherapy changes may include not talking over personal problems with her priest or other counselors, gradually letting go of the women's self-help group she has been in, reading the books suggested by the therapist, altering her daily schedule in order to have two appointments a week, having her husband come for a few visits to the therapist in order for the therapist to have the husband assist the patient in the changes she is undergoing. You can predict the kinds of extratherapy changes the therapist will work toward achieving when the therapist has the role of the good and caring parental figure, or the only real man in the patient's world, or the one who is always there in emergencies, or the one who knows the answers to life's problems, or the only one who can gradually steer the patient out of the debilitating "pathological state."

The bottom line is that the therapist truncates relationships that might compete with the relationship the therapist wants the patient to have with the therapist. However, the therapist rarely says, "I want you to give up your relationship with that woman and concentrate on being with me." Instead, the therapist wraps the behavior change in a justifying rationale. For example, the therapist says that because of the patient's diagnostic condition, it is best to reduce "inordinate stress," and therefore the patient should give up the relationship with the woman:

> . . . since the patient was schizophrenic, it was necessary to use the dreaming as something that might help him avoid overly demanding interpersonal relationships. He had to be forcibly dissuaded, for example, from becoming more deeply involved in a love relationship with a certain woman. (Boss, 1977, p. 126)

The second class of extratherapy changes includes those that enhance the role relationship that the therapist engineers with the patient. If their relationship is one in which the therapist is the tough big sister who is educating and guiding the patient toward feminine strength, then the extratherapy changes may include a more equal relationship with her husband, spending more time with women friends, volunteering at the women's center, dressing in less "feminine" ways. Whatever role relationship is established, it emphasizes those changes that are permitted by and enhance the particular role relationship.

All in all, there is a sharp difference between extratherapy changes that provide for the dream experiencing and those that enhance the role relationship the therapist establishes with the patient. Even more, the kinds of extratherapy changes flowing out of the experiential approach work toward explicitly defeating and diminishing the importance of the relationship with the therapist. Whatever the nature of the experiencing, the changes are to occur in the extratherapy world, with persons from the extratherapy world—rather than feeding the growing relationship with the therapist. Across the board, there is a sharp differentiation between the enlarged scope of experiential being-behavioral changes and the limited range of therapist-enhancing extratherapy changes.

Experiential being-behavioral change versus the supreme importance of the therapy situation. The net effect of this final step is to elevate the importance of the extratherapy world and symmetrically to diminish the importance of the therapy situation. The context in which this final step occurs is the extratherapy world. The patient lives and exists in prospective scenes of this imminent world, and correspondingly much less so in the context of being here in the office with the therapist. Indeed, there is a grating antinomy between the extratherapy world and the therapist-patient context, between the importance of being-behavioral change in the extratherapy world and upholding the supreme importance of the therapy situation.

In effect, you do have a choice. You can value being-behavioral change. This diminishes the importance of the therapy situation, for living in prospective scenes and experiences becomes more important than merely talking about what it is like to be and behave in these extratherapy scenes. On the other hand, you can value the therapy situation, in which case being-behavioral change is entertained only in ways that enhance the therapeutic context itself, including the role of the therapist and the relationship between therapist and patient.

PREPARATION AND READINESS FOR
BEING-BEHAVIORAL CHANGE

In an important sense, everything you have done so far in the session has been preparation and readiness for this final step. This means there are some indicators that you either are ready or not for this final step.

Being the dream potential versus reverting back into the ordinary operating personality. The patient is ready for behavior change when she is being the dream potential. It means that she is not wholly back to being the ordinary personality she was at the beginning of the session. Instead, she is now the deeper potential, speaking as the deeper potential, feeling and thinking as the deeper potential. She may be this all the way or only a little bit — the more the better.

When the patient is being the dream potential, behavior change is relatively easy. It is as if the new dream potential is quite ready for new behaviors, as if there is a behavioral vacuum and behaviors express what the potential is ready to express and to undergo. In this state of being the dream potential, the person is quite ready for new behaviors.

In contrast, picture the person who is back into being the ordinary operating personality. This person is not ready for the kinds of behaviors that go with the dream potential. Under this condition, the therapist would use methods of facilitating behavior change that are different from those called for when the patient is at least somewhat in the dream potential. Preparation and readiness are a function of who the patient is when we turn to behavior change.

Preparation consisted of being and behaving on the basis of the dream experiencing in the context of the dream, earlier and recent life situations (Chapter 10). These conditions were relatively safe—certainly safer than actually being as this dream experiencing in real life scenes when you leave the office. Yet all of this is preparation, readiness for being this dream experiencing in prospective scenes from tonight and tomorrow and next week in real life. If you did any of the earlier steps poorly, partially, less than all the way, or if you skipped any of them, then you are not completely ready for this final step.

Some indications that the patient is especially ready for this final step. Among the indications is a dream in which the dreamer is the main character and the feeling is good in both peaks. This means that the person has gone all the way into the guts of the deeper potential rather than going merely partway. These dreams virtually proclaim that the patient is ready to be the dream potential in the imminent future world. Perhaps the readiness lies in the personality state being sufficiently integrated and actualized to allow the sense of I-ness to enter all the way into the deeper potential in the dream state.

Corriere et al. (1980) use a somewhat similar indicator of readiness for opening up the dream feeling-experiencing into the real world:

> [In some dreams] . . . feeling is dominant. . . . The dreamer allows him- or herself to be aware of the feeling and permits it to occur to the fullest extent. . . . Such a dream indicates either that the dreamer is ready for and needs an increase in feeling in his or her life, or that such an increase has just occurred. (p. 42)

Mendel (1980) likewise sees the dream as indicating readiness or lack thereof for carrying out the dream feeling-experiencing in the imminent world. For example, if expressing assertiveness is followed by negative consequences in the dream, Mendel takes this as indicating a lack of readiness. By implication, if the consequences of such expression are positive, then perhaps the person is ready:

The assessment of emotional means is important in the conduct of psychotherapy. For example, if the dreaming existence cuts across a dream in which it is overwhelmed by the consequences of expressing an assertive attitude, such a patient is certainly not ready to express his assertiveness in the real world. Clearly, the expression of assertive and aggressive feelings is beyond the emotional means of that patient at that time. . . . (Mendel, 1980), p. 396)

In the experiential approach, every dream is used to go through all the steps, including being-behavioral change. If the dreamer is not the main character and the feeling is bad, then we have more work to do in each of the steps. On the other hand, if the dreamer is the main character in both peaks and the feeling is positive, then we accept these as indicators of special readiness.

In addition, there are two indicators of readiness provided in the course of dream work itself. One is that the patient enters wholly, easily, and wholesomely into being the dream experiencing in the context of the dream, the earlier situational context, and the recent scene. The second occurs when the patient finishes being the dream experiencing in the context of the recent scene and spontaneously turns to the real world out there. Usually the patient is still being the dream experiencing, only now she seems to lift her head from the context of the recent life scene and turns toward the imminent world. She mentions the real world. She seems to start to live in it. She says, "I wish I could be this way." "I'm thinking about my husband." "Maybe I could be this way with my daughter." "Richard would be surprised." "The court case is coming in a few weeks." "I'd never really act like that." "I'm thinking about the way I fight with my supervisor." "Being this way would be nice." The patient already is turning to the world of the imminently future.

CHAPTER 12

How to Do
Being-Behavior Change

THE PURPOSE OF THIS CHAPTER is to describe how to select an appropriate method of effecting being-behavior change, as well as the prospective scene-situation and the appropriate behaviors. This final step ends with trying out or rehearsing a few behaviors and a commitment to carrying out one or more of these behaviors.

SELECTING THE METHOD OF EFFECTING
BEING-BEHAVIOR CHANGE

If you are a therapist, you can use any of the seven methods that follow. There is a helpful guideline. Methods 1–3 are especially appropriate for the patient who is still more or less being the dream experiencing. On the other hand, if the patient has reverted to being the ordinary continuing operating personality, then methods 4–7 are useful. If you are working on your own dream, exclude methods 4 and 6 because they are designed especially for therapist and patient. You can use any of the other methods.

When the Patient is Still Being
he Dream Experiencing

When you as the therapist turn to this final step, some patients are still being the dream experiencing. They have just completed being the dream experiencing in the recent scenes linked to the dream itself, and they are still more or less inside of and being the dream experiencing.

This allows the therapist quite deliberately to talk to the patient as this new dream experiencing rather than to the ordinary operating personality who began the session:

T: You know what you want. You're a leader, a guy with self-confidence. Good for you. Now there's this other guy, Jeffrey. He only knows what it's like to fight with his mother, trying to please her and then trying to

be free of her, and nothing works. You're like a whole different person.
I like you. Well, I guess I like him too. Sort of.

Often a patient will be the new dream experiencing just a little bit,
or he will be in a kind of limbo, able to go either way. When this
happens, you can agree with the patient to play a game in which the
therapist says that she is going to talk to the new dream personality.
Would the patient agree to play the game and continue being the new
dream personality?

If you work on your own dreams, you can use the following three
methods of effecting being-behavioral change. The trick is to continue to be or pretend to be this new dream experiencing. Can you
permit yourself to play this game? If you can, then you can use these
three methods.

*(1) The patient, who is already being the dream experiencing,
fashions her own world and ways of being-behaving.* In effect, the
new personality is given wholesale freedom to describe her own (new)
world and her own (new) ways of being-behaving.

The therapist sets the stage as follows:

T: I love the way you are now. It seems so easy and right and natural. Would
   you be willing to be this way today, tonight, tomorrow? Do you want
   to feel this way from now on in your own world? Do you like being this
   way and feeling like this? It really is up to you. Does it feel like you are
   ready for this in your life, in your world? I mean the kind of world that
   you can have? Your world? Is this all right? Or would you rather not? It
   is your choice. It's up to you.

It is important that the therapist address the dream experiencing
and that this new personality is given plenty of freedom to sketch out
her own life, how and where she lives, what her own world is like:

T: I want to talk with you. You know what it is like to say no, to refuse, to
   stay away and not get caught in traps, right? Great! What is your life
   like? What do you do in your life? There ought to be lots of ways you
   can feel this, and you can do lots of things that are special like this.
   What is your world like? How do you like your life to be? What sort of
   person are you? What is your life like?

She can fill in her own extratherapy world, describe the ways she is
and the ways she acts in accord with this experiencing. The person

who fashions the world and her ways of being-behaving is this new dream personality.

(2) The patient, who is already being the dream experiencing, carries on the selfsame behaviors in the extratherapy world. During the session, as the dream experiencing, the person actually carried out new ways of behaving. This second method invites this continuing dream personality to behave in the very same ways in the prospective extratherapy world. If you actually did it here, you certainly can do it out there. It is just a matter of transferring or generalizing or doing the selfsame new behaviors in the extratherapy world.

The therapist tells the patient what she actually said and did in the session and invites her to be this selfsame way in the extratherapy world:

T: You were wonderful! You sat him down, told him to listen to what you have to say, and you said, "If you ever do that again I'm going to slug you!" That was delightful and it felt wonderful. You did it! I heard you. You heard you. We all heard you. How about doing it whenever you want to? You're a person who can do it, and you did it right here, about twenty minutes ago!

(3) The patient, who is already being the dream experiencing, can tell the ordinary patient how to be and behave in new ways. The dream personality can see the ordinary self, and can talk to this ordinary self, give the ordinary self a piece of her mind. By being the dream experiencing who talks to the ordinary everyday self, the person defines new ways of being and behaving:

T: Go ahead, tell her what you think of her and her life, the ways she carries on. You have any suggestions? Maybe ways that she can do things a little differently? Maybe a whole new life? Or just being different in little ways? You know what she's like, and what she maybe is missing, and here's your chance to give her a piece of your mind, a little advice. OK?

As the dream experiencing, the person can have a great deal to say to the ordinary self about how to be and what to do.

This calls for the person disengaging from her ordinary self. It is as if you were to step away from your physical self so that you could see yourself. Step back and see the person who is you as vividly and clearly as you can. Now you can talk to her.

When the Patient Reverts to the Old Personality

In the above three methods, the patient was being the dream experiencing. Often, however, after being the dream experiencing in the context of recent scenes, the person reverts back into the old personality, the ordinary operating domain. When this occurs, the following methods can be used.

(4) The therapist takes on the role of the dream experiencing, ready and willing to carry out the new ways of being and behaving. It is as if the therapist is the new experiencing, quite ready and willing to be and behave in all sorts of new ways that flow out of this dream experiencing. In effect, the therapist gives voice to the dream experiencing.

The therapist may be the dream experiencing with most of her attention onto the prospective situational context: "I can close the damned shop whenever I want, 'cause I'm the boss, and tonight we close early, and that's the way it is!" Or the therapist may be the dream experiencing and play with the patient: "Keep it open six days a week, 'cause if you shut it down someone'll scream at you, and then what'll you do?" or even order and command the patient: "One day this week you're going to shut the shop three hours early and put up a clever sign explaining why, and you are damned well going to do it or I will tell Edna that you broke her prize vase and lied your head off!" Whether the therapist is being the dream experiencing in the context of some scene or in interacting with the patient, the therapist takes on the role of the dream personality.

As the dream experiencing, the therapist can engage in a flat-out argument with the patient about the advantages of being the dream experiencing. The therapist can tell the patient that remaining as the ordinary person means having all those worries and troubles and problems, that the only effective way to free yourself of these worries and troubles and problems is to be the dream experiencing. Coerce the patient. Tell him your truth. Badger him. If you want to be free of the cancer pain, be the dream personality that is free of the cancer pain (cf. Erickson, 1985; Mahrer, 1980c). If you want to be free of those fears and disgusting ways of being and behaving, simply disengage from whom you are and be the dream personality. If you are attracted by the dream personality, the choice is easy.

In being the dream experiencing, the therapist can easily slide from being in the prospective situational context to being with the patient.

Here is the therapist being the dream experiencing (openly attracted to the older woman) in direct interaction with the patient:

T: It's time that you showed her. What are you waiting for? You want her to knock on the door and tear your clothes off?

Pt: She's almost fifty!

T: Eighteeen years more experience than you! Tell her she's a wonderful woman! Tell her you watch her when she washes her car!

Pt: No way!

T: You lying coward! All right. You win. I will.

Pt: What?

T: I'm going to tell her. "Hello Doris. Sam's too squeamish to tell you that he's attracted to you, but he is. Oh he really is!"

Pt: You can't say that!

T: Here, listen. "I think you are lovely, Doris. Now I think I'm going to collapse."

Pt: She'd think I'm a nut!

T: "And I know you think I'm a nut. I am! Bye!"

Pt: I could never say that.

T: Don't bother. I will. All by myself.

Pt: No! No, I'll do it. I'll tell her! I sure wish I could!

At the extremes, the therapist is fully being the dream experiencing behaving in some defined scene or fully being the dream experiencing talking directly to the patient. But it is easiest for the therapist to combine the two so that he both talks to the patient and acts in the scene. Here is the therapist being the dream experiencing of wicked and tabooed sexuality:

T: You really did nasty things, and with your younger sister yet . . .

Pt: Well, she's a mother now and has a daughter nearly 22.

T: Knowing you, you'll give the daughter a nice uncle kiss, and you'll stick your tongue in her mouth, and run your hand over her thighs, and she'll look in your eyes and see those awful thoughts you have about being in bed naked with her and her mother, your younger sister, both of them naked in bed with you.

Pt: I think her mother's still more attractive (lightly).

T: You can run your hands over their bodies and then say, "I think your mother's still more attractive." Then they can work with you so that the three of you can have simultaneous family orgasms. And then you can have family confessions.

Pt: If I could even think like that I'd be cured! Out loud. I have inner thoughts. I don't tell them to anyone. And that is rather silly, all these years!

This method relies on the therapist being, speaking, and expressing as the dream experiencing, and thereby carrying out or carefully describing the new behaviors. All of this is in the context of prospective scenes in the imminently future extratherapy world.

(5) The patient observes the differentiated dream experiencing carrying out the new ways of being and behaving. As the safely uninvolved, distant old personality, the patient sits on the sidelines, out of the action. The therapist paints a picture of the dream experiencing as the clone of the patient, or a twin sister, or an alternate personality, or an actress who takes the role of the new experiencing. The key to this method is that the patient is safely distant and uninvolved and yet can witness herself or some person like herself doing the being and behaving.

Differentiation can emphasize that what the patient is observing is not a whole new personality, but rather a blown-up version of one small quality or characteristic or potential. It is a mere caricature:

T: You know this quality in you, this thing in you that can put your foot down, and say "no," and mean it. It doesn't show much. It's not the way you are usually. It showed a little, especially when you were a little kid with your younger brother. It is just one little quality in you, and not shown much.

(6) The therapist infuses the patient into being and behaving as the dream experiencing. The therapist describes in magnetic detail exactly what it is like to be and behave as the dream experiencing. It is done in such painstaking detail that the patient is slowly infused into being and behaving as the new experiencing. It is like hypnogogically taking over the patient little by little.

As therapist you describe the outside face of the behavior, capturing every detail of the behavior. Then you describe the inside face of the behavior, including the inner thoughts and ideas, the bodily sensations, the inner sense of the physical movement. When you describe the outer and inner face of the behavior in such minute detail, the person is carried right along with you.

(7) The patient voluntarily tries out being and behaving as the dream experiencing. This is a matter of experimenting, merely trying out the dream experiencing and seeing how it feels. Once the patient is ready and willing to engage in the new ways of being and

behaving, the therapist sketches in what the patient is to do in whatever context is appropriate. Then it is up to the patient to undertake the dream experiencing and to try out the concrete new behavior. The premium is on the patient's voluntary and active readiness and willingness to try it out.

In encouraging the patient to volunteer, you are merely inviting the patient to do what he has already done several times in the session. That is, he voluntarily got into the dream experiencing, once in returning to the dream context, once in the context of the earlier scene, and once in the context of the recent life events. It also helps to be quite open and honest in describing this as a game. Clearly the patient can slide right back into being himself whenever he wishes. Clearly he is here in the office and not in some scene a week from now in the external world. It is naïvely and wholesomely a matter of trying out, pretending, game-playing.

T: Just for now, pretend that you can be this Doris person. She's incredibly grown-up and resourceful, she is sure of herself and confident, and when she makes huge mistakes she shrugs her shoulders and that's life. Letting yourself be Doris is pretend. I know it. You know it. Doris knows it. You're just going to let yourself see what it's like, like in the dream. You can always go back to you, any time at all. It's play time. This is really an office and you are really you, but you can let yourself see and feel what it's like to be this way, once, just once. What do you think?

It is true, refreshingly disarming, and quite helpful to point out how both therapist and patient know that we are here in the office and not in some prospective scene with the person. We both know that the other person in the scene is not really here, so the dreamer is free to pretend:

T: It's all right. All you're doing is pretending. It is all pretending. Marsha's not really here. You know that. So raise your voice and plead. Be frustrated. She's not going to hear you. Just pretend. It's a game. It's not even real. Marsha's probably home eating supper, so don't worry. She'll never know.

"Voluntary" means that you are doing the behavior just to see what it is like, to try it out. Tell the person beforehand that he can try out the behavior and check to see whether it gets something started in the body and, if so, what the body sensations are like. Sometimes nothing happens in the body. You try out the behavior and nothing happens. Try it again and again. Keep going until there are some bodily sensations. They may feel good or bad, but the sensations mean the behaviors are having some effect.

SELECTING THE PROSPECTIVE SCENE
OR SITUATION

It is essential, in any way of tasting and sampling being-behavioral change, that you live and exist and behave in some future scene-situation. You can start by selecting the prospective scene situation or you can start by selecting a behavior. If you begin by selecting a situational context, that somewhat determines the kinds of behaviors that are appropriate; if you start by selecting the behaviors, then the question is: What situation is called for by these behaviors in order to provide for that experiencing? The purpose of this section is to show how to start by selecting the scene situation.

There are four ways of selecting a prospective scene situation, and each can be used to generate a scene situation that is more or less realistic or unrealistic. Accordingly, you select a method and then you decide whether the scene situation is to be realistic or unrealistic. You can define a situation that could occur in the patient's realistic, actual life, or you can fabricate a situation that is admittedly impossible, far-fetched, fantastic, and quite unrealistic. In-between are scenes and situations that are risky but somewhat possible, or perhaps almost ideal but not very likely.

(1) Select a Scene–Situation From Those Already
Brought up in the Session

The session offers you at least four sources of scenes and situations: (a) moments of peak feeling in the dream, (b) earlier life situations, (c) recent life situations, and (d) scenes–situations mentioned by the patient before, during, and after actual dream work. You can select from any of these four sources.

The dream is a useful resource for selecting an appropriate extratherapy scene or situation in which the new experiencing can occur. Look at each of the two peaks. You can get a scene-situation from either of the peaks or from the way you put the two peaks together in identifying their common features. In any case, the challenge is to figure out how the dream peak scene or situation can be placed into the next few days or weeks so that the patient can have the experiencing in that future scene–situation.

You can also select and build future scenes from those identified in earlier life. The ones that are especially valuable are the ones in which the dream experiencing occurred fully and in its good form, rather than those in which the experiencing did not occur or occurred in a painful way. It is quite common that some dream experiencings do not occur in your present life, but they did occur in earlier times in your life, especially in childhood. Suppose that the dream experiencing is that of independent rebelliousness, something the patient rarely has today. Yet she recollected an earlier scene from when she was a young child and she indeed had this experiencing at the kitchen table when she absolutely refused to eat eggs. The question then is how she can get this experiencing of independent rebelliousness in prospective scenes situations involving meals or eating food.

From the dream, "Maniac with the knife, and controlling the maniac," the earlier life scene is one in which one person is in trouble or hurt or in need, there are others around who are all upset but doing nothing constructive, and the patient is prepared to take over and organize effective action. In another earlier life scene ("Late for the wedding, and watching the nurses"), the patient is at the table with her family, and she is receding into a withdrawn state, staring at a glass of milk. In "Surreptitious in the store, and avoiding one another," the earlier scene is one in which he has stolen pornographic photographs from his aunt and uncle and is lying on their bed, fascinated with the photographs. Given these earlier life scenes, the question is how these can be built into the person's imminent life.

A third source is the recent life situation. With one dream ("Late for the wedding, and watching the nurses"), two recent scenes were used. In one, she calls her ex-husband and he proceeds to tell her about his new woman. In the other, she has arranged for her brother to repair the back porch, and he responds snappishly to her pressure for him to hurry and get it done. Can these scenes and situations be approximated in the next few days or weeks?

A fourth source is those scenes and situations that the patient mentions in the session quite aside from actual dream work. She may mention such a scene before dream work begins or when she is thinking about the external world. She may cite some upcoming event such as the court hearing scheduled for a month from now, or the baby that is due in three or four weeks, or the visit from her aunt whom she hasn't seen in twenty years and who will be coming next week. Sometimes the scene is mentioned before dream work starts in the session, and once again when she is ready for the final step in the session. Just before dream work, she is considering whether to work on a dream or some other feelinged attentional center:

Pt: . . . so I'm starting to feel sexy again. I used to love sex. That was years ago, and it's starting again. But it was awful with Richard [her ex-husband]. He'd get mad, if I wanted sex . . .

Then she mentions that she had a dream and opts to work on a dream. After being the dream experiencing in the context of an earlier life scene she lifts her attention to the imminent future, and here is Richard once again:

Pt: . . . I was chosen to present the flowers because I am the most helpful in the class. The teacher chose me to present the flowers. That's an honor. Every year someone's chosen. Yes, I deserved it (light laughter). . . . Richard should hear something like that! He wouldn't believe it. To him I was nothing but a dumb servant, not even that!

She spontaneously introduces scenes involving her ex-husband, and therefore the situational context for the dream experiencing may well be that of interacting with him in the next few days or so.

Indeed, it is rather common that patients will finish being the dream experiencing in the earlier life scene and then turn toward some scene in the extratherapy world. After being the dream experiencing in an earlier scene, the experiencing of being a sneaky bastard, having the wicked inner pleasure of ducking out and leaving his buddy to be hurt ("The wino, the tough guys, and the hurt hand"), he spontaneously frames a situation from the imminent future:

Pt: . . . Now if only I can be this way when Todd comes back from Brazil! He's going to expect me to support him and I think I'll maybe, I can't do it, maybe I'll have a surprise for him! Oh, that's going to be some meeting!

Once you select a scene or situation from those already brought up in the session, the problem is how to duplicate it in the external world. If the scene were one in which she was a little girl gaining a sense of independent rebelliousness as she defiantly refused to eat the eggs, then the question is how some similar scene may be duplicated in the next few days or so. Perhaps you can order eggs at a restaurant, even though you rarely eat eggs today, and raucously refuse to eat them. Perhaps you can whip up a batch of eggs at home, and then belt out your refusal to eat them. Perhaps you can tell the friends who invited you to dinner next week the whole list of foods you stoutly refuse to eat. There are all sorts of realistic and unrealistic scenes and situations that can be fabricated to approximate the earlier incident around the eggs.

Suppose the dream experiencing is affection and fondness. How could she construct a prospective scene from those already brought up in the session? She used the recent situation from the linkage, a situation that happened last night, when she was telephoned by her supervisor who was drunk, complaining about the problems at higher levels at work and saying things that he should not have been saying. How could she be with her boss at work so as to gain a sense of affection and fondness? She framed a scene:

Pt: You and I are in the office, and you look sheepish about calling me. So I can grin at you. Yes, you called me last night, and yes you were a little high, and yes we both feel a little embarrassed about it. Well, you're a real person! Thank you for trusting me and calling me! There. Just a light touch! (Nice sigh) Ah! You're quite a guy! That feels good.

This method of selecting the prospective scene–situation can be used by therapists and by persons working on their own dreams. The question may be asked in this way: How may I use scenes and situations that were already brought up in the session to build a prospective scene for the experiencing? But this is only one way of selecting the prospective scene–situation.

(2) Select a "Problem Situation" in Which the Patient Feels Bad

A second way of selecting the prospective scene–situation is to think of the "problem situation" the patient feels bad or complains about, singles out as the worry or trouble. This method of selecting a scene–situation is open to both the therapist and the person who works on his own dreams. If you work on your own dreams, ask yourself: What is the situation that is my problem, the scene in which I feel bad, worried, troubled, the situation where I feel rotten because of what I do or because of what someone does to me? If you are a therapist, the "problem situation" should come from the patient, not from you.

Her bad feelings occur in scenes in which she is trying to be helpful to her brother Oswald, who drinks virtually all day long, who is in and out of medical and psychiatric hospitals because of diseases in various parts of his body. He hardly ever eats and is dangerously underweight. The therapist talks to the person who is still being the dream experiencing:

T: You are really quite a person. You are tough and commanding, right? And ballsy and sure of yourself, the authoritative bitch who takes charge, right? All right, now what the hell would you do with good old Oswald? There he is, in his apartment, and the physicians have laid it on you to try to get him in shape for the operation that Ossie is in no shape to undergo. So what would you do? I mean you! Huh? How would you handle this situation?

Pt: Easy! Listen, Ossie, this is the last time I'm ever coming over here! You can rot as far as I care! The doctors told you that if you keep on with this damned drinking you're going to kill yourself in a year. Less than a year! They wouldn't even operate on you till you got yourself in better shape, and THAT WAS MONTHS AGO! So kiss your little sister good bye, you nut! I am finished with you. When you're ready, you come and see me. If you want to keep on drinking, then DIE! Ha! Surprised you! Huh!

Once you know the dream experiencing and you identify a problem situation, there are some interesting match-ups. The dream experiencing is sexiness, seductiveness, provocativeness. The problem scene is the monthly big family meals at his parents' home, complete with his sister and brother, their spouses, his aunt and uncle, and about a dozen children. He always goes to pieces, beginning a couple of days before the big meal, a time the wife refers to as "Harry's time of the month, you know. . . . " The work, then, consists of Harry's being the dream experiencing in the context of the big monthly family meals at his parents' home.

Just about every patient will have some "problem situation" or two. This is a rich and easy source of prospective scenes and situations.

(3) Build a Situation That is Custom-Fitted for the Dream Experiencing

In using this method, you begin with the dream experiencing, and then build a custom-fitted prospective scene–situation. If you work on your own dream, ask yourself: What would be the perfect scene or situation for me to have this experiencing? How can my life be ideal so that I can have the dream experiencing of being special, putting on a show, being an accomplished performer?

You can build this situation out of building blocks that are realistic. As a variation, you could build scenes and situations that realistically could occur providing that there were some significant changes. She would have to lose over a hundred pounds, or would have to be married with two children and presently she is unmarried with no children. At the other extreme, you can build the situation out of quite unrealistic building blocks, highly imaginative and fantasized contexts that will never really occur and yet are tailor-made for the dream experiencing.

Usually you begin with just the dream experiencing, e.g., being helpful, providing, caring for, lending assistance. Just starting here, what sorts of situations would be custom-fitted? Invent situations that are perhaps realistic and doable and that would truly be ideal for this dream experiencing. She lives in an apartment house, and down the hall is an old woman, dutifully caring for her old brother who is dying of cancer. The patient can spend Wednesday afternoons relieving the old woman, giving her a full six hours of being able to leave the apartment knowing that a concerned and capable neighbor is caring for the brother. The patient reads to the brother, talks to him about whatever he wants to talk about, tends to his needs.

Another patient is 62 years old, and she has been divorced for nearly 30 years. She has two children, both in their thirties. She lives alone. The dream experiencing is that of soft and gentle sexuality, physical closeness, easy orgasms. The therapist allows this experiencing to build an ideal situational context.

T: You are married to a man, a fine gentleman who is in his sixties, is alive and vibrant and, like you, loves exercizing and especially regular swimming. He is warm and gentle and caring, and he loves being in bed with you, holding you close, touching you. It feels so good . . .

You can build the situation by starting from the dream experiencing and the behavior. The dream experiencing is being vulnerable and exposed. In the course of dream work the behavior that scored was simple crying. Now the question is: What scene–situation would optimally accommodate this experiencing (being vulnerable and exposed) and this behavior (simple crying)? You select being with Vin, your older cousin who lives in the next province, whom you grew up with, whom you can be very close to. Being with your cousin is the right situation for the ideal undergoing of this experiencing; you cry as you talk with Vin about yourself and your life.

(4) Build a Situation out of Exceedingly Threatening, Risky, Outrageous Elements

The dream experiencing is that of giving it up, letting it go, walking away from it. Whether you are the therapist or the person who works on his own dreams, ask yourself questions like these: In your life, in your current world, what scenes and situations would be the ones where you would absolutely *never* dare to give it up, let it go, walk away from it? If you were going to have that experiencing, what would be the scenes and situations in your current world where it would be exceedingly threatening, risky, outrageous for you to do it? What would be the last things in your life that you would give up, let go of, walk away from? Would you give up your good looks, gorgeous body, spouse, job, home, best friend?

You may select such a scene by starting from the dream. Given the situational context of the dream, look for a similar situational context in your current or imminent life in which you can experience giving it up, letting it go, walking away from it, even if the situational context is exceedingly risky, threatening, and outrageous:

T: Now think. In the dream you were involved with an association and with an important group. You have some association or group in your life? Maybe some meeting coming up or group or something?

Pt: Sure. We meet in Vancouver Thursday and Friday, the executive committee and the board. Important meeting. A whole day. Maybe 15 or 18 of us. Very heavy.

T: That's it!

Pt: Oh oh. Oh no. I got to drop out? (Laughs)

Start with the dream experiencing. It is one of shocking, doing wild and crazy things, being a nut. Scan your current life to find those situations in which you would have waves of horror at even the thought of carrying out such an experiencing. Try out this scene and that situation until you find a few that fill you with the right feelings. One is at departmental social functions where the big bosses say something in honor of this or that, and all the people are socially nice to one another. Another scene is in church, during the sermon. A third is at the forthcoming funeral of the fellow who was uniformly hated. These situations are threatening and risky if you imagine doing anything that opens up the experiencing of shocking, doing wild and crazy things, being a nut.

The dream experiencing consisted of opening up, showing the flaws in his personality, confessing the awful things, exhibiting his awfulness. In actuality he sneaks into houses of prostitution every two or three months or so. He would die if anyone even suspected. What would be the most threatening situation here? The answer is a scene in which his wife and a few of the prissy colleagues from the ministry were to see him entering the establishment and come into the room when he is ejaculating. We now have built a situation of exceedingly threatening, risky, outrageous elements.

SELECTING THE NEW BEHAVIORS

The final ingredient in being-behavior change is the selection of the right behaviors. There are at least three ways to do this.

Always begin with the dream experiencing. If the dream experiencing is being direct, open, and honest, then you either define the behavior and find the appropriate scene–situation, or you select the appropriate scene–situation and then look for the defined behavior. Given the dream experiencing, you may define the behavior of saying "No!" directly, openly, and honestly. The question is: What would be an appropriate situation in which you can stoutly declare "No" in a way that gives you a sense of being direct, open, and honest? Alternatively, given the dream experiencing, you may select a scene wherein your sister tearfully complains about her job and wants to know how you feel about her no longer working. Then the question is what you can do in that situation to provide the dream experiencing of being direct, open, and honest. Either the behavior helps determine the situation, or the situation helps determine the behavior.

(1) Use Behaviors That Were Actually Carried
Out in the Dream and in the Session

Here is where dream work has an advantage over therapeutic work without dreams: The dream and dream work offer you precise behaviors that may be carried out to provide for the new experiencing. These new behaviors can occur right here in the moment of peak feeling. Sometimes the behavior is muted and vague and hard to find.

Usually, however, there is a defined dream behavior that expresses the experiencing, carried out by the dreamer or perhaps by the other person or figure.

The question is whether or not that particular dream behavior provides for the dream experiencing in the prospective scene that you select. Some dream behaviors are suitable and some not. I try to give dream behaviors a fair hearing even though I may not find much use in such dream behaviors as murdering another person with an axe or shooting someone with a gun. In a sense, Boss is more cavalier in entertaining the extratherapy use of dream behaviors:

> By dismissing the patient's dreaming murders as reprehensible, the therapist prevents him from experiencing an increased wealth of behavioral possibilities. . . . (1977, p. 91)

The dream is one good source of new behaviors. A second source is what the patient actually did in the course of being the dream experiencing in returning to the dream context, in earlier life scenes, or in recent linked life scenes. Almost always, the patient behaved in new and different ways right here in the session.

In the earlier life scene ("Late for the wedding, and watching the nurses"), she was at the table, staring at the milk. Then she withdrew into her own separate world, an alternate state of consciousness where she was vividly aware of inner ideas and thoughts, and quite cut off from the persons, voices, actions around her. She also was able literally to get up from the table and walk away. What was occurring at the table was bothersome, and so she simply got up and walked away. These are behaviors she seldom uses today.

In the course of the session, in the context of the dream or the earlier life event or the recent scene, some behaviors (a) are accompanied with genuinely good feelings, (b) fully open up and express the dream experiencing, and (c) are rarely if ever shown in the patient's current life. One of these was a simple reaching out and light caressing of the face of the other person. Another was allowing tears to fill his eyes, instead of hiding and blocking them, when he sensed himself on the verge of tearfulness. Such behaviors were actually carried out in dream work, and are prime candidates for occurrence in the imminent external world.

Many of these behaviors feel great in the course of dream work but become quite risky which you consider using them today. For example, in the earlier life scene involving the bully, a patient allowed herself to go berserk, to actually strike him with a fist, to stick out her tongue in direct defiance. With another patient, the moment occurred in the earlier life scene when he was five years old; absolutely incensed about being scolded for not eating, he went directly to the garage and peed on the garage wall. While these behaviors are useful for the dream experiencing in the context of childhood scenes, enacting them would be quite risky for an adult.

(2) The Therapist Invents New Behaviors That Are Useful, Doable, Workable, Practical, Realistic, and Effective

The therapist can invent the new behaviors. It is a matter of starting from the dream experiencing and figuring out behaviors that are useful, practical, realistic and effective. The therapist must be inventive and creative, and yet in a way that is workable and realistic.

Suppose that the dream experiencing is that of being intruding, entering into others' lives in a friendly way. That is all you have to go on. Then you ask how and where can this occur. In the dream it occurred in the context of having dinner at an apartment of some friends, a couple whom he knows. Actually, he rarely has dinner at anyone's home. In fact, in the last year or so the only time this happened is when he went to visit his son and daughter-in-law and had a meal with them in their apartment when he was on a business trip. He and his wife seldom go to parties, rarely have meals at others' homes, and he never did this by himself. The therapist uses the method of taking on the role of this new personality and says the following:

T: OK, that is just fine for you maybe, but not me. Not me at all. I know Jane and Michael. I like them. Well, I am going to tell them that my wife is going to visit her sister for a week, and I damned well would like to come and have a meal with them. What is more, I am going to bring them some flowers, really nice flowers. Hello Jane. Martha's going to visit her sister for a week. Please, would you invite me for a meal then? Please? I will just stay for the meal and then I will go. What do you think? Yes? No? Oh, thank you. Yeah, Friday night would be great. You're a doll.

Her dream experiencing is that of manipulating and using. That is all we have to go on. We select a situation by identifying the problem situation. This is when the ex-husband just shows up, at randomly unannounced times, and she assumes a role in which she ends up giving him money, letting him sleep with her, and lending him her car. He has no steady job, and his appearances are constant sources of bad feelings. In this situation, the question is what behaviors could give her the opportunity of experiencing manipulation and using. The invented new behaviors are for her to get him to take the junk out of the basement and put it in front for the garbage truck, to get him to wash the second floor windows on the outside, and to inform him that she has called the city and volunteered his name as someone to help plant the trees around the city park.

These invented new behaviors are appropriate for a situation that will likely occur in the next week or so. That is, the ex-husband will just show up within the next week. On the other hand, some appropriate situations must be actively constructed by the patient. Constructing these situations calls for particular new behaviors; then, in the constructed situation, other behaviors provide for the dream experiencing. With the above patient, the situation occurs when her ex-husband shows up, and this happens whenever he wishes. She can also gain the dream experiencing of manipulation and using by first behaving in ways that set up the appropriate situation. For example, she knows that he likes to sleep late on Monday mornings, so the new behaviors include going to his room at 9:30 A.M., waking him up, informing him that she has just volunteered him to the city, and handing him the restraining order forbidding him to show up at her place unless he calls beforehand and she agrees to his visit, and furthermore, only when she has chores for him to do, starting with the removal of the junk from the basement, which he will do one week from today at 5:00 P.M. when a few of her burly male friends will be with her to insure that he does as told. Any questions? Going to his room and waking him up are behaviors that build the right situation. Her behaviors from then on provide for the dream experiencing.

There are behaviors that construct the right situation, as above, and there are behaviors that provide for the experiencing. Consider the passive experiencing of being cuddled, held, gentled. There are lots of very active behaviors that provide for quite passive experiencings. For example, you can carefully arrange the bathroom with the right scented water and suds, the right music and food and drink, and the right person to wash your back and read to you. Or you can actively arrange for two people to cuddle you—initiating the invitation, explaining what you want, perhaps arranging for a barter with these other people. You are the one who tells the pair where to recline, and what exactly to do — all in order for you then to have the passive experiencing of being cuddled, held, and gentled.

One set of behaviors can recreate the recent moment when the bad feelings surged up in you, and a second set allows for the dream experiencing. The recent moment may be when your wife was upset in the dining room, bitterly hurt by her grandmother and grandfather who were in the next room, and you froze in a state of automatic numbness. A special set of new behaviors can actually recreate that recent moment. These behaviors include being back in the dining room with your wife, inviting two old friends to play the role of grandmother and grandfather, stage-managing the whole setting to recreate that critical moment in which you froze. The second set of behaviors can then occur. With the dream experiencing of sheer explosion, the behaviors include roaring, swearing, jumping up and down, striding back and forth between wife and grandparents, bawling out everyone.

(3) The Therapist Invents New Behaviors That Are Zany, Wild, Outlandish, Risky, Dangerous, Impossible, Silly, Impractical, and Unrealistic

Whether you begin with a scene–situation or with a behavior, the aim is to invent behaviors that provide for the dream experiencing and are anything but useful, workable, practical, realistic, and effective. What unconstrained, wild, risky and unrealistic behaviors would provide for this dream experiencing?

By using behaviors that are so far-fetched, you are giving the patient plenty of safety and distance. Throwing a pie in your supervisor's face can be exaggerated, caricatured, burlesqued, and free of all reality constraints. You can pretend that you are seven feet tall and 300 pounds rather than your actual five foot four and 115 pounds. The pretense provides safety because you are not seven feet tall and you know that you will not throw a pie in your supervisor's face. None of these behaviors will really occur. All you want is to gain the dream experiencing, and the zany unreality allows this with plenty of insured safety.

The dream experiencing is a sense of absolute defiance and rebelliousness. What behaviors would provide this experiencing in an unrealistically zany and outlandish way? Spend an afternoon in one of those huge sky balloons with "The Hell With Everything" written in massive letters on the outside. Rent a whole page ad in the paper and have it read, "I refuse to do it anymore!" In the midst of the sermon, stand up and shout, "That is a load of bull shit!" Put a soap box in the middle of the city square and give a wild speech proclaiming that all the people who "have had it up to here" should join with you.

Feel quite free to be rather silly and whimsical in creating new behaviors. She is a nurse and the dream experiencing is that of being utterly passive, dependent, moved about. In the various situations at the hospital, with selected patients, physicians, and other nurses, there are lots of behaviors that provide for this experiencing as long as you assume a context of silliness and playfulness and absolute unreality. She can be physically limp, whispering that she will do whatever her supervisor wants. She falls to the floor and wraps her arms around the medical resident's knees in full obeisance. She bows her head. The least wish of anyone is her command.

The dream experiencing is that of actively intruding, interfering. When it comes to the imminent world, he immediately mentions the upcoming marriage between Sam, his friend and poker buddy, and Ellen, the sweet friend of his sister's. He knows Sam better than anyone, far better than Ellen does, and the marriage will not last a week.

T: You know that part where you're the best man, right? Where the preacher asks . . .

Pt: Yeah! Say it now or forever keep your mouth shut?

T: You move the preacher out of the way and you start singing, loud, with the band playing real loud, hard rock. You sing about Sam the screwing man, and all the women he's still screwing around with. No, no! Don't marry Sam. It won't last a week! Bring his mother on the stage. She tells how Sam was rotten from the time he started drinking milk, and his father says he tried to drown Sam and to blow him up and after a while he just gave up. Sam's evil!

Pt: I'll dress Sam as the devil with a long tail and horns, and Ellen will be in white, virginal. I'll bring all the pimps and whores that Sam hangs around with! Stop the marriage!

T: Never let this ceremony proceed! It's for good and against EVIL.

Pt: How many here know Sam? Raise your hand? NO ONE! SEE? WELL HE'S AN IRRESPONSIBLE IDIOT AND THIS MARRIAGE WILL END IN A WEEK. ELLEN WILL BE A DRUG ADDICT IN TWO DAYS AND SAM WILL TAKE ALL HER MONEY. I WILL NOT LET THIS HAPPEN! I AM SAVING ELLEN FROM A FATE WORSE THAN DEATH!

T: WHAT ARE YOU GOING TO DO FOR A FINALE?
Pt: THROW A NET AROUND SAM AND DRAG HIM FROM THE
    CHURCH!
T: HOORAY!

A special subclass includes behaviors typically carried out by the feared other person. The dream experiencing is that of superiority and bossing, and mother-in-law is the one who does this to the patient. The new behaviors are especially risky and unrealistic because they consist of doing to mother-in-law what she does to the patient. It means you are to boss your mother-in-law, tell her what to do, exactly as she ordinarily does to you. The practical question is: Who is it that carries out the dream experiencing unto you, and what behaviors does that person use? How about your reversing the action and doing to that person what that person does unto you?

The dream experiencing is being the center of attention, prized, looked at, attended to. Who is it that is the unquestioned center of attention, where it would be unthinkable for them to shower you with attention? Grandmother! Once a month you and Sid drive the thirty miles and attend the ritual dinner where you are expected to ask grandmother about every detail of her ailments and physical status. This time you take the play away by slumping in the chair that grandmother typically uses and reciting the lengthy story of all your current ailments, on and on and on. But this is only one way. You can also arrange a special party for yourself where the gift is for each of the twenty people to extol your selected virtues. "Tell me how wonderful I am! You have ten minutes, and the bell will ring when you are done. OK. Go!"

You must select some method of effecting being-behavioral change, the prospective scene–situation, and the new behaviors. I have discussed each of these separately, but in your actual work you will put them all together. We now turn to some illustrations.

A FEW ILLUSTRATIONS

While it seems artificial and contrived to identify and study separately methods of effecting being-behavioral change, of selecting the right scene-situation, and of selecting the new behavior, this is what you must do in order to become familiar with each method and to be able to use all of them. When you actually are engaged in dream work, however, you merely do whatever seems best at the time. In this section I will provide four illustrations of how you can more or less naturally use a method of effecting behavior change and of selecting the scene–situation and the behavior.

The first illustration is of a person who works on his own dream. The dream is "The fantastic skier and the dope shop," and the dream experiencing is performing, putting on a show, being special. In the earlier life scene, he was ten years old, at a family gathering at the home of two aunts. Because he was selected to be a lead singer in one song for a Christmas pageant to be put on at his school, his parents urge him to sing for the family. Too shy to be in the living room with the whole family, he goes to the dining room where he cannot be seen and he sings a bit of the song, all the while mortified with fear. In redoing this scene, however, he gets inside the dream experiencing and has a festival of performing, putting on a show, being special. In the recent scene, he is at home with some people who are at dinner, and his wife tells him to tell the funny story about what happened at customs in the airport when they returned from Mexico. The critical instant is when everyone faces him and he clutches up in tension. In being the dream experiencing, he thoroughly enjoys holding their captivated attention as he performs the story in dramatic style. Now he is ready to be and behave as this dream experiencing in prospective scenes. Here is his verbatim work on this final step:

Pt: If I wanted that, really performing, putting on a show. Where? Ideal, if it's ideal. Dreamlike, some special place. If I could. Just perform, put on a show. . . . All those talks. Deputy director so I have to say a few words. I hate doing that. With the microphone. Research and development is having awards. I got to welcome them, ten minutes.

"A few words from the great deputy minister. Thank you." Holding the microphone. Two hundred people and I'm supposed to say a few introductory. . . . "I want to make a few announcements. I am going to visit each of you once a year and find out what the hell you are doing. You are one of the finest departments and I haven't even met any one of you. And you don't know me. So I am going to schedule an appointment at your convenience and spend an hour finding out what you do and what you want. And I will take notes, so be careful. . . . And now I want to play my clarinet, you know why, 'cause I am the best clarinetist in Toronto except for eighteen real musicians. All right, now hear this. . . . You can't walk out! What's their names? Who are they? No walking out . . . And I am sick and tired of saying a few words that mean nothing. I am going to tell you all the problems you are facing and what I am going to do about them, and all in ten minutes! Are you listening to me? You're all fired! Get out! Wait! Wait! I'm just kidding! I don't really mean it! . . . "I hate those damned talks. . . .

My problem. Thing that bothers me. Oh shit. Drinking more. Not a drunk. But teetering. Drinking too much. Not telling anyone. Pretending. Lying. Oh Christ, I lie to Hillary. Damn. OK, I am . . . when, worst time. Let's see. I'll line up the family. No, really make this scary. I will have Stanley over, the big man, and the brass, all at my place, and I will tell them. Shit I would never ever do this. Hmmm. Dinner party. All dressed.

"I have an announcement! Everybody listen! I am not a drunk! I am not alcoholic! But I worry like hell about drinking! I get drunk about once a month, safely. On the weekend. In the kitchen. By myself. No one's there. Hillary is playing tennis or something. And I am so damned guilty that I pretend I am sick and go to bed and sleep. I tell Hillary that I have the flu or something and I sleep for hours. I am not a drunk. But I am a liar and I drink too much once a month. Now from now on I want to get drunk with someone. Does anyone want to get drunk about once a month? Secretly, with me?"

Wait a minute! That sounds like something I can really do! Find three or four other guys and get drunk. Fishing. I used to go fishing. I'm getting mixed up here. But I like that. Maybe it's really doable. You know what I'd love? I'd love to get away, just go fishing for three days with about four other guys, and . . . wait . . . Richard and Jack . . . my God, I could go with them. I think I really could. And the best thing is getting drunk with them. I could. I'm going to ask them. And I know I would love that. What the hell! I think I would.

There's something else. The Town Players. Wow! I could try out for a play. Wait a minute! I could! I really could! I have thought about, in the back of my mind . . . damned right. I could try out for one of their plays. I think I could do it. And even if I don't do it, what the hell. It would be fun. We could go to plays more. Hillary'd love that. So would I. But I could try out. I could! Why not?

He used several methods for selecting the scene–situation and several methods for selecting the new behaviors. However, he used only one method for effecting being-behavior change, i.e., the seventh method of voluntarily trying out being and behaving as the dream experiencing. Yet he succeeded in getting a taste of what it is like to be and behave as the dream experiencing in the external world. We now turn to three illustrations where therapist and patient work together in this final step.

From the dream, "Surreptitious in the store, and avoiding one another," the experiencing was that of being found out, seen, caught, exposed, opened up, exhibited. Being this experiencing in the context of the early scene meant being in his aunt and uncle's bedroom, having found some pornographic photographs. They come into the bedroom and he openly displays the discovered treasure in a festival of dream experiencing. He shows them the pictures, lays on their bed, let them catch him, confesses to sexual fascinations, asks to watch them have intercourse. In the context of a very recent scene, the same sense of being open, caught, found out, exposed, was experienced fully and delightfully by starting with an instant at the corner grocery. He is at the cash register, and there is the young lady whom he remembers as a little girl playing in the store. He exclaims how old he is, goes home and tells his wife about the incident, and starts telling her about his feelings, how he withholds thoughts from her. He has full and wonderful experiencings of being found out, welcoming his being caught and exposed, showing everything.

We turn now to being and behaving this way within the context of the imminent extratherapy world, using several methods:

T: (The patient is predominantly being the dream experiencing, almost dripping with this experiencing within the context of the recent scene. The therapist addresses the patient as this dream experiencing.) You are really some guy! Now I know that good old Harvey would never ever expose himself like that. He's never caught, at anything. But you! Good for you! It's about time that you were here. So go home and talk to your wife this way. You have a lot to tell her. Harvey doesn't.

Pt: (The I-ness is largely within the dream experiencing.) I wake up in the morning and I feel scared. I'm starting to remember things from when I was a little boy.

T: Tell her! You can do it! Harvey can't.

Pt: I'm going to tell her.

T: Tonight.

Pt: Yeah! I'm going to tell her that I eat my lunch by the playground and I watch the little elementary school kids and I remember the games we used to play when I was in elementary school.

T: (Oops. Here is a nubbin of threat and the therapist gives voice.) Wait a minute! Don't go too far, kiddo. Isn't that just a little too much?

Pt: No! I'm going to tell her.

T: She'll think you're a dirty old man!

Pt: Well I am! What the hell! I want to tell her everything.

T: What? What?

Pt: I gave some flowers to a girl in the office. No. I put them on her desk and didn't sign my name. I stare at her. I think I feel like a kid.

T: You're going to confess that to your wife? You're out of your mind!

Pt: (Laughing) No! I'm going to tell her everything. Everything! That's the worst thing I've done in years, and I want to tell her. It's awful! Right! Yeah, I want to tell her tonight. Everything.

T: Everything? There's more?

Pt: I'm tired of hiding. Tired of it. You know what? I want to take her to Kingston where I grew up. We've never been there. I want to show her where I lived, my house, and have her meet some of the kids I grew up with and where I used to steal things from stores and the tree I used to hide in and I never told my Mom and Dad about, and the things I used to read when I sat in the tree, and I want to tell her about Jack. Jack and I used to masturbate together and we touched each other's penis, and we thought we were homosexual and we got scared that other kids would find out, and I want her to meet Jack and I want to see Jack again and talk with him and tell her everything about myself.

T: You're going to expose everything!

Pt: Yeah, it's about time.

T: Are you really going to take her to Kingston?

Pt: I'm going to talk to her. I don't really talk with her. There's so much I want to tell her. You know the worst thing about this hiding all my life?

T: No.

Pt: It's that I don't even try to hide. I never think about hiding. I don't even feel bad about it. Just sail on, year after year. Well, it's disgusting!

T: (Here is something occurring as if he is actually saying this to his wife.) Listen, wife, here I am lying on your lap and I'm telling you that the worst thing about all this is that I never even think that I am hiding anything. So that is the worst thing, and it's disgusting!

Pt: And I love telling you this!

T: And if you want, I'll expose bunches of other things.

Pt: Like I sometimes make a fool of myself at the office. A conservative old fart and I make a fool of myself over a young girl.

T: (Screeching) Don't tell her that! She'll clobber you!

Pt: (Laughing) No she won't.

T: Listen, I got an idea. You know when you go at lunch, and watch the elementary school kids on the playground? And you feel old, really old, and you have all sorts of feelings about watching and when you watch? Well, how about asking Edna to bring a lunch and have a picnic, two old farts having feelings about watching the little kids.

Pt: Maybe we can get all sorts of old people to watch! (It is getting a little silly. He is half-kidding.)

T: I know! Get about 50 or 60 old farts and they can all sit on the playground and watch a token little girl and boy play together, and the old farts grunt and groan and make all sorts of senile wurps and wufs when the little kids stand around and play—or pick their noses.

Pt: You know I was scared that someone'd see me! I thought they'd think I was a pervert!

T: Get yourself a bright t-shirt that says "Stop me, I'm a pervert" on the back.

Pt: (Laughing) I'm a pervert! I'm a pervert! Oh shit. I want to talk to Edna. I just want to talk with her.

T: Are you really serious?

Pt: Yes!

T: Oh God, he's really thinking about doing it!

Pt: Right!

T: Well, good old Harvey won't.

Pt: He hides and pretends, and spends his time scared to death that some-one'll catch him or find out. What a scared old man. He glances at the girl in the office and has all sorts of little boy sexual thoughts. God, he can't even be honest with her!!

T: Listen, if you're so disgusted with old Harvey, tell him!

Pt: All your life! You are scared to death that someone'll find out something! Tell her! Tell her that you have a schoolboy crush on her! You don't have to hide anymore!!

T: Boy, do you sound disgusted with him!

Pt: He IS DISGUSTING!! Look at you! Why the hell don't you talk to Edna! . . . Never mind! I will!

T: (Laughs hard) That's telling him!

Here are all sorts of new ways of being and behaving, all providing for the experiencing of the dream potential and all befitting the patient, who was still being the dream experiencing as we entered this final step.

In the dream "Late for the wedding, and watching the nurses," the experiencing was that of staying away, being free and out of things, not being involved or caught, letting go of oppressive involvements. After we had gone through the early and recent scenes in which the patient was able to be the dream experiencing, she slid back into the operating domain. Accordingly, the methods were different from those used in the last example.

Pt: (Having just been the dream experiencing in the context of her calling her ex-husband) I wish I could really be like that. The trouble is that I act like a slave. I call him! That is really asking for it.

T: I'll tell you what. We can work together. You call him up in the next few days, and I'll fasten myself to you. The instant you start getting tense inside and go frozen, I'll say, "Oh shit, the kid's asking for trouble. Bye, Harry. Gotta go." And bang, I'll hang up. (The therapist is the being-behaving dream experiencing.)

Pt: (A little snicker) I never did that.

T: No problem. You won't have to do it. I will! I can do it easily. "So long, Harry, my body's all tensed up." Click. Off.

Pt: I could do that.

T: Step aside, little girl, I haven't even started yet. You know how you have quietly arranged to have all the big parties over at your place? Anniversaries, Christmas, Easter, picnics, parties at the pool, anything to celebrate, the whole family goes to your house? Well I got a surprise for you. I am going to call a family meeting — at Dad's apartment — not at my house, and I am going to say, "No more everything at my house! I am declining being the family social host and responsible one. Occasionally yes, but not exclusively. Any one want to argue with me?"

Pt: I couldn't do that!

T: Damned right. I will! First I am going to call Dad and tell him that the whole damned family is meeting at his place this Saturday.

Pt: Who's going to arrange for food and . . .

T: SHUT UP! You can do whatever the hell you want! Make a feast if you want! I'm going to get Evelyn and Sally to make all the calls, and then on Saturday I tell them the big news. I am going to abdicate! I've had it! So there!

Pt: You do it.

T: Course I will. Hello, family! I am going to say this quietly. No more hanging on me. I know that I arranged it, that I let you all come to my place for every get-together. I have done it. That is over now. I love you all, but I am going to be the big momma only sometimes. There is going to be a party for Jan's baby. I like that. It will be somewhere other than my place! This one is not on me! Are there any questions?

Pt: (Laughing and moving closer to this experiencing of letting go and being free) I'd love to be able to do that. Then I could take some time off. I don't know, maybe just be by myself sometime. I could do that. I mean I could stop running after Harry. It's up to me, and he doesn't call me. I'm the one who runs after him, and I'm the one who has everything over at my place. And the worst thing is that I resent it, you know. When I call Harry I get sick to my stomach and I get nauseous and bloaty and I retreat. I get depressed and stay alone. The same thing with the family. Everything's at my place, everything, and then I seem to get sick and I have to sleep for a day or so. I don't even stick around for the cleaning up. I'm in bed, dead tired, and I sleep till noon the next day and I drag around.

T: Listen, you don't have to do any of this. I'm going to take care of everything.

Pt: (Almost like practicing) Harry, you made my life miserable, and I asked for all of it! I even run after you and ask you to kick me in the teeth, and you do! You really do. Good-bye Harry! Enjoy yourself. I have more to do than that.

T: Wait a minute! That's my line!

Pt: It really is time!

T: Can I tell the family?

Pt: No! It's up to me. And I'm going to! (She is speaking quietly and with a sense of inner determination. All of this is a letting go of involvements and relationships that insure pain. The therapist goes beyond this.)

T: I am going to find your twin sister.

Pt: (Pause) I don't have a twin sister.

T: Yes you do. Her name is Alice.

Pt: That's my middle name.

T: Now you picture this. Alice looks just like you. Just picture her. Picture her going tonight to Dad's apartment. She is sitting in the kitchen with Dad. Just you stay out of the whole thing and picture her. Got her? OK. She tells Dad about her work. Then Dad says, "Todd and Janine and the kids are coming from Winnipeg for a couple of weeks. They called. I told them they could stay at your place."

Pt: Oh!

T: And now watch Alice. Just keep your eye on her. She has an instant clutching up in the belly. Tension city. Watch her. She closes her eyes and she gets up and she goes into the living room and she sits quietly on the floor, cross-legged, and she just sits there, for about ten minutes. Just quietly. She lets all of her attention be on the tension in her stomach. There are screamings in her head and she listens to them, just allowing them to go on. After some minutes she quietly opens her eyes and she goes back into the kitchen, and she says, "No, Dad. They are not going to stay with me unless they ask me. Now you can call them or I will, and right now. What is your choice? Do you want to tell them or should I?"

Pt: She is wonderful.

T: (Quietly) Yes she is.

Pt: There's this woman at the office. She's a silly thing and she says anything on her mind. But she is the only one at department meetings who can say here is the tense time. She actually says what everyone thinks. She says, "My head is getting dizzy and I'm all tense," and everyone laughs 'cause we're all feeling pretty much the same way. . . . I always wanted to be able to do that. I'm going to learn how to meditate.

T: What?

Pt: There are classes, and I'm going to learn. Allen does it. I'm going go ask him. He talks about being free. I want to learn how to do that. Yes. Yes. I feel good. I'm ready to let Harry go. That feels good. I think I will do it. And I'm going to call Todd and Janine. Tonight, I think I'm ready for the worm to turn — or to turn over a new leaf, or whatever it is!

In the dream, "Maniac with the knife, and controlling the maniac," the dream experiencing is a sense of control, of being in charge, of dominating, of having the other totally in your hands. This was first experienced in the context of an early scene in which her mother is slobbering drunk on the front lawn. Next the experiencing was within the context of a recent scene in which she is at her boyfriend's apartment and she yells at him. She had just finished a playful fantasy growing out of a recent scene at her boyfriend's apartment, a scene in which she had commanded him to do this and this. As we were winding down from this, she says:

Pt: (Coming down) I've never done anything like that.
T: What a damned pity.
Pt: Yes. Yes. It is a damned pity.
T: Well, it sure felt delicious.
Pt: It sure did. (Pause. We are leaning toward being-behavioral change.)
T: Look, let's pretend. You got this tendency to control, to be the big boss. I know it. You know it. Just pretend, just pretend that somehow, magically, you walk out of here as this person. You are the big boss. In this here relationship with Tom, you are the manager—it'll never really happen—and Tom totally is the controlled one. You know he'd never let that happen! But let's pretend. Here you are, the big controller, the tough boss. That's you. Got it? Feel it? Remember, this is all just fantasy. Feel it a little?
Pt: Uh-huh.
T: OK! Now you are going over to Tom's place tomorrow night. Got it? And you are going to do whatever you want to do. Anything at all. Just let yourself pretend. This is your show. It is all your way. Of course none of this can really happen. But now you are the controlling one, and you have Tom totally in your hands. Just try it out. Get the feel of what it is like. OK? (The scene is set. She can let the behaviors come.)
Pt: Yes! (She is laughing.)
T: Do it!
Pt: Tom, you're fat! I want you to stop drinking beer. Wait! I want you to get rid of all the beer!
T: Out the window. Open the window and dish it out!
Pt: Take all the beer and sling it out the window! Every damned can! DO IT! DO IT NOW! THERE! And now I order you to take off all your clothes. TAKE IT OFF! THERE! NOW JUMP UP AND DOWN! FASTER! FASTER! LOOK AT THAT BELLY JIGGLING! YOU'RE A FAT SLOB! LOOK AT YOU! MORE! FASTER! YOU'RE TOO DAMNED FAT! YOUR BOOBS ARE BIGGER THAN MINE! YOU ARE GOING TO LOSE WEIGHT OR . . . NO MORE SEX. I'LL

SLEEP WITH YOU WHEN YOU LOOK LIKE A HUMAN BEING INSTEAD OF A FLAT SLOB!

T: AND BY THE WAY, SPEAKING OF SEX . . .

Pt: YEAH! NO MORE OF YOUR DAMNED OTHER WOMEN! YOU HEAR? IF YOU FOOL AROUND WITH OTHER WOMEN I'M GOING TO BITE YOUR BALLS OFF!

T: They're too fat anyway!

Pt: (She is now quite giddy.) And no more disappearing for a week. You are going to move in with me. No! My place is too small. We're going to get an apartment together. Tomorrow we start looking for an apartment together. TOGETHER! AND I'LL DECIDE WHICH ONE WE GET! I WILL!

T: And make sure the apartment is big enough for all the guys!

Pt: That's it, I'll have lots of guys living there!

T: Ten men. You have ten lovers. They all can live there in a huge place.

Pt: (Screeching) There's this place! White stone. Gorgeous. Has eight bedrooms. We could all live there. I'm the boss and they all live there with me. Everybody line up! Naked. EVERYONE STAND IN A LINE. I AM INSPECTING YOUR PRICKS! HEY DAVID, WHERE DID YOU GET THAT RED SPOT ON THE HEAD? ARE YOU GETTING IT ON WITH TODD? NOT IN OUR PLACE! NOT UNLESS I JOIN IN!

T: HEY LOOK! THAT ONE'S AT ATTENTION.

Pt: WE START TONIGHT'S SEX! EVERYONE GET READY. ALL ON YOUR HANDS AND KNEES AND EVERYONE GETS A FEW LICKS! AH! THAT'S NOT SUCH A BAD IDEA. I COULD LIVE LIKE THIS, AND I COULD MANAGE ALL THOSE GUYS.

T: Oh, I don't know. George would be hard.

Pt: No one can manage George. He's a wild one. I'd put him in the room next to mine, and every day I'll screw him till he gets civilized. He'll never be civilized. (She is coming down a little, and becoming more serious and realistic.) It's at work that I wish. . . . There's where I . . . and with Mom and Dad. They're getting old . . . I always dreamed that I . . .

T: Here it comes, go ahead. Go ahead.

Pt: Dad's thinking about selling the firm, no one to manage it . . .

T: Yes, yes.

Pt: I could.

T: Sure.

Pt: That would really be something. Managing the whole place.

T: Where's the best place for you to talk seriously with the old man?

Pt: At home.

T: You tell him that you want to talk with him, alone. No mother. Not your brother or sister. Just you. You and Dad are alone in front of the fireplace. He loves a good cigar, so you have a fine cigar, and you give it to him. Just smoke it, Dad. And you listen. You just listen to me. Smoke and listen. Light up. There. Lean back. Good. Now just consider that for the next year I work at the firm. You show me how to be the boss . . .

Pt: Make me a member of the board . . .

T: . . . and for one year you keep the firm. You are the chairman and I learn the ropes. If I still want to take over after a year, and if you and I work together well and we both think that I can take over after a year, then you retire and I will take over. You took over from Grampa, and I will take over from you. You've always wanted to keep the firm in the family. All right, I'm the one, and I want to see if it can work out. I am ready to consider this, and I want you to think about it seriously. All right, now you can talk. What do you think, Dad?

Pt: He's always talked to me, told me he wanted Solly to take over when he retired, but Solly was never interested. I think maybe I am. Yes. I think maybe I could do it. I always dreamed about maybe taking over.

You now have had a taste and sample of what it can be like to be and to behave on the basis of the dream experiencing in the imminent external world. You have accomplished a great deal, but we are not quite done with this final step.

REHEARSAL FOR REALITY

When we taste and sample new ways of being and behaving, we sometimes come to a point where the patient is ready to carry out the new behavior for real. At this point we give the intended new behavior as realistic a dress rehearsal as possible to see if the person is ready to carry out the behavior in the next few days or so (step 5.1, Figure 1). In any case, the final procedure is to commit oneself to some kind of new behavior. Even when being-behavior change ends with no readiness or intentionality to actually carry out some new behavior, the session ends with some kind of behavioral commitment.

Quite frequently, the patient will be ready and even eager to carry out this new way of being and behaving in the real world. This is indicated, for example, when she says that there are already some ways in which she does behave like this. Suddenly the new ways of being and behaving are already familiar, part of what she already does, at least in some ways. She takes over the new way of being and behaving and lists a number of ways that it is already a part of the way she is. Or she mentions a whole series of ways of behaving that she could carry out. Typically she says something that indicates a serious intention to be and behave in this new way. She says, "I think I am going to do it. . . . It's about time that I go ahead. . . . Ted would be so surprised. . . . It would be easy, I could do it tomorrow. . . . I really want to do it."

As therapist your task it to give the new behavior as realistic a dress rehearsal as possible. Ask the patient if this is all right: "Let's try it out as realistically as possible and see whether it feels right or not to do it for real." If the patient agrees, then show the patient how to try it out in a scene or situation that is quite realistic. Actually try it out. Rehearse it right here in the session. The key is to pay close attention to bodily sensations. If they feel good, if they are solid and exciting, then the patient is indeed ready to go ahead and do the new behavior. Since the therapist will likely do this right along with the patient, the dress rehearsal is passed when bodily sensations in both patient and therapist are good ones.

If the bodily sensations are not good, if they are numb and dead, and especially if they are unpleasant, then the bodily sensation signs point away from actually undertaking the new behavior. You then have an option. One choice is to modify the behavior in some way and then try it out again, perhaps repeating this several times until you arrive at a specific behavior that feels right. The other is simply to conclude that your body says no to that behavior and stop there.

You are giving the ordinary operating domain a chance to react to how it feels about actually carrying out of the behavior. Usually the dream experiencing is in favor. The problem lies with the other potentials in the operating domain. If the session has done a good enough job of integrating relationships between the operating domain and the dream experiencing, then the operating domain can welcome the right behavior. If the operating domain has mainly disintegrative relationships toward the dream experiencing, then rehearsing the new behavior gives the operating domain its chance to decline the new behavior.

In any case, you should make the dress rehearsal as realistic as possible. Frame in the actual situation quite realistically. Carry out the new behavior quite realistically. Then stop and check bodily sensations. Are they strong or weak? Are they pleasant or unpleasant?

There is generally no problem when both patient and therapist have bodily sensations that are good or bad. There is also no problem when the patient's bodily sensations are not good and the therapist's bodily sensations are good. Under this condition, the patient is not ready to carry out the behavior for real and some modification is in order. The problem for the therapist comes when the patient's bodily sensations are good and the therapist's are bad. The patient is apparently quite ready and willing to carry out the behavior, but the therapist is clutched up against the new way of being and behaving. Here is where the therapist says:

T: I don't care what you think. That whole idea scares me. Just quitting your job scares me. It is just too much for me. I can't let you do that. I'm the one who's not ready. So I am going to do what I can to say no, no way.

T: My heart is beating faster. I am all tense inside. No way. That feels bad. Huh-uh. Do not do it. It is wrong and not fitting. My body says no, no way.

This situation occurs rarely, but when it does the therapist continues saying no until some mutually satisfactory outcome is reached.

Illustrations

It is the job of the therapist to introduce the rehearsal for reality. The transition is easy. In the dream, "Maniac with the knife, and controlling the maniac," the last few interchanges were as follows, after she considers talking to her father about taking over the firm when he retires:

Pt: He's always talked to me, told me he wanted Solly to take over when he retired, but Solly was never interested. I think maybe I am. Yes, I think maybe I could do it. I always dreamed about maybe taking over.
T: Hey! You sound half serious about this.
Pt: I am. I really am. It's always been there in the back of my mind.
T: Well, maybe now's the time.
Pt: I think so. Yes. I think so!

At this point the therapist invites the patient to rehearse this new behavior for reality.

T: All right. Let's try it out for real, and we can see how it feels. Make it as real as you can. Pick out a place where you can be with Dad. Is there a good place?
Pt: The back yard, on the patio. Just Dad and me. Sunday. In the afternoon. Just the two of us.

T: Makes sense. Now you have to see him and make it as real as possible. Make your offer, and make it real. When you're done, we can check our bodies and see how it feels. What do you think? Is this all right?

Pt: (Pause) You always wanted Solly to take over the firm. He won't. But you've known that I always wanted to. I have a proposition. I would like to work in the firm for two years to see. It would be a probation. You can see and I can see. . . . He'd love it. You really want this . . .

T: Check your body. Just check . . . what's it like?

Pt: Well, he'd be happy. But I don't feel much. It feels all right. A little warmth in my face. That's all.

T: Hmmm. Not much. (This particular behavior was not accompanied with even moderate bodily sensations. Keeping in mind the dream experiencing of power and control, perhaps we can modify the behavior.) Well, scratch that. Forget about being this way with old Dad. Want to try it again, but a little different this time? Or would you rather just drop it?

Pt: Dad, listen to me (she sounds more solid and even, balanced). I want to run the firm when you retire. I've always wanted to. It's time for us to talk. Sooner or later I want to take over from you. But I won't if you are opposed. But this is what I want, and I am going to do it unless you can talk me out of it. Are you ready to talk about this now?

T: How does that feel inside?

Pt: Strong. Like a fist. Good.

T: Are there little tinglings in your arms? I got them.

Pt: Yes, well, in my hands mainly. Like electricity.

T: Well, I don't know. Maybe you're ready to be this way. It feels right.

Pt: I feel good. I want to do it.

T: You sound ready. Seems like you feel ready. I feel good inside. You can do it. It sure as hell is up to you.

Pt: I think I will. I will!

T: Are you serious? Are you really ready to be this way with him and say this to him? Really?

Pt: I've been waiting all my life. I'm ready. I want to!

T: Are you going to do it? It really is up to you. But if you are really ready, then go ahead and do it.

Pt: I am. I am. I'm going over there tomorrow, and I'm going to do it!

T: Great!

In being and behavior change for the dream, "Late for the wedding, and watching the nurses," the experiencing was that of letting go of oppressive involvements, being free and out of things, not being involved or caught. We began this step with her turning to the way she enslaves herself in interactions with her ex-husband. Then we covered a number of appropriate behaviors, and ended with her mentioning her ex-husband again: " . . . I feel good. I'm ready to let Harry go. That feels good. I think I will do it. And I'm going to call Todd and Janine tonight. I think I'm ready for the worm to turn—or to turn over a new leaf, or whatever it is!" We are ready to rehearse these behaviors for reality.

T: If you're maybe ready to do these things, how about trying them out just to see? Maybe it'll feel all right, and maybe, who knows? Let's start with Todd and Janine. If you really are going to call, what would you say? Try it out. Make it as real as can be. Is this all right? If it feels right, then go ahead and do it. If not, forget it.

Pt: I'd make sure Dad was on the phone too.

T: So when would you do it and how? Can you do that? Just like as if you're really doing it.

Pt: Pick up the phone, Dad. I'm calling Todd and Janine now. I'll get the other phone. OK, now their number. Here it is. I'll tell you when to pick it up, Dad. Dial dial dial. Hi Todd, this is me, yeah. Dad's on the phone. He just told me that he said, wait, Dad, you tell it . . . Da da da da. That's right. Todd, I have great news for you. I've abdicated. I'm not big Momma anymore . . . oh, I'm getting nervous. My hands are shaking and . . . I don't think I can do it . . .

T: How about saying this out loud, just to see. "Todd, this isn't easy. I'm getting nervous and my hands are shaking.

Pt: No, I think it is up to me. I'll call them, myself. I'll do it. Todd, Dad told me that he said you can stay at my place when you are here for a couple of weeks. No! No Way! Stay at Sally's or with Evelyn. Stay with me for three or four days. . . . What? Yes, it is about time. Yes, they both have bigger places. I've stopped being mother superior for the family. I got my own life, and during those two weeks I've got plans for something. I don't know what. Something. Maybe even a vacation of my own. It's been so long I don't even remember. Yes!

T: Check your body! What's going on inside?

Pt: It feels great! Really great! Yes, dammit! I am going to call them! It's about time I did something like that . . . and I want to tell Harry I'm through. I'm going to call him. NO! I think I'll go to his place and tell him I'm through being his slave.

T: Go ahead. Make it as real as can be.

Pt: I'll go in the evening. Friday. Knock on the door. Harry . . . let me in. Harry, let me go. I'm finished with you. I've had enough of being your slave. It's over.

T: Kind of flat.

Pt: I don't really mean it.

T: Don't do it.

Pt: I felt numb.

T: Feelings sure weren't good.

Pt: I'm not ready.
T: No, neither am I.
Pt: But I am calling Todd and Janine. One thing at a time.
T: Right.

THE BEHAVIORAL COMMITMENT

There will be some occasions where you rehearse behaviors and there are wonderful bodily sensations. The rehearsal culminates in the person's committing herself to actually undertaking the new way of being and behaving, and almost always this is to occur in the next few days or so. But this leaves aside all those times when there is no special readiness and intentionality for truly carrying out the behavior, that is, when there is no "rehearsal for reality." It also leaves out those occasions when "rehearsal for reality" ends without strong positive bodily sensations. However, under all conditions and in every session, there is to be a behavioral commitment — regardless of what happens in the final being-behavioral step.

You are obligated to do *something,* to undertake some new behavior that (a) provides even a whisper of the dream experiencing, (b) is new and different for you, and (c) is to be carried out right away, within the next few days or so. Any such behavior will do. It may be tiny. It may be safe as can be, with no risk whatsoever. It may be personal and private so that only you know about it. Buy some flowers for the woman at the corner store who was so friendly and helpful when you dropped the bag and broke some eggs. You need not even give them to her. Instead of telling your uncle to go to hell, ask your husband to pretend he is Uncle Harry, and then whisper a few words of defiance.

Whether you are a person working on your own dreams or a therapist working with a patient, you are to end the session with a behavioral commitment of some kind. The target question is: Given this dream experiencing, what new behavior will you commit yourself to carry out in the next few days?

Here is the fellow who worked on this own dream ("Fantastic skier, and the dope shop") and the dream experiencing of putting on a show, performing:

Pt: OK, I am going to do something, getting a shot at the feeling of performing, putting on a show. I'll stand on the deck and flash to the people in the apartment. Sure. . . . What about the Town Players? Could I take a little step? That sounds all right. . . . I could investigate it, but that wouldn't give me the feeling . . . Hmmm. I have to do something. Juggle. I can juggle tennis balls. I'll practice somewhere, and maybe show someone. Wait. Where can I practice? I haven't done that in years. God, it's been years. All right, now where can I practice? Golf balls. I will practice at the club. No, I prefer tennis balls. Where? At home. Why not? Yeah, I'll practice in the living room and then I will . . . what? Where can I do it that's not going to be scary? On the porch. Sure, I will do it on the porch. I think I will! This is silly, but I think I like it. I will juggle tennis balls on the porch (laughs)! Unless there are people in the apartment. Then I'll flash. God, I sure want to flash. Not now. I can't do that. I'll juggle my balls (laughs). That's a compromise? I think I'll really do it too. Now I've got to look for a can of tennis balls. . . .

Beginning with the dream, "Surreptitious in the store, and avoiding one another," being-behavior change enabled Harvey to taste and sample all sorts of behaviors related to the dream experiencing of being found out, exposed, caught, seen. The behaviors included telling his wife that he secretly watches little kids on the playground and that he secretly gave flowers to the woman at work, going with his wife to the playground and watching the kids, taking her to the city where he grew up and confessing all his childhood sexual secrets, telling the woman at the office that he has a schoolboy crush on her, getting a t-shirt that says "stop me, I'm a pervert," and so on. Now we are ready for some behavioral commitment:

T: Well, you're really not going to do any of these things. Right?

Pt: I'd like to. But I won't. I know.

T: Think of something you'd be willing to do. A tiny little thing. But it gives you a little bit of a feeling of being exposed and found out. Confessing, or being caught. Just a wee tiny bit. Something that's a start. Tell you what. I'll mention one thing, and you think of another. OK?

Pt: I couldn't tell Edna.

T: Right. How about a little innocent confession to Edna. Something. Like you took some money from her purse. Innocent like. No! Tell her to watch you sneak some money from her purse. No, that's not good. Something that she could see you, something you don't show her.

Pt: I know. I know. I've been to Doc Parker, our doctor. I got a rash on my penis. It comes and goes away. I thought it was some disease. And I had him check these black moles on my back. I thought I had cancer. I never told her. I was embarrassed.

T: That's a lot to tell her.

Pt: I'm going to tell her.

T: How?

Pt: After supper, I'll . . . yeah, I'll take a shower and lie on the bed with her and tell her that I've been hiding it. I'll confess, and I'll show her the rash and the moles. And I'll tell her.

T: Are you really serious? You'll do it?

Pt: Uh-huh. Yeah. I don't usually. I'd want to. Yeah. I will!

T: Really?

Pt: I'm going to! Tonight! Yeah!

The person has had a taste and a sample of what it is like to be the dream experiencing and to behave in new ways in the extratherapy world. In addition to committing himself to behavior, he has become a new person who has a new experiencing, a new being-behaving person in a new extratherapy world. It may have lasted a few minutes or so, or it may be a profound change that lasts from here on. We have completed the dream work session.

The Dreams Referred to in the Text

THESE ARE 13 DREAMS REFERRED to in the text. You will notice that they are generally longer and more detailed than most dreams reported in many other approaches. This is because the experiential method encourages dreams of at least two peaks or episodes and because each peak is to be reported in detail. On the other hand, all linkages have been deleted to protect the confidentiality of the persons who had the dream and those referred to in the linkages.

A few of the dreams are from my own personal dream work or from other persons working on their own dreams. A few are from patients seen by my interns and postdoctoral trainees. Most are from my own patients.

Even though I had permission to use these dreams, I altered the content to protect the identity and confidentiality of the persons involved. I began with verbatim dreams and then made several changes. Proper names and places were altered. I changed the nature of the relationships of dreamed persons and figures to the dreamer. For example, a sibling was changed to a friend, a neighbor was changed to a person at work. Idiosyncratic words and phrases were altered. A scene or incident or situation that might identify the person was altered to a slightly different one. Furthermore, all changes were taken from other dreams of other persons so that bits and pieces of one person's dreams may well show up in another dream as given here. The net result is that these 13 dreams are illustrative rather than strictly verbatim, although the syntax of each recorded dream was preserved intact.

SHAKING THE HAND, AND THE NAME WAS SCRATCHED OUT

There is this episode about the guy with sort of reddish hair, older man shaking my hand. We were just shaking, talking, over this house that I think Peter and his wife rented, and it used to belong to, it was a big house like Andy owned it, but not really, and maybe it was a house where . . . anyhow, I know the house someplace, and it may have been in Haverford, like the house that I rented. Another one was where it was this party where I was handed this thing by Peter. He was in charge and oozing graciousness. He showed me this little brochure, or he thought there was something about me, and I looked through it and there was a little bit of, a word or two about me, or my name was listed and it was scratched out, and I didn't like that.

With this fellow, this big-boned guy, at Peter's place. He said, he introduced himself to me and I to him, and then he shook my hand, and I moved his finger here and moved it over there, 'cause it wasn't a good shake, and then, his hand was big, sort of, and I moved this guy's hands. I liked that, his fingers, and he was commenting to somebody else at the party, and Jane was at the party. Lots of people were at the party, and this guy was commenting that my wrist, something about my wrist. But the nice feeling I had was that this guy and I were engaging. He's not taking my little hand, and just moving it. We're really shaking, and I liked that. I really felt OK there, almost playful, partyish. We were just shaking hands and holding that shake.

The other one is where Peter handed me this little brochure and my name was scratched out or something I said was, and I didn't like that, I felt intruded upon or like this was his house. It wasn't that he was mad at me. I don't know why he scratched it out.

HE IS MOUNTING MY DOG, AND
TOO FAR TO WALK

Pete (my boy dog) was a girl dog, and this small, sort of mule or dog with a big head, like dark gray, this dog tries to mount Pete, and I have this awful feeling that Pete is going to get pregnant, and what are we going to do? And Pete is really nice. He is friendly, I mean that she is really nice and friendly. And this other dog is a little more insistent. I'm a little hesitant that this second dog might turn on me if I try to stop it. I yell "no, no" a couple of times, but the main thing is this dog or mule or funny-looking animal with the big head and big shoulders, neck, small body, it's like a scaled down jackass or mule, but it's all right. It tries to mount Pete from the rear, and I think it's going to. That's the strangest feeling, and I'm kind of annoyed and frustrated, and feeling oh my God, what am I going to do!

And then earlier, I'm figuring out a way that I want to go up this mountainside or go over to the other side or travel or move, and the main feeling is I can't do it. About 30 feet away is this small trailer bridge. It's made of wood, old wood, and I want to get up to the mountain. There is a lot of snow, and I see that the wooden, little camp trail can go down there. That would be OK, then I could do it. It would be all right, but it is a little too far away, and I have this same sense of "oh no." I have to walk all the way down there, around, and it's a bother or a waste of time, like I really do not want to. That's the main feeling. It's sort of winter time.

PROTECTING THE BONE, AND HOLDING
THE BREASTS

It's in a big house. Morning. Lots of different people, relatives, people older and younger. There's a big kitchen and a dining area, a table, and a sun room, and a back room. There are china cupboards and silver serving and chafing dish, a roasting pan of oak, carved, big bowls, windows, all the rooms, a sun room. The last one is closed with cabinets, an archway. Part of the idea is having a party. My grandmother is there, and uncles and aunts, sister. They are positive with me. It's Sunday morning. People are preparing food. My sister is there. She took the dog for a walk. I had taken a walk to go to Norm's. I went by his house, and off toward the other street. My sister is calling the dog, a collie. The dog came to me. Another dog came up. The dog that I called had a bone, and another dog came up, and the dog I called didn't fight, but was protective of its bone. You're not going to take it, and the other dog left. It just knew and went away.

Then I am with Mary Jo Auerbach, and we are flirting. I came up behind her, and put my hands on her breasts. She liked it, and there was a knowledge that we weren't going any further. I was struck by my putting my hands on her breasts. I was happy, enjoying all those people. My mother-in-law and her mother were not angry. We were going to mix in, and it was kind of flirtatious. It's fun.

THE OPPONENTS ARE SQUARING OFF FOR
THE KILL, AND I THROW THE BOMB TO
ONE OF THEM

These two guys were really having it out, with this sort of small, maybe 4 inches, but very heavy, black ball. It didn't bounce at all. They had a sort of net that they were hitting it back and forth in. I think both were black and very muscular, but these two guys were really out for the kill, really fighting one another. I was just an observer. I had nothing to do, and I was watching them, and they were really at it. They had this sort of ritual. Oh, there was something. The strange thing was that at the end I was involved! The ball, the thing, was thrown by one guy, over the head of the second one, and then it came toward me, and I wanted to be helpful, so I sort of just picked it up and tossed it at the one fellow, the good guy, the hero, the fellow I liked. He was a little bit older than the other one, and he did a strange thing. He caught it, sank to his knees on the grass, closed his eyes, and sort of hunched his back over it a little bit, and it was like it was all over. He turned his back, or his back was turned to the opponent, and the opponent didn't do anything. It was like it was over, and at the end there, I felt like I had interfered. I shouldn't. Like their fight was over. It was the end, and the feeling was that somehow I had done a bad thing. I finished things with them. I had interfered, or ended it, but they were no longer fighting. That was the end.

Then, what else? My feeling, earlier, when was the peak with that? They were having this ritualistic fight, like a confrontation. The peak was when, a fight, they fight. It's just an ominous, terrible feeling, especially as the opponent attacks by coming closer, and both crouching. It's the idea of throwing the black ball at the other one, and sometimes they would catch it or let it drop. I don't know what they were trying to do, but I did think it was a fight to the death, really to the death, and that one would kill the other, to the death. It was like they would throw the ball back, and it was a bad thing. They were exceedingly well built, the two guys, one much older, both black, and had quite dark skin, but their bodies were really well built. At the peak, I am watching them. They are both crouched, with this bomb, throwing it at one another, and maybe the peak was when the opponent got closer, and I almost wanted to say, "Watch out." I was scared he was going to grab my guy, the one I was in favor of. He was getting closer. Watch out! It was getting bad. Be careful. It was when they were squaring off.

SLAMMING THE INTRUDER, AND
PANICKED ABOUT THE GORILLA

I am hitting him with lefts and rights. His head is not moving much. He's not fighting back. I'm not having a helluva lot of impact on his head, but I am clobbering him again and again, and I am putting him away. The reason is I am in this huge kitchen where I called the police, 9142, about the gorilla. This guy just turns on the oven. It's in the wall. He turns it on. Just turns it on. I tell him to turn it off. He turns it on again and again even though I tell him not to. I get infuriated, and so I get enraged, go over to him and start smashing him. He has no right to be in my house. I was enraged. Who the fuck is he anyway?

I was, earlier, panicked, on the telephone. I was telling someone, I think the police, to come out here 'cause this wild gorilla is here in the neighborhood. It is a huge thing. I saw it near Annie McKenna's, it was about 40 feet high, even though I also saw it at another neighbor's and it was only a regular size. But I was panicked it would come into our house. I am yelling at the person on the phone, "It is a huge fucking gorilla, not some little chimp!" I am desperate, terrified it would come into our house, damned terrified. It's almost as if they won't believe me. The first policeman I reached didn't have much to say. Didn't take it seriously. But this time she did, and I was more terrified of the gorilla than anything else. It was all over the neighborhood.

THE WINO, THE TOUGH GUYS, AND THE HURT HAND

Here are the three episodes of the dream: (1) I'm going into a hospital, a small private room, for an operation on my eyes. There is an old man in one of the beds. He looks like a wino, with a stubbly beard and a veined nose, puffy cheeks, ragged hair, I don't know what we are in for. I'm walking into the room, and someone is behind me. The strongest feeling is when I'm seeing him, and I'm being a little repulsed.

(2) I'm out of the hospital, and I got out before this guy, Walter. I'm walking down the street with him, toward Front Street, in the slummy area of town. Some tough guys are there. We're near the Army and Navy store. I see four tough guys standing on the corner. I become extremely afraid. I tell Walter I have to get back to work. I'll see him later. This is an excuse because I'm scared and easing out. If I go by the four tough guys they will beat me up.

(3) In the hospital. Walter is in the room. My bed is scrunched up against the door. It is half inside and half on the other side of the door, widthwise. Half of the bed is covered by being on the other side. The half I see is a white hospital bed, and the other half is my own bed at home, with a blue comforter on top. It's put there so I

can't get into bed. It's crazy 'cause it is half in and half out. It shouldn't be this way. Walter is going to be going, leaving. His hand is hurt. I think the four tough guys have hurt him, but no, his hand is hurt legitimately. I think the four tough guys did it to him, and I wasn't there to help him. But then I feel relieved.

LATE FOR THE WEDDING, AND WATCHING THE NURSES

It was on a large pond, all ice. Everyone was on ice skates. There were lots of wedding parties, lots of weddings going on. I was skating around, all over, looking for my wedding. I was panicked, asking everyone where my wedding was. I was late, very late and getting later. I felt scared and full of panic because I couldn't find my wedding.

In the next part I am a nurse in a hospital and there are four other people besides myself. I knew the doctor. He was in a white coat. There were three other nurses and me. I was in a uniform too. I came there and the four were in the nursing station and I introduced myself, and I said that I didn't know what I as doing here and I would need a lot of help. No one spoke to me. No one spoke to me. They jumped up and started doing things. They were busy doing things. I didn't know what to do. The doctor said that he was sorry, he didn't have time. I said that I needed help. One of the nurses said, "You are a nurse, function." She said, "That is your problem." They were running around madly, and I just watched. I felt scared and not knowing what to do. They were running around madly, doing things and I stood back, feeling panic . . .

SURREPTITIOUS IN THE STORE, AND AVOIDING ONE ANOTHER

I remember very vividly, looking through the book, as if it had something to do with a New York publishing company. It was of two people, a blonde girl, young, very young, and a blonde fellow, and it was just soft black and white photographs of them making love. They were nice photographs, soft, not very vivid, and I'm just looking through it, and there's a strange feeling, mixture of feelings. I don't want to buy the book. It's more like a cheap collection of pictures, photographs. I don't want to do it because people may see me, especially the two neighbors who live next door. So there's a vigilance and an awareness that they may see me, 'cause I'm in this store with a lot of books. I pick it up. The feeling is a little bit of sexual, not terribly sexual. The girl is not very attractive, and she has something on her face sort of.

I also remember that I saw Nate, sort of walking across the street. It seems now that maybe he purchased one of those pornographic books, or he had something surreptitious. He is walking across the street. He doesn't see me, and the main feeling is again, a little bit of ominousness because the other neighbor, pretty far behind me, on a walk or a sidewalk, doesn't want to see Nate, really doesn't want to see Nate. I have sort of a strong sense that Nate seems disconcerted. What is he doing here? What's wrong with him? It's like he is at loose ends, and that's the feeling I have as I'm watching him. But I'm sensing how much the other neighbor doesn't want to see him, really doesn't want to see him. I'm a little surprised to see Nate, and also concerned that the other neighbor doesn't want to see him.

FLYING THE AIRPLANE, AND DRIVING THE PLANE ON THE GROUND

There were two peaks. In one, this woman is piloting the airplane, turning a little bit to her left, and she is saying something about that's what the airplane should be for. It's like a "memorial" airplane, a memory of somebody, a woman, some woman, a pilot. And my pilot looks like that famous actress, Katherine Hepburn. She's just like her. She makes no open and shorter answers to me. She's turning to her left, and I'm really in love with her. It's a kind of crush, but I really like her, partly because she thinks of me as somebody very very special somehow. I don't know why. But I think it has to do with my being somebody who is special, except that this woman really was Katherine Hepburn, the pilot, and she will tell, piloting the airplane and turning to the left. We were just going along, and I was to the right. I think there were just two seats. Her skin was smooth. She seemed almost strangely young, as if she had little on, but I don't think of her as nude, but she was turning to her left.

The other one is that right afterwards what I . . . She is still turned to her left or behind me, and this time the plane, which is big, really big, is on the ground, moving along, not terribly rapidly, like a car, and I'm holding the steering wheel which is black, round, small, and striated, not smooth. She's giving me a little bit of orders, like "left." I can see that because I have to move to avoid cars, and to avoid buildings, sidewalks, as we are moving along, not too fast. And then she'd say, "right." But that was obvious, and then "left," and the feeling I had was kind of a little bit scary, little bit excitement at maneuvering this big plane which I didn't want to hit or harm, but it was really beautiful, this plane. And the other is there is another sight of when we are flying, and the sky, maybe 20 airplanes moving, flying in a row, a couple already tightening up against one another, and I was kind of excited about being in the air, seeing other airplanes.

MANIAC WITH THE KNIFE, AND
CONTROLLING THE MANIAC

There was a neighborhood meeting. My husband wasn't there for some reason, but everybody else was. For some reason we all were spending the night across the street in a living room that had big picture windows looking out on the neighborhood. There were mats, like gym mats, laid out in this living room so that people could sleep. I didn't know why we were doing that but it was OK. I'm aware of Randy talking to some man. They were at the head of my mat, and I was getting real sleepy. They were whispering. Randy was explaining that the reason we were all sleeping there was that he had gotten into an argument with somebody and the guy had threatened to kill him and burn the neighborhood down, so we were there for safety and also so that Randy could keep an eye on the neighborhood from across the street.

All of a sudden, Randy said, "There he is. There he is." And he sounded really frightened. The guy was across the street. I hesitated and I didn't say anything, but what I was thinking was, "Why don't you call the police?" Randy didn't call them, and the next thing I knew the guy burst into the living room. He was wild-looking, about 40 years old, and wearing a checked shirt, crazy glint in his eye, and he was mad, really mad, and I sat up. Randy was about two feet away from me. The guy came running over. All he could see was Randy. He didn't even notice there were other people there. He took his knife and he stabbed Randy in the back of the neck. Randy pitched forward. Here's the first peak. The man looked up and realized there were other people there. He saw me because I was the closest. I was petrified. He came over and he took his knife and ran it down the right side of my neck to my shoulder. I was petrified. I know he could do anything he wanted and he was wild and crazy. I realized the other people were so scared they weren't going to help me. I was going to have to do something myself. I don't know whether it was the sense of I have to do something about this or whether it was this guy with all this power. I don't know which feeling is strongest. It's a sense of I'm all by myself and no one will help me and this guy's a lunatic and I'm going to have to handle it. He looked crazy.

The bad feeling went away when I realized I was going to have to do something about it and I couldn't get to a phone, and no one could help me. They were too scared to do anything. So I started talking to him and I said to the guy, "Why are you so angry at Randy? What happened? What's wrong? Tell me all about it." I was aware of being a therapist and this was the only skill I had that would pull me through the situation so I just kept, in good relationship style, asking him to tell me what was wrong, to describe it, to tell me more. He put his hands down, his body relaxed, and he sat down on the floor across from me. He started to tell me all about Randy, and his problem with Randy. He started to cry. When he started to cry, I realized I had the situation in complete control, that I was totally in charge of him, that he wasn't a wild, angry, deranged, killing maniac. He was a pathetic, crying, sad person. It was an incredible feeling. I was in charge of him, plus the neighbors were standing there frightened, dependent on me to be in charge, competent, and I was. I was going to get them out of this. It was a wonderful feeling.

Later he said that he had to go to the bathroom. I asked, "Do you want me to go with you? I'd be happy to go with you. Do you want me to hold your hand?" I had the same feeling of being in complete control. He said no, and I used paradoxical intention. I said, "Be sure you come right back here. Don't go anywhere else." When he left, the neighbors just stood there, and I said, "Call the cops." The whole thing had been a strategy on my part to disarm the situation. I was in total charge of the situation.

THE FANTASTIC SKIER, AND THE DOPE SHOP

We are driving along, or I am driving along by myself. Along the road we could see the mountain gorges. I see skiers. They are incredible. They are doing fantastic skiing tricks. One is skiing backwards and on one ski. It is almost as if they were ice skating. But it was most fantastic. The most fantastic was this Chinese fellow. He has a shirt on, and he's skiing down this mountain, and he looked like he would go over the gorge. He skis within two feet of it. He's really fantastic.

He skis backward and on one ski. That's all I remember. Next is this sort of tourist shop and I'm looking through these shelves. It's a head shop, and they're selling drugs, but not illegal drugs, things you can buy across the counter. It's mainly combinations of herbs that have a drug effect. There's another store next to it. They sold homemade pipes for smoking dope. That's all.

MOVING INTO THE DIRTY APARTMENT, AND HOLDING ONTO THE CAR

In the first one, Cassie and I are moving into a basement apartment, and it was really old and dilapidated. It was very dirty, and I remember that there was a toilet in the middle of the room. You couldn't see, like from the kitchen, where the toilet was, and you couldn't see outside the apartment. It had belonged to some people I knew. It was really dirty, and everything was makeshift. It had some furnishings. There was an old mattress on the floor, a puffy mattress, and two single ones, and it was just depressing to be in the apartment. It would take a lot of work to clean it up and do something with it.

In the next dream, we are going for a drive, and I'm standing, holding onto something. I'm outside the vehicle. I think it's a car. We're going along, and there is this river or waterfall surging over the top of a cliff. The water and the wind is so strong that I'm almost pulled out of the car. The river is overflowing, as if a lake is filled up and overflowing. It's a very wild scene, and very frightening and strange.

CUPPING THE WOMAN'S BREAST, AND THE TINY MINES EXPLODE

It starts off in the home in Wales. Lived there from about 8 to 15. I'm sitting on the gravel with someone. A World War II plane passes overhead. It looks small. It chokes, and blows two smoke rings, one from each of the wings, and then it disappears. I look for something on the ground. I'm crawling around, and I notice some little brass things. I heard them fall. I see some small brass shell casings, like from 38's. I thought that something else fell, and I see another bullet, another casing, and another bullet. It's as though the bullets were defective. It went "putt putt," making smoke rings. I was apprehensive. There were four objects, close together. I am down on my hands and knees and I notice other brass casings, like a little pyramid on the earth. What can they be? They are like mines, but very small. We used the driveway for years, but the mines never exploded. Maybe no one drove over them. I get some large stones and drop them on the mines and, holy shit, it explodes! It blows up. There's a tremendous crash right in front of a windshield of a neighbor's car. Like large fragments of granite. Like it blows a boulder into pieces, each about seven or eight pounds, right on the hood of a neighbor's car, and at that point we are called into lunch.

In the next episode I walk into a building. A young policeman says, "Where are you going?" and I say, "I'm going to the bathroom." He says, "We are taking you away," and I say, "Let me pee first." The police are rounding us up. One of our numbers, a girl, is tested for alcohol. We are amazed, and say, "You aren't even the slightest bit intoxicated, and you were drinking much more than the rest of us." She is a funky sort of girl, quite thin, and with wonderful hair, in an interesting cut, with the color of hair very much like mine. She seems strong, vibrant, and sparkling, and just genuinely lovely. I approach her as she is lying on the ground, and I embrace her. As I talk to her, her face is turned up to me, and I am aware of her blouse. She is flat chested. She is the first person I seem to have found with a decent hair cut. I ask her who's done her hair. I reach out and cup her breast, and ask her if this is all right, and she says yes, and does so nonchalantly. It is a lark and yet she can see the serious side. It is a wonderful feeling that such a delightfully kookie person might be here for me. Then I have a thought that this person is the love of my life. There is something really special about her. I feel really good after this dream, warm and right.

REFERENCES

Adler, A. (1983). *Social interest: Challenge to mankind*. London: Faber & Faber.

Adler, A. (1958). *What life should mean to you*. New York: Capricorn.

Adler, A. (1974). Dreams reveal the life style. In R. Woods and H. Greenhouse (Eds.). *The new world of dreams*, pp. 213–216. New York: Macmillan.

Alexander, F. (1930). About dreams with unpleasant content. *Psychoanalytic Quarterly, 4*, 447–452.

Altman, L. (1969). *The dream in psychoanalysis*. New York: International Universities Press.

Angyal, A. (1956). *Neurosis and treatment: A holistic theory*. New York: John Wiley and Sons.

Ansbacher, H., & Ansbacher, L. (1956). *The Individual Psychology of Alfred Adler*. New York: Basic Books.

Arlow, J. A., & Brenner, C. (1964). *Psychoanalytic concepts and the structural theory*. New York: International Universities Press.

Artemidorus (1975). *The Oneirocritica*, tr. Robert J. White. Hillsdale, New Jersey: Noyes Press.

Atwood, G., & Stolorow, R. (1984). *Structures of subjectivity: Explorations in psychoanalytic phenomenology*. Hillsdale, New Jersey: Analytic Press.

Bauer, R. (1985). Dream symbolization in light of analytic and experiential thinking. *Journal of Contemporary Psychotherapy, 15*, 20–28.

Baylor, G. W., & Deslauriers, D. (1987). Dreams as problem-solving: A method of study, Part 1: Background and theory. *Imagination, Cognition, and Personality, 4*, 105–118. Beck, A. T., & Ward, C. H. (1961). Dreams of depressed patients: Characteristic themes in manifest content. *Archives of General Psychiatry, 5*, 462–467.

Binswanger, L. (1958). The case of Ellen West: An anthropological-clinical study. In R. May, E. Angel & H. F. Ellenberger (Eds.). *Existence: A new dimension in psychiatry and psychology*, pp. 237–364. New York: Basic Books.

Binswanger, L. (1967). Dream and existence. In J. Needleman (Ed.). *Being-in-the-world: Selected papers of Ludwig Binswanger*, pp. 222–248. New York: Harper Torchbooks.

Bjerre, P. (1936). *Das trauman a/s heilungswey der seele*. Zurich: Rascher Verlag.

Black, A. (1971). *Dream diary*. New York: William Morrow.

Blum, H. (1976). Changing use of dreams in psychoanalytic practice: Dreams and free associations. *International Journal of Psycho-Analysis, 57*, 315–324.

Bonime, W. (1962). *The clinical use of dreams*. New York: Basic Books.

Bonime, W. (1969). The use of dreams in the therapeutic engagement of patients. *Contemporary Psychoanalysis, 6*, 13–30.

Bonime, W. (1984). Collaborative dream work. *Journal of the American Academy of Psychoanalysis, 14*, 15–26.

Bonime, W., & Bonime, F. (1987). Culturist approach. In J. L. Fosshage & C. A. Loew (Eds.). *Dream interpretation: A comparative study*. Pp. 79–124. New York: PMA.

Boss, M. (1957). *The analysis of dreams*. London: Rider.

Boss, M. (1959). The psychopathology of dreams in schizophrenic and organic psychosis. In M. F. DeMartino (Ed.). *Dreams and personality dynamics*. Pp. 124–139. Springfield, Illinois: Charles C. Thomas.

Boss, M. (1963). *Psychoanalysis and Daseins analysis*. New York: Basic Books.

Boss, M. (1977). "I dreamt last night . . . " New York: Gardner Press.

Boss, M., & Kenny, B. (1987). Phenomenological or Daseins analytic approach. In J. L. Fosshage & C. A. Loew (Eds.). *Dream interpretation: A comparative study.* Pp. 149–189. New York: PMA.

Breger, L. (1967). Function of dreams. *Journal of Abnormal Psychology Monograph, 72,* Whole No. 641.

Breger, L. (1980). The manifest dream and its latent meaning. In J. M. Natterson (Ed.). *The dream in clinical practice.* Pp. 3–27. New York: Jason Aronson.

Breger, L., Hunter, J., & Lane, R. W. (1971). The effects of stress on dreams. *Psychological Issues, 7,* 1–210.

Bressler, B., & Mizrachi, N. (1978a). The first dream as a psychodiagnostic tool: Its use by the primary physician with his psychosomatic patients. *Journal of Asthma Research, 15,* 179–189.

Bressler, B., & Mizrachi, N. (1987b). The first dream as a psychodiagnostic tool: Parameters. *Journal of Asthma Research, 14,* 1–14.

Bro, H. (1968). *Edgar Cayce on dreams.* New York: Paperback Library.

Buytendijk, F. J. J. (1967). The phenomenological approach to the problem of feelings and emotions. In T. Millon (Ed.). *Theories of psychopathology.* Pp. 254–260. Philadelphia: W. B. Saunders.

Byles, M. B. (1962). *Journey into Burmese Silence.* George Allen and Unwin.

Bynum, E. (1980). The use of dreams in family therapy. *Psychotherapy: Theory, Research and Practice, 17,* 227–231.

Caligor, L., & May, R. (1968). *Dreams and symbols: Man's unconscious language.* New York and London: Basic Books.

Cartwright, R. (1974). Problem solving: Waking and dreaming. *Journal of Abnormal Psychology, 83,* 451–455.

Cartwright, R. (1979). The nature and function of repetitive dreams: A survey and speculation. *Psychiatry, 42,* 131–137.

Cartwright, R. D., Kasniak, A., Borowitz, E., & Kling, A. (1972). The dreams of homosexual and heterosexual subjects to the same erotic movie. *Psychophysiology, 9,* 117.

Cartwright, R., Tipton, L., & Wicklund, J. (1980). Focusing on dreams. *Archives of General Psychiatry, 37,* 275–277.

Caruso, I. (1964). *Existential psychology.* New York: Herder & Herder.

Castaneda, C. (1972). *Journey to Ixtlan.* New York: Simon and Schuster.

Castaneda, C. (1977). *The second ring of power.* New York: Simon and Schuster.

Cavenar, J. C., & Nash, J. L. (1976). The dream as a signal for termination. *Journal of the American Psychoanalytic Association, 24,* 425–436.

Cavenar, J. C., & Spaulding, J. G. (1978). Termination signal dreams in psychoanalytic psychotherapy. *Bulletin of the Menninger Clinic, 42,* 58–62.

Cipolli, C., Baroncini, P., Fagioli, I., Fumai, A., & Salzarulo, P. (1987). The thematic continuity of mental sleep experience in the same night. *Sleep, 10,* 473–479.

Cirincione, D., Hart, J., Karle, W., & Switzer, A. (1980). The functional approach to using dreams in marital and family therapy. *Journal of Marital and Family Therapy, 6,* 147–151.

Cohen, D. B. (1974a). A test of the salience hypothesis of dream recall. *Journal of Consulting and Clinical Psychology, 42,* 699–703.

Cohen, D. B. (1947b). The salience hypothesis of dream recall: Further evidence. In M. H. Chase, W. C. Stern, & P. L. Walton (Eds.). *Sleep research,* Vol. 3. Pp. 118–137. Los Angeles: UCLA Brain Information Service/Brain Research Institute.

Condrau, G., & Boss, M. (1971). Existential analysis. In J. G. Howells (Ed.). *Modern perspectives in world psychiatry.* Pp. 488–518. New York: Brunner/Mazel.

Corriere, R., Hart, J., Karle, W., Binder, J., Gold, S., & Woldenberg, L. (1977). Toward a new theory of dreaming. *Journal of Clinical Psychology, 33,* 807-819.

Corriere, R., Karle, W., Woldenberg, L., & Hart, J. (1980). *Dreaming and working: The fundamental approach to dreams.* Culver City, California: Peace Press.

Crick, F., & Mitchison, G. (1983). The function of dream sleep. *Nature, 394,* 111-114.

Curtis, H. C., & Sachs, D. M. (1976). Dialogue on 'The changing use of dreams in psychoanalytic practice'. *International Journal of Psycho-Analysis, 57,* 343-354.

Davé, R. (1979). Effects of hypnotically induced dreams on creative problem solving. *Journal of Abnormal Psychology, 88,* 293-302.

de Becker, R. (1968). *The understanding of dreams and their influence on the history of man.* New York: Hawthorn.

De Koninck, J. M. (1987). Sleep and dreams in technostress management. In A. S. Sethi, D. H. J. Caro, & R. S. Schuler (Eds.). *Strategic management of technostress in an information society.* Pp. 338-356. New York: C. J. Hogrefe.

De Koninck, J. M., & Koulack, D. (1975). Dream content and adaptation to a stressful situation. *Journal of Abnormal Psychology, 84,* 250-260.

Delaney, G. (1981). *Living your dreams.* San Francisco: Harper & Row.

Dement, W., & Wolpert, E. (1958). Relationships in the manifest content of dreams occurring on the same night. *Journal of Nervous and Mental Diseases, 126,* 568-578.

De Monchaux, C. (1978). Dreaming and the organizing function of the eye. *International Journal of Psychoanalysis, 59,* 443-453.

Doweiko, H. E. (1982). Neurobiology and dream theory: A rapprochement model. *Individual Psychology: Journal of Adlerian Therapy, Research and Practice, 38,* 55-61.

Eckhardt, M. H., Zane, M., & Ullman, M. (1971). A dream workshop experience from 1965-1970. In J. H. Masserman (Ed.). *Science and psychoanalysis.* Pp. 89-113. New York: Grune and Stratton.

Edel, L. (1982). *The stuff of sleep and dreams.* New York: Harper and Row.

Edinger, E. F. (1972). *Ego and archetype.* New York: Putnams.

Ehrenwald, J. (1966). *Psychotherapy: Myth and method.* New York: Grune and Stratton.

Eisenstein, S. (1980). The dream in psychoanalysis. In J. M. Natterson (Ed.). *The dream in clinical practice.* Pp. 319-331. New York: Jason Aronson.

Eisler, K. (1953). The effects of the structure of the ego in psychoanalytic technique. *Journal of the American Psychoanalytic Association, 1,* 104-143.

Eliade, M. (1960). *Myths, dreams, and mysteries.* New York: Harper and Row.

Ellis, H. (1911). *The world of dreams.* Boston: Houghton Mifflin.

Enright, J. (1970). An introduction to Gestalt techniques. In J. Fagan and I. L. Shepherd (Eds.). *Gestalt therapy now.* Pp. 107-124. New York: Harper and Row.

Erickson, E. (1954). The dream specimen of psychoanalysis. *Journal of the American Psychoanalytic Association, 2,* 5-56.

Erickson, M. H. (1985). *Life reframing in hypnosis.* New York: Irvington.

Evans, C. (1983). *Landscapes of the night: How and why we dream.* New York: Viking.

Evans-Wentz, W. Y. (1967). *Tibetan yoga and secret doctrines.* New York: Oxford University Press.

Fairbairn, W. R. D. (1951). *An object-relations theory of the personality.* New York: Basic Books.

Fairbairn, W. R. D. (1958). On the nature and aims of psychoanalytic treatment. *International Journal of Psychoanalysis, 39,* 374-385.

Fantz, R. E. (1987). Gestalt approach. In J. L Fosshage & C. A. Loew (Eds.). *Dream interpretation: A comparative study*. Pp. 191–241. New York: PMA.

Faraday, A. (1972). *Dream power*. New York: Coward, McCann, & Geoghegan.

Faraday, A. (1974). *The dream game*. New York: Harper and Row.

Fenichel, O. (1953). Analysis of a dream. In H. Fenichel & D. Rapaport (Eds.). *The collected papers of Otto Fenichel: First series*. Pp. 160–164. New York: W. W. Norton.

Fisher, C. (1965). Psychoanalytic implicators of recent research on sleep and dreaming. *Journal of the American Psychoanalytic Association, 13,* 197–303.

Fiss, H. (1979). Current dream research: A psychobiological perspective. In B. Wolman (Ed.). *Handbook of dreams*. Pp. 20–75. New York: Van Nostrand Reinhold.

Fiss, H. (1983). Toward a clinically relevant experimental psychology of dreaming. *Hillside Journal of Clinical Psychiatry, 5,* 147–159.

Fiss, H., & Litchman, J. (1976). Dream enhancement: An experimental approach to adaptive function of dreams. Paper presented to Association for the Psychophysiological Study of Sleep. Cincinnati, Ohio.

Fleiss, R. (1953). *The revival of interest in the dream*. New York: International Universities Press.

Fodor, N. (1971). *Freud, Jung, and occultism*. New Hyde Park, New York: University Books.

Fosshage, J. L. (1983). The psychological function of dreams: A revised psychoanalytic perspective. *Psychoanalysis and Contemporary Thought, 6,* 641–669.

Fosshage, J. L. (1987a). New vistas in dream interpretation. In M. L. Glucksman & S. L. Wayner (Eds.). *Dreams in new perspective*. Pp. 23–43. New York: Human Sciences Press.

Fosshage, J. L. (1987b). A revised psychoanalytic approach. In J. L. Fosshage & C. A. Loew (Eds.). *Dream interpretation: A comparative study*. Pp. 294–318. New York: PMA.

Fosshage, J. L., & Loew, C. A. (1987a). *Dream interpretation: A comparative study*. New York: PMA.

Fosshage, J. L., & Loew, C. A. (1987b). Comparison and synthesis. In J. L. Fosshage & C. A. Loew (Eds.). *Dream Interpretation: A comparative study*. Pp. 243–295. New York: PMA.

Foulkes, D. (1982). *Children's dreams: Longitudinal studies*. New York: John Wiley and Sons.

Foulkes, D. (1985). *Dreaming: A cognitive-psychological analysis*. Hillsdale, New Jersey: Lawrence Erlbaum.

Foulkes, D., & Rechtschaffen, A. (1964). Presleep determinants of dream content: Effects of two films. *Perceptual and Motor Skills, 19,* 983–1005.

Fox, O. (1962). *Astral projection*. New York: University Books.

French, T. M., & Fromm, E. (1964). *Dream interpretation: A new approach*. New York: Basic Books.

Freud, S. (1900). The interpretation of dreams. In J. Strachey (trans.) *The standard edition of the complete psychological works of Sigmund Freud*. Vol. 485. New York: Norton.

Freud, S. (1959). Analysis of a case of hysteria. I. The clinical pictures. In E. Jones (Ed.). *Collected papers of Sigmund Freud*. Volume 3. Pp. 52–87. New York: Basic Books.

Fromm-Reichmann, F. (1958). *Principles of intensive psychotherapy*. Chicago: University of Chicago Press.

Garfield, P. (1976). *Dream notebook*. San Francisco: San Francisco Book Company.

Garfield, P. (1977). *Creative dreaming*. New York: Ballantine.

Garfield, P. (1984). *Your child's dreams.* New York: Ballantine.

Garma, A. (1966). *The psychoanalysis of dreams.* New York: Jason Aronson.

Garma, A. (1987). Freudian approach. In J. L. Fosshage & C. A. Loew (Eds.). *Dream interpretation: A comparative study.* Pp. 15–51. New York: PMA.

Gendlin, E. T. (1977). Phenomenological concept vs. phenomenological method: A critique of Medard Boss on dreams. In C. E. Scott (Ed.). *On dreaming: An encounter with Medard Boss.* Pp. 57–72. San Francisco, California: Scholar Press.

Gendlin, E. T. (1986). *Let your body interpret your dreams.* Wilmette, Illinois: Chiron.

Gillman, R. D. (1980). Dreams in which the analyst appears as himself. In J. M. Natterson (Ed.). *The dream in clinical practice.* Pp. 29–44. New York: Jason Aronson.

Gitelson, M. (1952). The emotional position of the analyst in the psychoanalytic situation. *International Journal of Psycho-Analysis, 33,* 1–10.

Glucksman, M. L., & Warner, S. L. (1987). *Dreams in new perspective.* New York: Human Sciences Press.

Gold, L. (1979). Adler's theory of dreams: An holistic approach to interpretation. In B. B. Wolman (Ed.). *Handbook of dreams.* Pp. 319–341. New York: Van Nostrand Reinhold.

Green, C. (1968). *Lucid dreams.* London: Hamilton.

Greenberg, R. (1987). The dream problem and problems in dreams. In M. L. Glucksman & S. L. Warner (Eds.). *Dreams in new perspective.* Pp. 45–57. New York: Human Sciences Press.

Greenberg, R., & Pearlman, C. (1975a). A psychoanalytic dream continuum: The source and function of dreams. *International Review of Psycho-Analysis, 2,* 441–448.

Greenberg, R., & Pearlman, C. (1975b). REM sleep and the analytic process: A psychophysiologic bridge. *Psychoanalytic Quarterly, 44,* 392–403.

Greenberg, R., & Pearlman, C. (1978). If Freud only knew: A reconsideration of psychoanalytic dream theory. *International Review of Psycho-Analysis, 5,* 71–75.

Greenberg, R., & Pearlman, C. (1980). The private language of the dream. In J. M. Natterson (Ed.). *The dream in clinical practice.* Pp. 85–96. New York: Jason Aronson.

Greene, T. A. (1979). C. G. Jung's theory of dreams. In B. B. Wolman (Ed.). *Handbook of dreams.* Pp. 298–318. New York: Van Nostrand Reinhold.

Greenleaf, E. (1973). "Senoi" dream groups. *Psychotherapy: Theory, Research and Practice, 10,* 218–222.

Greenson, R. (1970). The exceptional position of the dream in psychoanalytic practice. *Psychoanalytic Quarterly, 39,* 519–549.

Griesinger, W. (1867). *Mental pathology and therapeutics.* London: New Sydenham Society.

Guntrip, H. (1969). *Schizoid phenomena, object-relations, and the self.* New York: International Universities Press.

Gutheil, E. A. (1974). Universal (typical) dreams. In R. Woods and H. Greenhouse (Eds.). *The new world of dreams.* Pp. 118–124. New York: Macmillan.

Hall, C. S. (1947). Diagnosing personality by the analysis of dreams. *Journal of Abnormal and Social Psychology, 42,* 68–79.

Hall, C. S. (1962). Out of the dream came the faucet. *Psychoanalysis and Psychoanalytic Review, 49,* 113–116.

Hall, C. S. (1965). What people dream about. In R. S. Daniel (Ed.). *Contemporary readings in general psychology,* 2nd edition. Pp. 224–228. Boston: Houghton Mifflin, 1965.

Hall, C. S. (1966). *The meaning of dreams*. New York: McGraw-Hill.

Hall, C. S., & Domhoff, B. (1963). A ubiquitous sex difference in dreams. *Journal of Abnormal and Social Psychology, 66,* 278–280.

Hall, C. S., & Nordby, W. (1972). *The individual and his dreams*. New York: Signet Books.

Hall, C. S., & Van de Castle, R. L. (1966). *The content analysis of dreams*. New York: Appleton-Century-Crofts.

Hall, J. A. (1982). The use of dreams and dream interpretation in analysis. In M. Stein (Ed.). *Jungian analysis*. Pp. 123–156. La Salle, Illinois: Open Court.

Hall, J. A. (1983). *Jungian dream interpretation*. Toronto: Inner City Books.

Hall, J. A. (1984). Dreams and transference/countertransference: The transformative field. *Chiron, 5,* 31–51.

Hartmann, E. (1965). The D-state: A review and discussion of studies on the physiologic state concomitant with dreaming. *New England Journal of Medicine, 273,* 30–35.

Hartmann, E. (1967). *The biology of dreaming*. Springfield, Illinois: Charles C. Thomas.

Hauri, P. (1976). Dreams in patients remitted from reactive depression. *Journal of Abnormal Psychology, 85,* 1–10.

Henderson, J. L. (1980). The dream in Jungian analysis. In J. M. Natterson (Ed.). *The dream in clinical practice*. Pp. 369–387. New York: Jason Aronson.

Hernandez-Peon, R. (1965). A neurophysiological model of dreams and hallucinations. *Journal of Nervous and Mental Diseases, 141,* 632–646.

Hertz, D. G., & Jensen, M. R. (1975). Menstruating dreams and psychodynamics: Emotional conflict and manifest dream content in menstruating women. *British Journal of Medical Psychology, 48,* 175–183.

Hillman, J. (1967). *Insearch: Psychology and religion*. New York: Charles Scribners.

Hobson, J., & McCarley, R. (1977). The brain as a dream state generator: An activation-synthesis hypothesis of the dream process. *American Journal of Psychiatry, 134,* 1335–1348.

Hunter, I., & Breger, L. (1970). The effect of pre-sleep therapy upon subsequent dream content. *Psychological Issues Monograph Series*. New York: International Universities Press.

Jacobs, E. (1982). Dream theatre: Working from children's dreams. *Dreamworks, 3,* 7–9.

Jokipattio, L. (1982). Dreams in child psychoanalysis. *Scandanavian Psychoanalytic Review, 5,* 31–47.

Jones, E. 1971). *On the nightmare*. New York: Liveright.

Jones, R. M. (1962). *Ego synthesis in dreams*. Cambridge, Mass.: Schenkman.

Jones, R. M. (1964). The problem of "depth" in the psychology of dreaming. *Journal of Nervous and Mental Diseases, 139,* 507–515.

Jones, R. M. (1968). The psychoanalytic theory of dreaming. *Journal of Nervous and Mental Diseases, 147,* 587–603.

Jones, R. M. (1970). *The new psychology of dreaming*. New York and London: Grune and Stratton.

Jones, R. M. (1979). Foreword. In M. Ullman & N. Zimmerman, *Working with dreams*. Pp. 1–4. New York: Dell.

Jones, R. M. (1980). *The dream poet*. Cambridge, Mass.: Schenkman.

Jourard, S. M. (1976). Existential quest. In A. Wandersman, P. Poppen, & D. Ricks (Eds.). *Humanism and behaviorism: Dialogue and growth*. Pp. 35–53. New York: Pergamon.

Jung, C. G. (1933). *Modern man in search of a soul*. New York: Harcourt Brace.

Jung, C. G. (1954). *The practice of psychotherapy.* Princeton: Princeton University Press.

Jung, C. G. (1961). *Psychological reflections.* New York: Harper Torchbook.

Jung, C. G. (1974). *Dreams.* Princeton, New Jersey: Princeton University Press.

Kafka, J. S. (1980). The dream in schizophrenia. In J. M. Natterson (Ed.). *The dream in clinical practice.* Pp. 99–110. New York: Jason Aronson.

Karle, W., Corriere, R., Hart, J., & Woldenberg, L. (1980). The functional analysis of dreams: A new theory of dreaming. *Journal of Clinical Psychology, 36,* 5–78.

Kardiner, A. (1977). *My analysis with Freud.* New York: Norton.

Khan, M. M. R. (1976). The changing use of dreams in psychoanalytic practice. *International Journal of Psycho-Analysis, 57,* 325–331.

Koch-Sheras, P. E. (1985). *A re-examination of the difference between men's and women's dreams.* Paper presented at the Second Annual International Conference of the Association for the Study of Dreams, Charlottesville, Virginia.

Koestler, A. (1964). *The act of creation.* New York: Macmillan.

Kohut, H. (1977). *The restoration of the self.* New York: International Universities Press.

Kramer, M., Hlasny, R., Jacobs, G., & Ruth, T. (1976). Do dreams have meaning? An empirical inquiry. *American Journal of Psychiatry, 133,* 778–781.

Kramer, M., Whitman, R. M., Baldridge, B., & Lansky L. (1964). Patterns of dreaming: The interrelationship of the dreams of a night. *Journal of Nervous and Mental Disease, 139,* 426–439.

Kramer, M., Whitman, R. M., Baldridge, B., & Lansky, L. (1966). Dreaming in the depressed. *Canadian Psychiatric Association Journal, 11,* 178–192.

Kramer, M., Whitman, R. M., Baldridge, B., & Ornstein, P. H. (1968). Drugs and dreams: The effects of imipramine on the dreams of depressed patients. *American Journal of Psychiatry, 124,* 1385–1392.

Kramer, M., Whitman, R. M., Baldridge, B., & Ornstein, P. H. (1970). Dream content in male schizophrenic patients. *Diseases of the Nervous System, 31,* 51–58.

Krippner, S. (1980). Access to hidden reserves of the unconscious through dreams in creative problem solving. *Journal of Creative Behavior, 15,* 11–23.

Krippner, S., & Dillard, J. (1988). *Dreamworking: How to use your dreams for creative problem-solving.* Buffalo, New York: Bearly Limited.

Krippner, S., Posner, N., Pomerance, W., & Fischer, S. (1974). An investigation of dream content during pregnancy. *Journal of the American Society of Psychosomatic Dentistry and Medicine, 21,* 111–123.

Labruzza, A. L. (1978). The activation-synthesis hypothesis of dreams: A theoretical note. *American Journal of Psychiatry, 135,* 1534–1538.

Laing, R. D. (1962). *The self and others.* Chicago: Quadrangle Books.

Lane, R. W., & Breger, L. (1970). The effect of preoperative stress on dreams. *Psychological Issues Monograph Series.* New York: International Universities Press.

Langs, R. (1966). Manifest dreams from three clinical groups. *Archives of General Psychiatry, 14,* 634–643.

Langs, R. (1971). Day residues, recall residues, and dreams: Reality and the psyche. *Journal of the American Psychoanalytic Association, 19,* 499–523.

Langs, R. (1978a). Some communicative properties of the bipersonal field. *International Journal of Psychoanalytic Psychotherapy, 7,* 87–135.

Langs, R. (1978b). *The listening process.* New York: Jason Aronson.

Langs, R. (1980). The dream in psychotherapy. In J. M. Natterson (Ed.). *The dream in clinical practice.* Pp. 333–368. New York: Jason Aronson.

Langs, R. (1982). Supervisory crises and dreams from supervisors. *Contemporary Psychoanalysis, 18,* 575–613.

Levay, A. N., & Wessberg, J. (1979). The role of dreams in sex therapy. *Journal of Sex and Marital Therapy, 5,* 334–339.

Leveton, A. F. (1961). The night residue. *International Journal of Psychoanalysis, 42,* 506–516.

Levitan, H. (1980). The dream in psychosomatic states. In J. M. Natterson (Ed.). *The dream in clinical practice.* Pp. 225–236. New York: Jason Aronson.

Lévy-Bruhl, L. (1923). *Primitive mentality.* New York: Macmillan.

Lifton, R. (1976). *The life of the self.* New York: Simon and Schuster.

Little, M. (1951). Counter transference and the patient's response to it. *International Journal of Psycho-Analysis, 32,* 32–40.

Lorand, S. (1974). Dream interpretation in the Talmud. In R. Woods and H. Greenhouse (Eds.). *The new world of dreams.* Pp. 214–219. New York: Macmillan.

Lowie, R. H. (1935). *The Crow Indians.* New York: Farrar and Rinehart.

Lowy, S. (1942). *Foundations of dream interpretation.* London: Kegan Paul.

Maeder, A. (1916). The dream problem. *Nervous and Mental Disease Monograph.* No. 22. New York: New York Publishing Co.

Mahrer, A. R. (1962). A preface to the mind-body problem. *Psychological Record, 12,* 53–60.

Mahrer, A. R. (1966). Analysis of a fragment of a dream. *Voices: The Art and Science of Psychotherapy, 2,* 40–41.

Mahrer, A. R. (1967). The goals and families of psychotherapy: Implications. In A. R. Mahrer (Ed.). *The goals of psychotherapy* (pp. 288–301). New York: Appleton-Century-Crofts.

Mahrer, A. R. (1970). Self-change and social change. *International Journal of Interpersonal Development, 1,* 159–166.

Mahrer, A. R. (1971a). Personal life change through systematic use of dreams. *Psychotherapy: Theory, Research and Practice, 8,* 328–332.

Mahrer, A. R. (1971b). An emerging field of human relations.*International Journal of Interpersonal Development, 2,* 105–120.

Mahrer, A. R. (1971c). The expanded context of psychotherapy: Creative developments. In A. R. Mahrer & L. Pearson (Eds.). *Creative developments in psychotherapy.* Pp. 309–329. Cleveland, Ohio: The Press of Case Western Reserve University.

Mahrer, A. R. (1972a). Theory and treatment of anxiety: The perspective of motivational psychology. *Journal of Pastoral Counseling, 7,* 4–16.

Mahrer, A. R. (1972b). The human relations center: Community mental health from a motivational perspective. *Corrective Psychiatry and Journal of Social Therapy, 18,* 39–45.

Mahrer, A. R. (1973). Defining characteristics of a humanistic program of community change and a specimen: The facilitation of self-competence in the neonate. *The Ontario Pscyhologist, 5,* 45–50.

Mahrer, A. R. (1975). Metamorphosis through suicide: The changing of one's self by oneself. *Journal of Pastoral Counseling, 10,* 10–26.

Mahrer, A. R. (1978a). Sequence and consequence in the experiential psychotherapies. In C. Cooper & C. Alderfer (Eds.). *Advances in experiential social processes.* Pp. 39–65. New York: Wiley.

Mahrer, A. R. (1978b). The therapist-patient relationship: Conceptual analysis and a proposal for a paradigm-shift. *Psychotherapy: Theory, Research and Practice, 15,* 201–215.

Mahrer, A. R. (1978c). Turning the tables on termination. *Voices: The Art and Science of Psychotherapy, 13,* 24–31.

Mahrer, A. R. (1979). An invitation to theoreticians and researchers from an applied experiential practitioner. *Psychotherapy: Theory, Research and Practice, 16,* 409–418.

Mahrer, A. R. (1980a). Research on theoretical concepts of psychotherapy. In W. DeMoor and H. R. Wijngaarden (Eds.). *Psychotherapy: Research and training.* Pp. 33–46. Amsterdam: Elsevier, North Holland Biomedical Press.

Mahrer, A. R. (1980b). Value decisions in therapeutically induced acute psychotic episodes. *Psychotherapy: Theory, Research and Practice, 17,* 454–458.

Mahrer, A. R. (1980c). The treatment of cancer through experiential psychotherapy. *Psychotherapy: Theory, Research and Practice, 17,* 335–342.

Mahrer, A. R. (1982). Humanistic approaches to intimacy. In M. Fisher & G. Stricker (Eds.). *Intimacy.* Pp. 141–158. New York: Plenum.

Mahrer, A. R. (1983a). An existential experiential view and operational perspective on passive-aggressiveness. In R. D. Parsons & R. J. Wicks (Eds.). *Passive-aggressiveness: Theory and practice.* Pp. 98–133. New York: Brunner/Mazel.

Mahrer, A. R. (1983b). Humanistic approaches to intimacy. In M Fisher & G. Stricker (Eds.). *Intimacy.* Pp. 141–158. New York: Plenum.

Mahrer, A. R. (1984). The care and feeding of abrasiveness. *The Psychotherapy Patient, 1,* 69–78.

Mahrer, A. R. (1985a). *Psychotherapeutic change: An alternative approach to meaning and measurement.* New York: Norton.

Mahrer, A. R. (1985b). The essence of experiential psychotherapy. *The Humanistic Psychologist, 13,* 12–13.

Mahrer, A. R. (1985c). My alienness and foreignness: Therapeutic problems and no-problems. *Voices: The Art and Science of Psychotherapy, 21,* 19–24.

Mahrer, A. R. (1986a). *Therapeutic experiencing: The process of change.* New York: Norton.

Mahrer, A. R. (1986b). Is human destiny tragic? Psychoanalytic and humanistic answers. *The Humanistic Psychologist, 14,* 73–84.

Mahrer, A. R. (1986c). The steps and methods in experiential psychotherapy sessions. In P. A. Keller & L. G. Ritt (Eds.). *Innovations in clinical practice: A source book.* Volume 5. Pp. 59–69. Sarasota, Florida: Professional Resource Exchange.

Mahrer, A. R. (1986d). Introduction to symposium: Dreamwork in psychotherapy—Fading art or resurgence? *Psychotherapy in Private Practice, 4,* 107–108.

Mahrer, A. R. (1986e). A challenge to communication therapy: The therapist does not communicate with the patient. *Journal of Communication Therapy, 3,* 97–114.

Mahrer, A. R. (1987a). The depth of dreams: Some data and a model. *Psychiatric Journal of the University of Ottawa, 12,* 73–75.

Mahrer, A. R. (1987b). Joining the dreamer in having the dream. *Psychiatric Journal of the University of Ottawa, 12,* 74–81.

Mahrer, A. R. (1988a). Discovery-oriented psychotherapy research: Rationale, aims, and methods. *American Psychologist, 43,* 694–702.

Mahrer, A. R. (1988b). The briefest psychotherapy. *Changes, 6,* 86–89.

Mahrer, A. R. (1988c). Research and clinical applications of "good moments" in psychotherapy. *Journal of Integrative and Eclectic Psychotherapy, 7,* 81–93.

Mahrer, A. R. (1989a). *Experiencing: A humanistic theory of psychology and psychiatry.* Ottawa: University of Ottawa Press (original work published 1978).

Mahrer, A. R. (1989b). *The integration of psychotherapies: A guide for practicing therapists.* New York: Human Sciences Press.

Mahrer, A. R. (1989c). *Experiential psychotherapy: Basic practices.* (1989c). Ottawa: University of Ottawa Press (original work published 1983).

Mahrer, A. R. (1989d). *How to do experiential psychotherapy: A manual for practitioners.* Ottawa: University of Ottawa Press.

Mahrer, A. R., & Boulet, D. B. (1986). An experiential session with Edward and his "obsessional" thoughts and fears. *The Psychotherapy Patient, 3,* 143-158.

Mahrer, A. R., Dessaulles, A., Gervaize, P. A., & Nadler, W. P. (1987). An indictment of interpretation: The elevated role of therapist as grand interpreter. *Psychotherapy in Private Practice, 5,* 39-51.

Mahrer, A. R., & Gervaize, P. A. (1983). Impossible roles therapists must play. *Canadian Psychology, 24,* 81-87.

Mahrer, A. R., & Young, H. H. (1960). The onset of stuttering. *Journal of General Psychology, 67,* 241-250.

Marmer, S. S. (1980). The dream in dissociative states. In J. M. Natterson (Ed.). *The dream in clinical practice.* Pp. 163-175. New York: Jason Aronson.

Martin, J. (1982). The analyst in the dream: A reappraisal. *Journal for the Advancement of Psychoanalytic Education, 2,* 43-47.

Mattoon, M. A. (1978). *Applied dream analysis: A Jungian approach.* Washington, D.C.: V. H. Winston and Sons.

Mattoon, M. A. (1984). *Understanding dreams.* Dallas, Texas: Spring.

May, R. (1975). *The courage to create.* New York: Norton.

McCarley, R. W., & Hobson, J. A. (1977). The neurobiological origins of psychoanalytic dream theory. *American Journal of Psychiatry, 134,* 1121-1221.

Means, J. R., Palmadier, J. R., Wilson, G. L., Hickey, J. S., Hess-Homeier, M. J., & Hickey, C. S. (1986). Dream interpretation. *Psychotherapy, 23,* 448-452.

Meier, C. (1967). *Ancient incubation and modern psychotherapy.* Evanston, Illinois: Northwestern University Press.

Mendel, W. M. (1980). The dream in analysis of existence. In J. M. Natterson (Ed.). *The dream in clinical practice.* Pp. 389-403. New York: Jason Aronson.

Merrill, S., & Cary, G. L. (1975). Dream analysis in brief psychotherapy. *American Journal of Psychotherapy, 29,* 185-192.

Miller, J. B. (1969). Dreams during various stages of depression. *Archives of General Psychiatry, 20,* 560-565.

Miller, M. J., Stinson, L. W., & Soper, B. (1982). The use of dream discussions in counseling. *Personnel and Guidance Journal, 41,* 142-145.

Mindell, A. (1982). *Dreambody.* Boston: Sigo.

Monroe, R. (1955). *Schools of psychoanalytic thought.* New York: Holt, Rinehart and Winston.

Morris, J. (1985). *The dream workbook.* New York: Random House.

Murray, E. (1965). *Sleep, dreams, and arousal.* New York: Appleton-Century-Crofts.

Offenkrantz, W., & Rechtschaffen, A. (1963). Clinical studies of sequential dreams: A patient in psychotherapy. *Archives of General Psychiatry, 8,* 497-508.

Okuma, T., Sunami, Y., Fukuma, E., Takeo, S., & Motoike, M. (1970). Dream content study in chronic schizophrenics and normals by REM-awakening techniques. *Folia Psychiatrica et Neurologica Japonica, 3,* 151-162.

O'Neill, C. W. (1976). *Dreams, culture, and the individual.* Novato, California: Chandler and Sharp.

Ouspensky, P. D. (1962). *A new model of the universe.* New York: Vintage.

Padel, J. H (1987). Object relational approach. In J. L. Fosshage & C. A. Loew (Eds.). *Dream interpretation: A comparative study.* Pp. 125-148. New York: PMA.

Palombo, S. R. (1976). The dream and the memory cycle. *International Review of Psychoanalysis, 3,* 65-83.

Palombo, S. R. (1978). *Dreaming and memory: A new information-processing model*. New York: Basic Books.

Palombo, S. R. (1985). Can a computer dream? *Journal of the American Academy of Psychoanalysis, 13,* 453–466.

Parker, D., & Parker, J. (1985). *Dreaming: An illustrated guide to remembering and interpreting your dreams*. New York: Harmony Books.

Perlmutter, R. A., & Babineau, R. (183). The use of dreams in couples therapy. *Psychiatry, 46,* 66–72.

Perls, F. S. (1969). *Gestalt therapy verbatim*. Moab, Utah: Real People's Press.

Piatrowski, Z. A. (1986). *Dreams: A key to self-knowledge*. Hillsdale, New Jersey: Lawrence Erlbaum.

Pulver, S., & Renik, J. (1984). The clinical use of the manifest dream. *Journal of the American Psychoanalytic Association, 32,* 37–49.

Rapaport, D. (1959). The structure of psychoanalytic theory. *Psychological Issues Monograph Series,* Volume 2, No. 2. New York: International Universities Press.

Rechtschaffen, A., Vogel, G., & Shaikun, G. (1963). Interrelatedness of mental activity during sleep. *Archives of General Psychiatry, 9,* 536–547.

Reed, H. (1985). *Getting help from your dreams*. Virginia Beach, Virginia: Inner Vision.

Reiser, M. F. (1984). *Mind, brain, body: Towards a convergence of psychoanalysis and neurobiology*. New York: Basic Books.

Regush, J. V., & Regush, N. M. (1977). *Dream worlds*. Scarborough, Ontario: New American Library.

Rosenthal, H. R. (1978). A clinical note on the manifest content of dreams. *Modern Psychoanalysis, 2,* 228–243.

Rosenthal, H. R. (1980). *The discovery of the sub-unconscious in a new approach to dream analysis*. South Miami, Florida: Banyan Books.

Rossi, E. L. (1985). *Dreams and the growth of personality*. Second edition. New York: Brunner/Mazel.

Rycroft, C. (1962). *Imagination and reality*. London: Hogarth Press.

Rycroft, C. (1979). *The innocence of dreams*. New York: Pantheon.

Schachtel, E. G. (1947). On memory and childhood amnesia. *Psychiatry, 10,* 1–26.

Schonbar, R. A. (1961). Temporal and emotional factors in the selective recall of dreams. *Journal of Consulting Psychology, 25,* 67–73.

Schultz, K. L., & Koulack, D. (1980). Dream effect and the menstrual cycle. *Journal of Nervous and Mental Disease, 148,* 436–438.

Scott, J. A. (1982). The principles of rapid dream analysis. *Medical Hypoanalysis, 3,* 85–95.

Shaffer, J. B. P. (1978). *Humanistic psychology*. Englewood, New Jersey: Prentice-Hall.

Silberer, H. (1951). Report on a method of eliciting and observing certain symbolic hallucination-phenomena. In D. Rapaport (Ed.). *Organization and pathology of thought*. Pp. 195–207. New York: Columbia University Press.

Silberer, H. (1955). The dream. *Psychoanalytic Review, 42,* 361–387.

Sirois-Berliss, M., & De Koninck, J. (1982). Menstrual stress and dreams: Adaptation or interference? *The Psychiatric Journal of the University of Ottawa, 7,* 77–86.

Sloane, P. (1975). The significance of the manifest dream: Its use and misuse. *Journal of the Philadelphia Association for Psycho-Analysis, 2,* 57–78.

Snyder, F. (1963). The new biology of dreaming. *Archives of General Psychiatry, 8,* 381–391.

Snyder, F. (1969). The physiology of dreaming. In M. Kramer (Ed.). *Dream psychol-*

ogy and the new biology of dreaming. Pp. 7–31. Springfield, Illinois: Charles C. Thomas.

Snyder, F. (1970). The phenomenology of dreaming. In L. Madow & L. H. Snow (Eds.). *The psychodynamic implications of the physiological studies on dreams.* Pp. 124–151. Springfield, Illinois: Charles C. Thomas.

Spanjaard, J. (1969). The manifest dream content and its significance for the interpretation of dreams. *International Journal of Psychoanalysis, 50,* 213–228.

Spero, M. H. (1984). A psychotherapist's reflections on a countertransference dream. *American Journal of Psychoanalysis, 44,* 191–196.

Stern, P. (1977). Forward. In M. Boss, *"I dreamt last night . . . "* Pp. vii–xixx. New York: Gardner Press.

Stewart, K. (1953). Culture and personality in two primitive groups. *Complex, 9,* 3–23.

Stewart, K. (1954). *Pygmies and dream giants.* New York: Norton.

Stewart, K. (1969). Dream theory in Malaya. In C. Tart (Ed.). *Altered states of consciousness.* Pp. 185–207. New York: John Wiley.

Stolorow, R., & Atwood, G. (1982). The psychoanalytic phenomenology of the dream. *Annual of Psychoanalysis, 10,* 205–220.

Stout, G. F. (1899). *Manual of psychology.* New York: Hinds and Noble.

Stukane, E. (1985). *The dream worlds of pregnancy.* New York: Quill.

Swanson, E. M., & Foulkes, D. (1967). Dream content and the menstrual cycle. *Journal of Nervous and Mental Disease, 145,* 358–363.

Tart, C. (1969). *Altered states of consciousness.* New York: John Wiley and Sons.

Tart, C. (1970). Conscious control of dreaming: The post-hypnotic dream. *Journal of Abnormal Psychology, 76,* 304–315.

Taylor, J. (1983). *Dream work: Techniques for discovering the creative powers in dreams.* Ramsay, New Jersey: Paulist Press.

Trosman, H. (1963). Dream research and the psychoanalytic theory of dreams. *Archives of General Psychiatry, 9,* 9–18.

Trosman, H., Rechschaffen, A., Offenkrantz, W., & Wolpert, E. (1960). Studies in psychophysiology of dreams: Relations among dreams in sequence. *Archives of General Psychiatry, 3,* 602–607.

Ullman, M. (1961). Dreaming, altered states of consciousness, and the problem of vigilance. *Journal of Nervous and Mental Disease, 133,* 519–535.

Ullman, M. (1962a). Dreaming, life style, and physiology: A comment on Adler's view of the dream. *Journal of Individual Psychology, 18,* 18–25.

Ullman, M. (1962b). Foreword. In W. Bonine, *The clinical use of dreams.* Pp. vii–xvii. New York: Basic Books.

Ullman, M. (1965). Discussion: Dreaming—a creative process. *American Journal of Psychoanalysis, 24,* 19–21.

Ullman, M. (1987). The dream revisited: Some changed ideas based on a group approach. In M. L. Glucksman & S. L. Warner (Eds.). *Dreams in new perspective.* Pp. 119–130. New York: Human Sciences Press.

Ullman, M., & Zimmerman, N. (1979). *Working with dreams.* New York: Dell.

Van Bork, J. J. (1982). An attempt to clarify a dream-mechanism: Why do people wake up out of an anxiety dream? *International Review of Psychoanalysis, 9,* 233–277.

Van de Castle, R. L. (1971). *The psychology of dreaming.* Morristown, New Jersey: General Learning Press.

Van de Castle, R. L., & Holloway, J. (1971). Dreams of depressed patients, non-depressed patients, and normals. *Psychophysiology, 7,* 326–329.

Velikovsky, I. (1941). The dreams Freud dreamed. *Psychoanalytic Review, 28,* 487–511.

Vogel, G. W. (1978). An alternative view of the neurobiology of dreaming. *American Journal of Psychiatry, 135,* 1531-1535.

Von Gruenbaum, G. E., & Caillois, R. (Eds.). (1955). *The dream and human societies.* Berkeley, California: University of California Press.

Waldhorn, H. F. (1967). *Indications for psychoanalysis: The place of the dream in clinical psychoanalysis.* New York: International Universities Press.

Warner, S. L. (1987). Manifest dream analysis in contemporary practice. In M. L. Glucksman & S. L. Warner (Eds.). *Dreams in new perspective.* Pp. 97-117. New York: Human Sciences Press.

Warnes, H. (1982). The dream specimen in psychosomatic medicine in the light of clinical observations. *Psychotherapy and Psychosomatics, 38,* 154-164.

Webb, W. B., & Cartwright, R. D. (1978). Sleep and dreams. *Annual Review of Psychology, 29,* 223-252.

Webb, W. W. (1979). A historical perspective on dreams. In B. B. Wolman (Ed.). *Handbook of dreams: Research, theories, and applications.* Pp. 3-19. New York: Van Nostrand Reinhold.

Weiss, L. (1986). *Dream analysis in psychotherapy.* New York: Pergamon Press.

Werman, D. S. (1978). The use of dreams in psychotherapy: Practical guidelines. *Canadian Psychiatric Association Journal, 23,* 153-158.

Whiteman, J. H. M. (1961). *The mystical life.* London: Faber and Faber.

Whitman, R. M. (1980). The dream as a curative fantasy. In J. M. Natterson (Ed.). *The dream in clinical practice.* Pp. 45-54. New York: Jason Aronson.

Whitmont, E. C. (1987). Jungian approach. In J. L. Fosshage & C. A. Loew (Eds.). *Dream interpretation: A comparative study.* Pp. 53-77. New York: PMA.

Williams, S. K. (1980). *Jungian-Senoi dreamwork manual.* Berkeley, California: Journey Press.

Winget, C., Kramer, M., & Whitman, R. (1972). Dreams and demography. *Canadian Psychiatric Association Journal, 17,* 203-208.

Winson, J. (1985). *Brain and psyche.* New York: Doubleday.

Witkin, H., & Lewis, H. (1965). The relation of experimentally induced presleep experiences to dreams: A report on method and preliminary findings. *Journal of the American Psychoanalytic Association, 13,* 819-849.

Wolff, W. (1952). *The dream — Mirror of conscience.* New York: Grune & Stratton.

Wolman, B. B. (Ed.). (1979). *Handbook of dreams.* New York: Van Nostrand Reinhold.

Woods, R., & Greenhouse, H. (Eds.). (1974). *The new world of dreams.* New York: Macmillan.

Woodworth, R. S. (1929). *Psychology.* New York: Henry Holt.

Name Index

Subject Index